☑ **W9-BHM-747**

Business Data Communications and Networking:

A Research Perspective

Jairo Gutié—

DATE DUE

OCT 16 2008		
NOV 2 5 2008	OCT 2 8 2008	
	NOV 1 5 2008	

IDEA GROUP PUBLISHING

Hershey • London • Melbourne • Singapore

Acquisition Editor:	Kristin Klinger
Senior Managing Editor:	Jennifer Neidig
Managing Editor:	Sara Reed
Assistant Managing Editor:	Sharon Berger
Development Editor:	Kristin Roth
Copy Editor:	Nicole Dean
Typesetter:	Jamie Snavely
Cover Design:	Lisa Tosheff
Printed at:	Yurchak Printing Inc.

Published in the United States of America by
> Idea Group Publishing (an imprint of Idea Group Inc.)
> 701 E. Chocolate Avenue
> Hershey PA 17033
> Tel: 717-533-8845
> Fax: 717-533-8661
> E-mail: cust@idea-group.com
> Web site: http://www.idea-group.com

and in the United Kingdom by
> Idea Group Publishing (an imprint of Idea Group Inc.)
> 3 Henrietta Street
> Covent Garden
> London WC2E 8LU
> Tel: 44 20 7240 0856
> Fax: 44 20 7379 3313
> Web site: http://www.eurospan.co.uk

Library of Congress Cataloging-in-Publication Data

Business data communications and networking : a research perspective / Jairo Gutierrez, editor.
    p. cm.
  Summary: "This book addresses key issues for businesses utilizing data communications and the increasing importance of networking technologies in business; it covers a series of technical advances in the field while highlighting their respective contributions to business or organizational goals, and centers on the issues of network-based applications, mobility, wireless networks and network security"--Provided by publisher.
  Includes bibliographical references and index.
  ISBN 1-59904-274-6 (hardcover) -- ISBN 1-59904-275-4 (softcover) -- ISBN 1-59904-276-2 (ebook)
  1. Computer networks. 2. Wireless communication systems. 3. Data transmission systems. 4. Business communication--Data processing. I. Gutierrez, Jairo, 1960-
  TK5105.5.B878 2007
  004.6--dc22
                               2006031360

British Cataloguing in Publication Data
A Cataloguing in Publication record for this book is available from the British Library.

All work contributed to this book is new, previously-unpublished material. The views expressed in this book are those of the authors, but not necessarily of the publisher.

Business Data Communications and Networking:

A Research Perspective

Table of Contents

Section III: Wireless Deployment and Applications

Section IV: Network Security

Preface

Research in the area of data communications and networking is well and alive as this collection of contributions show. The book has received enhanced contributions from the authors that published in the inaugural volume of the *International Journal of Business Data Communications and Networking* (http://www.idea-group.com/ijbdcn). The chapters are divided in four themes: (1) network design and application issues, (2) mobility, (3) wireless deployment and applications, and (4) network security. The first two sections gathering the larger number of chapters, which is not surprising given the popularity of the issues presented on those sections. Within each section the chapters have been roughly organized following the Physical layer to Application layer sequence with lower-level issues discussed first. This is not an exact sequence since some chapters deal with cross-layer aspects; however, it facilitates the reading of the book in a more-or-less logical manner. The resulting volume is a valuable snapshot of some of the most interesting research activities taking place in the field of business data communications and networking.

The first section, *Network Design and Application Issues,* starts with Chapter I, "Design of High Capacity Survivable Networks," written by Varadharajan Sridhar and June Park. In it the authors define Survivability as the capability of keeping at least "one path between specified network nodes so that some or all of traffic between nodes is routed through". Based on that definition the chapter goes on to discuss the issues associated with the design of a survivable telecommunications network architecture that uses high-capacity transport facilities. Their model considers the selection of capacitated links and the routing of multicommodity traffic flows with the goal of minimizing the overall network cost. Two node disjoint paths are selected for each commodity. In case of failure of the primary path, a portion of the traffic for each commodity will be rerouted through the secondary path. The methodology presented in the chapter can be used by the network designer to construct cost-effective high capacity survivable ring networks of low to medium capacity.

In Chapter II, "A Data Mining Driven Approach for Web Classification and Filtering Based on Multimodal Content Analysis," Mohamed Hammami, Youssef Chahir, and Liming Chen introduce WebGuard an automatic machine-learning based system that can be used to effectively classify and filter objectionable Web material, in particular pornographic content. The system focuses on analyzing visual skin-color content along with textual and structural content based analysis for improving pornographic Web site filtering. While most of the commercial filtering products on the marketplace are mainly based on textual content-based analysis such as indicative keywords detection or manually collected black list checking, the originality of the authors' work resides on the addition of structural and visual content-based analysis along with several data mining techniques for learning about and classifying content. The system was tested on the MYL test dataset which consists of 400 Websites including 200 adult sites and 200 non-pornographic ones. The Web filtering engine scored a high classification accuracy rate when only textual and structural content based analysis are used, and a slightly higher classification accuracy rate when skin color-related visual content-based analysis is added to the system. The basic framework of WebGuard can apply to other categorization problems of Web sites which combine, as most of them do today, textual and visual content.

Chapter III, "Prevalent Factors involved in Delays Associated with Page Downloads," tackles an issue that concerns most Internet users: response times associated with Web page latencies. Kevin Curran and Noel Broderick studied the usage of images and the effect they have on page retrieval times. A representative sample of academic institutions' Websites which were image-intensive was selected and used in the research. Their findings showed that the prevalent factor that affects how quickly a Web site performs is the type of Web hosting environment that the site is deployed in. They also found that Web users are faced with a sliding scale of delays, with no one Web page taking the same time to load on two separate occasions. It is the number of application packets, not bytes, and the number of simultaneous users of the part of the Internet involved in the connection that determines the Web page latency and satisfaction levels. Finally, the authors discuss the fact that improvements on the coding of images can reduce latencies but some of the most efficient encoding techniques, such as PNG, only start to report benefits with larger (more than 900 bytes) images. A large number of images found during the testing fell in the sub-900 group.

The research reported in Chapter IV, "Network Quality of Service for Enterprise Resource Planning Systems: A Case Study Approach" by Ted Chia-Han Lo and Jairo Gutiérrez, studied the relevance of the application of network quality of service (QoS) technologies for modern enterprise resource planning (ERP) systems, explored the state-of-art for QoS technologies and implementations and, more importantly, provided a framework for the provision of QoS for ERP systems that utilise Internet protocol (IP) networks. The authors were motivated to conduct this research after discovering that very little had been investigated on that particular aspect of ERP systems, even though there was an increasing realisation about the importance of these types of applications within the overall mix of information systems deployed in medium and large organisations. Based upon the research problem and the context of research, a case study research method was selected. Four individual cases—including both leading ERP vendors and network technology vendors—were conducted. The primary data collection was done using semi-structured interviews and this data was supplemented by an extensive array of secondary material. Cross-case analysis confirmed that the traditional approaches for ensuring the performance of ERP systems on IP networks do not address network congestion and latency effectively, nor do they offer guaranteed network service quality for ERP systems. Moreover, a cross-case comparative data analysis was used to review the pattern of existing QoS implementations and it concluded that while QoS is increasingly being acknowledged by enterprises as an important issue, its deployment remains limited. The findings from the cross-case analysis ultimately became the basis of the proposed framework for the provision of network QoS for ERP systems. The proposed framework focuses on providing a structured, yet practical approach to implement end-to-end IP QoS that accommodate both ERP systems and their Web-enabled versions based on state-of-art traffic classification mechanisms. The value of the research is envisioned to be most visible for two major audiences: enterprises that currently utilised best-effort IP networks for their ERP deployments and ERP vendors.

The last chapter on this section, Chapter V, "Cost-Based Congestion Pricing in Network Priority Models Using Axiomatic Cost Allocation Methods," was written by Fernando Beltrán and César García-Díaz. The chapter deals with the efficient distribution of congestion costs among network users. The authors start with a discussion about congestion effects and their impact on shared network resources. They also review the different approaches found in the literature, ranging from methods that advocate for congestion-based pricing to methods that, after being critical about considering congestion, advocate for price definition based on the investors' need for return on their investment. Beltrán and García then proceed to introduce an axiomatic approach to congestion pricing that takes into account some of the prescriptions and conclusions found in the literature. The method presented in the chapter is defined on the grounds of axioms that represent a set of fundamental principles that a good allocation mechanism should have.

The second theme of this book is addressed in the second section, *Mobility*. The chapters in this section share that common denominator: the challenges addressed are introduced by that defining characteristic. The first contribution in this section, Chapter VI, "Mobile Multimedia: Communication Technologies, Business Drivers, Service and Applications," is written by Ismail Khalil Ibrahim, Ashraf Ahmad, and David Taniar. It serves as a great introduction to the topic of mobility and in particular the field of mobile multimedia which the authors define as "multimedia information exchange over wireless networks or wireless Internet." This chapter discusses the state-of-the-art of the different communication technologies used to support mobile multimedia, describes the key enabling factor of mobile multimedia: the popularity and evolution of mobile computing devices, coupled with fast and affordable mobile networks. Additionally, the authors argue that the range and complexity of applications and services provided to end-users also play an important part in the success of mobile multimedia.

Chapter VII, "Mobile Information Systems in a Hospital Organization Setting," written by Agustinus Borgy Waluyo, David Taniar, and Bala Srinivasan, deals with the issue of providing mobility in the challenging environment of a hospital. The chapter discusses a practical realisation of an application using push and pull based mechanisms in a wireless ad-hoc environment. The pull mechanism is initiated by doctors as mobile clients retrieving and updating patient records in a central database server. The push mechanism is initiated from the server without a specific request from the doctors. The application of the push mechanism includes sending a message from a central server to a specific doctor or multicasting a message to a selected group of doctors connected to the server application. The authors also discuss their future plans for the system which include the addition of a sensor positioning device, such as a global positioning system (GPS), used to detect the location of the mobile users and to facilitate the pushing of information based on that location.

Chapter VIII also tackles the issue of mobility but based on a study of the available types of data caching in a mobile database environment. Say Ying Lim, David Taniar, and Bala Srinivasan explore the different types of possible cache management strategies in their chapter, "Data Caching in a Mobile Database Environment." The authors firstly discuss the need for caching in a mobile environment and proceed to present a number of issues that arise from the adoption of different cache management strategies and from the use of strategies involving location-dependent data. The authors then concentrate on semantic caching, where only the required data is transmitted over the wireless channel, and on cooperative caching. They also discuss cache invalidation strategies, for both location and non location dependent queries. The chapter serves as a valuable starting point for those who wish to gain some introductory knowledge about the usefulness of the different types of cache management strategies that can be use in a typical mobile database environment.

In the last chapter of this section, Chapter IX, "Mining Walking Pattern from Mobile Users," John Goh and David Taniar deal with the issue of extracting patterns and knowledge from a given dataset, in this case a user movement database. The chapter reports research on the innovative examination, using data mining techniques, of how mobile users walks from one location of interest to another location of interest in the mobile environment. Walking pattern is the proposed method whereby the source data is examined in order to find out the 2-step, 3-step and 4-step walking patterns that are performed by mobile users. A performance evaluation shows the tendency for a number of candidate walking patterns with the increase in frequency of certain location of interests and steps. The walking pattern technique has proven itself to be a suitable method for extracting useful knowledge from the datasets generated by the activities of mobile users. These identified walking patterns can help decision makers in terms of better understanding the movement patterns of mobile users, and can also be helpful for geographical planning purposes.

The third section, *Wireless Deployment and Applications*, has two contributions. Chapter X, "Wi-Fi Deployment in Large New Zealand Organizations: A Survey," co-written by Bryan Houliston and Nurul Sarkar, reports on research conducted on New Zealand where 80 large organizations were asked about their level of Wi-Fi networks (IEEE 802.11b) deployment, reasons for non-deployment, the scope of deployment, investment in deployment, problems encountered, and future plans. The authors' findings show that most organizations have at least considered the technology, though a much smaller proportion has deployed it on any significant scale. A follow up review, included in the chapter, of the latest published case studies and surveys suggests that while Wi-Fi networks deployment is slowing, interest is growing on the issue of wider area wireless networks.

The second chapter in the section, by Subhankar Dhar, is "Applications and Future Trends in Mobile Ad Hoc Networks," and covers, in a survey style, the current state of the art of mobile ad hoc networks and some important problems and challenges related to routing, power management, location management, security as well as multimedia over ad hoc networks. The author explains that a mobile ad hoc network (MANET) is a temporary, self-organizing network of wireless mobile nodes without the support of any existing infrastructure that may be readily available on the conventional networks and discusses how, since there is no fixed infrastructure available for MANET with nodes being mobile, routing becomes a very important issue. In addition, the author also explains the various emerging applications and future trends of MANET.

The last section, *Network Security*, begins with Chapter XII, "Addressing WiFi Security Concerns." In it, Kevin Curran and Elaine Smyth discuss the key security problems linked to WiFi networks, including signal leakages, WEP-related (wired equivalent protocol) weaknesses and various other attacks that can be initiated against WLANs. The research reported includes details of a "war driving" expedition conducted by the authors in order to ascertain the number of unprotected WLAN devices in use in one small town. The authors compiled recommendations for three groups of users: home users, small office/home office (SOHO) users and medium to large organisations. The recommendations presented suggest that home users should implement all the security measures their hardware offers them, they should include WEP security at the longest key length permitted and implement firewalls on all connected PCs changing their WEP key on a weekly basis. The Small Office group should implement WPA-SPK; and the medium to large organisations should implement one or more of either: WPA Enterprise with a RADIUS server, VPN software, IDSs, and provide documented policies in relation to WLANs and their use.

Chapter XIII, "A SEEP Protocol Design Using 3BC, $ECC(F_2^m)$, and HECC Algorithm," by Byung Kwan Lee, Seung Hae Yang, and Tai-Chi Lee, reports on collaborative work between Kwandong University in Korea and Saginaw Valley State University in the U.S. In this contribution the authors propose a highly secure electronic payment protocol that uses elliptic curve cryptosystems, a secure hash system and a block byte bit cipher to provide security (instead of the more common RSA-DES combination). The encroaching of e-commerce into our daily lives makes it essential that its key money-exchange mechanism, online payments, be made more reliable through the development of enhanced security techniques such as the one reported in this chapter.

Finally, Chapter XIV deals with "Fighting the Problem of Unsolicited E-Mail Using a Hashcash Proof-of-Work Approach." Authors Kevin Curran and John Honan present the Hashcash proof-of-work approach and investigate the feasibility of implementing a solution based on that mechanism along with what they called a "cocktail" of antispam measures designed to keep junk mail under control. As reported by the researchers in this chapter, a potential problem with proof-of-work is that disparity across different powered computers may result in some unfortunate users spending a disproportionately long time calculating a stamp. The authors carried out an experiment to time how long it took to calculate stamps across a variety of processor speeds. It is concluded from the analysis of the results that due to this problem of egalitarianism, "hashcash" (or CPU-bound proof-of-work in general) is not a suitable approach as a stand-alone anti-spam solution. It appears that a hybrid (a.k.a. "cocktail") anti-spam system in conjunction with a legal and policy framework is the best approach.

We hope that you enjoy this book. Its collection of very interesting chapters gives the reader a good insight into some of the key research work in the areas of wireless networking, mobility and network security. Our goal was to provide an informed and detailed snapshot of these fast moving fields. If you have any feedback or suggestions, please contact me via e-mail at j.gutierrez@auckland.ac.nz.

Jairo A. Gutiérrez, Editor

Section I:

Network Design and Application Issues

Chapter I

Design of High Capacity Survivable Networks

Varadharajan Sridhar, Management Development Institute, Gurgaon, India

June Park, Samsung SDS Company Ltd., Seoul, South Korea

Abstract

Survivability, also known as terminal reliability, refers to keeping at least one path between specified network nodes so that some or all of traffic between nodes is routed through. Survivability in high capacity telecommunication networks is crucial as failure of network component such as nodes or links between nodes can potentially bring down the whole communication network, as happened in some real-world cases. Adding redundant network components increases the survivability of a network with an associated increase in cost. In this chapter we consider the design of survivable telecommunications network architecture that uses high-capacity transport facilities. The model considers selection of capacitated links and routing of multicommodity traffic flow in the network that minimizes overall network cost. Two node disjoint paths are selected for each commodity. In case of failure of the primary path, a portion of the traffic for each commodity is rerouted through the secondary path. The methodology presented in this chapter can be used by the network designer to construct cost-effective high capacity survivable networks.

Introduction

Optic fiber and high capacity transmission facilities are being increasingly deployed by Telecommunication companies for carrying voice, data, and multimedia traffic. Local (some times referred to as basic) telecom service providers are spending tens of billions of dollars on fiber-based equipment and facilities to replace or augment the existing facilities to provide high bandwidth transport. This has led to *sparse* networks with larger amount of traffic carried on each link compared to traditional bandwidth limiting technologies which deployed *dense* networks. One of such technologies is synchronous digital hierarchy (SDH) standardized by the International Telecommunications Union. SDH decreases the cost and number of transmission systems public networks need and makes it possible to create a high capacity telecommunications superhighway to transport broad range of signals at very high speeds (Shyur & Wen, 2001). Because of their sparse nature, these networks inherently have less reliability. Failure of a single node or link in the network can cause disruptions to transporting large volume of traffic, if alternate path is not provided for routing the affected traffic. Though backup links can be provided to improve the reliability of such sparse networks, it could increase the cost of the networks substantially. The challenge is to improve the reliability of the networks at minimal cost. Researchers have looked at methods of improving reliability of such networks. Detailed discussions on the importance of survivability in fiber network design can be found in Wu, Kolar, and Cardwell (1988) and Newport and Varshney (1991). Recently, vulnerabilities and associated security threats of information and communication networks have prompted researchers to define survivability as the capability of a system to fulfill its mission, in a timely manner, in the presence of attacks, failures or accidents (Redman, Warren, & Hutchinson, 2005).

Networks with ring architecture are also being increasingly deployed in high capacity networks to provide survivability. Synchronous optical network (SONET) uses a self-healing ring architecture that enables the network to maintain all or part of communication in the event of a cable cut on a link or a node failure. SONET networks are being increasingly deployed between central offices of the telecommunication companies and between point of presence (POP) of traffic concentration points. SONET-based transmission facilities are also being deployed increasingly to provide broadband facilities to business customers and government agencies. Operationally such self-healing ring networks divert the flow along an alternative path in the ring in case of failure of a node or link.

For a discussion of the use of rings in telecommunication networks, the reader is referred to Cosares, Deutsch, and Saniee (1995). Cosares et al. (1995) describes the implementation of a decision support system called *SONET toolkit* developed by Bell Core for constructing SONET rings. The SONET toolkit uses a combination of heuristic procedures to provide economic mix of self-healing rings and other architectures that satisfy the given survivability requirements. Chunghwa Telecom, the full service telecommunications carrier in Taiwan, has developed a tool for planning linear and ring architectures of high-capacity digital transmission systems (Shyur & Wen, 2001). The tool reduces planning and labor costs by 15 to 33%. Goldschmidt, Laugier, and Olinick (2003) present the case of a large telecommunication service provider who chose SONET ring architecture for interconnecting customer locations.

Organizations still use leased T1/T3 transmission facilities, especially in developing countries where the bandwidth is scarce, to construct private networks. These asynchronous transmission facilities use terminal multiplexers at customer premise and the multiplexers are interconnected using leased or privately owned links. Because of the flexibility offered by the time division multiplexing scheme to multiplex both data and voice traffic, it becomes economical to connect relatively small number of customer premise equipment using point-point lines. These networks connect few network nodes and often priced based on distance sensitive charges. It becomes important for the organizations to construct a minimum cost network to transport traffic between customer premise locations. At the same time, the network should be survivable in case of failure of a network node or a link so that all or portion of the network traffic can still be transported.

The problem described in this chapter is motivated by the above applications of reliable networks. Given a set of network nodes, each with certain processing and switching capacity, the objective is to install links at minimum cost between the network nodes to provide transport for the traffic between node pairs. The network so constructed should be survivable and that the routing of the traffic should be such that the capacity constraints at the nodes and the links should not be violated. In this chapter, we consider exactly two node disjoint paths between node pairs to provide survivability in case of a node or link failure. We consider non-bifurcated routing and that the traffic between any pair of nodes is not split along two or more paths. Under this routing strategy, a pair of node disjoint paths is predetermined for each pair of communicating nodes. One of them is designated as the *primary path* and the other as the *secondary path*. The latter is used only when a node or a link on the primary path becomes unavailable. If a node or arc fails along the primary path, the source reroutes all or portion of the traffic along the secondary path. Examples of this kind of routing can be found in bi-directional SONET networks (Vachani, Shulman, & Kubat, 1996), backbone data networks (Amiri & Pirkul, 1996), and in circuit switched networks (Agarwal, 1989).

One aspect of topology design is determining where to install transmission facilities of a given capacity between the network nodes to form a survivable network. The other aspect is to find routes for traffic between any pair of communicating pairs of nodes so that in case of failure of a node or a link along the primary path, a portion of the traffic can be re-routed through the secondary path. The multicommodity traffic between communicating nodes have to be routed such that the capacity constraints at the nodes and the links of the network are not violated. The problem addressed in this chapter combines the problem of topological design of *capacitated survivable network* with the problem of *routing multi-commodity traffic*. These problems are very difficult to solve, especially as the number of network nodes increase. We develop a mathematical programming approach to solving the above set of problems.

Literature Survey

There has been extensive research on the topological design of *uncapacitated* networks with survivability requirements. However, there have been only few studies on the topological design of *capacitated* networks with survivability requirements. Lee and Koh (1997) have developed a tabu search method for designing a ring-chain network architecture. But their work does not explicitly consider node and link capacity constraints. A general mathematical model is developed in Gavish, Trudeau, Dror, Gendreau, and Mason (1989) for circuit switched network. The model accounts for any possible state of link failures. Computational results are reported for small (eight nodes, 13 links) problem instances. A modification of the *cut-saturation algorithm* is proposed in Newport and Varshney (1991) for the design of survivable networks satisfying performance and capacity constraints. In Agarwal (1989) the problem of designing a private circuit-switched network is modeled as an integer linear program and solved by Lagrangian relaxation and branch-and-bound techniques. Agarwal considered only link capacity constraints and the survivability is provided. Design of multi-tier survivable networks has been studied by Balakrishnan, Magnanti, and Mirchandani (1998). Grotschel, Monma, and Stoer (1992) looked at the problem of providing two-node disjoint paths to certain special nodes in a fiber network and used cutting planes algorithms and graph-theoretic heuristics. For a comprehensive survey of survivable network design, the reader is referred to Soni, Gupta, and Pirkul (1999). In a paper by Rios, Marianov, and Gutierrez (2000), different survivability requirements for the communicating node pair are considered and a Lagrangian based solution procedure was developed to solve the problem. This paper also addresses only arc capacity constraints.

Kennington and Lewis (2001) used a node-arc formulation to model the problem of finding minimum amount of spare capacity to be allocated throughout a mesh network so that the network can survive the failure of an arc. Two-level survivable telecommunication network design problem to simultaneously determine the optimal partitioning of the network in to clusters and hub location for each cluster to minimize inter-cluster traffic is reported in Park, Lee, Park, and Lee (2000). In this study while a mesh topology is considered for the backbone network interconnecting the hubs, a ring or hubbed topology is considered for local clusters. Fortz, Labbé, and Maffioli (2000) studied a variation of survivable network design problem in which a minimum cost two-connected network is designed such that the shortest cycle to which each edge belongs does not exceed a given length.

Recently researchers have started looking at topology, capacity assignment and routing problems in wavelength division multiplexed (WDM) all optical networks. The problem of routing traffic, determining backup paths for single node or link failure, and assigning wavelengths in both primary and restoration paths, all simultaneously is addressed in Kennington, Olinick, Ortynsky, and Spiride (2003). Empirical study comparing solutions that forbid and permit wavelength translations in a WDM network is presented in Kennington and Olinick (2004).

A number of researchers have looked at the two terminal reliability problems of finding the probability that at least one path set exists between a specified pair of nodes. Chaturvedi and Misra (2002) proposed a hybrid method to evaluate the reliability of large and complex networks that reduces the computation time considerably over previous algorithms. Recently, Goyal, Misra, & Chaturvedi (2005) proposed a new source node exclusion method to evaluate terminal pair reliability of complex communication networks.

A number of researchers have looked at just the routing problems, given the topology of networks (see Gavish, 1992, for a survey of routing problems). These problems provide least cost routing solutions for routing commodity traffic in a given network topology. Vachani et al. (1996), and Lee and Chang (1997) have examined routing multicommodity flow in ring networks subject to capacity constraints. Amiri and Pirkul (1996) have looked at selecting primary and secondary route selection for commodity traffic, given the topology of the network and capacity of links of the network.

Models and solution procedures are developed in this chapter to address capacitated survivability network design problem. Unlike previous work in this area, we build a model that integrates both topology design and routing problems under specified survivability constraints. The problem is modeled as a mixed 0/1 integer nonlinear program and solved using Lagrangian relaxation and graph-theoretic heuristics. The remainder of the chapter is organized as follows. In the next section, we present the model. Then we present solution procedures and algorithms for obtaining lower and upper bounds on the optimal value of the problem. Computational results are presented next. Conclusions and future research directions are discussed in the last section.

Model Formulation

We consider a set of nodes with given traffic requirements (called as commodity traffic) between the node pairs. The objective is to install links between nodes at minimum cost so that two node disjoint paths can be designated for each commodity traffic and that the traffic carried on these paths are below the capacity constraints at the nodes and links on these paths. One of the paths designated as the primary path, carries the traffic between the node pairs during the normal operation of the network. The other path designated as the secondary path carries all or portion of the commodity traffic in the event of failure of a node or link along the primary path. The notations used in the model are presented in Table 1.

B_a in the above definitions refers to capacity of link which can be installed on arc a. In SONET and asynchronous networks, capacity of each link is determined by the *carrier rate* (T-3 at 45 Mbps, Optical Carrier (OC) - 3 at 155 Mbps, or OC-12 at 622 Mbps) of the multiplex equipment at the nodes at each end of the link. The multiplexing capacity of each node is normally much more than the capacity of links connecting them. We consider networks with homogeneous multiplexers and hence the carrier rate of each link is determined by the type of network (T-3, OC-3, OC-12). In these networks, the link capacity constraints dominate.

The problem, [P], of finding the optimal survivable topology and selecting a pair of node disjoint routes for each commodity is formulated as follows:

Problem [P]:

Minimize $\sum_{a \in A} C_a y_a$ (1)

Subject to:

$$f_a = \sum_{w \in Wr \in R_w} P_{ar} \lambda_w x_{rw} \quad \forall a \in A \tag{2}$$

Table 1. Notations used in the model

V	Index set of nodes; $i,j \in V$
A	Index set of arcs in a complete undirected graph with node set V; $a = \{i,j\} \in A$
W	Index set of commodities, i.e., pairs of nodes that communicate; for each commodity w, $O(w)$ and $D(w)$ represent the origin node and the destination node, respectively
λ_w	Traffic demand of commodity w, i.e., inter-node traffic demand between the node pair $w \in W$
C_a	Cost of installing a bridge on arc a
L_i	Capacity of node i
B_a	Capacity of links installed on each arc $a \in A$
R_w	Set of all candidate route pairs for commodity w; $r=(r1,r2) \in R_w$ defines a pair of node-disjoint *primary path* ($r1$) and *secondary path* ($r2$) that connect the pair of nodes w.
ρ_w	Portion of λ_w which must be supported by the secondary path in case of a node or an arc failure on the primary path
δ_{iw}	Descriptive variable which is one if $i=O(w)$ or $i=D(w)$; it is zero otherwise
P_{ar}	Descriptive variable which is one if arc a is in the primary path $r1$; it is zero otherwise
S_{ar}	Descriptive variable which is one if arc a is in the secondary path $r2$; it is zero otherwise
P_{ir}	Descriptive variable which is one if node i is in the primary path $r1$; it is zero otherwise
S_{ir}	Descriptive variable which is one if node i is in the secondary path $r2$; it is zero otherwise
y_a	Decision variable which is set to one if a link of capacity B_a is installed on arc $a \in A$; zero otherwise
x_{rw}	Decision variable which is set to one if route pair r is selected for commodity w; zero otherwise

$$f_{aj} = \sum_{w \in W} \sum_{r \in R_w} \{p_{ar}(1-p_{jr}) + (1-\delta_{jw})s_{ar}p_{jr}\rho_w\}\lambda_w x_{rw} \quad \forall a \in A, j \in V \tag{3}$$

$$f_{aj} = \sum_{w \in W} \sum_{r \in R_w} \{p_{ar}(1-p_{jr}) + (1-\delta_{jw})s_{ar}p_{jr}\rho_w\}\lambda_w x_{rw} \quad \forall a \in A, j \in V \tag{4}$$

$$f_i = \sum_{w \in W} \sum_{r \in R_w} p_{ir}\lambda_w x_{rw} \quad \forall i \in V \tag{5}$$

$$f_{ib} = \sum_{w \in W} \sum_{r \in R_w} \{p_{ir}(1-p_{br}) + s_{ir}p_{br}\rho_w\}\lambda_w x_{rw} \quad \forall i \in V \ b \in A \tag{6}$$

$$f_{ij} = \sum_{w \in W} \sum_{r \in R_w} \{p_{ir}(1-p_{jr}) + (1-\delta_{jw})s_{ir}p_{jr}\rho_w\}\lambda_w x_{rw} \quad \forall j \in V, i \in V \setminus j \tag{7}$$

$$f_a \leq B_a y_a \quad \forall a \in A \tag{8}$$

$$f_{ab} \leq B_a y_a \quad \forall b \in A, a \in A \setminus b \tag{9}$$

$$f_{aj} \leq B_a y_a \quad \forall a \in A, j \in V \tag{10}$$

$$f_i \leq L_i \quad \forall i \in V \tag{11}$$

$$f_{ib} \leq L_i \quad \forall i \in V, b \in A \tag{12}$$

$$f_{ij} \leq L_i \quad \forall j \in V, i \in V \setminus j \tag{13}$$

$$\sum_{r \in R_w} x_{rw} = 1 \quad \forall w \in W \tag{14}$$

$$y_a \in \{0,1\} \quad \forall a \in A \tag{15}$$

$$x_{rw} \in \{0,1\} \quad \forall r \in R_w, w \in W \tag{16}$$

$$f \geq 0 \tag{17}$$

In the model, the definitional variable f_i (respectively f_a) represents the flow of all commodities into node i (resp. the link on arc a if a link is installed on the arc), when none of the nodes and the links are in failure. Variables f_{ib} and f_{ab} represent the flow of all commodities into i and a, respectively, when the link on arc b has failed. Similarly, variables f_{ij} and f_{aj} represent the flow of all commodities into i and a, respectively, when node j has failed. Constraints (2) – (7) represent the definition of the above flows.

Constraints (8) to (13) require that, in the face of the failure of any node or link, none of the active nodes and links should be overloaded beyond their effective transmission capacities. Constraint set (14) requires that only one pair of node disjoint paths is selected for each commodity. The objective function captures the cost of links installed on the arcs of the network.

The above problem is a large-scale integer-linear program and integrates the problem of topology design, capacity assignment and routing. At least the topological design problem can be shown to be NP-hard as referenced in Rios et al. (2000). In this chapter, we develop methods to generate feasible solutions and bounds for checking the quality of these solutions, for realistically sized problems. We describe in the following section, the solution procedure we have developed to solve this problem.

Solution Procedure

Because of the combinatorial nature of the problem, we seek to obtain good feasible solutions and also present the lower bound on the optimal solution of the problem so that the quality of the feasible solution can be determined. Since the above model is normally one of the sub problems in a Metropolitan Area Network design as discussed in Cosares et al. (1995) our objective is to find a "good" but not necessarily optimal solution within reasonable computation time.

The number of node-disjoint route pairs for a commodity in a complete graph grows exponentially with the network size. We select apriori, a set R_w, of node-disjoint route pairs for each commodity w, a priori, based on the arc cost metric of C_a/B_a. This makes our model more constrained and hence provide an over-design of the network. But by selecting adequate number of node disjoint paths for each commodity, this shortcoming can be overcome. The selection of a subset of node disjoint paths is done to improve solvability of the problem. This approach has been used by Narasimhan, Pirkul, and De (1988), for primary and secondary route selection in backbone networks. The k-shortest path algorithm developed by Yen (1971) is employed in the route pair selection.

Let $G(V,A)$ be the graph where V is the set of all nodes and A is the set of all arcs which are present in any of the candidate route pairs, generated by the route generation algorithm. With all the reduction in the cardinality of R_w's, problem [P] is still a large-scale integer program. We describe in this section, a solution method based on Lagrangian decomposition that generates a good feasible solution, hence an upper bound (UB), as well as a lower bound (LB) on the optimal value of [P]. The Lagrangian relaxation scheme has been successfully applied by many researchers for solving network design problems (see Agarwal, 1989; Gavish, 1992; Amiri & Pirkul, 1996; Rios et al., 2000). For details on Lagrangian relaxation scheme, the reader is referred to Fisher (1981).

Lagrangian Sub Problems

After dualizing constraints (2) to (7) using multipliers $\alpha, \beta, \mu, \nu, \phi$ and ψ we get the following Lagrangian relaxation [LR(**D**)]. Here **D** represents the dual vector $[\alpha, \beta, \mu, \nu, \phi, \psi]$. In the sequel, OV[.] stands for the optimal value of problem [.] and OS[.] stands for the optimal solution of problem [P].

*Problem-LR(**D**):*

$$\min \sum_{a \in A} C_a y_a - \sum_{i \in V} \nu_i f_i - \sum_{i \in V} \sum_{b \in A} \phi_{ib} f_{ib} - \sum_{j \in V} \sum_{i \in V \setminus j} \psi_{ij} f_{ij} +$$

$$\sum_{w \in W} \sum_{r \in R_w} \left\{ \sum_{a \in A} \alpha_a p_{ar} + \sum_{b \in A} \sum_{a \in A \setminus b} \beta_{ab} \left\{ p_{ar} (1 - p_{br}) + s_{ar} p_{br} \rho_w \right\} \right. +$$

$$\sum_{a\in A}\sum_{j\in V}\mu_{aj}\left\{p_{ar}\left(1-p_{jr}\right)+\left(1-\delta_{jw}\right)s_{ar}p_{jr}r_{w}\right\}+\sum_{i\in V}\nu_{i}p_{ir}+$$

$$\sum_{i\in V}\sum_{b\in A}\phi_{ib}\left\{p_{ir}\left(1-p_{br}\right)+s_{ir}p_{br}\rho_{w}\right\}+$$

$$\left.\sum_{j\in V}\sum_{i\in V\setminus j}\psi_{ij}\left\{p_{ir}\left(1-p_{jr}\right)+\left(1-\delta_{jw}\right)s_{ir}p_{jr}\rho_{w}\right\}\right\}\lambda_{w}x_{rw}-$$

$$\sum_{a\in A}\alpha_{a}f_{a}-\sum_{b\in A}\sum_{a\in A\setminus b}\beta_{ab}f_{ab}-\sum_{j\in V}\sum_{a\in A}\mu_{aj}f_{aj} \qquad (18)$$

subject to (8)-(17).

Problem [LR(**D**)] can be decomposed into the following independent sub problems.

[LR$_1$(**D**)]   min $\sum_{i\in V}(-\nu_i f_i)$ s.t. (11) and (17).

[LR$_2$(**D**)]   min $\sum_{i\in V}\sum_{b\in A}(-\phi_{ib}f_{ib})$ s.t. (12) and (17).

[LR$_3$(**D**)]   min $\sum_{j\in V}\sum_{i\in V\setminus j}\left(-\psi_{ij}f_{ij}\right)$ s.t. (13) and (17).

[LR$_4$(**D**)]   min $\sum_{a\in A}\{C_a y_a - \alpha_a f_a - \sum_{b\in A\setminus a}\beta_{ab}f_{ab} - \sum_{j\in V}\mu_{aj}f_{aj}\}$
                        s.t. (8),(9),(10),(15), and (17).

[LR$_5$(**D**)]   min $\sum_{w\in W}\sum_{r\in R_w}\pi_{rw}x_{rw}$ s.t. (14) and (16).

                        where π_{rw} is the coefficient of x_{rw} in (18).

And OV[LR(D)] $= \sum_{i=1}^{5}$ OV[LR$_i$ (D)].

The best lower bound on OV[P] can be calculated as $Z_l = \text{OV}[\text{LR}(\text{D}^*)] = \max_{\text{D}}\{\text{OV}[\text{LR}(\text{D})]\}$ where Z_l is the best lower bound on OV[P]. The optimal set of multipliers D^* can be located by using a subgradient optimization procedure. The subgradient procedure has been effectively used by Amiri and Pirkul (1996), Gavish (1992), and others for solving network design problems. In this chapter, the following solution procedure based on subgradient procedure is developed for obtaining lower and upper bounds on OV[P].

The overall solution procedure is given in Figure 1.

Primal Heuristic for Generating Initial Primal Feasible Solution: *INITIALHEUR*

Since most of the networks, which use high capacity transport, are sparse networks, we have designed a primal heuristic that starts with a Hamilton circuit (Boffey, 1982). It then builds a bi-connected network to support traffic flow without violating capacity constraints of the nodes and arcs. The heuristic procedure is outlined in Figure 2.

Figure 1. Overall solution procedure

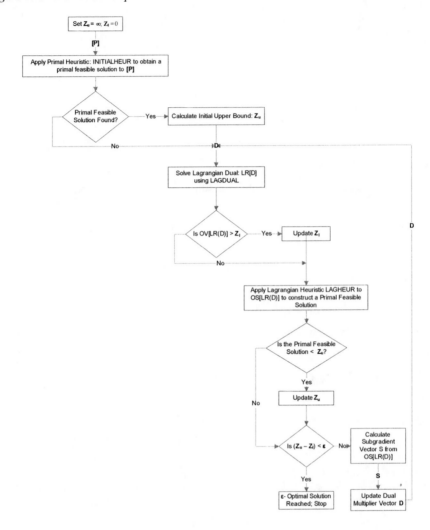

Procedure for Solving Lagrangian Subproblems: LAGDUAL

The individual Lagrangian sub problems of LR(**D**)], can be solved in polynomial time. Described below are the solution procedures for solving the different subproblems.

Problem $[LR_1(\mathbf{D})]$ can be decomposed in to $|V|$ sub problems for each $i \in V$. The solution to $[LR_1(\mathbf{D})]$ is: for each i, set $f_i = L_i$ if $v_i \geq 0$; else set $f_i = 0$. Similar closed form solutions are obtained for $[LR_2(\mathbf{D})]$ and $[LR_3(\mathbf{D})]$ by decomposing them into $|V| \times |A|$, and $|V|^2$ subproblems respectively. Problem $[LR_5(\mathbf{D})]$ can be decomposed over the set of commodities into $|W|$ subproblems. In each subproblem, set x_{rw} to 1 for which the coefficient π_{rw} is minimum; set all the other x_{rw} to 0.

Figure 2. Primal heuristic INITIALHEUR

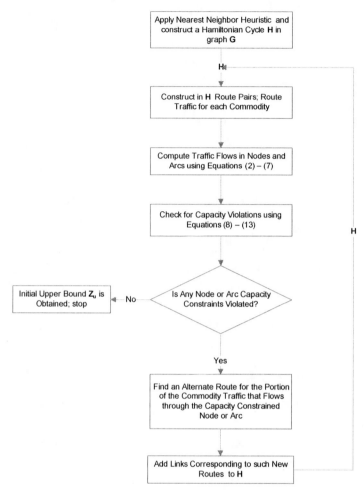

In [LR$_4$(**D**)], it is clear that $f_a^* = B_a y_a^*$ if $\alpha_a > 0$; 0 otherwise. Similar arguments can be made for variables f_{ab} and f_{aj}. Therefore, we can rewrite [LR$_4$(**D**)] as:

$$\min \sum_{a \in A} \left[C_a - B_a \left\{ \max(0, \alpha_a) + \sum_{b \in A \backslash a} \max(0, \beta_{ab}) + \sum_{j \in V} \max(0, \mu_{aj}) \right\} \right] y_a \; s.t. \; (15)$$

Given the vectors α, β and μ, [LR$_4$(**D**)] can be decomposed into $|A|$ subproblems, each of which can be trivially solved. Surrogate constraints can be added to [LR$_4$(**D**)] to improve the Lagrangian bound. We add constraints requiring that the topology implied by a **y**-solution should be connected and spanning. This constraint is a surrogate to constraint requiring two node disjoint paths between every pair of communicating nodes and hence if added will provide a lower bound to OV[P]. This strengthened version of $[LR_4(\mathbf{D})]$ is still solved in polynomial time using a variation of the minimum spanning tree algorithm.

After substituting for f_a, f_{ab}, f_{aj}, and adding the surrogate constraints, $[LR_4(D)]$ can be rewritten as follows:

$[LR_4{}'(D)]$: min $\sum_{a \in A} d_a y_a$ subject to (15) and **Y** forms a connected, spanning graph.

Next, we describe the procedure for solving $[LR_4{}'(D)]$.

- **Step 1:** The optimal solution to $[LR_4{}'(D)]$, contains arcs with negative coefficients. Set $y_a = 1$, $\forall a \in A$ such that $d_a \leq 0$ and call this set as A^1. Set lower bound on OV$[LR_4(\mathbf{D})]$ to be $z_{4l} = \sum_{a \in A^1} d_a y_a$. Let T be the set of all connected subgraphs formed after the inclusion of the arcs in set A^1 in the topology. If $|T|=1$, then a connected spanning graph is formed. Set $A^* = A^1$ and Stop.

  Otherwise, go to Step 2 to construct a minimal cost connected spanning subgraph.

- **Step 2:** Construct a new graph $G' = (T',A')$ where each connected sub graph $t \in T$ formed in *step:1* forms a corresponding node t' of graph G'. If subgraph t contains a single node, then the corresponding node $t' \in T'$ is called as a *unit node*. If t contains more than one node, then it is called as a *super node*. Let i and j denote nodes in the original graph G; s and t denote unit nodes in G'; u and v denote super nodes in G'. We say "$s = i$," if s in G' corresponds to i in G. We say "i in u" if super node u in G' contains node i in G.

  If there is an arc $\{i,j\}$ in G, and $s = i$ and $t = j$, then there is an arc (s,t) in G' with cost $d_{st} = d_{ij}$. If G has at least one arc between i and the nodes belonging to super node u, then there will be only one arc between $s = i$ and u in G' and the arc cost $d_{su} = \min_{\{i,j\} \in A} (d_{ij} \mid i = s, j \text{ in } u)$. If G has at least one arc between nodes in u and nodes in v, then there will be only one arc between $\{u, v\}$ in G' and the arc cost $d_{uv} = \min_{\{i,j\} \in A} (d_{ij} \mid i \text{ in } u, j \text{ in } v)$. Let E be the set of arcs in G corresponding to A' in G'.

  Go to Step 3.

- **Step 3:** Find the set of shortest paths P between every pair of nodes in G'. For every arc $\{p,q\} \in A'$, replace the arc cost d_{pq} by the cost e_{pq} of the shortest path between p and q. Now the cost of arcs in G' satisfies the triangle inequality. We can write the translated problem as:

$[LR_4{}''(\mathbf{D})]$: min $\sum_{a \in A} e_a y_a$ subject to (15) and **Y** forms a connected, spanning graph

and OV$[LR_4{}''(D)] \leq$ OV$[LR_4{}'(D)]$.

Go to Step 4.

- **Step 4. Held-Karp Lower Bound Algorithm - HELDKARP (Held & Karp, 1971):**
  As discussed in Monma, Munson, and Pulleyblank (1990), under the triangle inequality condition, the minimum cost of a two-vertex connected spanning network is equal to the minimum cost of a two-edge connected spanning network. Further, under the triangle inequality, the Held-Karp lower bound on Traveling Salesman Problem (TSP) is a lower bound on the optimal value of the minimum cost two-edge connected network design problem due to parsimonious property as discussed in Goemans and Bertsimas (1993). This yields the following condition: HK[TSP] $\leq$ OV[LR$_4$''(D)] where HK[TSP] refers to the Held-Karp lower bound on TSP applied to graph G'. We use Held-Karp algorithm based on 1-tree relaxation to compute the lower bound on TSP and hence a lower bound on OV[LR$_4$''(D)] .

  a. Apply *Nearest Neighbor Heuristic* (Boffey, 1982) to determine a salesman tour in graph G', and let the cost of the salesman tour be $\bar{z}$. If Nearest Neighbor Heuristic cannot find a salesman tour, then set $\bar{z} = \sum_{a \in A'} e_a$. Initialize Held-Karp lower bound z_l^{HK} and the dual vector π.

  b. Set $e_{pq} = e_{pq} + \pi_p + \pi_q \ \forall \{p,q\} \in A'$. Construct a minimum spanning 1-tree S_k based on modified weight (refer to Held & Karp [1970]) for 1-tree construction). Calculate the lower bound as:

$$z^{HK}(k) = \sum_{a \in S_k} e_a - 2 \sum_{i \in V'} \pi_i$$

  If $z^{HK}(k) > z_l^{HK}$, then set $z_l^{HK} = z^H(k)$. If $(\bar{z} - z_l^{HK}) < \varepsilon$, or if the degree of each node in S_k is two, then go to step:c. Otherwise, update the multiplier vector π and repeat this step.

  c. Let G''(V',A'') be the graph corresponding to the best subgradient. z_l^{HK} is the lower bound on OV[LR$_4$''(**D**)].

  Go to Step:5 to recover the solution on G.

- **Step 5:** Set lower bound on OV[LR$_4$(**D**)], $z_{4l} = z_{4l} + z_l^{HK}$. Map the arcs $a'' \in A''$ in G'' from Step:4, to the arcs in the shortest path set P as specified in Step:3 and further to the arcs in G as specified in Step:2. Let this arc set in G be A^2. Construct graph $G^*(V, A^*)$ by setting . Save this to be used in Lagrangian heuristic to recover primal feasible solution.

Lagrangian Heuristic: LAGHEUR

As described in the overall solution procedure, we try to recover primal feasible solution based on the Lagrangian solution obtained in each iteration of LAGDUAL. Such Lagrangian heuristics have been used by many researchers (Amiri & Pirkul, 1996; Gavish, 1992) to improve the upper bound on OV[P]. The Lagrangian based heuristic is described next:

- **Step 1. Build a biconnected graph $G'(V,A')$ from the Lagrangian solution:** Let $G^*(V,A^*)$ be the spanning graph obtained from *Step:*5 of the solution procedure for solving $[LR_4(\mathbf{D})]$. Set $A'=A^*$ and define graph $G'(V,A')$. If all nodes in G' have degree equal to two, then go to Step 2.

  Otherwise augment G' as follows:

  Let $V_1 \subset V$ be the set of leaf nodes in G' which have a degree less than 1. Add links between each pair of nodes in set V_1 to improve their degree to 2. If $|V_1|$ is odd, connect the lone node in V_1 to any other node in set $(V - V_1)$. Go to Step 2.

- **Step 2. Route flow and check for flow feasibility:** For each $w \in W$ construct a route pair $r = \{r_1, r_2\}$ in G' using the k-shortest path algorithm, such that r_1 and r_2 are node disjoint. If no node disjoint pair r could be found for any w, then graph G' is not biconnected and hence Stop.

  Otherwise, set $x_{rw}=1$. Using definitional equations (2) - (7), compute traffic flow f_i in nodes $i \in V$, f_a in arcs $a \in A'$. Check for capacity violations using the constraints (8) - (13). If there is capacity violation in any node or arc, go to Step 3. Otherwise, go to Step 4.

- **Step 3. Eliminate node and arc infeasibility:** Eliminate flow infeasibility in graph G_1 as described in the primal heuristic INITIALHEUR. If after rerouting commodity flow, there is still flow infeasibility, then primal feasible solution could not be found and stop. Otherwise go to Step 4.

- **Step 4:** If $\sum_{a \in A} c_a y_a > Z_u$ then set the upper bound $Z_u = \sum_{a \in A} c_a y_a$.

Computational Results

Since the model is applicable to a wide variety of networks, we designed our computational experiments to represent the different types of problem instance as given in Table 2.

The problem generation procedure generates 6, 10, and 15 node problem instances having 15, 45, and 105 y-variables. The route generation algorithm generates 20 route pairs for each traffic commodity and thus generates 60, 1800, and 4200 x-variables respectively. Nodes are randomly generated on a unit square. Since SONET and DS-3 based networks are either Wide Area Networks (WANs) or Metropolitan Area Networks (MANs), the distance are defined in hundreds of miles. The link cost c_{ij} consists of a constant term corresponding to interface cost plus a distance dependent component. The level of traffic demand is measured by (i) the ratio ρ_v of total traffic demand, $\sum_{w \in W} \lambda_w$ to the effective node capacity L_i for carrying originating, terminating and transit traffic through node i and by (ii) the ratio ρ_a of total traffic demand, $\sum_{w \in W} \lambda_w$ to the arc capacity B_a for carrying originating, terminating and transit traffic via arc a. In case of OC-12, OC-3 and DS-3 based WANs or MANs, the switches normally have enough switching capacity to support transmission across the link interfaces. In these cases, the node capacities are fixed at higher levels to make link capacity constraints more binding. For these problem instances ρ_v is set to be around 0.25 and ρ_a is set to 0.30. The parameters ρ_v and ρ_a are then used for generating the multicommodity

Table 2. Types of networks considered for problem generation

Problem Category	Type of Network	Link capacity
N-OC12	High-capacity N-node synchronous optical networks of type OC-12, typically used as private leased line networks or MANs.	622 Mbps
N-OC3	High-capacity N-node synchronous optical networks of type OC-3, typically used as private leased line networks or MANs.	155 Mbps
N-DS3	High-capacity N-node asynchronous private line network.	45 Mbps

traffic between each node pair. ε in the OVERALL procedure is set to 10%. Table 3 reports computational results for these problem categories.

For problems belonging to OC-12 category, LAGHEUR was not able to find a feasible solution. Larger gaps were observed. For networks belonging to OC-3 and DS3, LAGHEUR was effective in decreasing the upper bound. The average improvements in upper bound were 7.9%, 9.6% and 18.5% respectively for 6, 10 and 15-node problem. In all cases, LEGHEUR found optimal solutions. This indicates that the lower bounding procedure produces very tight lower bounds for problems in this category. The solution procedure took on the average, 11.4, 163.1, and 1936.1 seconds for solving 6, 10, and 15 node problems respectively in a Sun Sparc 5 workstation. Our solution procedure gives good results for designing low to medium capacity survivable networks. An example of a 10-node OC-3 backbone solution as given by our solution procedure, along with link costs, is illustrated in Figure 1.

For all problems, our solution procedure found a survivable ring network. This confirms the applicability of least cost ring network design being advocated for high-capacity optic fiber based telecommunication networks. Recently an architecture named HORNET (Hybrid Optoelectronic Ring NETworks) based on packet-over-wavelength division multiplexing technology is being proposed as a candidate for next generation Metropolitan Area Networks (White, Rogge, Shrikhande, & Kazovsky, 2003).

Conclusion and Future Reseach Directions

In this chapter we have studied the problem of selecting links of a network at minimal cost to construct a primary route and a node-disjoint secondary route for transfer of commodity traffic between nodes of the network, subject to capacity constraints at each node and link on the network. This problem is applicable to the design of high-capacity transport networks in the area of voice and data communications. We developed a Lagrangian-based solution procedure for finding the lower bounds of the problem. We developed effective heuristics to construct feasible solutions and upper bounds. We tested our solution procedure on four types of networks. Our computational study indicates that our solution procedure is effec-

Table 3. Computational results

Problem Category	LB from LAGDUAL	UB from INITIALHEUR	UB from LAGHEUR	% Improvement in UB	% Gap	Time (in Sec.)
6-OC12	2,410,462	2,587,345			6.84%	15.8
6-OC3	2,290,405	2,467,345	2,290,405	7.73%	0.00%	11.3
6-DS3	2,170,405	2,347,345	2,170,405	8.15%	0.00%	11.5
10-OC12	3,510,174	3,817,768			8.06%	183.7
10-OC3	3,310,077	3,617,768	3,310,077	9.30%	0.00%	179.8
10-DS3	3,110,077	3,417,768	3,110,077	9.89%	0.00%	180.2
15-OC12	3,988,659	4,641,755			14.07%	2157.8
15-OC3	3,688,547	4,341,755	3,688,547	17.71%	0.00%	2152.9
15-DS3	3,388,520	4,041,755	3,388,520	19.28%	0.00%	2159.6

Note: Blanks in the table indicate that either (1) LAGHEUR was not invoked as the epsilon optimal solution was found, or (2) LAGHEUR could not find a feasible solution

Figure 3. Optimal solution of an instance of 10 node OC-3 backbone network

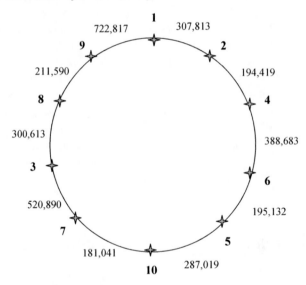

Note: Link costs are represented along side each link

tive in constructing optimal survivable ring networks of low to medium capacity. We were able to find optimal or near optimal solutions for networks having capacity as high as OC-3 (155 Mbps) transmission rate, and with up to 15 nodes in reasonable computation time. The effectiveness of the solution procedure, when ρ_v or ρ_a are high thus necessitating a dense topology, needs to be examined. As discussed in the solution procedure, we apriori generate the route set R_w for each commodity w. The set is large enough to provide a complete graph to start the solution procedure for the solved problems. But for larger problems, it might produce a subset of a complete graph. If it so happens, the upper bound from the solution procedure discussed in this chapter is an overestimate of the optimal solution. Hence more effective solution procedures need to be developed for larger problems. It would be ideal to integrate the route selection procedure endogenously into the model so that the limitations enumerated above on pre-selecting route pairs is overcome. Though our model allows for varying capacities across the network links, we have tested our solution procedure only against networks with homogeneous link capacities. An interesting study would be to test the performance of the solution procedure on networks with varying link capacities. Today's WANs operate at OC-48 (2.488 Gbps) and above. Such network instances need to be tested if the tool is to be used in the construction of high-speed survivable WANs.

References

Agarwal, Y.K. (1989, May/June). An algorithm for designing survivable networks. *AT&T Technical Journal*, 64-76.

Amiri, A., & Pirkul, H. (1996). Primary and secondary route selection in backbone communication networks. *European Journal of Operations Research, 93*, 98-109.

Balakrishnan, A., Magnanti, T., & Mirchandani, P. (1998). Designing hierarchical survivable networks. *Operations Research, 46*, 116-136.

Boffey T.B. (1982). *Graph theory in operations research.* Hong Kong: Macmillan Press.

Chaturvedi, S.K., & Misra, K.B. (2002). A hybrid method to evaluate reliability of complex networks. *International Journal of Quality & Reliability Management, 19*(8/9), 1098-1112.

Cosares S., Deutsch, D., & Saniee, I. (1995). SONET Toolkit: A decision support system for designing robust and cost-effective fiber-optic networks. *Interfaces, 25*, 20-40.

Fisher, M. (1981). Lagrangian relaxation method for solving integer programming problems. *Management Science, 27*, 1-17.

Fortz, B., Labbé, M., & Maffioli, F. (2000). Solving the two-connected network with bounded meshes problem. *Operations Research, 48*(6), 866-877.

Gavish, B., Trudeau, P., Dror, M., Gendreau, M., & Mason, L. (1989). Fiberoptic circuit network design under reliability constraints. *IEEE Journal on Selected Areas of Communication, 7*, 1181-1187.

Gavish, B. (1992). Routing in a network with unreliable components. *IEEE Transactions on Communications, 40*, 1248-1257.

Goemans, M., & Bertsimas, D. (1993). Survivable networks: Linear programming relaxations and the parsimonious property. *Mathematical Programming, 60,* 145-166.

Goldschmidt, O., Laugier, A., & Olinick, E. (2003). SONET/SDH ring assignment with capacity constraints. *Discrete Applied Mathematics, 129*(1), 99-128.

Goyal, N.K., Misra, R.B., & Chaturvedi, S.K. (2005). SNEM: A new approach to evaluate terminal pair reliability of communication networks. *Journal of Quality in Maintenance Engineering, 11*(3), 239-253.

Grotschel, M., Monma, C,L., & Stoer, M. (1992). Computational results with a cutting plane algorithm for designing communication networks with low-connectivity constraints. *Operations Research, 40,* 309-330.

Held, M., & Karp, R. (1970). The traveling-salesman problem and minimum spanning trees. *Operations Research, 18,* 1138-1162.

Held, M., & Karp, R. (1971). The traveling salesman problem and minimum spanning trees: Part II. *Mathematical Programming, 1,* 6-25.

Kennington, J., & Lewis, M. (2001). The path restoration version of the spare capacity allocation problem with modularity restrictions: Models, algorithms, and an empirical analysis. *INFORMS Journal on Computing, 13*(3), 181-190.

Kennington, J., Olinick, E., Ortynsky, A., & Spiride, G. (2003). Wavelength routing and assignment in a survivable WDM mesh network. *Operations Research, 51*(1), 67-79.

Kennington, J., & Olinick, E. (2004). Wavelength translation in WDM networks: Optimization models and solution procedures. *INFORMS Journal on Computing, 16*(2), 174-187.

Lee, C.Y., & Chang, S.G. (1997). Balancing loads on SONET rings with integer demand splitting. *Computers and Operations Research, 24,* 221-229.

Lee, C.Y., & Koh, S.J. (1997). A design of the minimum cost ring-chain network with dual-homing survivability: A tabu search approach. *Computers and Operations Research, 24,* 883-897.

Monma, C., Munson, B.S., & Pulleyblank, W.R. (1990). Minimum-weight two-connected spanning networks. *Mathematical Programming, 46,* 153-171.

Narasimhan, S., Pirkul, H., & De, P. (1988). Route selection in backbone data communication networks. *Computer Networks and ISDN Systems, 15,* 121-133.

Newport, K.T., & Varshney, P.K. (1991). Design of survivable communications networks under performance constraints. *IEEE Transactions on Reliability, 4,* 433-440.

Park, K., Lee, K., Park, S., & Lee, H. (2000). Telecommunication node clustering with node compatibility and network survivability requirements. *Management Science, 46*(3), 363-374.

Redman, J., Warren, M., & Hutchinson, W. (2005). System survivability: A critical security problem. *Information Management & Computer Security, 13*(3), 182-188.

Rios, M., Marianov, V., & Gutierrez, M. (2000). Survivable capacitated network design problem: New formulation and Lagrangian relaxation. *Journal of the Operational Research Society, 51,* 574-582.

Shyur, C., & Wen, U. (2001). SDHTOOL: Planning survivable and cost-effective SDH networks at Chunghwa Telecom. *Interfaces, 31,* 87-108.

Soni, S., Gupta, R., & Pirkul, H. (1999). Survivable network design: The state of the art. *Information Systems Frontiers, 1*, 303-315.

Vachani, R., Shulman, A, & Kubat, P. (1996). Multicommodity flows in ring networks. *INFORMS Journal on Computing, 8*, 235-242.

White, I.M., Rogge, M.S., Shrikhande, K., & Kazovsky, L.G. (2003). A summary of the HORNET project: a next-generation metropolitan area network. *IEEE Journal on Selected Areas in Communication, 21*(9), 1478-1494.

Wu, T., Kolar, D.J., & Cardwell, R.H. (1988). Survivable network architecture for broadband fiber optic networks: Model and performance comparison. *Journal of Lightwave Technology, 6*, 1698-1709.

Yen, J.Y. (1971). Finding the K-shortest loopless paths in a network. *Management Sciences, 17*, 712-716.

Chapter II

A Data Mining Driven Approach for Web Classification and Filtering Based on Multimodal Content Analysis

Mohamed Hammami, Faculté des Sciences de Sfax, Tunisia

Youssef Chahir, Université de Caen, France

Liming Chen, Ecole Centrale de Lyon, France

Abstract

Along with the ever growing Web is the proliferation of objectionable content, such as sex, violence, racism, and so forth. We need efficient tools for classifying and filtering undesirable Web content. In this chapter, we investigate this problem through WebGuard, our automatic machine-learning-based pornographic Web site classification and filtering system. Facing the Internet more and more visual and multimedia as exemplified by pornographic Web sites, we focus here our attention on the use of skin color-related visual content-based analysis along with textual and structural content based analysis for improving pornographic Web site filtering. While the most commercial filtering products on the marketplace are mainly based on textual content-based analysis such as indicative keywords detection or manually collected black list checking, the originality of our work resides on the addition of structural and visual content-based analysis to the classical textual content-based analysis along with several major-data mining techniques for learning and classifying. Experimented on a testbed of 400 Web sites including 200 adult sites and 200 nonpornographic ones, WebGuard, our Web filtering engine scored a 96.1% classification accuracy rate when only textual and structural content based analysis are used, and 97.4% classification accuracy rate when skin color-related visual content-based analysis is driven in addition. Further experiments on a black list of 12,311 adult Web sites manually collected and classified by the French Ministry of Education showed that WebGuard scored 87.82% classification accuracy rate when using only textual and structural content-based analysis, and 95.62% classification accuracy rate when the visual content-based analysis is driven in addition. The basic framework of WebGuard can apply to other categorization problems of Web sites which combine, as most of them do today, textual and visual content.

Introduction

In providing a huge collection of hyperlinked multimedia documents, Web has become a major source of information in our everyday life. With the proliferation of objectionable content on the Internet such as pornography, violence, racism, and so on, effective Web site classification and filtering solutions are essential for preventing from socio-cultural problems.

For instance, as one of the most prolific multimedia content on the Web, pornography is also considered as one of the most harmful, especially for children having each day easier access to the Internet. According to a study carried out in May 2000, 60% of the interviewed parents were anxious about their children navigating on the internet, particularly because of the presence of adult material (Gralla & Kinkoph, 2001). Furthermore, according to the Forrester lookup, a company which examines operations on the Internet, online sales related to pornography add up to 10% of the total amount of online operations (Gralla & Kinkoph, 2001). This problem concerns parents as well as companies. For example, the company Rank Xerox laid off 40 employees in October 1999 who were looking at pornographic sites during their working hours. To avoid this kind of abuse, the company installed program packages to supervise what its employees visit on the Net.

To meet such a demand, there exists a panoply of commercial products on the marketplace proposing Web site filtering. A significant number of these products concentrate on IP-based black list filtering, and their classification of Web sites is mostly manual, that is to say no truly automatic classification process exists. But, as we know, the Web is a highly dynamic information source. Not only do many Web sites appear everyday while others disappear, but site content (especially links) are also frequently updated. Thus, manual classification and filtering systems are largely impractical and inefficient. The ever-changing nature of the Web calls for new techniques designed to classify and filter Web sites and URLs automatically (Hammami, Tsishkou, & Chen, 2003; Hammami, Chahir, & Chen, 2003).

Automatic pornographic Web site classification is a quite representative instance of the general Web site categorization problem as it usually mixes textual hyperlinked content with visual content. A lot of research work on Web document classification and categorization has already brought to light that only textual-content based classifier performs poorly on hyperlinked Web documents and structural content-based features, such as hyperlinks and linked neighbour documents, help greatly to improve the classification accuracy rate (Chakrabarti, Dom, & Indyk, 1998; Glover, Tsioutsiouliklis, Lawrence, Pennock, & Flake, 2002).

In this chapter, we focus our attention on the use of skin color related visual content-based analysis along with textual and structural content-based analysis for improving automatic pornographic Web site classification and filtering. Unlike the most commercial filtering products which are mainly based on indicative keywords detection or manually collected black list checking, the originality of our work resides on the addition of structural and visual content-based analysis to the classical textual content-based analysis along with several major-data mining techniques for learning and classifying.

Experimented on a testbed of 400 Web sites including 200 adult sites and 200 nonpornographic ones, WebGuard, our Web-filtering engine scored a 96.1% classification accuracy rate when only textual and structural content-based analysis are used, and 97.4% classification accuracy rate when skin color-related visual content-based analysis is driven in addition. Further experiments on a black list of 12,311 adult Web sites manually collected and classified by the French Ministry of Education showed that WebGuard scored 87.82% classification accuracy rate when using only textual and structural content-based analysis, and 95.62% classification accuracy rate when the visual content-based analysis is driven in addition. Based on a supervised classification with several data mining algorithms, the basic framework of WebGuard can apply to other categorization problems of Web sites combining, as most of them today, textual and visual content.

The remainder of this chapter is organized as follows. In the next section, we first define our MYL test dataset and assessment criterion then overview related work. The design principle together with MYL learning dataset and overall architecture of WebGuard are presented in the following section. The various features resulted from textual and structural analysis of a Web page and their classification performance when these features are used on MYL test dataset are described in the section afterwards. The skin color modelling and skin-like region segmentation are presented in the subsequent section. Based on experimental results using MYL test dataset, a comparison study of strategies for integrating skin color-related visual content-based analysis for Web site classification is discussed in the next section. The experimental evaluation and comparison results are then discussed. Some implementation issues including in particular image preprocessing are described in the following section. The final section summarizes the WebGuard approach and presents some concluding remarks and future work directions.

State of the Art and Analysis of the Competition

In the literature, there exists an increasing interest on Web site classification and filtering issue. Responding to the necessity of protecting Internet access from the proliferation of harmful Web content, there also exists a panoply of commercial filtering products on the marketplace. In this section, we first define some rather classical evaluation measures and describe our Web site classification testbed, MYL test dataset which is used in the subsequent to assess and compare various research work and commercial products. Then, we overview some significant research work within the field and evaluate different commercial products using MYL test dataset. Finally, we conclude this state-of-the-art section with findings from the research work overview and the analysis of commercial product competition.

MYL Test Dataset and Measures of Evaluation

A good Web content-filtering solution should deny access to adult Web site while giving access to inoffensive ones. We thus manually collected a test dataset, named *MYL test dataset* in the subsequent, consisting of 400 Web sites; half of them being pornographic while the other half being inoffensive. The manual selection of these Web sites was a little bit tricky so as to have a good representativeness of Web sites. For instance, for pornographic Web sites of our MYL test dataset, we manually included erotic Web sites, pornographic Web sites, hack Web sites presenting pornographic nature images, and some game Web sites, while inoffensive on the day, presenting illicit text and images in the night.

The selection of nonpornographic Web sites includes the ones which may lead to confusion, in particular the ones on health, sexology, fashion parade, shopping sites on under-wear, and so forth.

The performance of a classifier on a testbed can be assessed by a confusion matrix opposing assigned class (column) of the samples by the classifier with their true original class (row). Figure 1 illustrates a confusion matrix for a two-classes model.

In this matrix, $n_{A,B}$ gives the number of samples of class A but assigned by the classifier to class B and $n_{B,A}$ the number of samples of class B but assigned to class A, while $n_{A,A}$ and $n_{B,B}$ give the number of samples correctly classified by the classifier for both classes A and B. In our case for pornographic Web site classification, suppose that a Web filtering engine is assessed on our MYL test dataset, we would have two classes, for instance A denoting of pornographic Web sites while B that of inoffensive Web sites. Thus, a perfect Web site filtering system would produce a diagonal confusion matrix with $n_{A,B}$ and $n_{B,A}$ set to zero.

From such a confusion matrix, one can derive not only the number of times where the classifier misclasses samples but also the type of misclassification. Moreover, one can build three global indicators on the quality of a classifier from such a confusion matrix:

Figure 1. Confusion matrix for a model of 2 classes A and B

	Assigned class	
Original class	A	B
A	$n_{A,A}$	$n_{A,B}$
B	$n_{B,A}$	$n_{B,B}$

- **Global error rate:** $\varepsilon_{global} = (n_{A.B} + n_{B.A})/card(M)$ where $card(M)$ is the number of samples in a test bed. One can easily see that the global error rate is the complement of *classification accuracy rate* or success classification rate defined by $(n_{A.A} + n_{B.B})/card(M)$.

- **A priori error rate:** this indicator measures the probability that a sample of class k is classified by the system to other class than class k. $\varepsilon_{a\,priori}(k) = \Sigma_{j \neq k} n_{k.j}/\Sigma_j n_{k.j}$ where j represents the different classes, i.e., A or B in our case. For instance the a priori error rate for class A is defined by $\varepsilon_{a\,priori}(A) = n_{A.B}/(n_{A.A} + n_{A.B})$. This indicator is thus clearly the complement of the classical *recall rate* which is defined for class A by $n_{A.A}/(n_{A.A} + n_{A.B})$.

- **A posteriori error rate:** this indicator measures the probability that a sample assigned to class k by the system effectively belongs to class k. $\varepsilon_{a\,posteriori}(k) = \Sigma_{j \neq k} n_{j.k}/\Sigma_j n_{j.k}$ where j represents the different classes, i.e., A or B in our case. For instance the a posteriori error rate for class A is defined by $\varepsilon_{a\,posteriori}(A) = n_{B.A}/(n_{A.A} + n_{B.A})$. This indicator is thus clearly the complement of the classical *precision rate* which is defined for class A by $n_{A.A}/(n_{A.A} + n_{B.A})$.

All these indicators are important on the assessment of the quality of a classifier. When global error rate gives the global behaviour of the system, a priori error rate and a posteriori error rate tell us more precisely where the classifier is likely to commit wrong results.

Related Research Work

There exist four major pornographic Web site filtering approaches which are Platform for Internet Content Selection (PICS), URL blocking, keyword filtering, and intelligent content-based analysis (Lee, Hui, & Fong, 2002). PICS is a set of specification for content-rating systems which is supported both by Microsoft Internet Explorer, Netscape Navigator and several other Web-filtering systems. As PICS is a voluntary self-labelling system freely rated by content provider, it can only be used as supplementary mean for Web content filtering. URL blocking approach restricts or allow access by comparing the requested Web page's URL with URLs in a stored list. A *black* list contains URLs of objectionable Web sites while a *white* list gathers permissible ones. The dynamic nature of Web implies the necessity of constantly keeping to date the black list which relies in the most cases on large team of reviewers, making the human based black list approach impracticable. Keyword filtering approach blocks access to Web site on the basis of the occurrence of offensive words and phrases. It thus compares each word or phrase in a searched Web page with those of a keyword dictionary of prohibited words or phrases. While this approach is quite intuitive and simple, it may unfortunately easily lead to a well known phenomenon of "overblocking" which blocks access to inoffensive Web sites for instance Web pages on health or sexology.

The intelligent content-based analysis for pornographic Web site classification falls in the general problem of automatic Web site categorization and classification systems. The elaboration of such systems needs to rely on a machine-learning process with a supervised learning. For instance, Glover et al. (2002) utilized SVM in order to define a Web document classifier, while Lee et al. (2002) made use of neural networks to set up a Web content filtering solution. The basic problem with SVM which reveals to be very efficient in many classification applications is the difficulty of finding a kernel function mapping the initial feature vectors into higher dimensional feature space where data from the two classes are roughly linearly separable. On the other hand, neural networks, while showing its efficiency in dealing with both linearly and non linearly separable problems, are not easy to understand its classification decision.

A fundamental problem in machine learning is the design of discriminating feature vectors which relies on our a priori knowledge of the classification problem. The more simple the decision boundary is, the better is the performance of a classifier. Web documents are reputed to be notoriously difficult to classify (Chakrabarti et al., 1998). While a text classifier can reach a classification accuracy rate between 80%-87% on homogeneous corpora such as financial articles, it has also been shown that a text classifier is inappropriate for Web documents due to sparse and hyperlinked structure and its diversity of Web contents more and more multimedia (Flake, Tsioutsiouliklis, & Zhukov, 2003). Lee et al. (2002) proposed in their pornographic Web site classifier frequencies of indicative keywords in a Web page to judge its relevance to pornography. However, they explicitly excluded URLs from their feature vector, arguing that such an exclusion should not compromise the Webpage's relevance to pornography as indicative keywords contribute only a small percentage to the total occurrences of indicative keywords.

A lot of work emphasized rather the importance of Web page structure, in particular hyperlinks, to improve Web search engine ranking (Brin & Page, 1998; Sato, Ohtaguro, Nakashima, & Ito, 2005) and Web crawlers (Cho, Garcia-Molina, & Page, 1998), discover Web communities (Flake, Lawrence, & Giles, 2000), and classify Web pages (Yang, Slattery, & Ghani, 2001; Fürnkranz, 1999; Attardi, Gulli, & Sebastiani, 1999; Glover et al., 2002). For instance, Flake et al. (200) investigated the problem of Web community identification only based on the hyperlinked structure of the Web. They highlighted that a hyperlink between two Web pages is an explicit indicator that two pages are related to one another. Started from this hypothesis, they studied several methods and measures, such as bibliographic coupling and co-citation coupling, hub and authority, and so forth. Glover et al. (2002) also studied the use of Web structure for classifying and describing Web pages. They concluded that the text in citing documents, when available, often has greater discriminative and descriptive power than the text in the target document itself. While emphasizing the use of inbound anchortext and surrounding words, called extended anchortext, to classify Web pages accurately, they also highlighted that the only extended anchortext-based classifier when combined with only textual content-based classifier greatly improved the classification accuracy. However, none of these works propose to take into account the visual content for Web classification.

Analysis of Market Competition

To complete our previous overview, we also carried out a study on a set of best known commercial filtering products on the marketplace so as to get to know the performance and functionalities available at the moment. We tested the most commonly used filtering software over our MYL test dataset. The six products we tested are: Microsoft Internet Explorer (RSACi) [Content Rating Association (ICRA)], Cybersitter 2002 (www.cybersitter.com),

Figure 2. Classification accuracy rates of six commercial filtering products on MYL test dataset

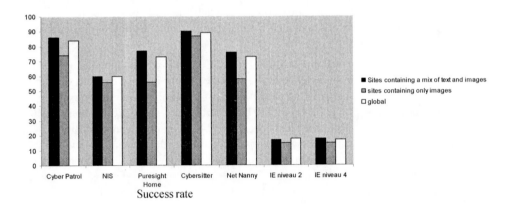

Netnanny 4.04 (www.netnanny.com), Norton Internet Security 2003 (www.symantec.com), Puresight Home 1.6 (www.icognito.com), and Cyber Patrol 5.0 (www.cyberpatrol.com).

Most of them support PICS filtering, URL blocking and but only keyword-based content analysis. Figure 2 shows the results of our study. It compares the success rates of the most common software on the market today. As we can see, the success classification rate can reach 90% for the best of them. Interestingly enough, another independent study on the most 10 popular commercial Web-filtering systems was driven on a dataset of 200 pornographic Web pages and 300 nonpornographic Web pages and gave similar conclusion on performance (Lee et al., 2002).

In addition to drawbacks that we outlined in the previous section, these tests also brought to light several other issues that we discovered. A function which seems very important to users of this kind of product is the configurability of the level of selectivity of the filter. Actually there are different types of offensive content and our study shows that, while highly pornographic sites are well handled by the most of these commercial products, erotic sites or sexual education for instance are unaccounted for. That is to say they are either classified as highly offensive or as normal sites. Thus, good filters are to be distinguished from the less good ones also by their capacity to correctly identify the true nature of the pornographic or non-pornographic sites. Sites containing the word "sex" do not all have to be filtered. Adult sites must be blocked but scientific and education sites must stay accessible.

Another major problem is the fact that all products on the market today rely solely on keyword based textual content analysis. Thus, the efficiency of the analysis greatly depends on the word database, its language, and its diversity. For instance, we found out that a product using an American dictionary will not detect a French pornographic site.

Overview Outlines

To sum up, the most commercial filtering products are mainly based on indicative keywords detection or manually collected black list checking while the dynamic nature and the huge amount of Web documents call for an automatic intelligent content-based approach for pornographic Web site classification and filtering. Furthermore, if many related research work suggest with reason the importance of structural information, such as hyperlinks, "keywords" metadata, and so on, for Web site classification and categorization, they do not take into account the visual content while the Internet has become more and more visual as exemplified by the proliferation of pornographic Web sites. A fully efficient and reliable pornographic Web site classification and filtering solution thus must be automatic system relying on textual and structural content-based analysis along with visual content-based analysis.

Principle and Architecture of WebGuard

The lack of reliability and other issues that we discovered from our previous study on the state of the art encouraged us to design and implement WebGuard with the aim to obtaining an effective Web-filtering system. The overall goal of WebGuard is to make access to Internet safer for both adults and children, blocking Web sites with pornographic content while giving access on inoffensive ones. In this section, we first sketch the basic design principles of WebGuard; then, we introduce the fundamentals of data mining techniques which are used as the basic machine learning mechanism in our work. Following that, two applications of these data mining within the framework of WebGuard are shortly described. Finally, the MYL learning dataset are presented.

WebGuard Design Principles

Given the dynamic nature of Web and its huge amount of documents, we decided to build an automatic pornographic content detection engine based on a machine learning approach which basically also enables the generalization of our solution to other Web document classification problem. Such an approach needs a learning process on an often manually labelled dataset in order to yield a learnt model for classification. Among various machine learning techniques, we selected data mining approach for its comprehensibility of the learnt model.

The most important step for machine learning is the selection of the appropriate features, according to the a priori knowledge of the domain, which best discriminate the different classes of the application. Informed by our previous study on the state of the art solutions, we decided that the analysis of Web page for classification should rely not only on textual content but also on its structural one. Moreover, as images are a major component of Web documents, in particular for pornographic Web sites, an efficient Web filtering solution should perform some visual content analysis.

In order to speed up navigation, we decided to use a black list whose creation and update is automatic thanks to the machine learning based classification engine. We also decided to use a keyword dictionary as occurrence of sexually explicit terms is an important clue for textual content and its use in the current commercial products, while reaching a classification accuracy rate up to 90%, showed its efficiency.

Fundamentals of Data Mining Techniques

A number of classification techniques from the statistics and machine learning communities have been proposed (Quinlan, 1986, 1993; Weiss & Kulikowski, 1991; Zighed & Rakotomala, 1996). As highlighted in the studies (Chen & Liu, 2005; Fu & Wang, 2005) on the use of data mining techniques in various applications, each one has its advantages and drawbacks. But the most important criterion for comparing classification techniques remains the classification accuracy rate. We have also considered another criterion which seems to us very important: the comprehensibility of the learned model which leads us to a well-accepted method of classification, that is the induction of decision trees (Breiman, Friedman, Olshen, & Stone, 1984; Quinlan, 1986; Zighed & Rakotomala, 1996; Jeong & Lee, 2005).

A decision tree is a flowchart-like structure consisting of internal nodes, leaf nodes, and branches. Each internal node represents a decision, or test, on a data attribute, and each outgoing branch corresponds to a possible outcome of the test. Each leaf node represents a class. In order to classify an unlabeled data sample, the classifier tests the attribute values of the sample against the decision tree. A path is traced from the root to a leaf node which holds the class predication for that sample.

Let Ω be the population of samples to be classified. To each sample ϖ of Ω one can associate a particular attribute, namely its class label C. We say that C takes its value in the class of labels. For a problem of two classes c_1, c_2, one can thus write:

$$C: \quad \Omega \rightarrow \Gamma = \{c_1, c_2\}$$
$$\varpi \rightarrow C(\varpi)$$

For instance, c_1 might be the label representing the class of pornographic Web sites while c_2 the nonpornographic ones. Direct observation of $C(\varpi)$ usually is not easy; therefore we are looking for other way φ to describe the classifier C on the basis of a combination of well selected features. Thus, from each sample ϖ we derive a feature vector $X(\varpi) = [X_1(\varpi), X_2(\varpi), \ldots, X_p(\varpi)]$ which are also called *exogenous variables* or *predictive attributes*. The supervised learning consists of building a model φ from a learning dataset to predict the class label of ϖ.

The process of graph construction is as follows: We begin with a learning dataset and look for the particular attribute which will produce the best partition. We repeat the process for each node of the new partition. The best partitioning is obtained by maximizing the variation of uncertainty $\Im_\lambda$ between the current partition and the previous one. As $I_\lambda(S_i)$ is a measure of entropy for partition S_i and $I_\lambda(S_{i+1})$ is the measure of entropy of the following partition S_{i+1}.

The variation of uncertainty is:

$$\Im_\lambda(S_{i+1}) = I_\lambda(S_i) - I_\lambda(S_{i+1})$$

For $I_\lambda(S_i)$ we can make use the quadratic entropy (a) or Shannon entropy (b) according to the method being selected:

$$I_\lambda(S_i) = \sum_{j=1}^{K} \frac{n_j}{n} \left(-\sum_{i=1}^{m} \frac{n_{ij} + \lambda}{n_j + m\lambda} (1 - \frac{n_{ij} + \lambda}{n_i + m\lambda}) \right) \qquad \text{(a)}$$

$$I_\lambda(S_i) = \sum_{j=1}^{K} \frac{n_j}{n} \left(-\sum_{i=1}^{m} \frac{n_{ij} + \lambda}{n_j + m\lambda} \log_2 \frac{n_{ij} + \lambda}{n_j + m\lambda} \right) \qquad \text{(b)}$$

where n_{ij} is the number of elements of class i at the node S_j with $I \in \{c_1, c_2\}$; n_i is the total number of elements of the class i, $n_i = \sum_{j=1}^{k} n_{ij}$; n_j the number of elements of the node S_j $n_j = \sum_{i=1}^{2} n_{ij}$; n is the total number of elements, $n = \sum_{i=1}^{2} n_i$; $,m = 2$ is the number of classes $\{c_1, c_2\}$. λ is a variable controlling effectiveness of graph construction, it penalizes the nodes with insufficient effectives.

There exists in the literature several decision tree building algorithms, including ID3 (induction decision tree) (Quinlan, 1986), C4.5, Improved C4.5 (Quinlan, 1993) and Sipina (Zighed & Rakotomala, 1996). C4.5 and Improved C4.5 mainly differ from ID3 by the way of discretising continuous values of predicative attributes while the control and support the fusion between summits is a major specificity of Sipina which stops if no changes in uncertainty occur.

Applications to Pornographic Web Site Classification and Skin Color Pixel Classification

Within the framework of WebGuard, we applied the above data mining techniques to two classification problems (Hammami, 2005). The first one is of course pornographic Web site classification where Ω is the population of Web sites with c_1 representing for instance pornographic Web pages while c_2 the nonpornographic ones. To each Web site s is thus associated a class attribute $C(s)$ which takes two values, for instance 0 for adult Web sites while 1 for normal ones:

C: $\Omega \rightarrow \Gamma = \{Adult, Non\_Adult\}$

            $s \rightarrow C(s)$

As direct observation of C is not easy, we look for setting up a prediction model φ which describes the class attribute $C(s)$ on the basis of a well selected feature vector : $X(s) = [X_1(s),$

Figure 3. Data mining process from data

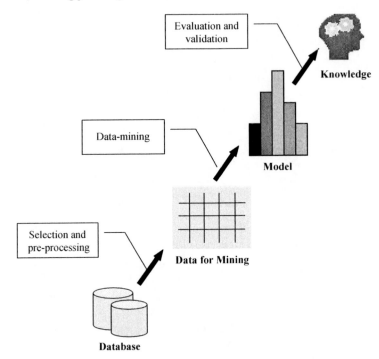

$X_2(s)$, ..., $X_p(s)$] that we can extract from an automatic analysis of a Web site content s. The supervised learning by the aforementioned data mining algorithms consists of building a decision tree based model φ from a learning dataset to predict the class attribute of each Web site s. As illustrated by Figure 3, a whole data mining process consists of three major steps:

- Selection and pre-processing step which consists of select the features which best discriminate classes and extract the feature vectors from the learning dataset;
- Data mining step which looks for a synthetic and generalizable model by the use of various algorithms;
- Evaluation and validation step which consists of assessing the quality of the learnt model on the learning dataset but preferably other dataset.

In much a similar way as we will detail in the following sections, the second problem is visual content-based analysis, namely skin color like pixel classification. According to such a classification, all the pixels of an image are divided into two classes: c_1 with all pixels labelled as skin color while c_2 with all non skin pixels.

The MYL Learning Dataset

From the previous sections, we see that the data mining process for pornographic Web site classification requires a representative learning dataset consisting of a significant set of manually classified Web sites. In our case, we collected a large number of Web sites in each category: 1,000 pornographic Web sites and 1,000 non-pornographic ones. This number of 2,000 is necessary not only to simulate a good representation of Internet content but also because we are collecting a great deal of different information. In the subsequent, we will call this database of 2,000 Web sites for learning purpose as MYL learning dataset.

We have collected these sites manually from the internet because we wanted our base to be as representative as possible. Within the adult sites we find content ranging from the erotic to the pornographic, and within the non-adult sites we find health-based information, anti-pornographic and anti-AIDS sites, and so forth.

Textual and Structural Content-Based Analysis

The selection of features used in a machine learning process is a key step which directly affects the performance of a classifier. Our study of the state of the art and manual collection of our test datasets helped us a lot to gain intuition on pornographic Web site characteristics and to understand discriminating features between pornographic Web pages and inoffensive ones. These intuition and understanding suggested us to select both textual and structural content-based features for better discrimination purpose. The prediction model learnt from MYL learning dataset using these textual and structural content-based features leads to WebGurad-TS, our first version of pornographic Web site classification and filtering solution displaying high filtering effectiveness as evidenced by the experiments on MYL test dataset.

Textual Content-Based Features and Keyword Dictionary

The very first and evident discriminating feature is frequency of prohibited keywords within a Web page. We thus introduced n_x_words and $\%x\_words$, respectively number of prohibited keywords and their percentage, as the first two discriminating features. However, as we evidenced in a previous section, the effectiveness and the quality of a classifier when using keyword filtering approach depend on the nature, language, and diversity of the word database (or dictionary). We did take care of this dictionary elaboration, and unlike a lot of commercial filtering products we built a multilingual dictionary including currently French, English, German, Spanish, and Italian keywords.

Structural Content-Based Features

As evidenced by the work in Glover et al. (2002), Web structure analysis when combined with text analysis improves Web page classification and description. The structure of a Web page is introduced by tags which describe their type: hyperlinks, images, words, and so on. For instance, it has been shown that hyperlinks among Web pages are important indicator of Web communities (Flake et al., 2003). We thus introduced *n_xxx_link* that counts the number of "black listed" links as another feature. This attribute may describe the degree of membership of the current URL in the "black listed" community.

However, outbound links of a Web page under classification are not always classified at the time of the classification. A hyperlink has two components: the destination page, and associated anchortext describing the link which is provided by a page creator. Much as the search engine Google which may return pages based on keywords occurring in inbound anchortext, we also use as feature *n_x_links* which counts the number of hyperlinks having prohibited keywords in the associated achortext.

Similarly, it is an evident intuition that a pornographic Web site has a lot of images. Prior to a true visual content-based analysis of images which is investigated in the next section, we also count in *n_x_images* the number of images whose name contains sexually explicit keywords.

Other features that we introduced from analysis of various tags include:

- ***n_x_meta***: the number of sexually explicit keywords in "keywords" metadata as compared to *n_meta*, the total number of words in "keywords" metadata within a Web page;
- ***n_x_url***: the number of sexually explicit words in the URL of the current Web page under investigation.

Synthesis of Textual and Structural Content-Based Feature Vectors

To summarize the above, the feature vector that we proposed to characterize a Web site includes the following attributes: *n_words* (total number of words on the current Web page), ;*n_x_words* (total number of words occurring in the dictionary), *n_images* (total number of images), *n_x_images* (total number of images whose name has a keyword of the dictionary), *n_links* (the total number of links), *n_x_links* (the number of links which contain sexually explicit words), *n_xxx_links* (the number of links that have been classified as sex-oriented in the black list), *n_x_url* (the number of sexually explicit words in the url), *n_meta* (the total number of words in "keywords" metadata), *n_x_meta* (the number of sexually explicit keywords in "keywords" metadata), *pcxwords* (the percentage of sexually explicit keywords), *pcxmeta* (the percentage of sexually explicit keywords in "keywords" metadata), *pcxlinks* (the percentage of links containing sexually explicit words), *pcximage* (the percentage of images whose name contains a sexually explicit word).

Skin Color Related Visual Content-Based Analysis

It is a fact that Web has been a major vehicle of multimedia document dissemination. A study on more than four million Web pages reveals that 70% of them contain images and there are on average 18.8 images per Web page (Stayrynkevitch, Daoudi, Tombelle, & Zheng, 2002). Accurate Web site classification should thus take into account its visual content counterpart. While content-based image retrieval (CBIR) has been the focus of a lot of works in the literature (Chahir & Chen, 2000; Yang & Hurson, 2005), the easy intuition of appropriate visual content regarding pornographic Web site is evidently skin related (Hammami, Tsishkou, & Chen, 2004; Tang, Liew, & Yan, 2005). In this section, we describe our skin model which also results from a supervised learning process by a data mining technique. We further improve the skin related visual content-based analysis by a region growing based image segmentation technique. The study of strategies in order to take into account the resulting skin related visual feature for improving pornographic Web site classification will be discussed in the next section.

Skin Color Modelling

Skin-color modeling is a crucial task for several applications of computer vision (Hammami, Chen, Zighed, & Song, 2002). Problems such as face detection in video are more likely to be solved if an efficient skin-color model is constructed. Classifying skin-color pixels for Web based adult content detection and filtering is also fundamental to the development of accurate and reliable solution. Most potential applications of skin-color model require robustness to significant variations in races, differing lighting conditions, textures and other factors. Given the fact that a skin surface reflects the light in a different way as compared to other surfaces, we relied once again, on data mining techniques to define a skin color model which enables the classification of image pixels into skin ones or non skin ones (Hammami et al., 2003).

Skin Color Learning Datasets

A machine learning process requires a learning dataset in order to train a model. In our case, large datasets composed of tens of millions of pixels are necessary to explore various types of lighting conditions, races, and so on. Two large datasets were used in our work for skin color modelling. The first one is CRL dataset of skin-color and non-skin color images (Jones & Regh, 1998) which results from a set of 12,230 images collected by a Web crawler, consisting of 80,377,671 skin pixels and 854,744,181 nonskin pixels.

In order to further capture the lighting conditions of video images that are often encountered in pornographic Web pages, we also collected our own dataset, ECL SCIV dataset, consisting of over 1,110 skin-color images of more than 1,110 people, which resulted from

Figure 4. Color images (left) and their corresponding skin binary mask (right)

30 hours of various video sources (Karpova, Tsishkou, & Chen, 2003). These 1,110 skin-color images cover five races, two sexes, exterior/interior, and day/night conditions. They were manually segmented for skin binary mask, as illustrated in Figure 4, discriminating skin pixels from the non skin ones.

Data Preparation and Data Mining Based Learning

Let the set of pixels Ω be extracted and pre-processed automatically from training images and corresponding binary masks. We thus have a two classes classification problem, each pixel ϖ being associated with its label $C(\varpi)$: skin-color or non skin-color.

The observation of $C(\varpi)$ is not easy, because of lighting conditions, race differences and other factors. Given that skin color is perceived color of light reflected by a skin surface, we therefore looked for an efficient mean φ to describe class C of each pixel in different color spaces. Several color spaces have been proposed in the literature for skin detection applications. YCbCr has been widely used since the skin pixels form a compact cluster in the Cb-Cr plane. As YCbCr is also used in video coding and then no transcoding is needed, this color space has been used in skin detection applications where the video sequence is compressed (Albiol, Torres, Bouman, & Delp, 2000; Wang & Chang, 1997). In Wang and Sung (1999) two components of the normalized RGB color space (rg) have been proposed to minimize luminance dependence. And finally CIE Lu*v* has been used in Yang and Ahuja (1998). However, it is still not clear which is the color space where the skin detection performance is the best.

In our work, we computed for each pixel its representation in various normalized color spaces: RGB, HSV, YIQ, YCbCr, CMY in order to find the most discriminative set of color axes. This leads to a feature vector V composed of 14 exogenous variables: V=[r,g,b,H,S,V

Figure 5. Color images (left), skin pixels classification (middle) and skin regions after segmentation (right)

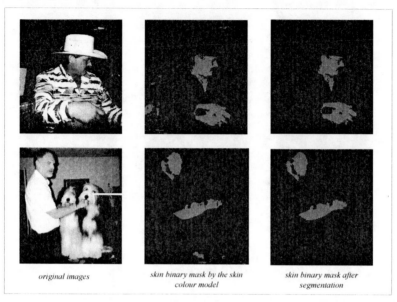

original images   *skin binary mask by the skin colour model*   *skin binary mask after segmentation*

,Y,I,Q,Cr,Cb,C,M,Y]. Both CRL and ECL SCIV datasets were used to generate the learning population. Associated with each pixel feature vector is its class label C: 1 for skin color and 0 for non skin color (Hammami, Chahir, Chen, & Zighed, 2003). SIPINA (Zighed & Rakotomala, 1996) technique was used for training. As result, a hierarchical structure of classification rules of the type "IF...THEN..." is created. Figure 5 illustrates some skin color pixel classification examples where the images in the middle correspond to the direct application of these decision rules.

Skin Color Region Growing

As we can see from the middle images in Figure 5, there exist some pixels misclassified as skin color by our learnt skin model. In order to improve the classification reliability, we further segment the skin color binary mask into skin regions by a region growing technique. The basic intuition is that a skin region is a significant area with a minimum of skin pixels; otherwise this region is a noisy skin like area which needs to be filtered.

The region growing process consists of gathering neighbor pixels from a starting point on the basis of homogeneity criteria. A skin color homogeneous area within an image is a coherent area formed by all 1 pixels in its skin binary mask. More precisely, the process starts from a skin color pixel in the binary mask, and tries to determine whether neighboring pixels are also skin color pixels according to a visiting order illustrated by Fig.6. This process eventually leads to grow a skin like region until no more neighboring skin color

Figure 6. Visiting order of neighboring pixels starting from a pixel p

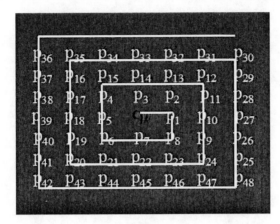

Figure 7. Skin region detection results showing the effectiveness of our approach on various ethnic races, lighting conditions and complex background

pixels can be added to the same region. In order to extract all skin like regions, the region growing process has to be repeated for all unvisited pixels in an image.

All the skin like regions are then filtered on a minimum surface criterion. Indeed, a skin like region is considered as skin region only when its area represents more than λ % of the original image. The images of the last column in Figure 5 illustrate the result of such a process. As we can see, small skin-like regions are filtered after the region growing based segmentation process.

Figure 7 illustrates some other skin region detection results showing the effectiveness of our approach.

Strategy Study for Integrating Skin Color Related Visual Content-Based Analysis

From the previous skin region segmentation technique, two strategies can be used to combine skin color related visual content feature in the Web filtering process. A first straightforward strategy, that we can call *strategy of homogeneity* in the subsequent, consists of extending the fourteen textual and structural content-based features by a new skin color related feature, for instance *%SkinPixels* within a Webpage. We thus need to make a new training on MYL learning dataset using the new feature vector in order to obtain a new prediction model for classifying and filtering Web sites. The second strategy consists of cascading WebGuard-TS, our Web site filtering engine only based on textual and structural content-based features, with a second Web site filtering engine, noted as WebGuard-V, only based on skin color related feature. Experiments were carried out on MYL test dataset in order to evaluate and compare these two strategies.

Strategy of Homogeneity

According to this strategy, the visual content of a Web page is used along with the textual and structural content for better discriminating pornographic Web sites from the normal ones. We thus proposed to extend the 14 textual and structural features as described in the previous section by the following 11 other features related to visual content of a Web page:

- Number of adult images within a Web page;
- Percentage of adult images within a Web page;
- Number of adult images whose name contains a keyword of the dictionary;
- Percentage of adult images whose name contains a keyword of the dictionary;
- Number of logos within a Web page;
- Percentage of logos within a Web page;
- Number of logos whose name contains a keyword of the dictionary;

Figure 8. Experimental results by the strategy of homogeneity on MYL test dataset

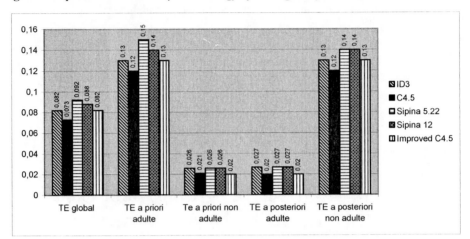

- percentage of non skin pixels within a Web page;
- Number of normal images;
- Percentage of normal images;
- Percentage of skin pixels within a Web page;

Figure 8 summarizes the experimental results which are obtained by the five data mining algorithms on MYL test dataset using this new feature vector.

As we can see from the figure, the strategy of homogeneity for visual content integration displayed bad performance as compared to WebGuard-TS which only used textual and structural features. This is explained by the fact that visual features such as skin pixels within images are not features having the same granularity as compared to textual and structural features.

Strategy of Cascading

The basic idea is the following. As WebGuard-TS displayed very good performance, we can consider a strategy of cascading which applies first WebGuard-TS and then an engine only based on skin color related visual content analysis, called in the subsequent *WebGuard-V*, which further examines normal Web sites classified by WebGuard-TS. However, there are again two variants that we study in the subsequent.

The First Variant of Cascading Strategy Using Percentage of Pornographic Images

The first variant of our cascading strategy, that we note WebGuard-V (%Pornographic Images), integrates skin related visual analysis by computing a percentage of potential pornographic images within a Webpage. When this percentage exceeds a threshold, then the Web site under analysis is classified as pornographic. According to such as variant, we need to first determine a threshold setting the percentage of skin color pixels within an image from which the image can be considered as potentially pornographic. For this purpose, we collected a dataset of 6,000 images extracted from the Internet. The analysis of this dataset gives an average of 18% of skin pixels per image for 4,000 nonpornographic images which include 700 portray images, and an average of 45% of skin pixels per image for the remaining 2000 pornographic images of our dataset. After several experiments, we chose 26% as the threshold of skin color pixel percentage from which an image is classified as potentially pornographic. According to such a threshold, 78% of pornographic images are effectively classified as pornographic while misclassification occurred for 23% of nonpornographic images.

Figure 9 displays the various performances when this strategy, coupled with WebGuard-TS, is experimented on MYL test dataset. As we can see from the figure, the results are much better as compared to the ones obtained when using the first strategy of homogeneity. They even improve slightly the performance achieved by WebGuard-TS.

The Second Variant of Cascading Strategy Using Percentage of Total Skin Color Pixels within a Web Page

The second variant of the cascading strategy, that we note as WebGuard-V (%skin color), proposes to consider rather the percentage of the total skin pixels from all the images within a Web site. When this percentage exceeds a threshold, the Webpage is then considered as pornographic. Using all the images included within our MYL learning dataset, we obtained the two curves of skin color pixel percentage depicted in Figure 10 for normal Web sites and pornographic ones. As we can see, these two curves depict a gaussian behaviour and the best threshold for discriminating pornographic Web sites from the normal ones is 24%. Using such as threshold, the performance that we achieved was very similar to the one by the previous variant using percentage of potential pornographic images.

When carrying out a detailed analysis on these results, we discovered that many images are actually logo images or images containing only text. Once eliminated these logo or text images by an automatic process that we will explain in the section on implementation issue, we obtained a threshold of 34% of skin pixel percentage which discriminates much better pornographic Web sites from normal ones as we will see in the next section.

Comparison Synthesis

The previous comparison study on visual content integration strategies led us to choose the cascading strategy with the second variant using the total percentage of skin pixels within

Figure 9. Experimental results of the cascading strategy – WebGuard-V (% pornographic images)

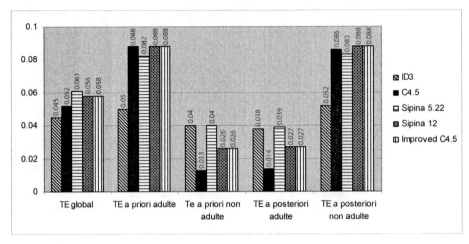

a Web page. In summary, if we designate WebGuard-V our Web site classification engine only based on skin color related analysis, our global Web site classification engine, that we note as WebGuard-TSV, consists of applying first WebGuard-TS for classification then WebGuard-V for further checking, thus cascading WebGuard-V over WebGuard-TS which only relies on textual and structural content-based analysis.

Experimental Results

In order to validate our Web filtering system, WebGuard was evaluated by intensive experiments. Actually, we carried out two series of tests: The first used only textual and structural content-based analysis, resulting in a first Web filter engine WebGuard-TS, while the second one took into account both textual, structural content-based analysis and visual content-based analysis, giving birth to a cascaded version of WebGuard. This section presents the results of these experiments. However, in order to make clear the experimental conditions, we first describe shortly the validation techniques and conditions.

Validation Conditions

In order to show the behaviour of textual and structural content-based classification from the one integrating visual content analysis, two series of experiments were carried out: the first one used only the textual and structural content-based features, leading to the first Web filter engine WebGuard-TS, while the second one added visual content-based features in the learning and classification process, cascading WebGuard-TS and WebGuard-V.

In the first series of experiments focusing on textual and structural content-based features, we first experimented with five data mining techniques on the MYL learning dataset and validated the quality of the learnt model using *random error rate technique*. The stability of the learnt model is further validated using *cross-validation* and *bootstrapping techniques*.

The evaluation measures are the ones defined in a previous section, namely *global error rate, a priori error rate,* and *a posteriori error rate*. As global error rate is the complement of classification accuracy rate while *a priori error rate* (respectively *a posteriori error rate*) the complement of the classical *recall rate* (respectively *precision rate*). Thus, the lower *a priori* error rate is achieved; the better is the recall rate. The same applies to the relationship between global error rate and global classification rate, and the couple between *a posteriori* error rate and precision rate.

However, an efficient model on a learning dataset might reveal poor performance on real data because of the so called "overfitting" phenomena or the lack of generalization ability of the learnt model. A good decision tree obtained by a data mining algorithm from the learning dataset should not only produce good classification performance on data already seen but also on unseen data as well. In order to ensure the performance stability of our learnt model from MYL learning dataset and validated by random error rate technique, cross-validation, and bootstrapping, we thus also tested the learned model on our MYL test dataset consisting of 400 Web sites. Thanks to our textual and structural content-based features, the results from these experiments showed that WebGuard-TS already outperformed the existing commercial products on the market by four or five points.

The second series of experiments integrated visual content-based analysis to further improve the previous experimental result. For comparison purposes with other commercial products, we carried out the experiment on MYL test dataset and WebGuard directly, cascading textual, structural and visual analysis reaching a classification accuracy rate up to 97.4%. In the following, we describe in more detail these two series of experiments.

Experiments by Textual and Structural Content-Based Classification

During this series of experiments, only textual and structural content-based features extracted from a Web page were considered. Five data mining algortithms were studied, including ID3, C4.5, Improved C4.5, Sipina with λ=5.22 and admissibility constraint fixed at 20, noted Sipina (5.22) and Sipina with λ=12 and admissibility of 50, noted Sipina (12). The MYL learning dataset composed of 2000 manually labeled pornographic and nonpornographic Web sites was used as the learning dataset and the test dataset according to the three evaluation techniques.

Figure10. Gaussian curves of skin color pixel percentage (left for normal Web sites and right for pornographic ones)

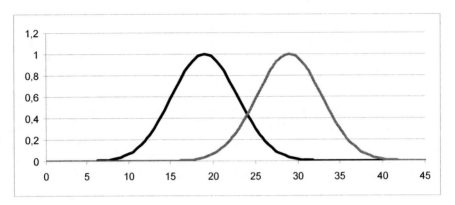

Random Error Rate Method

According to the random error rate method, MYL learning dataset was divided into two subsets: the first one for learning, composed roughly of 70% samples from the MYL learning dataset, the other one for testing composed of the remaining samples. This process was repeated three times with random choice of the two subsets, however keeping the ratio between the subset for learning and the one for testing. The three error rates, in other words, global error rate, a priori error rate, and a posteriori error rate, were averaged on these three experiments. The experimental results on the different data mining algorithms are depicted in Figure 11.

As we can see in the figure, all the five data mining algorithms echoed very similar performance on the feature vector, displaying a global error rate of less than 4% and only 2.6% for the best one (Improved C4.5). There is clearly a tradeoff between a priori error rate on pornographic Web sites and nonpornographic ones, and the much the same between a posteriori error rate on pornographic Web sites and nonpornographic ones. For instance, when Sipina (12) displayed the best performance on pornographic Web sites with a priori rate of 1.5%, it recorded on the other hand a priori error rate of 5.2% on nonpornographic Web sites which is the second-worst performance. The same tradeoff was also observed on a posteriori error rate side. When Sipina (12) achieved, with 1.7%, the best a posteriori error rate on nonpornographic Web sites, it recorded on the other hand a 5.9% of a posteriori error rate on pornographic Web sites which is the second worst performance among the five algorithms. It seems that the best average behavior was achieved by improved C4.5 which recorded the best global error rate of 2.3%, a priori error rates and a posteriori error rates ranging from 1.7% to 2.9% on pornographic Web sites and nonpornographic ones.

Cross-Validation and Bootstrapping

The experimental results by the random error rate technique are thus very encouraging as all the five algorithms only on the basis of textual and structural content-based features outper-

Figure 11. Experimental results by random error rate technique

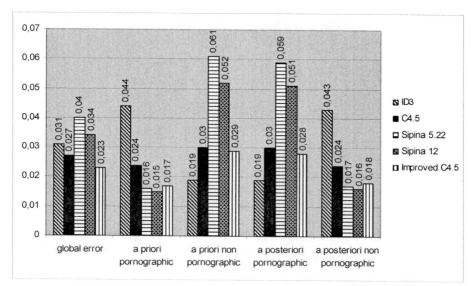

Figure 12. Global comparison results on the three validation techniques

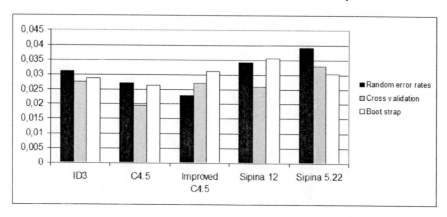

form by six points the best performance displayed by commercial products that we tested. We therefore used the two other more systematic evaluation methods, namely cross-validation and bootstrapping to further confirm these results. Figure 12 summarizes the performance of WebGuard-TS according to the three validation techniques. As we can see from the figure, even though the global error rates for the five data-learning algorithms by the random error technique are higher than the figures by the two other validation techniques, the performance obtained for each algorithm is globally in accordance as the various error rates by the three validation techniques do not differ from one another by more than 1%.

To conclude, the tests allow us to say that the error rates of the data mining algorithms, when using an appropriate dictionary and well chosen parameters, are individually less than 4%. This rate is further lowered by a majority-voting based smoothing mechanism discussed in the following section.

Experimental Results on MYL Rest Dataset and Classification Results Smoothing

Encouraged by the previous validation results, we then tested the five data mining algorithms on the MYL test dataset which was used to compare commercial products in a prior section. The experimental results are summarized by Figure 13. As we can see in this figure, the average global error rate by the five data mining algorithms is roughly 6% which corresponds to a classification accuracy rate of 94%, thus four points higher than the best performance of the commercial products we evaluated. We observe again the tradeoff between a priori error rate on pornographic Web sites and the nonpornographic ones and the same for posteriori error rate between the two classes. When Sipina 12 displayed the worst performance on pornographic Web site classification, it achieved at the same time the best performance of a priori error rate on nonpornographic Web site classification. The best result was scored by Sipina 5.22 with only 3% on global error rate.

While displaying different performances, we discovered that the five data mining algorithms did not make errors in the same way. We thus decided to smooth the classification result by majority voting, leading to the first Web filter engine, WebGuard-TS. That is to say that a Web site will be classified as a pornographic one if only three of the five algorithms achieve such a classification. Using this principle in our experiment on the MYL test dataset, WebGuard-TS further improved the performance and achieved a global error rate of 3.9% only.

Figure 13. Experimental results by the five algorithms on MYL test dataset

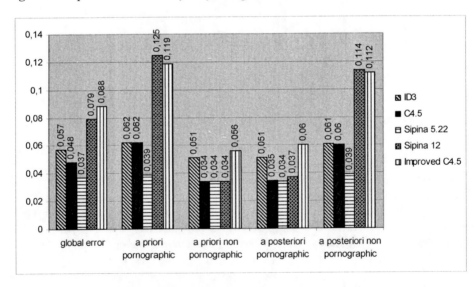

Experimental Result on WebGuard Combining Textual, Structural and Visual Content-Based Analysis

In order to highlight the performance improvement by considering skin color related content analysis (Hammami, Chahir, Chen, & Zighed, 2003) we carried our a first experiment which compares, on the basis of MYL test dataset, WebGuard-TSV with WebGuard-TS which already displayed a low global error rate. Figure 14 illustrates the improvement of classification accuracy compared to the performance achieved by WebGuard-TS when only textual and structural content-based features are used.

As we can see from Figure14 cascaded WebGuard-TSV further improved the performance obtained by WebGuard-TS, achieving a priori pornographic Web site error rate down to 2.5% while the global error rate was only 2.6%.

Figure 15 further highlights the performance of WebGuard-TSV compared to other adult content detection and filtering systems, including CyberPatrol, Norton Internet Security, PureSight, Cybersitter, NetNanny, and Internet Explorer (RSACi).

This result encouraged us to further experiment cascaded WebGuard on a black list of 12,311 pornographic Web sites manually collected and classified by French Ministry of Education. Tables 1 and 2 displayed classification results. While we might be a little bit disappointed by the slight improvement on global error rate from 3.9% by WebGuard-TS to 2.6% by cascaded WebGuard-TSV, WebGuard-TSV improved significantly the performance, as we can see from these tables, scoring a 95.55% classification accuracy rate by cascaded WebGuard from a 87.82% classification accuracy rate by WebGuard-TS.

When carrying out this experiment, we first discovered that 3,723 Web sites have disappeared, illustrating the extreme dynamic nature of the Internet. Furthermore, according to these tables, 1,723 Web sites were classified as normal ones both by WebGuard-TS and WebGuard-TSV. After a laborious phase of manual checking, we effectively discovered that

Figure 14. Classification accuracy of cascaded WebGuard compared to WebGuard-TS

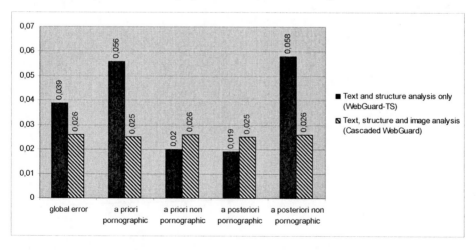

Figure 15. Classification accuracy rate of cascaded WebGuard-TSV compared to some products

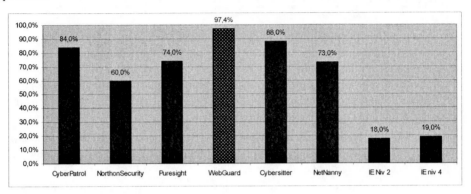

Table 1. Classification results by WebGuard-TS on the black list from French Ministry of Education

WebGuard-TS	Classification results	
Web site category	Adult Web sites	Normal Web sites
Adult Web sites	5819	1046
Normal Web sites		1723
Vanished Web sites	3723	
Classification accuracy rate :	**87.82%**	

Table 2. Classification results by WebGuard-TSV on the black list from French Ministry of Education

WebGuard-TSV	Classification results	
Web site category	Adult Web sites	Normal Web sites
Adult Web sites	6489	376
Normal Web sites		1723
Vanished Web sites	3723	
Classification accuracy rate :	**95.62 %**	

these Web sites are normal ones. Their content had simply been changed when our experiment was carried out. These discover reinforce again the necessity for automatic Web site classification engines.

Implementation Issues

WebGuard Web site classification engine was implemented in C++ on a PC platform while the rule based knowledge by all the data mining process described in this chapter was generated using a Sipina platform. Some other miscellaneous implementation issues include extraction of texual and structural content-based features, image preprocessing and WebGuard configurability. They are described in the subsequent.

Textual and Structural Content-Based Features Extraction

In order to gather dataset for learning, testing and feature vector of a Web site for classification, WebGuard relies on the principle of analyzing the HTML code of a Web page. We thus should be equipped with a set of functions that make it possible to read from a server then to analyze a page. The analyzer is composed of three main functions: an http client used to connect to the Web server and retrieve the source code, an html flag analyzing function, and a content analyzer to make an initial treatment of the raw data.

Logo Image Discrimination

WebGuard-V uses the percentage of skin pixels within a Web page to discriminate pornographic ones from the nonpornographic ones. In order to obtain a discrimination threshold δ on percentage of skin pixels, we relied again on our MYL learning dataset composed of 2,000 pornographic Web sites and 2,000 nonpornographic ones. However, some precautions were needed in proceeding in such a way. Indeed, we found out, on the one hand, that a lot of logo images are inserted within Web pages as illustrated by Figure 16, distorting this discrimination threshold δ, and on the other hand that some "smart" pornographic content providers escape from the vigilance of keyword-based pornographic Web site filters by inserting pornographic text content into images. We thus developed a specific engine discriminating logo images from non logo ones on the basis of image grey level histogram analysis. As logo images tend to have very few picks as compared to non logo images, we built a very simple discrimination decision as follows: once computed the grey level histogram of an image under analysis, we count the number of picks; if the number of picks exceeds an empirical threshold, the image under analysis is considered as non logo image.

Once performed all this pre-processing, we computed the histograms on percentage of skin pixels from our MYL learning dataset both on pornographic Web site class and the nonpornographic one. The threshold δ on percentage of skin pixels discriminating the both classes is set to the intersection of the two Gaussian like curves and the optimal value was found to be 34%.

Figure 16. Logo and no logo image samples and their histograms

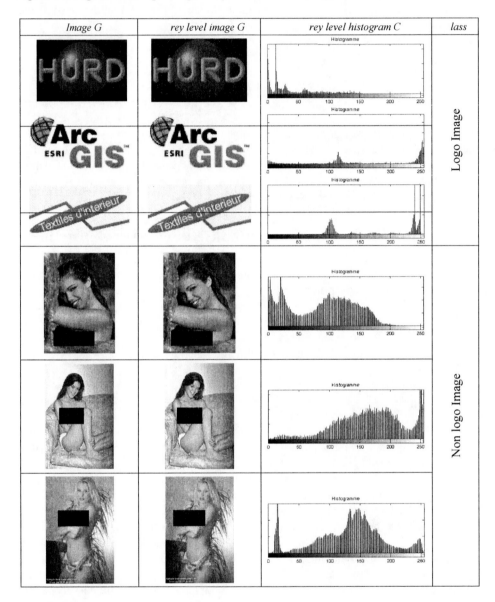

For Web sites inserting textual pornographic content into images, another pre-processing is needed which consists of text detection and recognition within an image (Schüpp, Chahir, Elmoataz, & Chen, 2002; Mahdi, Ardebilian, & Chen, 2002).

Weighting System for Configurability of Objectionable Content Level Selectivity in WebGuard

As evidenced in a prior section from our study on several commercial filtering systems, an important functionality which lacks to most of commercial products is the selectivity of objectionable content. Having precise behaviour of each of five data mining algorithms from our experiments on both MYL learning and test dataset, we answered this question by setting up a weighting system combining the five data mining algorithms so that we can tune the selectivity of objectionable content by moving a threshold.

As we can see from Figure 13, the five data mining algorithms, in other words ID3, C4.5, SIPINA 12, Sipina 5.22, and Improved C4.5, displayed different performances on the various error rate. We might choose Sipina 5.22 for classification as it was the best algorithm achieving minimum of various error rates on MYL test dataset. Instead, we decided to combine the five data mining algorithms together in the classification process as they produced different classification errors. However, the more reliable a data mining algorithm is, the more it should contribute in the final classification decision. We thus affected a weight γ_i associated to the classification decision χ_i of each data mining algorithm according to the formula:

$$\gamma_i = \alpha_i/(\Sigma_{i=1,N}\alpha_i) \text{ with } \alpha_i=(1-(\varepsilon_i-\delta))^n$$

where:

- γ_i : the a priori error rate of the i-th algorithm;
- N : the number of algorithms used for classification, here N = 5;
- n : the power in order to emphasize the difference in weight;
- δ : a threshold value that we take away from the error rate again to emphasize the difference in weight;
- γ_i : the classification decision by the i-th data mining algorithm on a Web site, 0 for nonpornographic class while 1 for pornographic class.

In WebGuard, we have chosen the a priori error rates from the cross validation results on MYL learning dataset in order to ensure that the pornographic Web sites are filtered at maximum. We might also choose other validation results as they differ quite few or global error rates in our formula if we want to a have the best balanced behaviour of our filter both on pornographic and nonpornographic classes. As the best a priori rate was a little bit more than 0.03, we set $\delta = 0.03$. After several experiments, we fixed n = 5 giving the best result on MYL test dataset. Using data from Figure 13, we obtained the relative weight of

Figure 17. Relative weights of the five data mining algorithms in classification decision

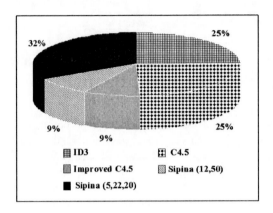

the five data mining algorithms as illustrated in Figure 17. The following figure shows the individual success rates of these algorithms:

As we can see from Figure 17, the algorithm having the best performance on MYL test dataset, otherwise known as Sipina 5.22, received the most important weight. The final classification decision of a Web site is made thus on the basis of the following formula:

$$\chi = \Sigma_{i=1,N}\gamma_i\chi_i \geq \tau \text{ with } \chi \text{ ranging from 0 to 1}$$

τ is defined as the sensitivity to "objectionable" content. Indeed, if τ is set to 0, WebGuard is the most sensitive as a Web site is classified as pornographic if just one data mining algorithm does so. On the contrary, if if τ is set to 1, WebGuard appears as less sensitive as it classifies a Web site as pornographic only if all the five data mining algorithms do so. The principle of majority voting used in our experiments for smoothing the classification results corresponds to set $\tau = 0.42$.

Concluding Remarks and Future Work

In this chapter, we studied and highlighted the use of skin color related visual content-based analysis along with textual and structural content-based analysis for improving Web filtering through our machine learning based pornographic Web site classification engine WebGuard. Using MYL test dataset consisting of 200 adult Web sites and 200 nonpornographic Web sites, we compared WebGuard-TS using only textual and structural content-based analysis of a Webpage with WebGuard-TSV when WebGuard-TS is further cascaded with a skin color related visual content based classification engine (WebGuard-V). The experimental results first showed that structural content-based analysis, such as hyperlinks, used in WebGuard-TS along with classical textual content-based analysis, has a very good discriminative power (Chakrabarti et al., 1998; Flake et al., 2003; Glover et al., 2002) as WebGuard-TS already achieved 96.1% classification accuracy rate. Moreover, the visual content-based analysis can further improve the classification performance as WebGuard-TSV scored 97.4% classification accuracy rate when cascading WebGuard-TS and WebGuard-V. The experiment of WebGuard-TSV on a black list of 12,311 adult Web sites manually collected and classified by the French Ministry of Education further confirms the interest of considering visual content based analysis as WebGuard-TSV scored 95.62% classification accuracy rate compared to 87.82% classification accuracy rate displayed by WebGuard-TS. The basic framework of WebGuard can apply to other categorization problems of Web sites which combine, as most of them do today, textual and visual content.

We can thus summarize our major contribution by the use of both structural and visual analysis along with classical keyword based textual content analysis for Web document classification and filtering problem. However, it would be unfair to say that all the good performances were only results of textual and structural content-based analysis combined with visual content-based analysis. Actually, the dictionary of indicative keywords also played a big role in the improvement of all these performances (Velásquez, Ríos, Bassi, Tasuda, & Aoki, 2005). Currently, our dictionary contains more than 300 indicative keywords extracted from six languages. Its elaboration was manual, thus quite laborious and probably only possible thanks to the comprehensibility of decision trees from our data mining algorithms.

Overcoming this drawback of laborious elaboration of dictionary is one of the directions of our future work. Actually, finding automatically discriminative indicative keywords or sentences is also typically a data mining problem. From a corpus of hyperlinked documents for one class and another one for the second class, the problem is to find indicative keywords or sentences which discriminate the best the two classes.

The other direction of our future work is to leverage mutual classification capabilities both from textual and structural content-based analysis and multimedia content-based analysis. This is a fact that Web has become more and more multimedia, including music, images and videos. The work described in this chapter suggests that Web document classification can benefit from visual content-based analysis; we also think on the other hand that textual and structural content-based analysis can greatly help automatic classification of images embedded within Web documents.

Acknowledgments

Our acknowledgements go to our students Peter Bungert, Mathieu Capou, Hervé Guignot, Benjamin Herzog, Elie Huvier, Thomas Lesinski, Vincent Rocher, Florian Gérus, Nicolas Jouffroy, Audrey Licini, Fabien Perdriel, and Phan Le Bao Tuy who carried out the most of the experiments described in this chapter. This work was partly funded and carried out within the French national RNTL MUSE (Multimedia Search Engine) project.

References

Attardi, G., Gulli, A., & Sebastiani, F. (1999). Automatic Web page categorization by link and context analysis. *THAI-99, 1ˢᵗ European Symposium on Telematics, Hypermedia and Artificial Intelligence* (pp.105-119).

Albiol, A., Torres, L., Bouman, C.A., & Delp, E. J. (2000, September). A simple and efficient face detection algorithm for video database applications, *IEEE International Conference on Image Processing* (pp. 239-242). Vacouver, Canada.

Brin, S., & Page, L. (1998). The anatomy of a large-scale hypertextual Web search engine. *WWW7*. Brisbane, Australia.

Breiman, L., Friedman, J., Olshen, R., & Stone, C. (1984). *Classification of regression trees.* Belmont, CA: Wadsworth.

Chahir, Y., & Chen, L. (2002). Efficient Content-based image retrieval based on color homogeneous objects segmentation and their spatial relationship characterization. *Journal of Visual Communication and Image Representation, 11*(1), 302-326.

Chakrabarti, S., Dom, B., & Indyk, P. (1998). Enhanced hypertext categorization using hyperlinks. *The 1998 ACM SIGMOD International Conference on Management of Data.*

Chen, S.Y., & Liu, X. (2005). Data mining from 1994 to 2004: An application-orientated review. *Intl J of Business Intelligence and Data Mining* (pp. 4-21).

Cho, J., Garcia-Molina, H., & Page, L. (1998). Efficient crawling through URL ordering. *Computer Networks and ISDN Systems* (pp. 161-172).

Cybersitter. (2002). Copyright © 1995-2003, Solid Oak Software, Inc. All Rights Reserved. Retrieved from www.cybersitter.com.

Cyber Patrol 5.0 (n.d.). Copyright © 2003 SurfControl plc. All Rights Reserved. Retrieved from www.cyberpatrol

Flake, G.W., Lawrence, S., & Giles, C.L. (2000). Efficient identification of Web communities. *The 6th International Conference on Knowledge Discovery and Data Mining.* Boston.

Flake, G.W., Tsioutsiouliklis, K., & Zhukov, L. (2003). Methods for mining Web communities: Bibliometric, spectral, and flow. In A. Poulovassilis & M. Levene (Eds.), *Web dynamics.* Springer Verlag.

Fu, X., & Wang, L. (2005). Data dimensionality reduction with application to improving classification performance and explaining concepts of data sets. *Intl. J. of Business Intelligence and Data Mining,* 65-87.

Fürnkranz, J. (1999). Exploiting structural information for text classification on the WWW. *Intelligent Data Analysis,* 487-498.

Glover, E.J., Tsioutsiouliklis, K., Lawrence, S., Pennock, D.M., & Flake, G.W. (2002, May). Using Web structure for classifying and describing Web pages. *WWW2002,* Honolulu, Hawaii, USA.

Gralla, P., & Kinkoph, S. (Eds.). (2001). *Internet et les enfants*. CampusPress ISBN 2-7440-0979-2, 74.

Hammami, M. (2005). Modèle de peau et application à la classification d'images et au filtrage des sites Web. *Thèse de doctorat*, Ecole Centrale de Lyon.

Hammami, M., Chahir, Y., & Chen, L. (2003, October 13-17). WebGuard: Web based adult content detection and filtering system. In *The 2003 IEEE/ WIC International Conference on Web Intelligence* (pp. 574-578). Halifax, Canada.

Hammami, M., Chahir, Y., Chen, L., & Zighed, D. (2003). Détection des régions de couleur de peau dans l'image. *Revue RIA-ECA, 17*, 219-231.

Hammami, M., Chen, L., Zighed, D., & Song, Q. (2002, Juin). Définition d'un modèle de peau et son utilisation pour la classification des images. *MediaNet'02*, 186-197.

Hammami, M., Tsishkou, D., & Chen, L. (2003, September 22-24). Data-mining based skin-color modeling and applications. *Third International Workshop on Content-Based Multimedia Indexing* (pp. 157-162).

Hammami, M., Tsishkou, D., & Chen, L. (2004, June 6-9). Adult content Web filtering and face detection using data-mining based skin-color model., *IEEE International Conference on Multimedia and Expo ICME 2004* (pp. 403-406).

Jeong, M., & Lee, D. (2005). Improving classification accuracy of decision trees for different abstraction levels of data. *Intl. J. of Data Warehousing and Mining*, 1-14.

Jones, M.J., & Regh, J.M. (1998). *Statistical color models with application to skin detection*. Cambridge Research Laboratory, CRL 98/11.

Karpova, E., Tsishkou, D., & Chen, L. (2003, June). The ECL skin-color images from video (SCIV) database. *International Conference on Image and Signal Processing* (pp. 47-52), Agadir, Maroc.

Lee, P.Y., Hui, S.C., & Fong, A.C.M. (2002). Neural networks for Web content filtering. *IEEE Intelligent Systems*, 48-57.

Mahdi, W., Ardebilian, M., & Chen, L. (2002, July). *Text detection and localization within images*. PCT/ FR03/ 02406.

Net Nanny 4.04. (2002-2003). BioNet Systems, LLC. Retrieved from www.netnanny.com

Norton Internet Security. (2003). Symantec Corporation. Retrieved from www.symantec.com

Puresight Home 1.6. (n.d.). I Cognito Technologies Ltd. Retrieved from www.icognito.com

Quinlan, J.R. (1986). Induction of decision trees. *Machine Learning, 1*, 81-106.

Quinlan, J.R. (1993). *C4.5: Programs for machine learning*. San Mateo, CA: Morgan Kaufmann.

Recreational Software Advisory Council on the Internet. (n.d.). Association that became the Internet Content Rating Association (ICRA) in 1999. Retrieved from www.icra.org

Schüpp, S., Chahir, Y., Elmoataz, A., & Chen, L. (2002). Détection et extraction automatique de texte dans une vidéo: une approche par morphologie mathématique. *MediaNet2002* (pp. 73-82).

Sato, K., Ohtaguro, A., Nakashima, M., & Ito, T. (2005). The effect of a Web site directory when employed in browsing the results of a search engine. *Intl. J. of Web Information Systems,* 43-51.

Stayrynkevitch, B., Daoudi, M., Tombelle, C., & Zheng, H. (2002, December). *Poesia Software architecture definition document.* Technical report, Poesia consortium.

Tang, J.S.S., Liew, A., & Yan, H. (2005). Human face animation based on video analysis, with applications to mobile entertainment, *Journal of Mobile Multimedia,* 133-148.

Velásquez, J.D., Ríos, S., Bassi, A., Yasuda, H., & Aoki, T. (2005). Towards the identification of keywords in the Web site text content: A methodological approach. *Intl. J. of Web Information System,* 53-57.

Wang, H., & Chang, S.F. (1997, August). A highly efficient system for automatic face region detection in mpeg video. *IEEE Transactions on Circuits and System for Video Technology,* 615-628.

Wang, J. G., & Sung, E. (1999, October). Frontal-view face detection and facial feature extraction using color and morphological operators. *Pattern recognition letters,* 20(10), 1053-1068.

Weiss, S. M., & Kulikowski C. A. (1991). *Computer systems that learn: Classification and prediction methods from statistics, neural nets, machine learning, and expert systems.* San Mateo, CA: Morgan Kauffman.

Yang, B., & Hurson, A. R. (2005). Hierarchical semantic-based index for ad hoc image Retrieval. *Journal of Mobile Multimedia,* 235-254.

Yang, M. H., & Ahuja, N. (1998, October). Detecting human faces in color images. *International Conference on Image Processing* (pp. 127-130). Chicago.

Yang, Y., Slattery, S., & Ghani, R. (2001). A study of approaches to hypertext categorization. *Journal of Intelligent Information Systems.*

Zighed, D.A., & Rakotomala, R. (1996). *A method for non arborescent induction graphs.* Technical report, Laboratory ERIC. Lyon, France: University of Lyon 2.

Chapter III

Prevalent Factors Involved in Delays Associated with Page Downloads

Kevin Curran, University of Ulster at Magee, UK

Noel Broderick, University of Ulster at Magee, UK

Abstract

Over the years the number of Web users has increased dramatically unfortunately leading to the inherent problem of congestion. This can affect each user's surfing experience. A large percentage of sites use a combination of text and image-heavy design with the use of images contributing heavily to slow-loading sites. Studies have shown that surfers spend a lot of time impatiently waiting for pages to emerge on screen and HCI guidelines indicate 10 seconds as the maximum response time before users lose interest. This chapter presents research into the observed usage of images by academic institutions and the effects on page retrieval times.

Introduction

Web users spend a lot of time impatiently waiting for Web pages to emerge on screen. HCI guidelines indicate 10 seconds as the maximum response time before users lose interest (Selvidge, Chaparro, & Bender, 2002). Such delays impact the sites' success and are expensive in terms of lost business opportunity or users productivity (Saiedian & Naeem, 2001). When a user launches a browser and requests an action to be performed the browser interprets the request. It sends information to the appropriate site server where the requested information is stored and this site server sends the information back. The Internet is actually a packet switching network which sends requests via packets of data (datagram's). Each packet contains the IP address of sender and receiver, and the information being requested. On any one request there can be more than one packet. This is because each packet is of a fixed size and some requests may need more than this. This means the request must be broken up into the appropriate number of packets. The route taken to obtain the requested information depends on the sender's geographic location and that of the receiver. If there are a lot of packets along a certain route they will all be queued or find a different route until they reach their destination. The destination cannot send any information until all the associated packets have been received. When all the packets have been received the destination sends the requested information back in packets via routers to the sender (Comer, 2000).

Findings of this study will provide a better understanding and help to devise a strategy on what can one do to eliminate or at least reduce potentially harmful effects of very slow page retrieval times. The top level domains (TLD), in other words, home pages, of 47 academic Web sites were chosen. They span across five different countries: UK, Ireland, Canada, U.S., and Australia. They have many Web users and typically they all hit the same home page. There will be potential students checking out the course prospectus. Perhaps commercial users are looking for consultancy. The five countries under scrutiny have their own private multi-gigabit data communication network reserved specifically for research and education use and are linked to international peer networks. The first study examines network latency by visiting the Web sites for the first time. The efficiency of cache mechanism in reducing the client latency was also assessed. Latency measurements were obtained from two different sources, from a workstation at the author's institution and from a Web performance monitoring service provided by TraceRT.[1] The second study surveys the academics' Web sites and account for variations in page retrieval times particularly to images which was the interest of this study. The final study explores image compressions and assesses how efficiently Web developers are optimising images for their Web sites. Another topic awaiting exploration was to trim the file size of images while retaining visual fidelity. The effects of reduced image size (in bytes) have on page retrieval times had been looked into.

Network Delay Components and Related Work

What follows is a description of some of the main factors influencing Web page delay.

A modern server uses path maximum transmission unit discovery (PMTUD) heuristics to determine the maximum segment size (MSS) which is the safe packet size that can be transmitted

(Mogul & Deering, 1990). This technique was adopted to address the poor performance and communication failures associated with oversized packets which are fragmented at routers with small MTU (Kent & Mogul, 1987). Today, the PMTUD concept is imperfect as it uses the Internet control message protocol (ICMP) which some network administrators view as a threat and block them all, disabling PMTUD, usually without realising it (Knowles, 1993). This led to increased packets overheads due to retransmissions and eventually connection time-outs. Lahey (2000), suggested a workaround where after several time-outs, the server network should be reconfigured to accept an altered ICMP packet with the "Do Not Fragment" bit disabled. Consequently the PMTUD feature is bypassed, but detection can take several seconds each time, and these delays result in a significant, hidden degradation of network performance.

Transmission Control Protocol's (TCP) Flow Control

The flow control mechanism of TCP uses slow start and congestion avoidance algorithms as a mechanism to control the data transmission rate (Floyd & Fall, 1999). This helps to reduce packets loss caused by congested routers. However, lost packets can be recovered using TCP's retransmission feature, but this incurs added delivery time. The aggressive behaviour of multimedia applications involving audio and video, in which developers employ UDP compounds the problem of congestion. UDP are not TCP friendly and they do not respond to packet drops which typically hint congestions. This aggressive behaviour degrades and even shuts out TCP packets such as hypertext transfer protocol (HTTP) and prevents them from obtaining their fair share of their bandwidth when they battle for bandwidth over a congested link. Lee, Balan, Jacob, Seah, and Ananda (2002) examined the use of TCP tunnels at core routers to isolate different types of traffic from one another. Benefits include reduced TCP's retransmission per connected by over 500% and more packets can be processed using the same amount of memory resources. This concept is not used extensively on the current Internet infrastructure.

Domain Name Servers (DNS) Lookup

DNS are the nub of the Internet infrastructure. They are responsible for translating domain names into an equivalent IP address needed by the Internet's TCP. The latency between DNS request and response is a random variable as the DNS lookup system uses the client's cache file, the hierarchical nature of the domain name and a set of DNS operating at multiple sites to cooperatively solve the mapping problem. A survey from Men and Mice (Menandmice, 2003) showed that 68% of the DNS for commercial sites (e.g., .COM zones) has some configuration errors, thus making them vulnerable to security breach and denial of service. They are normally handled by novices who do not fully understand the operation of DNS very well. An intelligent DNS management system was recently developed by Liu, Tseng, and Chen (2004) which offers administrators support in DNS system configuration, problem diagnosis and tutoring.

HTTP Protocol

The network delay for Web page loading is dominated by the current version of the HTTP/1.1 standard. It is an application level protocol for transfer of Web contents between clients and servers. Due to increasing Internet traffic, HTTP/1.1 makes inefficient use of the network and suffers from high latencies for three reasons: (1) it takes time to transmit the unnecessarily large number of bytes, (2) TCP's three-way handshakes for opening a connection adds extra round trip time delay, and (3) multiple parallel TCP streams do not share the same congestion avoidance state. Spreitzer (2000), have composed a prototype for HTTP "next generation" which should address these latency issues.

Cache Mechanism

The caching mechanism is available ubiquitously. It exists on the client's local disk and is also provided by DNS, network servers and Internet service providers. Commercial providers such as Akamai[2] use cache server technology to help companies get their Web pages faster to potential customers. Its rationale is to assuage congestion, reduce bandwidth consumption, improve retrieval times by temporary storing Web objects closer to the clients and reduce the burden on the site server as it handles fewer requests. Caching is often deliberately defeated as not all Web contents are cacheable. A modern day Web page contains both dynamic and static contents. Dynamic items are non-cacheable and typically they contain interactive and changeable items that provide a far richer experience for users, but they are not happy to wait for them (Nielsen et al., 1997). Cached components characteristically contain items that do not change, in other words, they are static. An intelligent cache engine has emerged recently that serves dynamic elements of Web page and reduces the latency time by 90% (Govatos, 2001). It works by estimating future client's behaviour at a site based on pass and present access patterns. The downside with caching is that if the user does not use the cached items, then congestion may have been caused needlessly.

File Size of Embedded Objects

Recommendations that were made to improve Web page designs have positive impact to page retrieval times as well as usability. The adoption of cascaded style sheets (CSS) (Lie & Bos, 1996) and more compact image representations, Portable Network Graphics (PNG), have added value of reducing the file size and speeding up page downloads without sacrificing graphics design (Nielsen et al., 1997). PNG was designed to be successor to the popular GIF files, but it was not until the late 1997 when browser wars came to an end as many old browsers finally caught up and are able to read PNG formats. Another Web image format is JPEG which uses lossy compression and exploits known limitations of the human eye. Weinberger, Seroussi, and Sapiro (2000) have created a new lossless/near-lossless image compression format called JPEG-LS. This standard is for continuous tone images and is currently awaiting approval from the World Wide Web Consortium.

Next Generation Internet

Network connection quality can be described in terms of availability, latency, jitter, and capacity. Availability is the assurance that traffic will reach its destination successfully, and forms the basis of most service-level agreements. Latency is the delay that traffic experiences as it travels across the network while jitter is the change in this latency over time. Establishing a particular QoS level for a connection is a complex process, in part because of the stateless, best-effort paradigm upon which the Internet is based and the fact that one must balance all of the QoS parameters above. There are two main approaches to QoS: the integrated services model (Crawley et al., 1998) and the differentiated services model (Fulp & Reeves, 2001). The integrated services model negotiates a particular QoS at the time it is requested. Before exchanging traffic, the sender and receiver request a particular QoS level from the network. Upon acceptance, the intermediate network devices associate the resulting traffic flow with a specific level of jitter, latency, and capacity. Resource Reservation Protocol (RSVP), a protocol for signalling QoS requirements for a particular traffic flow, is a key component. Differentiated services takes a different approach using traffic handling classes with various levels of service quality. These are established by the network administrator so when the sender needs a particular kind of handling, it marks each individual packet. Through the migration from resource-based to service-driven networks, it has become evident that the Internet model should be enhanced to provide support for a variety of differentiated services that match applications and customer requirements, and not stay limited under the flat best-effort service that is currently provided (Bernet et al., 2000).

Methodology

Data Collection

Forty seven TLD sites belong to universities; 12 UK's sites, 10 USA's sites, nine Canadian's sites, eight Ireland's sites and eight Australian's sites; were chosen and that they contain images which was the interest in this study. This was a large sample size to ensure a high level of statistical power. Universities selected for this research was identified through search engine results and that they are linked to the NRENs—Ja, Abilene, Aarnet, Canarie, and Heanet. Information about the network topology for the five NRENs was gathered and checks were made to ensure that there were no intermittent brief outages or reported performance issues. For this study, the response time was obtained from two sources. From the author's institution, the response time was the period it took for the requested Web page to be fully presented on the browser window. This measured the performance of Web pages delivered within the international NRENs infrastructure via the UK's JANET network. The test was conducted using Netscape Navigator 6.2 on Windows 2000 Professional, with a 10Mbit/s link to JANET. The experimental method was to request a Web page via specially prepared bookmarks. The download timer in Navigator gave the loading time measurements. Two types of request were used:

1.   **First time retrieval:** equivalent to a browser visiting a site for the first time. In Navigator the memory and file cache was cleared.

2.   **Cache request:** equivalent to revisiting a site online. The static contents were already available in the client's local cache. This meant that static items are displayed on screen more quickly the next time the page is visited and any dynamic items had to be retrieved from the server.

To account for network idiosyncrasies, latency measurement was collected three times and the measured mean was used. The second measurement source was provided by TraceRT. This service was used to measure the speediness of Web sites as seen from six measurement points (called agents) around the world. The agents are commercial sites and operate outside the NRENs infrastructure. To account for changing server loads and different time zones, the response time investigations was repeated at approximately the same time in the morning, afternoon and evening (in British Summer Time) for seven consecutive days. A snapshot of the various statistics held for each site tested on one particular day is shown in Figure 1.

Long latency link may have a major influence on the total response time for serving a set of Web page objects from the server to the client. The location of site servers was gathered using a diagnostic tool from NeoTrace Express (Networkingfiles, 2006). To account for variations in retrieval times, statistics on the quantity and size of objects that a Web page contains was collated. The number of embedded objects gave an indication of how many server requests must be made and the file size implicates how quickly the heterogeneous network could present them.

Figure 1. Snapshot of site details

	Thursday (9-04-2004)							
	Total Web Page Size (bytes)	Visible Text Size (bytes)	Size of HTML Tags (bytes)	Text to HTML Ratio %	Number of Images	Largest Image Size (bytes)	Size of all Images (bytes)	Total: Images + HTML = (bytes)
Dublin City University	7630	1302	6328	17.56	7	21197	63364	70994
National University of Ireland	13207	3692	9515	28.45	20	7279	39823	53030
National University of Ireland Galwy	7901	1075	6826	14.1	29	40857	81485	89386
Queens University Belfast	17552	3656	13896	21.32	30	8883	59448	77000
Royal College of Surgeons in Ireland	25078	6994	18084	28.38	15	27578	62065	87143
University College London	13070	2970	10100	23.22	23	15461	61258	74328
University of York	4065	661	3404	16.75	4	16467	23281	27346
Imperial College, London	26723	16091	10632	60.71	18	34644	49363	76086
University of Nottingham	8015	1290	6725	16.59	22	40054	221923	229938
University of Warwick	24702	5662	19040	23.42	28	14829	79312	104014
King's College London	14786	2640	12146	18.35	28	4968	23055	37841
University of Toronto	18804	2850	15954	15.65	21	23495	66705	85509
University of Saskatchewan	error	0	0	0	0	0	0	0

Figure 2. Statistics from Australian agents on Friday 11th March 2005

Agent	adelaide			anu			monash			unimelb			unsw		
	morn	aft	eve	morn	aft	eve	morn	aft	eve	morn	aft	eve	morn	aft	eve
#77 USA Active-Server.com	12	14	12	12	11	12	2	2	1	14	14	14	14	14	14
#80 USA Marketing Internet Ltd	120	120	120	120	120	120	11	11	12	120	120	120	120	120	120
#81 USA Teal Networks	10	10	9	10	10	10	1	1	1	12	11	12	10	10	8
Hosting	12	12	11	12	12	11	1	1	1	15	14	14	14	14	14
#75 USA IDCL	13	13	13	13	12	12	1	1	1	14	14	14	13	14	12
#46 Canada Vancouver Webpages	9	41	11	10	25	15	1	1	1	14	34	19	13	31	18
GmbH	20	16	16	17	17	17	2	1	1	18	19	19	18	18	19
#60 UK Shellnet	21	17	17	17	17	17	2	2	2	20	20	17	18	18	18
#45 Spain Grupo Intelideas	19	17	19	18	17	18	2	2	2	21	21	18	19	102	102
#13 Hungary N@plo- Pók Webstudio	78	19	18	39	20	23	12	2	2	36	22	20	33	21	21
#88 Russia WebHost	20	26	19	18	17	20	2	7	2	22	23	21	32	28	20
#42 USA Internet Young Polonia	25	28	21	39	56	41	3	1	1	47	120	47	59	92	63

Figure 3. Statistics from Canadian Agents on Friday 11th March 2005

Agent	mcgill			queensu			toronto			ualberta			ubc		
	morn	aft	eve	morn	aft	eve	morn	aft	eve	morn	aft	eve	morn	aft	eve
#77 USA Active-Server.com	1	1	1	1	3	1	2	3	4	2	3	2	6	4	16
#80 USA Marketing Internet Ltd	11	10	10	120	120	120	120	120	120	92	93	96	120	120	120
#81 USA Teal Networks	2	1	1	5	5	5	8	7	9	2	2	3	6	26	4
Hosting	1	1	1	4	3	3	4	5	6	2	3	2	13	6	6
#75 USA IDCL	1	1	1	2	2	2	4	4	3	2	3	2	8	6	6
#46 Canada Vancouver Webpages	3	1	1	11	5	6	9	9	11	1	11	1	5	28	5
GmbH	1	1	1	6	7	7	11	11	11	120	120	120	11	15	11
#60 UK Shellnet	1	1	1	6	11	7	11	12	11	9	5	5	11	11	11
#45 Spain Grupo Intelideas	1	1	1	7	8	7	13	14	12	5	5	5	28	23	22
#13 Hungary N@plo- Pók Webstudio	11	1	1	113	12	9	120	12	13	35	6	6	82	16	12
#88 Russia WebHost	1	2	1	12	9	9		14	13		6	6	18	13	14
#42 USA Internet Young Polonia	2	1	1	31	34	35	53	60	50	32	27	34	15	9	19

In the course of this research, over 300 graphs were compiled in order to provide detailed analysis of the delay involved in Web page download. A snapshot of the various statistics held for each site tested on one particular day from the Australian Web sites are shown in Figure 2 and the statistics from Canadian Web sites are shown in Figure 3.

Using GIF files that were extracted from the sample sites, these images were converted into compact PNG formats. Where possible an attempt was made to create transparent PNGs so that images could rely on the background colour of the site's home page. With Adobe Photoshop 8.0, all JPEG images were optimised for the Web using 60 as the quality factor. This setting was perfectly acceptable on the Web while retaining visual fidelity. The optimised JPEG images were compared with the original to see if Web developers have used appropriate compressions. The author went one step further and took a shot at trimming the file size of optimised JPEG images by saving them, unchanged, as JPEG in Microsoft Paint v5.1. The file size for the new PNG, optimised JPEG and trimmed JPEG images was recorded.

Figure 4. First time retrieval and cache validation response time results (for pages requested within the NRENs)

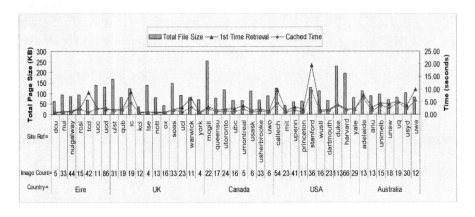

Figure 5. Speed of USA's Web sites as seen by an agent in Spain

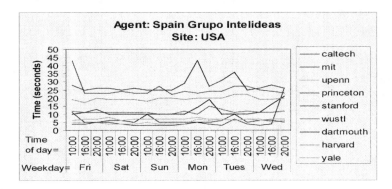

Thresholds of Interest

Web users tend to be sensitive to variations in loading delays and for this study there are two natural thresholds of interests: that of insignificant and that of pain. Delays that are less than the threshold of insignificant are not minded by the user. Delays that is greater than the threshold of pain result in users abandoning the system. Delays that fall between these thresholds normally results in a minor whinge from the user. Absolute values for these natural thresholds are not known as patience varies from user to user. In this study, values for insignificant and value for pain were taken to be three seconds and eight seconds, respectively.

Figure 6. Percentage of cache misses within the NREN infrastructures

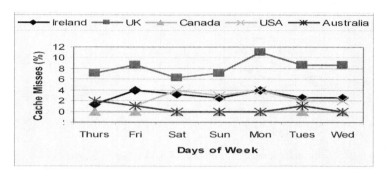

Figure 7. Effects of compression to JPEG images in the USA

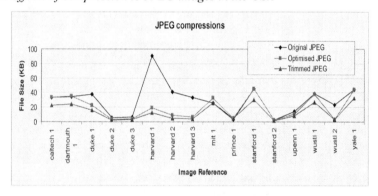

Findings

The first time retrieval and cache validation tests for Web pages downloaded via the JANET infrastructure is shown in Figure 4. This graph includes the image counts with histograms showing the total page sizes (in KB). No obvious relationship was found with the file sizes or image counts to justify the response times.

Long latency link could possibly explain the high retrieval times as experienced from two U.S.'s site servers, "Caltech" and "Stanford," as they are the only site servers in the west coast of USA. Other USA sites are located in the east. Figure 5 illustrates the speed (in seconds) of nine USA's Web sites as observed by a commercial agent in Spain.

While the Internet was behaving in a fluctuating manner it can be seen that five USA's sites would have missed out on possible business opportunities as they were in the pain zone. The other four sites fell inside the whinge sector. U.S. lags behind Spain by five to eight hours, therefore a safe assumption was made whereby on Monday afternoon (Spanish

Figure 8. Effects of compression to loading times as seen by six agents.

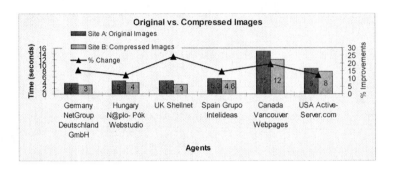

time) the condition of site servers became heavy as Web users in the U.S. went online after the weekend break. Comparing the latency results shown in Figure 4 and Figure 5, pages requested within the NREN infrastructure was presented much quicker.

To seek out additional reasons behind the sliding scale of delays as seen in Figure 4 and Figure 5, a packet sniffer[3] was used to count the number of packets involved for the transmission of images. When a sniffer was applied during individual requests for images from sample site servers, some interesting effects were noticed. Based on visual inspection of Figure 4, it has been noticed that no two images of equal size (in bytes), from five Australian sites, arrived at the author's workstation with the same number of packets. As the file size of images increased the packet counts increased exponentially and without doubt so did the image loading time. Similar behaviours have been observed for sample sites in U.S., Canada, UK, and Ireland. Dissimilar PMTUD schemes used by site servers, server loads, congestion levels or fragmentation of oversized packets may have attributed to varying packet counts.

The outcome of the first time retrieval tests (from Figure 4) showed that five sites were in the pain sector, ten sites fell inside the whinge region and twenty eight sites in the insignificant zone. With the cache mechanism in place, the author noticed that for the five sites that were in the pain sector, one went to the insignificant zone while three moved to the whinge region. The last one stayed, but its response time improved by ten seconds. Three cache misses took place, but the user would not have cared or noticed because the average added time was 236ms and the affected sites did not shift from the insignificant zone. The cache system was very effective in reducing the retrieval times and made Web browsing more pleasurable. While cache misses augment page retrieval times the author carried out a survey to obtain the frequency of these misses. The results are depicted in Figure 6.

While there were no cache misses for Canada, UK had the highest percentage of misses due to a large number of sites containing dynamic items which had to be fetch from the site servers when the page was reloaded. It has been noticed that new items may increase the overall page size and this impacts how quickly the Internet could present the page's contents. The author took a peek at Navigator's temporary cache folder and noticed that only image files are readily cached than text files.

Forty seven test sites held a total of static 904 GIF images. Of these only 476 were successfully converted to PNG format. GIF images that were successfully converted totalled 1,048,299 bytes, while PNG equivalent resulted in a total 919,298 bytes, saving 129,001 bytes. The savings are modest because many of the images are very small. PNG conversion did not perform well on very low depth images in the sub-900 bytes category. It is thought that checksums and related data were added which made the file bigger. It is clear from Figure 7 that some sites in the USA did not optimise their JPEG images for the Web. By optimising the JPEG images and trimming the file size, the author was able to compress 452,250 bytes of original JPEG images down to 194,150 bytes. This represents a saving of 57.1%. Similar behaviour was also observed for sites in Australia, Canada, UK and Ireland. It is thought that by saving the optimised JPEG images in Microsoft Paint, it removed supporting bytes used by Photoshop.

Based at the author's institution there are two public Web sites, each containing thirteen images. The total page size for Site A is 83.3KB and is composed of six GIFs and seven original JPEG images. Site B totalled at 51.9KB includes matching images as in Site A, but only compressed versions are used. The effects of reduced file size to loading times as seen by six foreign agents are depicted in Figure 8. It is evident that by making attempts to reduce file size, it will reduce user visible latency.

Conclusion and Future Work

The prevalent factor that affects how quickly a Web site performs is the type of Web hosting environment that the site is deployed in. Web users are faced with sliding scale of delays in reality, with no one Web page taking the same time to load on two separate occasions. It is the number of application packets, not bytes, and the number of simultaneous users of the part of the Internet involved in the connection that determines the Web page latency and satisfaction levels. It is arguable that the magnitude and variance of network delay between a client and server are generally proportional to the distance spanned, assuming that all other influencing factors remain constant. If Web developers take the time to tweak different file sections then the loading time of their Web sites may improve. While it is highly documented that PNG is a more compact image representation, they are not suited on low depth images in the sub-900 bytes group. Of the 904 GIF images sampled, 48% of them fell in the sub-900 group, but they do not graphically capture the meaning of the page.

To achieve the graphical and functional goals of Web sites within the technological limitations of the Internet infrastructure, the author wish to research the possibility of developing a Web-authoring tool that will trim the file size of images autonomously. One technique as was adopted in this paper is to convert GIF images above 1KB to PNG formats. In addition, using known limitations of the human eye, the tool can further optimise the JPEG images to acceptable quality levels. An option would be available for developers to override these features. .

References

Bernet, Y., Ford, P., Yavatkar, R., Baker, F., Zhang, L., Speer, M., Braden, R., Davie, B., Wroklawski, J., & Felstaine, E. (2000). *A framework for integrated services operation over DiffServ networks* (RFC2998). IETF, ISSLL Working Group.

Comer, D.E. (2000). *Internetworking with TCP/IP, Vol 1: Principles, protocols and architecture.* Upper Saddle River NJ: Prentice Hall.

Crawley, E., Berger, L., Berson, S., Baker, F., Borden M., & Krawczyk, J. (1998, August). *A framework for integrated services and RSVP over ATM* (RFC 2382).

Floyd, S., & Fall, K. (1999). Promoting the use of end-to-end congestion control in the Internet. *IEEE/ACM Transactions on Networking, 7*(4), 458-472.

Fulp, E.W., & Reeves, D.S. (2001). Optimal provisioning and pricing of differentiated services using QoS class promotion. *Jahrestagung,* (1), 144-150.

Govatos, G. (2001). Accelerating dynamic Web site performance and scalability. *Chutney Technologies, Inc.* Available at: http://www.caching.com/pdf/Preloader_final.pdf

Kent, C.A., & Mogul, J.C. (1987, December). *Fragmentation considered harmful* (Research Report No. 87/3). Digital Western Research Laboratory. Retrieved from http://research.compaq.com/wrl/techreports/abstracts/87.3.html

Knowles, S. (1993, March). *IESG advice from experience with path MTU discovery* (RFC1435). Retrieved March 1993, from http://www.faqs.org/ftp/rfc/pdf/rfc1435.txt.pdf

Lahey, K. (2000). *TCP problems with path MTU discovery* (RFC2923). Retrieved from http://www.faqs.org/ftp/rfc/pdf/rfc2923.txt.pdf

Lee, B., Balan, R., Jacob, L., Seah, W., & Ananda, A. (2002). Avoiding congestion collapse on the Internet using TCP tunnels. *Computer Networks, 39*(2), 207-219.

Lie, H., & Bos, B. (1996, December 17). *Cascading Style Sheets, level 1* (W3C Recommendation). Presented at the World Wide Web Consortium, revised 11th Jan 1999. Retrieved January, 2004, from http://www.w3.org/TR/REC-CSS1

Liu, C.L., Tseng, S.S., & Chen, C.S. (2004). Design and Implementation of an intelligent DNS management system. *Expert Systems with Applications, 27*(2), 223-236.

Menandmice. (2003). *Domain Health Survey for .COM.* Retrieved February, 2003, from http://www.menandmice.com/6000/61_recent_survey.html

Mogul, J., & Deering, S. (1990). *Path MTU discovery* (RFC1191). Retrieved November, 1991, from http://www.faqs.org/rfcs/rfc1191.html

Nielsen, H.F., Gettys, J., Baird-Smith, A., Prud'hommeaux, H., Lie, H., & Lilley, C. (1997). Network performance effects of HTTP/1.1, CSS1, and PNG. *Computer Communication Review, 27*(4).

Networkingfiles. (2006). Retrieved from http://www.networkingfiles.com/PingFinger/Neotraceexpress.htm

Saiedian M.Z.H. & Naeem, M. (2001). Understanding and Reducing Web Delays. *IEEE Computer Society Press, 34*(12), 30-37.

Selvidge, P.R., Chaparro, B.S., & Bender, G.T. (2002). The world wide wait: Effects of delays on user performance. *International Journal of Industrial Ergonomics, 29*, 15-20.

Spreitzer, M., & Janssen, B. (2000). HTTP 'next generation'. *Computer Networks*, 33, 593-607.

Weinberger, M., Seroussi, M., & Sapiro, G. (2000, August). The LOCO-I lossless image compression algorithm: Principles and standardization into JPEG-LS. *IEEE Trans. Image Processing, 9*, 1309-1324.

Endnotes

[1]   http://www.tracert.com/

[2]   http://www.akamai.com

[3]   http://www.etherdetect.com/

Chapter IV

Network Quality of Service for Enterprise Resource Planning Systems:
A Case Study Approach

Ted Chia-Han Lo, University of Auckland, New Zealand

Jairo Gutiérrez, University of Auckland, New Zealand

Abstract

The research reported in this chapter studied the relevance of the application of network quality of service (QoS) technologies for modern enterprise resource planning (ERP) systems, explored the state-of-art for QoS technologies and implementations, and finally provided a framework for the provision of QoS for ERP systems that utilise Internet protocol (IP) networks. The motivation for conducting this research has been the fact that, to date, there is a dearth of literature on the realisation of network QoS for mission-critical ERP systems. Nor have the current implementations of QoS been studied with the objective of developing a practical framework, based on the knowledge and experiences of the practitioners, to allow a structured approach for the provision of QoS for modern ERP systems. Due to the intent and the nature of the research, an interpretivist research paradigm underlies the work and informed a qualitative research method. Based upon the research problem and the context of research, a case study research method has been selected. Four individual cases—including both leading ERP vendors and network technology vendors—were conducted. The primary data collection was done using semi-structured interviews and this data was supplemented by an extensive array of secondary material. The case data collected was then analysed using qualitative data analysis strategies derived from the existing literature. Cross-case analysis confirmed that the traditional approaches for ensuring the performance of ERP systems on IP networks do not address network congestion and latency effectively, nor do they offer guaranteed network service quality for ERP systems. Moreover, a cross-case comparative data analysis was used to review the pattern of existing QoS implementations and it concluded that while QoS is increasingly being acknowledged by enterprises as an important issue, its deployment remains limited. The findings from the cross-case analysis ultimately became the basis of the proposed framework for the provision of network QoS for ERP systems. The proposed framework focuses on providing a structured, yet practical approach to implement end-to-end IP QoS that accommodates both ERP systems and their Web-enabled versions based on state-of-art traffic classification mechanisms. The value of the research is envisioned to be most visible for two major audiences: enterprises that currently utilise best-effort IP networks for their ERP deployments and ERP vendors.

Introduction

According to Kumar and Hillegerberg (2000), ERP systems are configurable information system packages that integrate information and information-based processes within and across functional areas in an organisation. Other definitions may differ in their wording, but a common theme surfaces upon closer inspection: the integration of enterprise information.

Traditionally ERP systems have targeted the large, complex business organisation, facilitating the integration and the flow of information between functions within an enterprise in a consistently visible manner. Even with the current movement of repackaging their systems for small to medium enterprises (SMEs) by the ERP vendors, the governing concept remains: how can ERP systems support the integration of enterprise information across functional boundaries in an enterprise, across geographical boundaries for multi-site enterprises, or even across organisational boundaries to reach external entities such as suppliers and customers. It has been suggested that IS academics have been asleep at "the wheel of the ERP phenomenon," and most of the early research has not examined the implications and complexities of enterprise-wide information integration (Kumar & Hillegerberg, 2000).

To support enterprise-wide information integration, the enterprise network infrastructure should be considered as a critical component of the overall IT strategy and ERP system deployments. This is largely due to the fact that modern ERP systems have evolved from centralised mainframe systems to the more scalable client-server architecture. The client-server ERP systems are inherently distributed, and therefore are capable of supporting large, multi-site enterprises. However, ERP client and server communicate with each other mainly through network connections and the quality of the network connections therefore has a very strong influence on the stability and performance of the entire ERP system.

The quality of the network has traditionally been measured mainly in terms of bandwidth. According to Delcroix and Green-Armytage (2002), between 1998 and 2003, Wide Area Network (WAN) bandwidth use in multinational companies was driven by Internet applications and database applications such as ERP. In the 2002-2003 periods, bandwidth requirements are being driven by an increased used of these applications and by the natural growth of computer applications and of graphical screen presentations.

Bandwidth in general is expected to become more of a commodity in the long-term. In fact, enterprises are already enjoying the benefits of high-capacity local area networks (LAN) at prices lower than ever before (Hiller, 2002). In the meantime, however, the WAN bandwidth price and the availability vary significantly from one location to another. Delcroix and Green-Armytage (2002) suggested that the long-distance markets offer sufficient bandwidth at acceptable prices in the United States and Western Europe. However, in less deregulated countries, bandwidth tends to be less available and hence more expensive. Enterprises constrained with IT budgets and local bandwidth availability will have to manage their network traffic effectively or face congestion on the enterprise networks. Globally, it has been predicted that some form of bandwidth management will be necessary during at least the next five-year period to bring bandwidth use in line with the acceptable cost for enterprises in various locations (Delcroix & Green-Armytage, 2002).

Furthermore, enterprises are experiencing heavy increases in bandwidth demand. A significant issue, that leads enterprise network managers to doubt that the current enterprise networks will meet business requirements over the next two years, is the continuing growth in volume of traffic. A study conducted by Ashton, Metzler & Associates, and Sage Research (2001) showed that the vast majority of enterprises surveyed in the study has data traffic growing by eleven percent or more on an annual basis and about a quarter of surveyed enterprises have data traffic growing by 51% on an annual basis. Roughly 1 in 12 has data traffic doubling in a year or less. As the traffic volume continues to grow, enterprises are expected to increasingly encounter congestion-related problems, especially the enterprises that deploy multiple applications on the same network infrastructure. Nonetheless, there are a growing number of converged enterprise networks that support all the enterprise's communication requirements. A large part of the network convergence movement can be attributed to the increasing popularity of Internet protocol (IP) applications (Pultz, 2001; Hafner, 2003; Chatterjee, Abhichandani, Tulu, & Li, 2005).

Network congestion in enterprise networks have traditionally been dealt with additional bandwidth (Delcroix & Green-Armytage, 2002; Ashton, Metzler & Associates, 2002; Melia, 1999). While this is considered as an intuitive, quick-and-easy way to alleviate the issue, the WAN bandwidth availability and cost of bandwidth often render this solution less attractive, or in some cases impossible. Moreover, the inherent nature of the IP-based applications makes adding bandwidth less effective in dealing with network congestion, as some applications tend to, in the long-term, consume all of the available bandwidth on the network regardless of how much bandwidth there is. These "bandwidth hungry" applications are typically applications such as Web applications, e-mail and file transfer protocols (FTP). While the importance of an application is highly dependent on the business activities and goals of the organisation, these applications are generally considered as being less important to enterprises. When these applications happen to consume most, if not all, of the available resources on the network, other applications such as ERP systems or VoIP suffer and perform at sub-optimal levels.

In addition to bandwidth, enterprises must also take into account the latency, or response time, required by applications and end users. The latency, or round-trip delay, is the time required to move a bit of information from one location to another and back again. When networks become saturated, latency increases. Historically latency problems encountered have also been tackled by upgrading the network bandwidth capacity. However previous literature has also suggested that the strategy of adding more bandwidth is ineffective by itself to deal with latency problems (Adams & Bawany, 2002; Cisco Systems et al., 2001).

Over the past few years, both academics and practitioners in the field of network management have searched for an alternative, or a complementary strategy, to network bandwidth. The result is what has been termed quality of service (QoS). QoS is a relatively new technology that has primarily been shaped by the practitioners including numerous Internet technology workgroups and key network technology vendors. QoS is considered as a general term referring to the technologies that classify network traffic and then ensure that some of that traffic receives special handling (Siegel, 2000; Huston, 2000; Armitage, 2000a; Soldatos, Vayias, & Kormentzas, 2005). QoS in theory allows an enterprise to efficiently utilise the existing network resources by providing tools for managing a set of parameters, including bandwidth and latency, for an arbitrary amount of network traffic. This can be desirable where a single network infrastructure supports a multitude of applications.

QoS can be a compelling alternative to sheer bandwidth because it has the potential to be more cost-effective and provides more control on the network. QoS, as a subject, has a diffuse body of literature. In the academic world, the various techniques and architectures of QoS are well studied. However, most of the studies to date have not examined in detail the complexity and the implications of implementing QoS on a converged network for data applications. While numerous studies on implementation of QoS for voice applications over IP networks have been carried out and published, such as in Fineberg (2002) and Siegel (2000), very little is known about the network requirements of today's ERP systems and how QoS technologies can be deployed to satisfy these requirements.

In theory, ERP systems should make great targets for network QoS. As with most client-server applications, network quality heavily impacts the performance and the stability of the entire ERP system. ERP systems are generally regarded as mission-critical to most enterprises hence it would be legitimate to provide preferential treatment in the times of network congestion for ERP traffic. Moreover, the inherent nature of ERP systems and their typical deployment in the business environment implies that the cost and the availability of WAN bandwidth are potential limiting factors in the system deployment and performance. Therefore the research into how QoS technologies have been, or can be, used for ERP systems should be of high priority, but is not.

Moreover, numerous research papers and articles that appeared in influential trade press publications and information systems journals, from authors such as Anderson (2001), Sheer and Haberman (2000) and Comport (2001), suggested that ERP, like many other mission-critical enterprise applications, is in the process of a makeover. Gartner Research coined the term ERP II and suggested that ERP II puts an outward focus on ERP. This is expected, at least technically, to involve a fast move towards Web-based systems. The rationale behind this movement, in large part, is due to the popularity of the Internet. Rao (2000a) pointed out that the biggest challenge facing ERP suppliers is to address the global access issues that would cater to intra-organisation and extra-organisation needs effectively. Anderson (2001) suggested that the way most ERP vendors address these issues is by utilising native Internet technologies and network infrastructures. However, today's Internet is largely based on best-effort IP networks and its technologies, such as HTTP and HTML, were not developed to offer mechanisms for ensuring the performance of applications that use them. QoS, therefore, is potentially valuable for Web-based ERP applications.

Furthermore, the market for enterprise networks has always been characterised by innovations and rapid advancement of technologies. The latest advancements in traffic classification such as Layer 7 traffic classification, for instance, are potentially valuable enhancements to current QoS technologies—as traffic flows must be identified to allow differentiated treatment. However, Layer 7 traffic classification is a relatively new concept and has not been widely tested and adopted. A framework to explore the potential of this technology for the provision of QoS for applications such as ERP systems does not exist in the current literature.

In summary, the gaps within the present literature related to network QoS and ERP systems, identified here have limited the practicality of QoS implementations for ERP systems. Moreover, an array of interrelated marketing and technical trends highlights the importance of this research, including:

- ERP systems are increasing being deployed on IP networks.
- The movement towards converged networks is observable among enterprises.
- WAN bandwidth cost and availability varies significantly.
- IP networks largely remain as best-effort networks.
- The maturing of QoS technologies and advancements in traffic classification technologies.
- The popularity of the Internet as a platform for wide area network applications and the evolution of ERP systems.

The overarching purpose of this chapter is therefore to explore the ways QoS can be implemented for ERP systems that utilise IP networks, and then use the results as a guide and benchmark to develop the first framework for the provision of QoS to ERP systems.

Research Objectives and Questions

The first objective is **to explore and identify the reasons to provide network QoS for ERP systems that utilise IP networks**. To achieve this objective the research must answer the following question:

RQ 1: *Why is it necessary to provide network QoS for ERP systems?*

The answer to RQ 1 should address the technical, as well as the business-oriented aspects of the question.

The second research objective is **to explore how is QoS currently implemented on IP networks that support ERP systems**. As revealed through reviewing the existing literature on network QoS, a wide array of QoS technologies and mechanisms is available. This allows network managers and system implementers to be selective and implement the technologies that are most appropriate for providing network QoS to ERP systems. The deployment of these technologies is likely to depend on a number of factors, including ease of deployment, scalability and the organisational context. The second research objective is defined to provide insights into the following research questions, including:

> **RQ2:** *What are the available QoS technologies that can be implemented to pro-vide end-to-end network QoS for ERP systems? And, RQ 3: What is the current status of deployment and common deployment topologies of the available QoS technologies to provide end-to-end network QoS for ERP systems?*

While for the first and the second research objectives a sequential relationship does not exist, it is envisioned that the completion of research objective one and two is required to achieve the third research objective. Based on the knowledge acquired from the first and second objectives, the final objective of the research is **to propose a framework for the provision of network QoS for ERP systems that utilise IP networks**.

Research Methodology Overview

With a diffuse body of literature on network QoS and the largely exploratory nature of the research questions, qualitative research methodologies were the preferred choice from the outset. Moreover, the specific markets related to this research are characterised by oligopolic vendors dominating the majority of the market. This research would have to embrace both technical and organisational issues, as well as the current trends in these markets, and therefore needed to focus on a small number of leading vendors rather than a large number of smaller, "second-tier" vendors. For this reason, case study research seemed to be more appropriate than survey techniques.

The case study research methodology, as set out by Yin (1984), is primarily oriented towards testing of hypotheses that have been derived from previous theoretical propositions. Eisenhardt (1989) and Yin (1994) later extended this to cases where the researcher has no preconceived ideas and thus is independent from prior literature or past empirical observations. This then seemed to be an appropriate methodology for the research.

The interpretive nature of the research suggested the use of a methodology that is capable of and can be focused on gaining a deeper understanding into the phenomenon under study—in this case, the scope of the research method must be able to include technological, as well as organisational and behavioural factors and relationships related to the ERP systems and QoS. Moreover, interpretive research is usually conducted to understand phenomenon in the context of situations. The authors felt that quantitative research methods—including experiments and surveys—did not offer the required "realism" for this kind of research.

Benbasat, Goldstein, and Mead (1987), however, suggested that a case study methodology might be better suited in the context of this type of research: the information systems (IS) field is characterised by constant technological change and innovations. IS researchers, therefore, often find themselves trailing behind practitioners—this is particularly true in the disciplines of ERP and computer networking. It has been suggested that researchers often learn by studying the innovations put in place by practitioners. These factors also helped to persuade the authors that, for this research, the case study might be the best-suited research method to capture the knowledge of the practitioners.

For this research the authors selected a holistic, multiple-case design (Yin, 1994). The unit of analysis has been determined to be "organisations" which is expected to allow the research to most effectively acquire the information needed for answering the specific research questions. The target population has been defined to include "leading vendors in the markets of ERP applications and network technologies." The market status of each identified vendor was assessed using metrics such as market share and size of their installed base, based on information published by third party organisations and general word-of-mouth. Four organisations were eventually selected to be included in this research. Face-to-face (8) and e-mail interviews (3) were used to collect data. The interviews produced around 150 pages worth of transcripts. Additionally the authors used approximately 1800 pages of secondary data (company reports, white papers, Web sites information, etc.). The e-mail interviews conducted were based on the framework provided by Chadwick (1996) for collecting case study information via the Internet. The data analysis strategy that has been custom-built for this research focuses on the identification of common patterns and themes among the cases through the use of data reduction and display methods as in Huberman and Miles (1998), and the use of the within-case analysis and cross-case comparative analysis methods suggested in Eisenhardt (1989).

According to Alter (1996), information systems can have three different dimensions: organisational, technical, and managerial. For the research objects of this work: ERP systems and network QoS, the three dimensions were identified and adapted as:

- The organisational, or the "vendor" dimension
- The "technology" dimension
- The "market" dimension

The need to adapt the model of IS viewpoints presented in Alter (1996) for this research arise from the tight coupling of ERP systems and network QoS to the various trends in the relevant markets.

The three dimensions of the research objects were effectively used in the categorisation of case data, which allowed a reduced set of case data to be presented for each dimension. Cross-case comparative analysis was conducted for the three dimensions with the aim of identifying patterns that were relevant to the issues informed by research questions. Tables were used as the primary presentation tools for reduced data sets and identified patterns. The cross-case patterns were used to answer the specific questions of the research—RQ 1, RQ 2, and RQ 3.

Case Studies: The Network Vendors

The primary source of data was semi-structured, face-to-face interviews with key vendor engineers and consultants. However, a significant portion of the case study data came from a number of secondary sources, including articles and books published by the companies, internal training documents, product documentation, downloaded Web material, and archival records.

Company A

Company A, though headquartered in the U.S., has offices in more than 50 countries, and employs more than 35,000 people around the world. The company's strategy is to be prominent in advancing the development of IP, which it considers to be the basic protocol of the Internet and private networks. The company aims to position itself as being innovative, a technology leader, and to push "everything into the network." According to The Yankee Group (2002) Company A has 50% to 90% market share in the enterprise network market, depending on the product category. Company A offers a broad line of network solutions for LAN, MAN, WAN, optical and wireless networks.

Company A's hardware product lines such as hubs, switches, routers, and access servers are the basic building blocks to its network solutions for small, medium-sized and large networks. Within each product line Company A offers a number of product series, each differing in terms of price, performance and functionality, targeted to support different types of networks. In particular, Company A has an extensive range of routers and switches—both product lines have more than twenty product series and combine to give over one hundred product models. A number of Company A's flagship routers and switches families are managed by proprietarily developed operating system software which provides a common interface across the hardware platforms. The operating system has been regarded as an important software solution that performs a number of critical functions, including routing and switching, network management, security, MPLS tunnelling, multicasting, support for voice and video applications and quality of service (QoS).

This case provides a detailed description of company A, its perspective on network QoS, its QoS tools and its recommended network solutions and QoS implementations for ERP systems. Due to the space limitations of this chapter the authors present just a summary of the cases. Full details of the four case studies, including interview quotations, reference to source documents, diagrams, and so forth can be found in Lo (2002).

Company A, while in an active effort to push its QoS solutions to its customers, also recognises the importance of upgrading the network capacity. However there are certain classes of enterprise applications, identified by Company A, that require more than sheer bandwidth to perform satisfactorily on a converged IP network. These applications include voice, video and ERP systems. Company A considers QoS as critical to ensure ERP system performance, particularly over the WAN links, and provides a comprehensive set of per-hop QoS mechanisms and full support for the various QoS network models to deliver end-to-end QoS for ERP network traffic.

The specific approach of Company A toward implementing QoS for ERP systems is also described in the case. In general, network traffic is usually classified and prioritised using Layer 2-4 header information. The class-based prioritisation is then honoured throughout the network with, mainly, multi-queue congestion management: WRED for congestion avoidance and traffic shaping based on token-bucket metering. These per-hop QoS mechanisms are usually coordinated by DiffServ or IP precedence, as Company A considers IntServ as inappropriate for ERP traffic, given its specific traffic patterns.

Company B

Company B, founded in 1996 in the U.S., is a network technology vendor in the enterprise and service provider network markets that specialises in the provision of quality of service (QoS) for networked applications and managed services. Company B received net revenue of $46.6 million for the 2001 fiscal year. It currently employs approximately 200 employees and its products are sold by more than 100 resellers, distributors, and system integrators in more than 50 countries. The products and services provided, according to Company B, are designed to enable enterprise and service providers to measure, control and validate the performance of network applications. It is considered as a dominant player in that particular market niche. Its products, according to Company B, are being deployed worldwide. Current statistic shows that more than 18,000 units of the company's flagship product have been shipped worldwide to date (Company B, 2001h).

This case presents detailed descriptions of Company B, focusing on its perspective on QoS, its QoS tools—particularly on its Layer 7 classification engine and TCP rate control technologies—and how it implements QoS for ERP systems.

Company B considers QoS as necessary for enterprise applications such as ERP, VoIP and real-time video. Over-provision of the network in its pure form is seen as short-term solution to issues arisen from network resource contention on best-effort networks. Moreover, Company B also recognises the need to provide preferential treatment for certain classes of Web traffic, whereas Web traffic in general has been treated as secondary in terms of its importance to the enterprise. In the views of Company B and its consultants, Layer 7 classification is critical to provide effective implementations of QoS for ERP systems on modern networks.

The patented QoS technology played an important role in defining the concept of QoS for the company. With TCP rate control, bandwidth and network delay stated as the major parameters for defining QoS for Company B—since TCP rate control in theory eliminates queuing and loss of packets due to router queuing management and policing. The QoS implementation as recommended by Company B is also discussed in the case study, which places a focus the provision of QoS for network connections that tend to span LANs and WANs.

This section of the chapter contains case studies for two network technologies vendors that are both currently considered as leading vendors in their own market niche. Both cases focused on issues informed by the research problem and objectives that include:

- The network technology vendors' perspective towards QoS

- The tools and technologies available to achieve network QoS

- The ERP traffic profiles and network requirement as understood by the network technology vendors

- The vendor-specific QoS deployment topologies recommended by the network technology vendors for ERP systems

Case Studies: The ERP Vendors

The first section of each case study contains a brief overview of the company. This is followed by a description of the company's flagship ERP systems, focusing on issues that centre on system architecture, network traffic patterns, and requirements. The case study then proceeds to explore the approaches of the vendors toward network performance issues and the QoS concepts and technologies.

Company C

Company C was founded in the late 1970s in the U.S. It has been amongst the leading vendors in the ERP market worldwide—it received annual revenue of $894 million for Year 2001 and currently has approximately 6500 mid-market and large customers with sites in over 100 countries. To support this scale of operation, Company C employees close to 5000 staff in 18 U.S. offices and 60 international offices. Company C also has over 300 partners from consulting firms to small organisations, providing service to customers in remote locations (Company C, 2002c, 2002d). Company C offers a wide range of software solutions, including ERP systems, supply chain management (SCM) systems, customer relationship management (CRM) systems, and various collaboration tools.

The company's first ERP product was named "C0" and released in the late 1980s. At the time it was released, "C0" was not designed to be implemented in a distributed environment. According to Company C, "C0" uses a "monolithic," or host-centric system architecture. Its successor was released in the mid-1990s, and it was named "C1," which has since become Company C's flagship ERP system.

Recent statistics shows that there are approximately 1,700 customers worldwide "live" on C1 to date (Company C, 2002a). One of the major differences between C1 and C0 is an architecturally defined one—C1 was designed to be a platform-independent, distributed client-server system in order to provide both performance and scalability over the underlying network infrastructure.

While single to multi-tier implementations are possible, the most common implementation of C1 has been the three-tiered architecture. The client tier supports a traditional "fat client" configuration, using the proprietary Win32 client executables, storing C1 logic and static data elements. The Win32 client has C1-specific middleware and APIs to handle the message-based communication between application elements and servers. Other supported clients include Web-based clients, using a Web server, and server-based technologies such as Windows Terminal Service and Citrix´s MetaFrame.

The server tiers include the application servers, database servers, and for Web-based clients, Web servers. The "enterprise server" is the term given to the server that hosts both the application functions and the database functions. When C1 users choose to implement the Enterprise Server, the system architecture is termed the "virtual," or "logical" three-tiered architecture. While the Enterprise server approach has its pros and cons when compared to the physical three-tiered architecture, they do not directly relate to the use of network resources.

Company C, as well as its customers, in general have moved away from the traditional Win32 client, to the fully Web-enabled ERP solution. From a network perspective, this approach has been able to reduce the volume of traffic being injected into the network by the ERP system. However, Company C and its ERP systems currently, do not provide QoS at the application level. The typical recommendations from the consultants at Company C focus on bandwidth upgrades.

The increasing adoption of the Web-enabled C1 system implies a new set of traffic characteristics and requirements that Company C and its clients must take into consideration during various stages of ERP implementation and operation. Some of the major considerations include the use of HTTP and HTTPS protocols over WAN networks, encapsulated print data and multimedia object attachments.

Company D

Company D was founded in the early 1970s in Europe and has since grown to be the world's leading software vendor in the ERP market with a market share of about 36%. Company D currently has an installation base of 44,500, serving approximately 10 million users at 17500 organisations in 120 countries. Company D currently employs approximately 28,000 staff in more than 50 countries. The reported annual revenue for Company D for Year 2001 was €7340.8 millions. Company D offers the broadest ERP functionality among its competitors, providing solutions to over 20 industries, including both manufacturing and services. These solutions incorporate the so-called "best practice" for conducting businesses in these industries. In recent years Company D has been committed to the development and implementation of functionalities such as supply chain management (SCM), customer relationship management (CRM), and database warehousing.

The two predecessors of the Company D's flagship ERP system, D1 and D2 were released in the 1970s. Both D1 and D2 were developed to satisfy the business needs of mainframe users. D2 became the major product of Company D in the 1980's when the centralised computing paradigm prevailed. D3 is the logical evolution of the D2 systems, and it is the product that has actually fuelled the expansion of Company D since its introduction in the early 1990s (D Info, 1998).

D3 is a real-time, client-server software solution whose functionalities are based on the concept of business processes. D3 itself, since its initial release, has undergone a series of expansions in functionality and technology enhancements. The version of D3 released in 1996 marked a significant step forward for Company D, as D3 was Internet-enabled through the use of open, Web-based technologies such as Java, Web browsers, and Web servers. The next major release of D3, while maintaining the commitment to open technologies, was focused on achieving fast implementation of componentised D3 systems.

The D3 system, from a software perspective, is structured in a three-tiered client-server architecture, with each tier having a distinct function. Conceptually, all data is stored in a database, and the data is processed in the application layer on the application servers. The client programs, or the presentation layer, are the interface to the user. All three layers communicate with each other through the network. Physically, the three-tiered architecture has been the most common implementation. It is possible, however, to implement D3 with single to N-tiered architecture. Moreover, with the introduction of HTML clients, D3 systems are now considered to be structured in a multi-tiered architecture (Company D, 2001d, 2001e, 2002a).

There are three types of D3 client programs, including the Win32 clients, the Java clients, and the HTML clients. The Win32 client is the best-known client program for D3. The advantage of the Win32 client is its singular range of functions. The Java client can be implemented on most known platforms. The HTML client uses a preinstalled Web browser to show the application and data.

While each network connection supported by D3 has its own set of requirements that must be satisfied by the supporting network infrastructure, which is derived from both the business requirements of the enterprise and the technical requirements of the D3 system and communication protocols, the network requirements of D3 network connections have in general been described as being "qualitative."

Due to its distributed nature, all the tiers of the D3 system are connected by networks, usually TCP/IP networks. This study, adhering to Company D's conventions, roughly divided the network connections into two categories based on the type of supporting network infrastructure. Server communication, which includes connections between the servers that are usually supported by LANs, is considered vital to D3 system performance. To ensure the supporting LANs fulfil the stringent network requirements for server communications, Company D strongly recommends D3 users to take advantage of low-cost LAN bandwidth. For this reason, experience suggests that the LAN connections very rarely become performance bottlenecks of D3 systems. The access communication, however, can become the focal point for network performance tuning when network connections span over LANs as well as WANs. This is especially the case for Web-enabled D3 systems.

Other than the continuous effort to reduce and control network load created by D3 systems, Company D has recently QoS-enabled its flagship ERP system by providing software support for RSVP (IETF RFC 2205). Nonetheless, QoS through resource reservation has yet to find its way to current D3 implementations. Most D3 consultants and D3 partner consultants remain supporters of the "over-provisioning" approach for issues such as network congestion and long response times.

Cross-Case Analysis

This section contains the cross-case analysis of the case studies. The following discussion focuses on answering questions posed by the first two objectives of the research:

- **Objective one:** to explore and identify the reasons to provide network QoS for ERP systems that utilise IP networks.

- **Objective two:** to explore how is QoS currently implemented on IP networks that support ERP systems.

The completion of the first two research objectives provided the fundamental architectural "blueprint" to inductively achieve the final research objective:

- **Objective three:** to propose a framework for the provision of network QoS for ERP systems that utilise IP networks.

The cases encountered contrasting organisational values, business practices and technology adoption processes. The selection and number of cases allowed a rich, representative description of the research domain and provided an opportunity to establish external validity, in which the selected issues described are examined in a cross-case analysis. These issues, which are referred to as the "focal issues" throughout this chapter, include:

- ERP systems and the supporting network infrastructure
- ERP traffic profiles
- Perspective towards QoS
- QoS tools available
- QoS implementations for ERP systems
- Current implementations to ensure ERP performance on the network

Three dimensions—the "vendor," "market" and "technology"—are used for the comparative analysis and pattern clarification across the cases.

The "vendor" dimension provides a description of the issues centred on the values, the speculations, the preferences, and the strategies of the vendors described in each individual case study. The vendor dimension provides a valuable insight to the research problem as these vendors, with their large installed base and commanding share in their respective markets, are expected to have the ability to shape the current and future markets relevant to this research. The summarised case descriptions from the vendor dimension are presented in Table 1. Across the cases, the first and foremost pattern that can be observed is the clear separation of duties between the ERP vendor and the network technology vendor. The ERP vendors effectively considered themselves as providers of enterprise application software—while they provide consultancy services and guidelines for hardware sizing during ERP implementation, they do not actively participate in the design and implementation of the underlying network infrastructure. The focus of the ERP vendors has been to develop software solutions that are highly extendable, configurable and can implemented in a reasonable timeframe. The hardware requirements of the ERP systems, including servers and network infrastructure, are passed onto the hardware vendors, who in turn are expected to design and deliver the necessary hardware infrastructure.

Table 1. Cross-case analysis: The vendor dimension

Focal issues	Company A	Company B
ERP System and the supporting network infrastructure	■ ERP considered as a mission-critical application. ■ Confined awareness of the growth and development Web-based ERP systems. ■ Provides a network methodology for building ERP supporting network.	■ ERP considered as a mission-critical application. ■ Shows explicit awareness of Web-based ERP systems. ■ Provides no recommendation for building the underlying network infrastructure.
Perspective towards QoS	■ Explicit recognition of the importance of QoS, company-wide ■ Leading provider and supporter of both QoS and bandwidth technologies. ■ Considers over-provisioning as the best option and QoS as the more intelligent and way to utilise exiting bandwidth. ■ ERP is considered as a top QoS candidate.	■ Explicit recognition of the importance of QoS, company-wide. ■ Strong supporter and specialised provider of QoS. ■ Considers over-provision as only short-term solution and QoS as necessary to ensure application performance. ■ ERP is considered as a top QoS candidate.
QoS Tools	■ Mainly incorporated into the routers and switches offered by the company ■ Based open standard and/or proprietary technologies.	■ Entirely incorporated into a single product unit offered by company ■ Based on proprietary, technologies.
QoS implementation for ERP systems	■ Can be achieved through the concatenation per-hop QoS mechanisms implemented routers / switches. ■ Focused on end-to-end, class-based QoS.	■ Should be achieved through TCP rate control rather than the per-hop mechanism in routers / switches. ■ Focus on Layer 7 traffic classification.
Current implementations to ensure ERP performance on the network	■ Recommends high-redundancy at network and server level. ■ Recommends Fast / Gigabit Ethernet for LAN. ■ End-to-end QoS recommended for ERP systems. ■ Very few networks are QoS enabled but there is positive speculation for the future.	■ QoS recommended for ERP systems ■ Recommends data compression for Web-based ERP. ■ Very few networks are QoS enabled but there is positive speculation for the future.

The ERP and network technology vendors, following their own visions and missions, have specialised in the areas where their expertise and competences lay. This specialisation provides a strong business case for the common separation of duties in ERP system deployments.

The technology dimension adds another layer of detail that is focused on providing an in-depth, technical description to the focal issues of this research. The technology dimension is mostly fabricated from "hard," quantitative data elements from the cases studies and is presented in a summarised form in Table 2.

The market dimension adds the third and final layer of detail that is focused on providing a description of markets trends, as observed by the ERP and network technology vendors, regarding the focal issues identified previously. The market dimension is mostly fabricated from interviewee experiences in providing products and services to their respective client enterprises and is presented in a summarised form in Table 3.

Table 1. continued

Company C	Company D
■ Considers its ERP application as a mission-critical application. ■ The company is moving towards Web-based solutions and provides fully Web-enabled version of C1. ■ Considers the network infrastructure as critical for the C1 but offloads most designing and sizing responsibilities to the network hardware suppliers.	■ Considers its D3 as a mission critical application and a core component of the e-business & e-commerce strategy ■ Provides equal support for Web and original version of its flagship ERP offering. ■ Considers the network infrastructure as critical for the D3 but offloads most responsibilities to the network hardware suppliers. ■ Known for its hardware sizing methodologies.
■ No explicit recognition of QoS by the company. However the company is currently working in partnership with a server hardware vendor to explore the value of QoS. ■ Supporter of over-provision in general.	■ The company has a confined, but slowly growing recognition of the importance of QoS. ■ Working in partnership with operating system vendors to deliver QoS. ■ The consultants are supporter of over-provisioning in general. ■ The company recognises two types of network QoS: qualitative and quantitative QoS
■ Does not provide any QoS solution	■ Provides the means to support QoS signalling in recent releases of its flagship ERP application
■ Company C considers implementing QoS for C1 as the responsibilities of the enterprise network managers and network technology suppliers.	■ Recommends QoS based on prioritisation and/or resource reservation. ■ Network-level QoS implementation is offloaded to the network managers and technology vendors.
■ Moved to the Web-based solution specifically to reduce the network load. ■ Recommends over-provision the network where possible when congestion occurs. ■ The tuning of networks is usually the responsibility of the network hardware suppliers.	■ Committed to minimise the D3 network load ■ Usually recommends over-provisioning the network where possible. Recently embraced the QoS concepts at the application level but very few networks have been enabled to provide QoS for the company's flagship ERP systems. ■ The network tuning is usually the responsibility of the network technology vendors.

Analysis of Cross-Case Patterns

The patterns or themes identified provide valuable insights into the main research issues. The specialisation or separation of duties in a typical ERP system implementation appeared to be the grand pattern underlying many of the themes identified. For instance, the network technology vendors generally support network QoS, while the ERP vendors continue to be committed to the approach of having over-powered networks and running ERP systems that have been optimised in terms of network requirements. Network technology vendors, on the other hand, have a general understanding of the requirements of a typical ERP system. However this understanding is somehow limited to the earlier versions of the ERP systems—versions not enabled for Web-browser access.

This observable specialisation, however, does not appear to completely insulate the two types of vendors from each other. It can be expected that as long as their targeted markets

Figure 1. Relationships between the vendor, technology and market dimensions

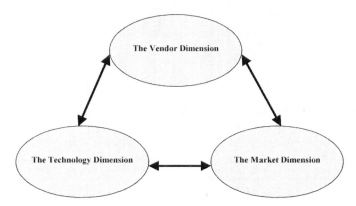

intersect with each other, the ERP vendors are likely to be aware of technologies offered by the network technology vendors and vice versa. The likelihood of any one side devoting an extra effort to better understand and utilise the technologies offered by the other—such as Company D enabling D3 to support traffic identification and RSVP signalling—is likely to depend on a series of interrelated factors. For ERP vendors, the factors are likely to include the value of network QoS as perceived by the company and its consultants in comparison with bandwidth cost, the attitudes of other ERP vendors, and ultimately the level of demand for QoS from established or prospective clients. As for the network technology vendors, the single most important factor is likely to be the perceived demand for QoS from organisations deploying or running ERP systems.

The cross-case, multi-dimensional analysis also revealed a number of interrelationships between the cross-case patterns identified from the description of three dimensions (see Figure 1).

The inter-relationships between the patterns appeared to be relationships of dependency. A strong, directional dependency appeared to exist between:

- Patterns identified from the vendor dimension and the patterns identified from the technology dimension—the technology depends on the organisational value, mission, and vision.

- Patterns identified from the market dimension and the patterns identified from both the technology and vendor dimensions.

Table 2. Cross-case analysis: The technology dimension

Focal issues	Company A	Company B	Company C	Company D
ERP System and supporting networks	• ERP systems have tiered system architecture • Application server and database server usually connected by LAN • Clients connect to the application servers via LAN/WAN/Internet/telephone network • The IA network architecture.	• ERP systems have tiered system architecture, including the Web-enabled versions. • Application server and database server usually connected by LAN • Clients connect to the application servers via LAN/WAN/Internet.	• C1 support multi-tiered deployment • Latest release of C1 is based on Web technologies. • C1 Supports both Win32 and HTML clients • Application and data server can be implemented on the same machine. • Win32 client communicates to the application and database server using the proprietary communication middleware via TCP/IP networks • HTML client communicates to the Web application server using HTTP / HTTP-S via TCP/IP networks • Server-to-server communication also uses the communication middleware via TCP/IP networks.	• D3 is three-tiered in nature but the Web-enabled D3 is multi-tiered. • D3 supports Win32, Java and HTML clients • Win32 and Java clients communicate to the application servers via TCP/IP networks, using DIAG protocol • HTML client communicates to the HTML middleware layer via TCP/IP networks, using HTTP / HTTP-S. • The HTML middleware layer communicates to the applications layer via TCP/IP networks, using the DIAG protocol. • The application servers communicate to the database servers using remote database calls TCP/IP networks
ERP system traffic profile	• ERP systems usually create more than one network connections. • The interactive network connections have stringent latency requirements, relatively low per-user bandwidth requirements, and tolerate some jitter • The per-user bandwidth requirements vary with transaction, application and software version. • For two-tiered ERP systems, the clients and the servers usually engage in more intensive exchanges of date for a given transaction — high data volume and greater number of round-trips — when compared to their three-tiered implementation. • Other network connections usually include communication between databases, communication between applications servers and printing. The delay, bandwidth, and jitter requirements of these connections vary in individual circumstances	• ERP systems usually generate more than one network connection • The interactive traffic between the client and server is delay-sensitive. • Low per-user bandwidth requirement and non-bursty for interactive traffic between clients and servers (for non-Web ERP systems) • Print traffic is not delay-sensitive and has a tendency to be burst. • Possible per-user higher bandwidth requirement and somewhat bursty for Web-based, interactive network connections between the client and server. • ERP network connections are usually not prone to jitter. • The delay, bandwidth requirement, burstiness and jitter requirements of other ERP flows vary individual circumstances.	• Web-enabled C1 is less demanding in terms of network resources required • Supports a number of major connection types: client-server, server-server and server-printer network connections. All network connections uses static TCP ports. • Clients-server network connections are characterised by delay-sensitive, interactive traffic. The bandwidth requirement depends on user, transaction, application, system release, and deployment and range from 4-40KB per active user, without media objects attached • Server-server connection are characterised by database access traffic and have high bandwidth and latency requirements. The network load depends on number of user, transaction and application. • Print traffic is bursty and capable of creating network load from 1KB to 100MB plus depending on the size of the print job	• Web-enabled D3 is more demanding in terms of network resources required. • Supports access and server communications, each include multiple connection types. All network connections use non-registered static TCP ports. • Access communication includes the delay-sensitive, interactive client-application server traffic whose bandwidth requirements depend mainly on system release, user, transaction, and application data and ranges from 2KB to 23KB per dialog step. • Both printing and communication with other bandwidth requirements depend on the content size and protocol. • D3 systems can be bursty and bandwidth-demanding - they require varying bandwidth depending on the content size and protocol. • Application server- database server connections are highly delay-sensitive and bandwidth intensive.
Network-induce performance bottlenecks	• At the WAN access links or anywhere on the network link capacity disparities exist, the ERP traffic experiences buffering delays and packet loss just as any other application traffic flows in times of network congestion. • The overall latency equates the round-trip delay multiplied by the number of round trips involved for each client-application server interactions. The WAN contributes much of the total network latency	• At the WAN access links where the speed usually exists, network congestion forces routers to queue the ERP packets as with any other packet, which introduces latency and packet loss. A packet loss in turn causes packet retransmission that also uses the existing bandwidth.	• Using C1 Win32 client on the WAN incurs high bandwidth and intensive exchange of information, which caused congestion and latency issues • WAN bandwidth can be consumed by other applications on a converged network. • Sending print traffic over the WAN often overloads the network	• Using the Web-enabled D3 on the WAN incurs higher bandwidth consumption than the Win32 and Java clients. • WAN bandwidth can be consumed by other applications on a converged network. • Sending print traffic over the WAN often overloads the network

Table 2. continued

Perspective towards QoS	• QoS is relevant on LANs and WAN, wherever congestions can occur. • QoS is measured by bandwidth, delay, jitter and packet loss. • Regardless of the bandwidth, congestions will occur on TCP/IP networks. QoS will protect the important the prioritised traffic flows in times of congestion but will not create bandwidth. • QoS is needed to ensure ERP response-time needs are met consistently	• Congestion is most noticeable at WAN access links and is the appropriate place to implement QoS • QoS is measured mainly be bandwidth and network delay. • Additional bandwidth is only short term solution does not protect important traffic flows like QoS. • Queuing and policing causes delay, jitter, packet loss, and packet retransmission,	N/A	• Considers qualitative QoS as based on specific, quantifiable size of network resources, including bandwidth and delay. Qualitative QoS, on the other hand, is considered as suitable for applications that do not have specific, consistent requirements on the network • QoS is valuable in dividing and prioritising the available network resource among applications but the prioritisation of one application comes at the expense of another
QoS Tools	• Router/switch hardware and software work together to deliver QoS. • Layer 2-4 classification based on ACLs. • Software Layer 4-7 traffic classification. • Packet marking based on CoS, IP Precedence, DSCP and MPLS. • FIFO, PQ, CQ, CB-WFQ LLQ queue management and scheduling. • WRED congestion avoidance. • Policing and shaping based on token bucket metering. • Supports RSVP, COPS, and SBM QoS signalling.	• Software-based solution • Rely on the performance of microprocessor QoS implemented in appliance • Layer 7 classification engine that allows automatic and user-defined classification • TCP rate control that manipulates the sliding-window control to allow logical bandwidth partitioning, establishing rate and priority policies • Packet marking/remarking based on IP precedence/DSCP and MPLS	N/A	• The QoS component of the D3 system allows the QoS requirements of different D3 network connections to be signalled using policy string locators.
QoS implementations for ERP systems	• Classifies ERP traffic flows at network edges, preferably at access switches. • Classifies ERP traffic flows by input interface and Layer 2-4 header fields • Mark packets and enforce priority using CoS at in LAN • Mark packets and enforce priority using DSCP or IP Precedence at Layer 3 and in WAN • ERP traffic flows maybe of different importance. Interactive flows should be marked with highest priority among data applications	• Classifies ERP traffic on the LAN side of WAN access links. • Classifies ERP traffic at Layer 7. • Interactive ERP traffic has highest priority and priority of other ERP flows varies. • Logically partition the available bandwidth and reserve that for the ERP traffic at aggregate level, or set the minimum / maximum rate for each ERP traffic flow identified. • Mark or remark the IP Precedence, DSCP or MPLS header if needed.	N/A	• Implements qualitative QoS. • Prioritise D3 traffic based on TCP ports and IP addresses, or alternatively D3uses the policy string locator and accesses the host-based APIs to signal flow-based QoS requirements via RSVP. • Client-application server traffic has the highest priority while the print traffic has lower priority. Communication between applications servers should also receive preferential treatment.
Current implementations to ensure ERP performance on the network	• The required QoS technology is matured but the adoption remains limited. • Implements high-throughput LAN switches/ WAN routers. • Implements devices and designs for improving availability through network level redundancy • Implements Layer 7 switching for server load balancing.	• The required QoS technology is matured but the adoption remains limited. • Implements Web content acceleration appliance for Web data compression, file transformation and caching.	• Bandwidth is preferred over QoS to deal with network congestion and delay. • Separate networks for C1 • Implements high-speed LAN (100MB – Gigabit). • Implements FDDI connection between database and application servers to control latency. • Web compression utilities can be implemented on the network to regulate response time for Web-enabled C1	• The QoS technology is available is rarely implemented — bandwidth is usually preferred over QoS to solve issues of congestion and long response time. • Usually separate network is implemented for D3 systems. • Implements 100MB plus LAN. • Uses data compression to optimising protocols to minimise D3 network load. • Provides comprehensive guides to minimise network protocol overheads

Figure 2. The need to provide QoS: An overview of relevant factors

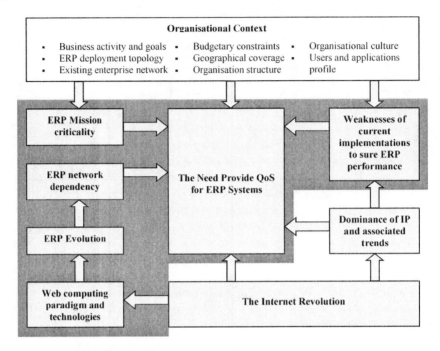

Achieving the Research Objectives

This section starts with the first research question:

RQ1. *Why is it necessary to provide network QoS for ERP systems?*

The case study data analysis and the literature both suggested that the necessity to provide network QoS for ERP systems ultimately arises from the mission criticality of ERP systems and its dependency on the underlying network infrastructure, and is under the influence of the combined effect of organisational, market and technology factors (refer to Figure 2). Some of such factors are trends that have been identified and discussed in the Introduction section, including:

- The Internet revolution
- The increasing ubiquity of IP networks and several contemporary trends associated with IP, including growth of network traffic and demand for IP bandwidth, network convergence, IP bandwidth cost and availability
- The evolution of ERP networks

Table 3. Cross-case analysis: The market dimension

Focal issues	Company A	Company B	Company C	Company D
ERP System and supporting networks	• Most enterprises implements three-tiered ERP systems. • Most enterprise allows the local users to access their systems via LAN, remote user via WAN, and connects the application server and the databases using Fast Ethernet or Gigabit Ethernet. • Most enterprises have frame relay connections in the WAN.	• Most enterprises implements three-tiered ERP systems. • The market is seeing the growth of web-based ERP systems. • Most enterprise allows the user to access their systems locally via LAN and remotely via WAN, and the application server and the databases using Fast Ethernet or Gigabit Ethernet. • Most enterprises have frame relay connections in the WAN.	• C1 is deployed worldwide • Most enterprises implement three-tiered C1. Some implement the enterprise server. • Most enterprises have moved to the web-based C1 and Citrix-published C1. • Some enterprises implement multiple application / enterprise server. • Most enterprise allows the client to access C1 system via LAN and / or WAN. • Application servers are usually connected to database server via FDDI connection.	• D3 is the world's most deployed ERP system. • Most enterprises implements three-tiered D3. • Most enterprises continue to use D3 Win32 client, while a movement towards the HTML client maybe expected in the future. • Some enterprises implement multiple application servers. • Most enterprise allows the client to access D3 system via LAN and/ or WAN. • Application servers are usually connected to database server via high-speed LAN (100MB+)
ERP network-performance bottlenecks	• Many enterprises are troubled by WAN bandwidth and latency issues. • Shared token ring / FDDI network can be performance bottlenecks in large ERP implementations.	• Many enterprises are troubled by WAN bandwidth cost and availability. • Some ERP systems perform inconsistently due to bandwidth contention with other IP traffic.	• Enterprises have found C1 Win32 client does not perform well over WAN and enterprises with web-enabled C1 have also been troubled by WAN bandwidth and latency issues	• Enterprises have found WAN capacity to be the performance bottleneck when remote sites begin to access more bandwidth intensive applications, or when D3 HTML clients consume significantly more bandwidth.
Perspective towards QoS	• There is growing awareness of QoS in the enterprise market. • Majority of the enterprises prefer additional bandwidth over QoS	• There is growing awareness of QoS in the enterprise market. • Senior management largely remain as supporters of over-provisioning	• Growing awareness of QoS in the enterprise market is shown in recent RFPs • Majority of the enterprises prefer additional bandwidth over QoS	• Enterprises still need to be convinced that QoS deliver the values it claims. • Majority of the enterprises prefer additional bandwidth over QoS
QoS Tools	• Most enterprises know that there is wide array of QoS tools and architectures available in the market. • IP precedence CoS and DiffServ are considered as more popular than IntServ. MPLS is seen as more relevant in service providers' networks.	• Most enterprises know that there is wide array of QoS tools available in the market.	N/A	N/A
QoS implementation for ERP systems	• Most enterprises implements router-based QoS and classify ERP traffic at layer 2-4 • Most enterprises mark packets in CoS, IP precedence and DSCP.	• Most enterprises implement router-based QoS and classify ERP traffic at layer 2-4. • Some enterprises implement TCP rate control for their ERP systems, web-based ERP systems, or for their Citrix-published ERP systems.	• Little is know about how enterprises implements QoS for C1. • The client-server traffic usually has the highest priority. However, this priority then varies with time and application. • The priority of print traffic range from being less important to mission-critical, depending on the time and C1 application.	• Some enterprises implements prioritisation based on TCP / IP address for the D3 traffic. • Enterprises usually give the client-application server traffic usually has the highest priority. • Enterprises usually consider print traffic as of lower priority.
Current implementations to ensure ERP performance on the network	• Most enterprises choose to add more bandwidth whenever possible when network congestion becomes an issue. • Some enterprises are exploring methods of utilising Company A's QoS solutions • A large number of enterprises continue to have separate networks for ERP system.	• Most enterprises choose to add more bandwidth whenever possible when network congestion becomes an issue • A large number of enterprises continue to have separate networks for ERP system.	• Most enterprises choose to add more bandwidth whenever possible when network congestion becomes an issue • Enterprises continue to have separate networks for C1 system	• Few enterprises have implemented QoS for their D3 deployments. • Most enterprises choose to add more bandwidth whenever possible when network congestion becomes an issue. • Enterprises continue to have separate networks for D3 system. • Users typically follow the guidelines provided by company D to minimise network load.

Figure 2 illustrates the case for research objective one: the unshaded area includes the factors and relationships (represented as arrows) that have been suggested in the existing literature. The shaded area on the other hand includes additional factors and relationships that are identified and studied in this research. The factors and relationships that are included in the shaded area are considered "additions" to the existing literature in the sense that they have not been studied from the perspective of this research—for instance, the Web computing paradigm and the evolution of ERP systems may have been well studied for purposes other than to provide network QoS for ERP systems—and therefore these factors and relationships are the centre of discussion here.

Generally, the mission-criticality of any enterprise application depends mostly on the organisational context. However, modern ERP systems, unlike any other enterprise applications, have been deployed and used in such a way that the continuation of the business operation relies on those systems to perform at the level that is required by its users. The performance of any ERP system is in turn measured against what it is designed to achieve. According to Davenport (1998), ERP systems are designed to solve the problem of fragmentation of information in business organisations—"if a company's systems are fragmented, its business is fragmented." This contention can be used to provide a set of fundamental user requirements to evaluate the performance of any ERP system, based on the following key terms: fragmentation of information and business organisations.

- **The fragmentation of information:** It has at least two technical implications for ERP systems. Firstly, the system must be able to facilitate the integration of enterprise information flowing through a company. This requires the collaboration from all system components—both the software and hardware infrastructure. Secondly, the term "information" places additional requirements onto ERP systems. Information, by its definition, has a number of characteristics that distinguish it from raw data—information is "meaningful," meaning that it should be accurate and presented in ways that can be interpreted by its users, and its value depends on the "timeliness" of the information. This implies that the system infrastructure not only has to support the integrated information flows, but it has to do so in a way that the information retains its meaningfulness and timeliness.

- **Business organisations:** ERP systems are inherently business-oriented. ERP have been deployed in enterprises to manage various business functions in order to achieve whatever goals the enterprises have defined for their deployments—from cost reduction to competitive advantage, from business process reengineering, to improved customer satisfaction. With such clear business-oriented intention, the performance of an ERP system needs to be evaluated in terms of its ability to react to the dynamics of the business environment. Globalised markets and product demand, for instance, often mandates the highest performance ERP system to facilitate the flow of enterprise information—in terms of timeliness, cost-effectiveness, reliability and security—over technically heterogeneous environments. The market versatility—including forces of customer demand and intra-market competitions—requires any ERP system to perform in a consistent, desired manner at all times without being affected by functional, organisational, technical, or geographical boundaries.

Table 4. Weaknesses of major performance-ensuring methods in relation to ERP network requirements

Methods	Qualitative	Quantitative
Network sizing	• Typically lack of consideration for future growth	• Recursive cost of network sizing.
Separate network infrastructure (IP)	• Best effort service for all ERP network connections. • Management complexity	• High, ongoing cost of maintenance.
Additional bandwidth over-provisioning (IP)	• Best effort service for all network traffic • Theoretically unable to avoid network congestion in the long term.	• High, ongoing cost of bandwidth upgrades. • Possible limited bandwidth availability.
Data compression / file transformation	• Does not provide guaranteed service level nor differentiate service. • Provide little value for highly interactive and / or encrypted data.	• Cost of infrastructure • Trade-off exists between size of transmission and latency – increased CPU / memory usage.
Caching	• Does not provide guaranteed service level nor differentiate service. • The value of caching is highly contingent to the user behaviour, and application.	• Cost of infrastructure. • Only applicable for Web applications.

It is clear that, due to its mission criticality, ERP systems need to perform at the level defined by the systems users with regards to the requirements discussed above. The current literature suggested that modern ERP systems depend heavily on the underlying network infrastructure for this purpose. This reliance on the network can be traced back as early as the MRP era when the major access method to the system was through "dumb" terminals that were connected to the mainframe systems. The reliance on the network infrastructure to provide the necessary connectivity for system access has been growing continuously, as MRP evolved into MRP II, and from MRP II to current ERP systems—ever since the emergence of ERP, its deployments have become more and more distributed due to the changing business environment and the increasing prevalence of the client-server paradigm.

The current ERP systems, from the functional perspective, are developed to support multi-tier implementations. Most enterprises, as described before, have implemented three-tiered ERP systems and rely on the TCP/IP network's infrastructure to provide the connectivity required for interactions that occur between-tier, within-tier and between ERP systems. The literature on ERP evolution, as well as the observable trend toward Web-based computing in the case studies, provided evidence that modern ERP systems should be viewed as "networked" enterprise applications. As the dependency on the underlying network infrastructure grows, the abilities of ERP systems to perform at the level defined by the systems users are increasingly related to the quality of the underlying network infrastructure.

The ERP vendors, the enterprises and the network technology vendors have gone to great lengths to ensure the quality of the network. They use network sizing guidelines for designing and implementing the networks for ERP systems that are expected to fulfil pre-determined capacity, availability, and scalability characteristics.

Common methods that have been used for reducing the likelihood of network-induced performance bottlenecks include the use of dedicated network rings for ERP communications, network over-provisioning and minimisation of per-user transactional network requirements at the application and network levels—using technologies such as data caching and compression, file transformation, Web-based computing (such as C1), and proprietary optimising protocols for data transmission (such as the protocols used in D3). The ERP implementation and maintenance strategies adopted by most enterprises, as revealed by the interviewees, are to use some combination of the above methods. For instance, when an enterprise deploys its chosen ERP application suite, the deployment is likely to utilise at least part of the existing enterprise network. Depending on the organisational context, the enterprise may or may not implement separate networks for newly deployed ERP systems. However, regardless of the implementation decision—new or existing, converged or separate network infrastructure—the conventional wisdom has been to equip the underlying network infrastructure with more than sufficient transmission and processing capacity to facilitate overall, average communication needs of the entire enterprise, thereby providing a "safety net" that increases the likelihood of consistent ERP performance. Data compression and caching, file transformation, and other transmission-optimising techniques can also be installed and configured during the implementation and maintenance stages. The post-implementation strategy for alleviating network performance bottlenecks due to the natural growth of enterprise network traffic—including the components of organisational growth and the general trend of enterprise application development—has been to continuously add more bandwidth.

The literature review and the individual cases studies, however, revealed that these network-related, performance-ensuring methods have numerous inherent characteristics and weaknesses that limit their effectiveness in guaranteeing the level of performance dictated by the mission criticality of ERP systems. A summary of these limiting characteristics and weaknesses is presented in Table 4. This table highlights the fact that currently the most common implementations for ensuring ERP systems performance on the enterprise network are "imprecise" approaches in term of satisfying one of the most important requirements of modern ERP systems and their enterprises users—they are unable to recognise network connections of ERP systems and provide controllable, guaranteed network service quality for these connections. The fact that the parameters of service quality—including bandwidth, latency, jitter, and packet loss – of the networks supporting ERP systems cannot be controlled and guaranteed means the enterprise risks sub-optimal ERP system performance with regards to fundamental user requirements discussed previously (refer to the discussion of fundamental ERP user requirements based on Davenport, 1998). Given the current dominance of best-effort IP networks and the possibility of congestion over WAN links, the probability of network ERP systems performing at the less-than-satisfactory level cannot be overlooked – the findings from the individual cases also support this speculation. QoS technologies, on the other hand, have been developed with the specific purpose to address the limitations of IP networks, which appeared to be root of the weaknesses of the traditional implementations to ensure ERP performance on the network. The advantage of QoS over, for instance, over-provisioning and separate network rings is increasingly being recognised by business enterprises and practitioners. Fundamentally, QoS technologies firstly allow the enterprise users to control the various service quality parameters and enforce such controls, end-to-end, for all network connections that deserve differentiated service. Secondly, the financial costs of QoS technology are usually the cost of infrastructure that tends to be a one-off expenditure. Over-provisioning a converged or multiple network infrastructures, however, is often associated with increasing both the infrastructure cost and the ongoing subscription cost for WAN connections.

In summary, it is proposed here that it is necessary to provide network QoS for ERP systems due to the combined effects of numerous organisational, market-oriented and technological trends. The fact that ERP systems are currently deployed and used in such a way that the enterprise needs to guarantee the end-to-end service quality of the underlying network in order to ensure optimised system performance implies that network QoS is needed for ERP systems—as IP networks, as well as the current implementations aimed to ensure ERP performance, do not offer the mechanisms required to control and guarantee network service quality. Contemporary trends in the markets of ERP systems and IP networks—including market globalisation, IP ubiquity, network convergence, the Internet revolution and ERP's evolution—also amplified the necessity of network QoS for ERP systems. The organisational context can be another major reason that QoS is needed for ERP systems—for instance, modern ERP systems are increasing being deployed by SMEs around the world. The sheer cost of bandwidth and/or the cost of maintaining multiple network rings to ensure ERP system performance may not be a viable option for a large number of SMEs.

Achieving Research Objective Two

The achievement of research objective two involves addressing the following research questions:

> **RQ 2.** *What are the available QoS technologies that can be implemented to provide end-to-end network QoS for ERP systems?*

and

> **RQ 3.** *What is the current status of deployment and common deployment topologies of the available QoS technologies to provide end-to-end network QoS for ERP systems?*

The literature review suggested that QoS is a rapid growing discipline and the use of ambiguous terms has opened a schism in the networking industry and the academics where the issue of QoS is concerned. The cross-case analysis presented above supported this suggestion. For instance, out of the three network technology vendors that offer mechanisms to achieve network QoS, at least two major kinds of QoS tools are identified: firstly, tools that concentrate on utilising the intrinsic abilities of modern routers and switches to provide per-hop guarantees and enforce end-to-end quality through various QoS network architectures appeared to be the most common implementation of the QoS tools available today for two reasons:

- Classification and marking, queuing and scheduling are the basic functions of any modern router or switch. It is then logical to utilise these basic functions—and further enhance them if necessary—to achieve per-hop QoS. According to the interviewees, most modern routers offer basic QoS functions—including Layer 2-4 traffic classification, congestion management, multi-queue management and QoS-enabled scheduling. This implies that to enable per-hop QoS little infrastructure cost and implementation efforts are involved in most cases. Moreover, rapid advancing hardware implementations of classification, queuing, scheduling and switching—using technologies such as ASICs — have increased the performance of router and switches by several orders of magnitude.

- Numerous network QoS architectures—including IEEE 802.1 Q/D (CoS), IntServ, DiffServ, and MPLS—and the related service models—including GF and CL of IntServ, AF, and EF for DiffServ—have been standardised by the relevant IETF working groups. The standardisation of these network architectures and service models fuelled greater interoperability between the QoS tools offered by different network technology vendors. Moreover, existing and emerging research on topics including QoS mappings across different layers of the OSI model and internetworking of various network layer QoS protocols (Gutiérrez & Wee, 2001; Fineberg, 2002; Le Faucheur et al., 2002; and Gutiérrez & Ting, 2005) showed the strengths of various network architectures to develop an end-to-end, QoS-enabled network.

The other approach, which focuses on achieving network QoS through the manipulation of the TCP/IP sliding window protocol, is also a recognised technology. Due to the fundamental philosophies of TCP rate control, its effectiveness largely relies on the ability to pace the packets so that the predetermined bandwidth and latency requirements are met. Moreover, the fact that the TCP rate control intercepts and manipulate the ACK messages appeared to violate the original intent of TCP. Its users, however, have suggested that TCP rate control is an effective tool to control and enforce application-level QoS policies (Ashton, Metzler & Associates, 2002).

One of the most important findings from the case studies is the usage and importance of Layer 7 traffic classification technologies in the provision of network QoS. As indicated by the limited literature on traffic classification that uses Layer 4 through 7 packet information, such technologies have only emerged recently and their adoption remains limited. Moreover, it has also been suggested that the implementations of Layer 4-7 classification are usually vendor-specific. The case studies in fact showed two different implementations of Layer 7 classification, and provided insights into the intended usage of each implementation classification. While the implementation of Layer 4-7 classification may differ technically—for instance, the hardware implementation, the classifier architecture and classification algorithms typically differ from vendor to vendor—the case studies suggested that for the provision of network QoS, software-based classifiers appeared to be the main approach among the network technology vendors. According to the interviewed practitioners, the software-based traffic classification provided the highest flexibility—including sub-application classification by variable text strings, multi-media object types and user host information. This ability to achieve sub-application traffic classification can be a considerable advantage for complex networked enterprise applications, such as ERP systems that are supported by best-effort IP networks.

Table 5. Examples of router / switch QoS tools for the provision of QoS for ERP systems

Router/switch-based QoS Tools	Specific Example
Classification	■ Input interface ■ Packet header fields (Layer 2-4) – single or multi-field classification key ■ Packet content (Layer 5-7)
Marking and Policing	■ Metering (Token bucket) ■ DSCP ■ IP ToS ■ CoS (IEEE 802.1 Q/P) ■ MPLS label
Queuing and scheduling	■ ECN tagging ■ RED ■ WRED ■ FIFO ■ PQ ■ CQ ■ CB-WFQ
QoS protocols and architecture	■ IntServ ■ DiffServ ■ MPLS ■ RSVP ■ SBM ■ COPS

The case studies also revealed an alternative to achieve sub-application traffic classification. Instead of parsing and/or scanning the packets for the occurrence of pre-defined strings or objects, a new class of enterprise applications allows their users to identify the sub-applications network connections by utilising host-based QoS functionalities.

Considering the typical ERP deployment strategies, the ERP traffic profiles as the result of such deployment strategies, common network-induced performance bottlenecks, and the technical characteristics of the various QoS technologies, it appeared the tools, in the two major categories surveyed, can all be used in an integrated fashion to provide end-to-end network QoS for ERP systems that utilise IP networks. Table 5 provides a list of well-known examples of QoS tools that utilise the intrinsic functions of router and switches, and highlights the fact that QoS implementers are allowed to be selective when QoS-enabling the supporting network infrastructure for ERP systems.

Network QoS in general has not yet been widely deployed—the existing literature, as well as the case study data, suggested that QoS-enabled networks remain only a fraction of existing IP networks. The main drivers for existing and foreseeable future QoS deployments have been to provide guaranteed, preferential services for the following enterprise applications:

•   Real-time, streaming audio and video, including VoIP and video conferencing applications.

•   Highly interactive thin-client applications, including applications published in the Citrix and /or Windows systems.

•   Terminal service environments. Mission-critical, interactive applications such as ERP systems.

The case study data suggested that real-time applications of voice and video have generally been the leading candidates for network QoS. ERP systems, however, are increasingly being considered as top candidates for QoS by various organisations that use or are planning to deploy ERP systems—according to the interviewees, ERP systems are the number-one QoS candidate among data applications largely due to its mission criticality and to their dependency on the supporting network infrastructure. However, early adopters of QoS as a means to provide preferential services for ERP systems on IP networks are also confronted with numerous difficulties, including:

- Determining the traffic profile and requirements of ERP systems on the network for optimised system performance
- The technical complexity of QoS installations and configuration

Voice and video applications are known to have consistent performance requirements that need to be somehow enforced across the enterprise networks. ERP systems on the other hand, as with most networked data applications, have "qualitative" network performance requirements, which add complexity to the goal of providing QoS for them. Usually, the associated network requirements tend to vary for different environments and must be profiled prior to the implementation of QoS. In fact, the case study data showed that the complexity of QoS implementations and cost of bandwidth are often decisive factors in the adoption of QoS for ERP systems.

The case data suggested that the stage of "mass market" on the traditional technology adoption curve can be expected when enterprises in general become more familiar with QoS technology and the complexities associated with providing qualitative QoS are somewhat lessened. Moreover, as QoS technologies evolve over time, the network technology vendors are expected to be increasingly capable of quantifying the value of QoS to enterprises that use ERP systems and service providers.

Due to the potential complexity associated with QoS implementations, the ease of deployment and scalability of a particular QoS architecture have become one of the governing considerations for current implementations of QoS for ERP systems.

Achieving Research Objective Three

The motivation of research objective three arise from the fact that the review of existing literature on network QoS suggested a general lack of practicality in terms of actual implementation for networked data. The proposed framework aims to provide a set of practical guidelines to implement end-to-end IP QoS for ERP systems, which is expected to allow a more structured implementation process.

The Proposed Framework

It was expected that the achievement of research objectives one and two would provide the fundamental architecture "blueprint" to propose the first framework for the provision of network QoS for ERP systems. The answers to RQ1 revealed the reasons that network QoS is needed for currently ERP deployments, and the answers to RQ2 and RQ3 described the current implementations of network QoS for ERP systems. Upon close scrutiny, the answers to RQ1, RQ2 and RQ3 have led the proposed framework to focus on the following issues:

- For ERP systems, it appeared that it would be most cost-effective to provide sub-application QoS so that each ERP network connection receives the service quality it deserves.

- The provision of QoS must be extended to cover the entire spectrum of ERP deployments, ranging from Win32 clients to HTML clients deployments.

Focusing on these issues, the proposed framework contains three major components: ERP profiling, evaluation of alternatives, and the implementation of an end-to-end, QoS-enabled network infrastructure.

ERP Profiling

As with most networked applications with qualitative network requirements, the requirements of the network connections supported by ERP systems depend on factors such as user expectations, applications, transactions and time. An effective QoS implementation for ERP systems therefore must be based upon an accurate, up-to-date traffic profile of the planned or existing ERP deployment.

Due to the mission criticality of ERP deployments, there are several reasons to believe that a formal, structured approach to profile the traffic patterns and requirements of ERP systems on the enterprise network can be advantageous in this stage, such as:

- Structured methodologies to profile traffic patterns and requirements of networked applications, such as the NRP (network resource planning) methodology typically have a cyclic nature which when properly implemented allows these methodologies to provide an accurate and up-to-date traffic profile of the applications under examination.

- A structured application profiling methodology can potentially avoid major network problems early in the application implementation process, which can yield substantial financial and operational efficiencies (Clewlett, Franklin, & McCown, 1998).

- The cyclical nature of some structured application profiling methodologies allows such methodologies to support multiyear ERP systems rollouts and the evolution of ERP systems and networks. ERP implementations have been known to be extremely complex; hence the implementation project team usually consists of experts from all relevant disciplines. A formal, structured application profiling methodology can potentially facilitate a better coordination between the application developers and implementers, and network managers.

- Certain application profiling methodologies are implemented within a software suite, such as the operating systems running on Company B's network monitoring appliance, which allows automatic documentation of the traffic profile over the period of study.

Considering the advantages of a structured methodology for traffic profiling of ERP systems for QoS implementation, the proposed framework contends that methodologies such as NRP would be appropriate in this stage. Figure 3 (adapted from Clewlett et al., 1998) outlines NRP diagrammatically.

While a structured approach towards profiling ERP traffic patterns and requirements may lead to the advantages discussed above, a very important objective of this stage of the proposed framework is to obtain the profile with application and sub-application details. To address the issues stressed in this section, content-aware traffic classification, monitoring and profiling is required.

Figure 3. ERP profiling: The NRP methodology

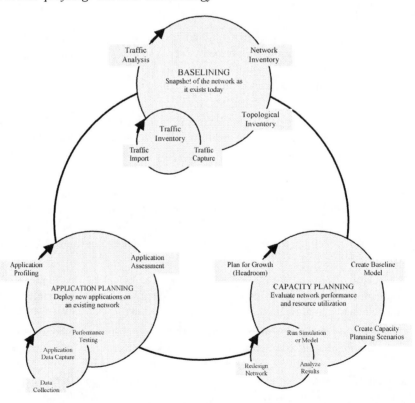

Evaluating Alternatives

While the underlying philosophies and technologies differ, bandwidth, separate network rings and Web-acceleration tools are often considered strong alternatives to network QoS with regards to ensuring the performance of ERP systems on the network. Based on the application and sub-application ERP traffic profile acquired from the previous stage of the proposed framework, as well as other organisational factors that influence the necessity of QoS for ERP systems, two related decisions must be made:

- At the higher level, the cost-effectiveness of QoS as a method to ensure the performance of ERP systems must be evaluated against other alternatives. It is also quite conceivable that the most cost-effective solutions are some combinations of the available options—for instance, adding more bandwidth as well as QoS-enabling the underlying network infrastructure supporting the ERP system.
- If the most cost-effective solution involves QoS, another critical decision, which relates to the selection of appropriate QoS tools, must be made.

The Implementation of an End-to-End, QoS-Enabled Network Infrastructure

The third component of the proposed framework contains a practical architecture for implementing end-to-end QoS:

- Firstly a practical architecture for implementing end-to-end QoS is presented. This architecture is based on Fineberg (2002) and adapted to provide network QoS to ERP systems that utilise IP networks. Thereafter,
- A set of implementation guidelines developed from the findings of RQ1, RQ 2 and RQ3 is discussed.

In Fineberg (2002), a practical architecture for implementing end-to-end QoS in an IP network for VoIP is proposed. Upon close inspection, it appears that this architecture can potentially be adapted to provide network QoS for ERP systems that are supported by IP networks:

- The architecture includes many of the latest QoS technologies and architecture that can be used to provide end-to-end QoS for ERP systems.
- The architecture provides explicit recommendations on the selection of QoS tools—based on present and speculated future adoption.
- The architecture focus on delivering end-to-end QoS and therefore focuses on enforcing QoS on LAN, WAN and the internetworking of LANs and WANs. This is critical for ERP systems due to the fact that ERP systems are often deployed over a geographically dispersed area.

Figure 4. Architecture for implementing IP QoS for ERP systems

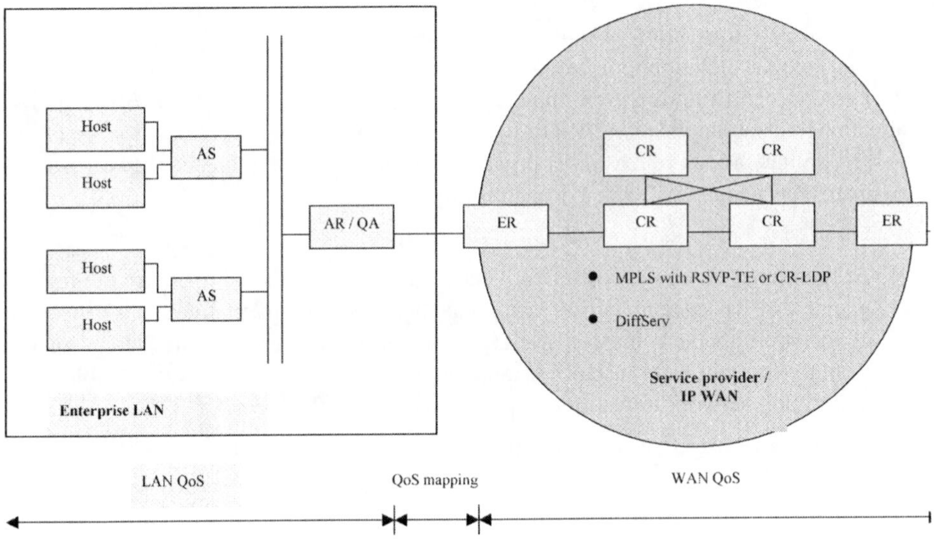

The architecture from Fineberg (2002) is therefore used and adapted for the purpose of achieving research objective three, and is presented in Figure 4.

The LAN QoS

The findings from research objective two—the answers to RQ 2 and RQ3—suggested that CoS (Ethernet), DSCP, ToS and RSVP can all be used in the LAN to provide LAN QoS. The deployment of IntServ with RSVP signalling has been limited due to its complexity and scalability limitations. However the deployments of IntServ with RSVP can be realistic in an enterprise LAN for a few reasons, including:

- Hosts on the edges of the network now have the ability to utilise RSVP signalling. A host can be an ERP client or server. An ERP client running on the Microsoft platform, for example, may be able to signal its QoS requirements to the network by using the QoS APIs of the operating system.

- On the enterprise LAN, it is quite conceivable that the number of network connections is much lower than the number of connections typical of service provider networks. This can potentially make the flow-based IntServ QoS a practical option on the enterprise LAN.

The WAN QoS

DiffServ and MPLS appeared to be the two dominant technologies in the WAN. TCP rate shaping, however, is also another recognised QoS technology in the WAN. Additionally, the internetworking of LAN and WAN QoS involves:

- Translation of enterprise LAN QoS setting as the packets leave the access router (AR) for the edge router (ER) (refer to Table 5)—for instance, the private DSCP or ToS settings may need to be redefined as the packet leaves the boundary of the enterprise LAN.
- Mapping of QoS requirements from one architecture to another—for instance an enterprise may use IntServ on the enterprise LAN, but on the WAN the service provider uses DiffServ.

Specific Guidelines for Implementing QoS for ERP Systems

The following guidelines are developed from the answers to RQ1, RQ2, and RQ3:

- The network must allow traffic classification by application type—classifying the network traffic at Layer 4. This is a basic requirement for implementing QoS for ERP systems that are running on a converged IP network infrastructure. Application level traffic classification can currently be implemented at many places on the architecture presented in Figure 4: firstly the QoS-enabled applications and hosts have the capability of identifying themselves through QoS APIs and RSVP signalling. Secondly the Access Switch (AS) to which the hosts are connected to can be used to classify and mark the traffic based on TCP/IP port numbers—the AS, however, needs to operate at Layers 2-4. The Access Router (AR) can also classify and mark the packets using Layer 4 packet information as packets pass through it.
- The network should also allow traffic classification using packet content information. This can be considered as a necessity to provide QoS for Web-enabled ERP systems—to distinguish HTTP ERP traffic from other HTTP traffic, Layer 2-4 classification is considered insufficient for the provision of QoS and for ERP systems whose network requirements are highly qualitative. Currently the traffic classification at Layer 7 can be implemented within AR. Alternatively the enterprise can also implement Layer 7 classification and packet marking through the use of specialised QoS appliances (QA) such as the ones offered by Company C.

Conclusion and Future Research Directions

This findings and the proposed framework from this research are expected to provide value for both theory and practise. The proposed framework for the provision of QoS for ERP systems provides new insights into a number of areas that have largely been ignored by ERP-related research.

The findings from this research may also provide value for practitioners, particularly for organisations with ERP deployments that utilise best-effort IP networks and professional ERP implementers, including consultants from ERP and network technology vendors. It is expected that the value of the research will not diminish significantly in the foreseeable future, as long as the follow assumptions hold:

- The ERP evolution will continue to be influenced by the Internet and the various Web-based technologies.

- ERP systems will continue to be deployed—even by SMEs around the world—and used to support the core business activities of the enterprises.

- The number of converged IP networks will gradually increase.

- The demand for IP bandwidth from the enterprises will continue to grow and WAN bandwidth will remain contested.

- The processing power of network nodes, such as routers and switches, will continue to grow.

Two directions for future research are identified: firstly, wireless QoS for mobile ERP access. Similar to the "wired" QoS for ERP systems—which has been the focus of this research—wireless QoS technologies have also been largely neglected by enterprises, ERP system vendors and implementers. There are, however, reported trends for an increasing number of mobile users and growing usage of wireless devices that provide access to ERP systems (Mello, 2002a, 2002b). Finally, the potential impact of QoS implementations for ERP systems on the enterprise and system users has to be taken into account. Prior to network QoS, ERP systems that utilise IP receive no more than two types of network services: the best-effort service provided by the network infrastructure that is dedicated to EPR systems and the best-effort service provided by converged network infrastructure. With the presence of network QoS, enterprises have the ability to provide differentiated services based on user and user activity, office location, application, content, time as well as any other information that is accessible to the network. It would be conceivable that network QoS could influence the existing "power user" structures in enterprises, particularly for users of mission-critical applications such as ERP.

References

Adams, K., & Bawany, K. (2001). *Quality of service over IP networks*. Gartner Research, Inc.

Anderson, R. (2001). The survivor's guide to 2002: Business applications. *Network Computing, 12*(26), 59-66.

Armitage, G. (2000a). *Quality of service in IP networks: Foundations for a multi-service Internet.* Indianapolis: Macmillan Technical Publishing.

Ashton, Metzler & Associates, & Sage Research, (2001). *Bandwidth management strategies.* Retrieved September, 3, 2002, from http://www.kentrox.com/library/techpapers/servicepoint/03-12-012.pdf

Benbasat, I., Goldstein, D. K., & Mead, M. (1987, September). The case research strategy in studies of information systems. *MIS Quarterly, 11*(3), 369-385.

Chatterjee, S., Abhichandani, T., Tulu, B., & Li, H. (2005, October). SIP-based enterprise converged network for voice/video over IP: Implementation and evaluation of components. *IEEE Journal on Selected Areas in Communications (JSAC).*

Chadwick, D. W. (1996). A method for collecting case study information via the Internet. *IEEE Network, 10*(2), 36-38.

Cisco Systems (2001). *Internetworking technology handbook.* Indianapolis: Cisco Publication.

Clewett, A., Franklin, D., & McCown, A. (1998*). Network resource planning for SAP/R3, Baan IV, and PeopleSoft.* New York: McGraw-Hill.

Company B. (2002f). *Enterprise deployment topologies.* Retrieved December 5, 2002. URL not disclosed due to confidentiality agreement.

Company C. (2002a). *Company C & Company – Historical business metrics* (title disguised due to confidentiality agreement). Retrieved October 6, 2002. URL not disclosed due to confidentiality agreement.

Company C. (2002c). *Company C & Company – Historical pro forma results* (title disguised due to confidentiality agreement). Retrieved October 6, 2002. URL not disclosed due to confidentiality agreement.

Company C. (2002d). *Company C & Company – Q3 2002 earning release* (title disguised due to confidentiality agreement). Retrieved October 6, 2002. URL not disclosed due to confidentiality agreement.

Company D. (1999a). *Company D D3 document: The D3 and Web architecture* (title disguised due to confidentiality agreement). Retrieved October 12, 2002. URL not disclosed due to confidentiality agreement.

Company D. (2001d). *Network integration of D3 servers: D3 technical infrastructure* (title disguised due to confidentiality agreement). Personal communication (electronic mail). Retrieved November 6, 2002.

Company D. (2001e). *D3 system architecture overview* (title disguised due to confidentiality agreement). Retrieved October 16, 2002. URL not disclosed due to confidentiality agreement.

Company D. (2002a). *D3 GUI technical infrastructure* (title disguised due to confidentiality agreement). Personal communication (electronic mail). Retrieved November 6, 2002.

Comport, J. (2001). ERP II technology and architecture trends for 2002. *Gartner Research, Inc.*

Delcroix, J., & Green-Armytage (2002). *Bandwidth needs of enterprises, SMBs and teleworkers through 2006.* Gartner Research, Inc.

Eisenhardt, K. M. (1989). Building theories from case study research. *Academy of Management Review, 14*(4), 532-550.

Fineberg, V. (2002, January). A practical architecture for implementing end-to-end QoS in an IP network. *IEEE Communications Magazine,* 122-130.

Gutiérrez, J., & Ting, W. (2005). Quality of service issues associated with Internet protocols. In M. Pagani (Ed.), *Encyclopedia of multimedia technology and networking* (pp. 869-874). Idea Group Reference.

Hafner, B. (2003). *Predicts 2003: Network convergence on the horizon (again).* Gartner Research, Inc.

Hiller, K., (2002). *LAN switching: Overview.* Gartner Research, Inc.

Huberman, A., M., & Miles M. B. (1998). Data management and analysis methods. In N.K. Denzin & Y.S. Lincoln (Eds.), *Collecting and interpreting qualitative materials.* Thousand Oaks, Calif.: Sage Publications.

Huston, G. (2000). *Internet performance survival guide: QoS strategy for multiservice networks.* New York: John Wiley & Sons.

Kumar, K., & Hillegersberg, J. V. (2000). ERP experience and evolution. *Communications of the ACM, 43*(4), 23-26.

Le Faucheur, et al. (Ed.). (2002). *Multi-protocol switching support for differentiated services* (RFC 3270). The Internet Society. Retrieved October 11, 2002, from http://www.ietf.org/rfc/rfc3270.txt

Lo, T. C.-H. (2003). *A framework for the provision of network quality of service for enterprise resource planning systems: A case study approach.* Unpublished MCom thesis, The University of Auckland.

Melia, A. (1999). Quality of service in Enterprise Networks, *IEEE Colloquium*, 2/1 -2/4.

Mello, A. (2002a). *Are you ready to go mobile?* Retrieved on December 29, 2002, from http://techupdate.zdnet.com/techupdate/stories/main/0,14179,2842201,00.html

Mello, A. (2002b). *4 trends shaping ERP.* Retrieved on December 30, 2002, from http://techupdate.zdnet.com/techupdate/stories/main/0,14179,2844338-4,00.html

Pultz, J. (2001). *Emerging network technologies for the decade.* Gartner Research, Inc.

Rao, S. S. (2000a). Enterprise resource planning: Business needs and technologies. *Industrial Management and Data Systems, 100*(2), 81-88.

Scheer, A., & Habermann, F. (2000). Making ERP a success. *Association for Computing Machinery, Communications of the ACM, 43*(4), 57-61.

Soldatos, J., Vayias, E., & Kormentzas, G. (2005). On the building blocks of quality of service in heterogeneous IP networks. *IEEE Communications Surveys, 7*(1), 70-89.

Siegel, E. D. (2000). *Designing quality of service: Solutions for the enterprise.* New York: John Wiley & Sons.

Yin, R. K. (1984). *Case study research: Design and methods.* Beverly Hills, CA: Sage Publications.

Chapter V

Cost-Based Congestion Pricing in Network Priority Models Using Axiomatic Cost Allocation Methods

César García-Díaz, University of Groningen, The Netherlands

Fernando Beltrán, University of Auckland, New Zealand

Abstract

Congestion effects are the negative externalities or social costs that users generate on each other when using a shared network resource. Under a congestion-based pricing scheme, networks with enough slack capacity should reflect a very low priced negative externality, while a network with reduced capacity to provide one more unit of the requested resource should reflect the negative effects in the form of higher prices for the use of network resources. This chapter deals with the efficient distribution of congestion costs among network users. First, we present a review of different approaches found in the literature, ranging from methods that advocate for congestion-based pricing to methods that, after being critical about considering congestion, advocate for price definition based on the investors' need for return on their investment. We then proceed to introduce an axiomatic approach to conges-

tion pricing that takes into account some of the prescriptions and conclusions found in the literature. The method presented here is defined on the grounds of axioms that represent a set of fundamental principles that a good allocation mechanism should have.

Background

Pricing of broadband multiservice networks has been a topic that has notably attracted researchers in the last two decades, due especially to the widespread use of Internet. The sustained, increasing demand for bandwidth on the Internet, the development of highly sophisticated applications that require more network resources, the need for offering QoS guarantees and the call for of a sense of economic efficiency to the commercial operation of digital communication networks have made explicit the need for pricing mechanisms that help to regulate the use of broadband network resources (Falkner, Devetsikiotis, & Lambadaris, 2000). Along with economic and network efficiency, provisioning of individual quality-of-service (QoS) is an important criterion to assess the integrity of a pricing mechanism (Falkner et al., 2000). However, "[t]hese objectives are often conflicting or even contradictory" (Li, Iraqi, & Boutaba, 2004, p. 88), as we see below.

Conventional approaches to standardization of quality-of-service (QoS) architectures include Intserv, Diffserv, and MPLS (multiprotocol label switching). As found in the literature (O'Donnell & Sethu, 2002, 2003; Li et al., 2004; Jin & Jordan, 2004) those protocols depend on cooperation among users in implementing end-to-end congestion control; their main feature is the distinction that each makes between different types of flows.

Congestion control through pricing mechanisms has integrated economic and engineering elements in search for a sensible set of criteria for network resource regulation (Falkner et al., 2000). Such economic elements include optimization approaches and assumption of well-known utility functions. However, in line with Shenker (1995), if congestion is realized in very short time frames, it is difficult to really know the user's utility function and link it to a long-term demand (Falkner et al., 2000). Optimization approaches usually assume a centralized topology, making evident the scalability problems of implementing them in environments like Internet (Li et al., 2004). Although pricing schemes using several optimization frameworks have been proposed in a number of papers (Yaiche, Mazumdar, & Rosenberg, 2000; Jin & Jordan, 2004; Fulp & Reeves, 2004) some other rise their concerns about having complete end-to-end price mechanisms based on optimisation techniques (Shenker, 1995; Li et al., 2004) because of the lack of feasibility for implementation.

Pricing has been considered as a tool for congestion control and proper distribution of network resources (Falkner et al., 2000). Using microeconomic principles to guarantee fair allocation has been a concern in flow control (Fulp, Ott, Reininger, & Reeves, 1998), as well as congestion control (Mackie-Mason & Varian, 1995a, 1995b). These recent, alternative approaches have been developed to attempt to account for the asymmetry of information between users and the network's nodes of decision-making. Yet, others argue that congestion price is not an issue because what network providers need to resolve is the financial viability of their network operation including assuring return on investment. These perspectives will be presented in the upcoming paragraphs.

Information Revelation as a Basis for Congestion-Pricing

Gibbens and Kelly (1999), for instance, provide two reasons that should make us rethink TCP's approach to congestion control: the increasing heterogeneity of applications and the modifications to TCP to turn it into a version that more aggressively takes available bandwidth or into a protocol that avoids congestion at all. Their approach does not attempt to discriminate among services to restrict the bandwidth allocated to different flows or families of flows. Instead their objective is to implement the idea of letting end-nodes know about the resource implications of their actions, expecting the end-nodes to determine their demands upon the network resources. So, instead of having the users classify their flows into categories and send such information to the network, the information can be conveyed from the network to the end-nodes. Based on MacKie-Mason and Varian's (1995a) "smart market" approach to pricing, in which price is set for each packet depending upon the level of demand, Gibbens and Kelly propose to use a single bit to mark some packets. Jin and Jordan (2004) state that these packet-based pricing approaches have moved on to bandwidth unit pricing in the recent years, since per-packet pricing has difficulties addressing QoS metrics, although per-packet pricing is still being proposed and investigated (Ros & Tuffin, 2004).

Two factors determine the optimal allocation of resources: utilities users attach to their flows and the properties of the resources within the network. When utilities are concave functions of attained throughput, an optimal allocation of network resources is characterised by shares proportional to the users' willingness to pay for them (Kelly, 1997). The use of the weighted proportional fairness criterion in several works (Chiu & Jain, 1989) (Kelly, Maulloo, & Tan, 1998; Crowcroft & Oechslin, 1998) has illustrated the possibility of congestion control parameters that may be altered by end-nodes. The most prominent feature of such approach is that users may alter those parameters in an incentive-compatible manner.

A simple model introduced by Courcoubetis and Weber (2003) may help illustrate the basic ideas of congestion pricing. Suppose n users demand quantities of a service and a seller has capacity k of the service at cost c(k); suppose, in addition, that each user i is represented with a utility function $u(x_i, y)$ where x_i is i's demanded quantity of service and $y= \Sigma x_i /k$. Here the utility function does not only depend on the level of consumption from each user but on the aggregate use relative to the total available capacity. Maximising social welfare given by the sum Σu_i over all users minus the total cost at capacity k, c(k), prices can be obtained that represent the marginal decrease in social welfare due to congestion by a marginal increase in usage. It is shown that as long as users are presented with the mentioned price, the quantity x^*_i that maximizes i's individual utility is the one that also maximizes the social welfare. Thus, the combination of optimal individual consumption levels, x^*_1, x^*_2, ..., x^*_n, is a Nash equilibrium.

The model reveals a very interesting and complex issue: as the computation of the congestion price depends on the users' sensitivities to degradation of performance due to congestion—the derivatives of their utility functions—how can we expect users to truthfully reveal such sensitivities? A form of the Vickrey-Clarke-Groves (VCG) mechanism (Krishna, 2002) can be used that provides incentives to users to reveal their true valuation for the resource being offered while achieving socially optimal levels of demand. The VCG mechanism is a direct, incentive compatible and efficient mechanism, implying that VCG calls for truthful revelation of users' values. Semret (1999) introduces an iterative mechanism that inherits the VCG properties: the progressive second-price (PSP) auction. PSP is used as a congestion control mechanism; a bidder will keep adjusting his bids as a way of trading off benefits obtained by access to bandwidth and charges made upon him by the PSP payment rule, which is aimed at recognising the cost that his presence exerts on other bidders.

The auction proceeds with bidders submitting bids, each consisting of a pair (p,q) of values: the amount q of resource requested and the price p for one unit of the resource. The PSP allocation mechanism sorts the incoming bids according to the unit price indicated by the bidder and allocates resources to all bidders up to the maximum resource capacity Q. The intuition behind PSP is an exclusion-compensation principle: user i pays for its allocation so as to exactly cover the "social opportunity cost" which is given by the declared willingness to pay of the users who are excluded by i's presence. With incentive compatibility in PSP auctions, it is a weakly dominant strategy for all bidders to truthfully report their valuation. Therefore, the bidding behaviour can be modelled by using the individual demand function of each bidder.

It is clear that congestion-based pricing increase economic efficiency: for instance, Wang and Schulzrinne (2000) explore pricing based on level of service, usage, and congestion. Pricing is used as an equitable incentive for application to adapt their transmission rates. They propose a dynamic, congestion-sensitive pricing algorithm and develop the demand behaviour of adaptive users based on a physically reasonable user utility function. A simulation framework is introduced to compare the performance of a network supporting static pricing to that supporting congestion-sensitive pricing and adaptive reservation. Results show that congestion-sensitive pricing takes advantage of application adaptation to achieve significant gains in network availability, revenue and user-perceived benefit relative to fixed-price policy. Users are seen to fairly share bandwidth, even when their demand elasticity differ.

On the other hand, in Garg, Kamra, and Khurana (2002) it is explained how, in the presence of selfish users, end-to-end congestion control based on "voluntary end-user cooperation" lead to congestion collapse. The authors claim that all currently proposed router and switch mechanisms (service disciplines, buffer management) either encourage the behaviour that leads to congestion or are oblivious to it. They go ahead to propose a technique called diminishing weight schedulers, a service discipline that punish misbehaving users and reward congestion-avoiding well-behaved users, and a sample service discipline, rate inverse scheduling (RIS) from DWS. They also show that RIS solves the problem of excessive congestion due to unresponsive flows, aggressive versions of TCP, and multiple parallel connections.

Return on Investment as a Price Driver

From a radically different approach to those explained before Roberts (2004) claims that because return-on-investment can be assured by sharing network capital and operational costs between users, congestion pricing is not a satisfactory charging basis for a commercial network operator. Price discrimination is economically efficient but should be based on criteria other than QoS guarantees.

Thus, Roberts explains how traffic characteristics impact the realisation of QoS guarantees and proposes to study traffic through a broader approach using a flow-based traffic model. Flows occur within sessions and the Poisson model of session arrivals is quite suitable for modelling them. Two basic types of flows are identified: streaming and elastic. The former are associated with real-time audio/video, whereas the latter correspond to traffic sources less demanding of packet loss and delay.

His so-called "flow-aware networking" approach is able to stand up to performance requirements for individual flows with no need for class-of-service differentiation. Based on measurement-based admission control (MBAC) and on the implementation of a per-flow scheduler called priority fair queuing (PFQ), he proposes a router mechanism named cross-protect. PFQ realizes unweighted start-time fair queuing.

Axiomatic Framework for Efficient Pricing

In the rest of the chapter we emphasize the use of axiomatic-based solutions. We call axioms those fundamental properties that a good mechanism should have. Mechanisms with a no well-grounded set of principles may give light to incentive misbehavior that might lead a pricing scheme to collapse. To give an idea of an axiomatic-based solution, we refer the reader to the star network allocation distribution problem presented by Henriet and Moulin (1996). In this work, it is shown that many distribution mechanisms might sound sensible in principle, but not all accomplish such minimum requirements that avoid incentive deviation and sustainability of the price mechanism.

Although we recognize the efforts develop from a technological point of view, the ever higher incremental use of networks (Falkner et al., 2000) makes us think of a solution in economic terms dealing with the problem of efficiently allocate network resources. Apart from technology-based solutions to guarantee required levels of QoS (IntServ and DiffServ networks), and, consequently, acceptable levels of congestion, pricing becomes an economic alternative for congestion control, as we have argued throughout this chapter (Falkner et al., 2000). Thus, we approach this problem from a rather economic point of view.

If pricing is to be regarded as a congestion control mechanism, it would be natural to think that such mechanism has to fairly distribute congestion costs (e.g., the negative externalities exert by the shared use of a resource) among network users. We argue that such pricing scheme has to be based on an efficient congestion distribution mechanism. The approach developed in this chapter takes the work of McLean and Sharkey (1994, 1998) as a starting point. We go further in the sense of adding non-preemptive priority service differences to user heterogeneity, in which high-priority users are guaranteed less delays in their information transmission[1]; we also show a series of applied cases where efficient distribution mechanism might take place for congestion-based network pricing.

Although at a first glance consumer valuation and the establishment of priorities might go hand in hand, as we observe in further pages they are actually decoupled. They mainly depend on what it is intended to mean with the term "valuation": priority might be associated with high capacity of spending from users (i.e., they are able to pay high-quality services); however, low priority users might have the highest valuation just to stimulate Internet use as a welfare governmental policy.

Finally, it has been argued that priority pricing mechanisms (Gupta, Stahl, & Whinston, 1998), do not emphasize social fairness (Falkner et al., 2000), and, as a consequence, poor users are just left out. In more recent works, O'Donnell and Sethu (2002, 2003) show how to guarantee a QoS level for multiple classes in a DiffServ environment using priority pricing. In our approach, as we will see later, poor users might have a guaranteed service, due to the fact that priority service and information value are decoupled. Also, due to the potential problems of scability offered by IntServ networks and the further attention that DiffServ networks have drawn (Li et al., 2004), we believe that a pricing mechanism that efficiently distribute costs in shared resources with small number of classes might offer a light that leads to applicable pricing mechanisms.

Axiomatic Distribution Mechanisms

The Aumann-Shapley (AS) Prices in the Data Network Framework

Let us define a set of user profiles by $N = \{1,...,n\}$. Each user profile i has its own consumption pattern characterized by an arrival rate λ_i. Each λ_i might represent, say, the average amount of consumers (with profile i) that request service, the amount of data packets (per profile i) to be transmitted per unit of time or, simply, the incoming data rate to the system (e.g. in Mbps). Such set of arrival rates is represented by $\{\lambda_1, \lambda_2,..., \lambda_n\}$, where $\lambda_i > 0$, $i=1,...,n$. Consequently, let us assume that the vector of arrival rates, $\lambda = (\lambda_1, \lambda_2,...,\lambda_n)$, is defined in the positive region of the n-Euclidean space $\mathbf{R}^n$, $\mathbf{R}^n_+$. We consider a cost allocation problem as a pair (F, λ), where $\lambda \in \mathbf{R}^n_+$ and F: $\mathbf{R}^n_+ \rightarrow \mathbf{R}_+$ is a function that represents congestion costs. As we will see in following pages, F is continuous, differentiable, and equal to zero when in total absence of congestion $F(\mathbf{0})=0$. This is, the fixed cost of using the network is not included in the analysis (e.g. costs related to network infrastructure, maintenance, and so on, which does not depend on the amount of traffic de network handles). We define the the class of all cost allocation problems in $\mathbf{R}^n_+$ with F and λ defined as above as c^n. The price mechanism is defined as a function M:

$$\bigcup_{n=1}^{\infty} c^n \longrightarrow \bigcup_{n=1}^{\infty} R^n$$

that maps each problem (F, λ) in c^n to the price vector $(P_1(F, \lambda), ..., P_n(F, \lambda))$ in $\mathbf{R}^n$ (McLean and Sharkey, 1998).

In the price computation mechanism, each price vector $\mathbf{P} = (P_1, P_2,..., P_n)$ should fulfill several desirable properties in order to be considered a "fair" mechanism. These properties are summarized as follows (McLean & Sharkey, 1998):

a.   **Cost sharing:** This is a fundamental property that simply states that the total income must exactly cover total congestion costs. Strictly speaking, the price mechanism is rather a cost allocation mechanism in which congestion costs are distributed among users in a fairly manner.

b.   **Monotonicity:** This fundamental property implies that the user types that have a non-negative arrival rate and a non-negative contribution to congestion costs should have a non-negative price assigned. Different to adjustment pricing mechanism like the one found in Fulp et al. (1998), where a minimum non-negative price is set a will, the efficient allocation mechanism incorporates such requirement as a default characteristic.

c.   **Additivity:** This implies that if the cost function can be decomposed into two totally independent functions, then the price for congestion found according to the total cost function should be equal to the sum of the contributions derived from each of the component functions. This property just makes irrelevant the way congestion costs are disaggregated and avoid depending on specific accounting allocation procedures.

d.   **Rescaling invariance:** This property indicates that if a linear change in the units of measurement occurs, a similar or proportional change takes place in prices. This property is especially important because the unit of measurement does not generate any distortion in the allocation mechanism and allows easy conversion from one measurement system to another.

e.   **Consistency:** This property roughly implies that user profiles that have the same effect on congestion cost must bear the same price.

According to Billera and Heath (1982) and Mirman and Tauman (1982), there exists a unique mechanism that satisfies all of the aforementioned properties, and that mechanism is the *Aumann-Shapley* price mechanism. This mechanism is defined for each $i \in N$, as:

$$P_i^{AS}(F,\lambda) = \int_0^1 \frac{\partial F}{\partial \lambda_i}(t\lambda)dt \qquad (1)$$

Let the vector of arrival rates to the network λ consist of $(\lambda_1, \dots, \lambda_n)$, where The A-S prices reflect somehow the marginal costs of each user profile per unit of time.

The Shapley Value Approach to Data Networks

Next, we considered an alternative approach in which the network is seen as a cooperative game. Following McLean and Sharkey (1994, 1998), let us define a game with a set of *n* user profiles or user types. Suppose that this game is related to the cost allocation problem (F,λ), where F represents the total congestion cost, just as in the previous section, and λ, similarly, represents the vector of demand rates. Let us define the set of game participants as $N=\{1,\dots,n\}$. The problem consists in efficiently distributing the congestion F among the *n* players, in a way that the distribution criteria meet a series of desirable properties (McLean & Sharkey, 1998).

Let us consider a set of possible functions ψ from which we can extract a solution. Also define a function $v: 2^n \to \mathbf{R}$ assuming that $v(\varnothing) = 0$ and $v(N)=F$. For each of the possible subsets $S \subseteq N$, $v(S)$ represents the cost incurred by the subset or *coalition* S when using the network resources (i.e., bandwidth).

If G_N denotes the space of all of the possible games in N, then formally it is possible to describe the aforementioned class of functions $\psi: G_N \rightarrow \mathbf{R}^n$ where for each $v \in G_N$ and every $i \in N$, $\psi_i(v)$ is the distribution of costs that user profile i receives when the effects of joint actions of the coalitions are quantified by v. In the same fashion of the Aumann-Shapley prices, it is desirable that the class of functions ψ fulfills the following properties (McLean & Sharkey, 1994):

a. **Additivity:** This means that if the original problem may be separated into two distinct problems (for example, in the case of finite queuing models, the original total cost distribution problem can be divided into the problem of cost distribution due to service delays and problem of cost distribution due to system blocking), it is desirable that the sum of the solutions to the components of the problem is equal to the solution to the original problem.

b. **Efficiency:** refers to the fact that the sum of the charges assigned to each player in N should be the same as the total cost to be allocated.

c. **Symmetry:** means that if individuals contribute the same costs to each coalition, then they should pay the same charge.

d. **Monotonicity:** This requires that if the player contributes a non-negative cost to the coalition, then the fee for that player should also be non-negative.

Among all of the possible functions ψ, there exists only one function $\varphi: G_N \rightarrow \mathbf{R}^n$ that fulfills the aforementioned properties. Such function is the *Shapley value*. In order to define more specifically the Shapley value, it is necessary to define the set Ω of n! possible orderings of the members in N. For each user profile $i \in N$ and each ordering $P \in \Omega$, define the set $X_i(P)$ = $\{j_1, ..., j_{k-1}\}$ as the set of predecessors of i in the order P, with $i = j_k$, $N = \{j_1, ..., j_n\}$. Note $Xi(P) = \varnothing$ if $i = j_1$. From the previous paragraph, recall that v is the function of costs derived from the cost distribution problem F and that it represents the cost or penalty assigned to a specific group of users. We denote $v(S) = F(\lambda^S)$, where $\lambda^S \in \mathbf{R}^n$ is a vector with $\lambda_i^S = \lambda_i$ if $i \in S$, and $\lambda_i^S = 0$ if $i \notin S$. The Shapley value may be defined as follows:

$$\varphi_i(v) = \sum_{R \in \Omega} \frac{1}{n!}[F(\lambda^{X_i(R) \cup \{i\}}) - F(\lambda^{X_i(R)})] \tag{2}$$

In this case, the price that user profile i should pay for each resource unit request is defined as:

$$P_i^{SV}(F,\lambda) = \frac{\varphi_i(v)}{\lambda_i} \tag{3}$$

An Illustration: The Priority Service Model and the Congestion Function

We now extend McLean and Sharkey's models to the case where entry disciplines are different from FIFO. Although we acknowledge the existence of sophisticated scheduling disciplines in telecommunication networks (fair queueing, weighted fair queueing, class-based weighted fair queueing, etc.), we consider a simple non-preemptive priority service with two user profiles, for the sake of clarity and clear representation of results. The same approach is followed in some recent papers, in which classic queuing models are used to exemplify pricing mechanisms: for instance, in order to present a possible application of the Paris metro pricing scheme (see Falkner et al., 2000), Ros and Tuffin (2004) developed a mathematical representation for packet pricing and present numerical results using M/G/1 models. We will now describe two models to represent an ISP that satisfies the Internet service application needs of a set of users, such as e-mail, video Web commercials, bank transactions, Web purchasing, and so forth. For the sake of clarity, we also assume we have two user profiles.

Each profile can be characterized by an arrival rate λ_i and a service rate μ_i, i = 1,2 (e.g. offered bandwidth). The arrival process is described as a Poisson process, which means that the aggregated arrivals may be represented by a unique rate $\lambda = \lambda_1 + \lambda_2$, while the service times of each user are represented by an exponential distribution with mean $1/\mu_i$. Additionally, we assume that user type 1 has priority over user type 2. We consider two separate cases for analysis: a model (this is, model 1) when service distribution rates is unique for the whole network ($\mu_1 = \mu_2$), and a case (i.e. model 2) when the service rates differ depending on user type ($\mu_1 \neq \mu_2$). We define the capacity of the profile i service as $\rho_i = \lambda_i/\mu_i$, i=1,2. The capacity for the overall network is represented by $\rho = \rho_1 + \rho_2$. It can also be seen that ρ may be equal to λ/μ (the ratio beween the global arrival and service rates), where $1/\mu = P_1(1/\mu_1) + P_2(1/\mu_2)$, and $P_i = \lambda_i/\sum\lambda_i$.

We also assume there is no open exclusion of user's needs for those who arrive to the system, and arriving users are simply placed in a line to wait until they receive the corresponding service.

A user with high priority is expected to pay a price that ensures some service quality and, consequently, some amount of delay. Since it is expected that users with the high priority pay more that a user with the low priority, in our model we consider delay only as a proxy for QoS. Of course, users with the high priority generate delay on lower priority users' service. This is important to define the congestion function, F.

The function F is defined as $F(\gamma,\lambda,\mu) = \gamma_1\lambda_1 d_1 + \gamma_2\lambda_2 d_2$, where d_i corresponds to user i's average wait time in line and γ_i to the value of each packet (also for user profile i). Following standard queuing theory (Wolff, 1989), these wait times are defined in the following way for systems that operate with non-preemptive priorities:

$$d_i = \frac{\lambda \, E(S^2)}{2(1 - \sum_{j<i}\rho_j)(1 - \sum_{j\leq i}\rho_j)} \tag{4}$$

where $\sum_{j \leq i} \rho_j < 1$ and $\sum_{j < i} \rho_j < 1$, $i = 1,2$, and S is a random variable that represents the service time, based on the exponential distribution. It can be easily shown that, for model 1, the cost function $F(\gamma,\lambda,\mu)$ corresponds to the following expression:

$$F(\gamma,\lambda,\mu) = \gamma_1 \frac{\lambda_1 \rho}{\mu(1-\rho_1)} + \gamma_2 \frac{\lambda_2 \rho}{\mu(1-\rho_1)(1-\rho)} \qquad (5)$$

where $\rho_1 = \lambda_1/\mu$ y $\rho = \rho_1 + \rho_2$.

For model 2, the function $F(\gamma,\lambda,\mu)$ is represented by:

$$F(\gamma,\lambda,\mu) = \gamma_1 \lambda_1 \frac{\lambda E(S^2)}{2(1-\rho_1)} + \gamma_2 \lambda_2 \frac{\lambda E(S^2)}{2(1-\rho_1)(1-\rho)} \qquad (6)$$

where $\rho_1 = \lambda_1/\mu_1$, $\lambda = \lambda_1 + \lambda_2$, $\rho = \rho_1 + \rho_2$, and additionally (Wolff, 1989):

$$E(S^2) = \int_0^1 t^2 \left[\frac{\lambda_1}{\lambda} \mu_1 e^{-\mu_1 t} + \frac{\lambda_2}{\lambda} \mu_2 e^{-\mu_2 t} \right] dt = \sum_{i=1}^2 \frac{\lambda_i}{\lambda} \left[\frac{2}{\mu_i^2} \right] \qquad (7)$$

In Appendices A and B the price calculation for AS and SV prices is shown.

Behavior of Shapley Value (SV) Prices

Numerical examples indicate the consistent ordering of prices according to priorities in some cases. For instance, if we consider the case where user profile 1 (i.e., the users who have the high priority) are characterized by $\lambda_1 = 4$, $\lambda_2 = 2$, $\gamma_1 = 2$, $\gamma_2 = 1$, $\mu = 10$ (model 1), we get the following prices: $P_1^{SV} = 0.223 > P_2^{SV} = 0.204$.

However, there are cases where this ordering is not maintained. Let us consider the case when there is only one service rate (model 1), information has the same value ($\gamma_1 = \gamma_2$) and $\lambda_1 > \lambda_2$. This may be the case when valuations have the same societal value (this is, there is no difference regarding the social "importance" of the information submitted to the network, but one consumer profile is willing to pay for a higher preferential service). Although the cost distribution is efficient, it can be shown that it always necessary to introduce a correction mechanism to ensure that $P_1^{SV} > P_2^{SV}$ (for an explanation of the weighted Shapley Value, see McLean and Sharkey, 1994).

A numerical example shows that when $\gamma_1 = \gamma_2 = 2$, $\lambda_1 = 2$, $\lambda_2 = 1$ and $\mu = 5$, the prices result in 0.56 and 0.68 for user types 1 and 2, respectively. If we would like the price of user type 1 to be greater, we can use weighted Shapley value with a weighting vector $w = (2,1)$. The resulting prices would be 0.66 and 0.49, for user types 1 and 2, respectively. This implies that, in this case, the coherence of the cost allocation method depends on a weighted mechanism that is up to the network administrator. As seen in Figure 1, the difference between the two prices tends to stabilize as the difference between the weights increases.

Figure 1. Changes in SV prices under the weighted shapley value mechanism for model 1. Parameter values are $\mu = 10$, $\gamma_1 = \gamma_2 = 2$, $\lambda_1 = 2$, $\lambda_2 = 1$. X axis shows the values of the high priority weight, w_1, while we keep the low priority weight $w_2 = 1$. Solid line is the behavior of high priority user price, P_1^{SV}; dashed line shows the behavior of low priority user price, P_2^{SV}.

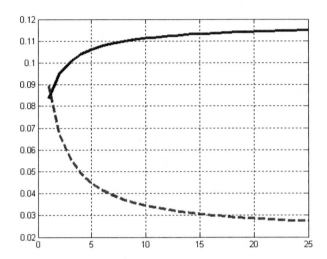

A similar result is found in model 2, if we assume that $\mu_1 > \mu_2$ and $\gamma_1 > \gamma_2$ (but neither $\gamma_1 >> \gamma_2$ nor $\mu_1 >> \mu_2$). Then, a value of λ_1 larger than λ_2 makes clear that $P_1^{SV} < P_2^{SV}$, although they tend to be similar when congestion is low. Figure 2 shows the behavior of Shapley Value prices before the weighted mechanism has been applied.

We do not want to mean that the application of the weighted mechanism correspond to a general case. Obviously, the richness of the parameter possibilities would force the network administrator to apply a weighted mechanism in some specific situations. To cite a different example, for model 2 it can be shown that it is possible to guarantee that $P_1^{SV} > P_2^{SV}$ if (a) γ_1 tends to be much greater than γ_2 and, (b) $\rho_1^2 > \lambda_1(\lambda_1 - \lambda_2)E(S^2)/2$. Figure 3 shows that when γ_1 tends to be very large, the price for user profile 1 becomes greater than the price assigned to user profile 2 ($\rho_1^2 = 0.44 > \lambda_1 E(S^2)(\lambda_1 - \lambda_2)/2 = 0.19$).

Also, let us assume that it is up to the network administrator to assign priorities to user profiles. For model 1, if the arrival rates are equal and $\gamma_1 > \gamma_2$, it is guaranteed that $P_1^{SV} > P_2^{SV}$ and the congestion cost might be minimized if the network administrator assigns the high priority to the user profile that has the high valuation. Let us assume that $\lambda_1 = \lambda_2 = 2$, $\mu_1 = \mu_2 = 5$. If $\gamma_1 = 2$ and $\gamma_2 = 1$, we observe that $P_1^{SV} = 1$ and $P_2^{SV} = 0.87$. If the network administrator assigns the high priority to the high valuation user, total congestion costs will add up $F(\gamma, \lambda, \mu) = 3.73$; otherwise, $F(\gamma, \lambda, \mu)$ takes the value 5.87.

Figure 2. Behavior of SV Prices before the application of the weighted mechanism under variation of λ_1 (high priority arrival rate at X axis): $\mu_1=10$, $\mu_2=5$, $\lambda_2=1, \gamma_1=2$, $\gamma_2=1$ (Solid line $\equiv$ total congestion cost; dashed line $\equiv$ price for user profile high priority; dotted line $\equiv$ price user profile low priority).

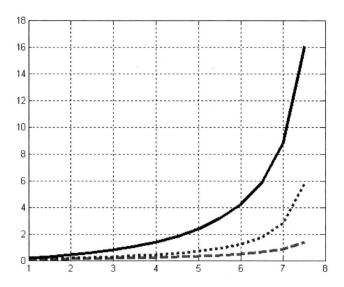

Behavior of Aumann-Shapley (AS) Prices

Numerical examples also show, as in the SV prices, the consistent ordering of prices according to priority setting in some cases. For instance, in the case where $\lambda_1= 4, \lambda_2=1, \gamma_1 = 5, \gamma_2 = 2, \mu = 10$ (model 1), we get the following prices: $P_1^{AS} = 0.429 > P_2^{AS} = 0.283$.

As in the SV prices, if $\lambda_1 = \lambda_2$, $\mu_1 = \mu_2$ and $\gamma_1 > \gamma_2$, it is guaranteed that $P_1^{AS} > P_2^{AS}$ and the congestion cost minimized if the network administrator assigns the high priority to the user profile that has the high valuation. Also, it can be shown that, when $\mu_1 = \mu_2, \gamma_1 = \gamma_2$, the AS prices are always equal, independent from the value that λ_1 and λ_2 take (Beltran & Garcia-Diaz, 2005).

In the AS prices, there might also be cases where a weighted mechanism is needed in order to ensure a coherent set of prices. Let us consider the case where $\gamma_1 > \gamma_2$ (but not $\gamma_1 \gg \gamma_2$) and $\lambda_1 = \lambda_2$. Then $\mu_1 \ll \mu_2$ implies that $P_1^{AS} > P_2^{AS}$, but $\mu_1 \gg \mu_2$ leads to get $P_1^{AS} < P_2^{AS}$.

In order for $P_1^{AS} > P_2^{AS}$, it is necessary to apply a weighting mechanism analogous to the one shown for the SV prices. (see McLean, Pazgal, & Sharkey, 2004). Let us consider the limit case where $\lambda_1 = \lambda_2 = 1, \gamma_1 = 2, \gamma_2 = 1, \mu_1 = 10$ and $\mu_2 = 5$. In this case, $P_1^{AS} = 0.08$ and $P_2^{AS} = 0.11$. Under the weighted the AS mechanism and using weights $w_1 = 2$ and $w_2 = 1$, the prices transform to $P_1^{AS} = 0.10$ and $P_2^{AS} = 0.09$.

Figure 3. Behavior of SV under variation of γ_1 (high priority user valuation at X axis): μ_1 = 3, μ_2 = 4, λ_1 = 2, λ_2 = 1, γ_2 = 5 (Solid line ≡ total congestion cost; dashed line ≡ price for user profile high priority; dotted line ≡ price user profile low priority)

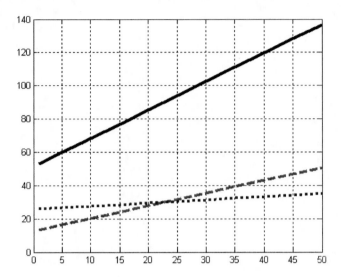

Admission charges may be included by extension of AS prices and adopt a different approach from what we have presented so far. AS-based two-part tariffs take into account both the arrival and the service rate. Let us assume $\mu_1 = \mu_2 = 1$. For model 1, we can show that $\partial F(\gamma,\lambda,\mu)/\partial\lambda_1 = [1/\mu]\{\gamma_1(\rho+\rho_1-\rho_1^2)/(1-\rho_1)^2 + \gamma_2\rho_2\,(1+\rho-\rho_1-\rho^2)/[(1-\rho_1)^2(1-\rho_1)^2]\}$. Letting α = $1/\mu,^2$ we get the following inputs for the AS prices calculation:

$$\frac{\partial F(\gamma,\lambda,\alpha)}{\partial\lambda_1} = \gamma_1\frac{2\lambda_1\alpha^2 + \lambda_2\alpha^2 - \lambda_1^2\alpha^3}{(1-\lambda_1\alpha)^2} + \gamma_2\frac{\lambda_2\alpha^2 + \lambda_2^2\alpha^3 - (\lambda_1+\lambda_2)^2\lambda_2\alpha^4}{(1-\lambda_1\alpha)^2(1-\lambda\,\alpha)^2} \tag{8}$$

$$\frac{\partial F(\gamma,\lambda,\alpha)}{\partial\lambda_2} = \gamma_1\frac{\alpha^2\lambda_1}{(1-\lambda_1\alpha)} + \frac{\gamma_2\alpha}{(1-\lambda_1\alpha)}\frac{(\lambda_1\alpha + 2\lambda_2\alpha)(1-\lambda_1\alpha-\lambda_2\alpha)+\lambda_2(\lambda_1+\lambda_2)\alpha^2}{(1-\lambda_1\alpha-\lambda_2\alpha)^2}$$

$$\tag{9}$$

$$\frac{\partial F(\gamma,\lambda,\alpha)}{\partial\alpha} = \gamma_1\lambda_1(\lambda_1+\lambda_2)\left[\frac{2\alpha(1-\lambda_1\alpha)+\alpha^2\lambda_1}{(1-\lambda_1\alpha)^2}\right]$$

$$+\gamma_2\lambda_2(\lambda_1+\lambda_2)\frac{2\alpha(1-\lambda_1\alpha)(1-\lambda_1\alpha-\lambda_2\alpha)+\alpha^2(2\lambda_1+\lambda_2-2\lambda_1^2\alpha-2\lambda_1\lambda_2\alpha)}{(1-\lambda_1\alpha)^2(1-\lambda_1\alpha-\lambda_2\alpha)^2} \tag{10}$$

Figure 4. Behavior of AS prices under variation of μ_1 (high priority user service rate at X axis) before the application of the weighted mechanism under variation: $\mu_2 = 10$, $\lambda_1 = 2$, $\lambda_2 = 2$, $\gamma_2 = 1.1$, $\gamma_2 = 1$ (Solid line $\equiv$ total congestion cost; dashed line $\equiv$ price for high priority user profile; dotted line $\equiv$ price for low priority user profile)

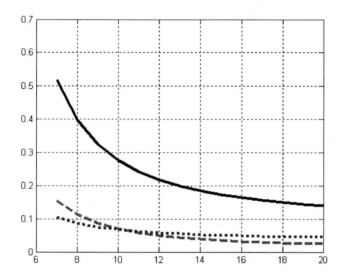

In Appendix C there is a summary of the AS prices for the case $\mu_1 = \mu_2 = 1$. Let us assume that $\lambda_1 = 0.4$, $\lambda_2 = 0.2$, $\gamma_1 = 2$, $\gamma_2 = 1$. Prices result in $P_{\lambda 1}^{AS} = 1.181$, $P_{\lambda 2}^{AS} = 0.889$, $P_\alpha^{AS} = 0.65$. Notice that the high priority user has a higher admission charge that the low priority user, despite the service is charged at the same rate for both user profiles.

Final Discussion

Although in many instances, the AS and SV price mechanisms give a set a coherent set of prices (respect to user profile priority), in many others, and due to the richness of the parameter space, it is necessary to complement them with weighted mechanisms. At first glance, weighted mechanisms give room for "unfair" allocations since it is up to the network manager to assign the corresponding weights to user profiles. First, it can be shown that weighted mechanisms adhere to the slightly modified set of axioms that keep the fundamental properties mentioned in 3.1 and 3.2 (see for instance, McLean et al., 2004). Second, as seen in Figure 1, prices might become insensitive to large differences in weights. Third, we will expect that market (e.g., price elasticity) forces regulate how preferential the weights set would be to one or another user profile. So, in the end, we do not think that the potential use of a weighted mechanism would obscure the axiomatic properties of the price mechanism.

Figure 5. Example of behavior of AS prices under varying entry rate

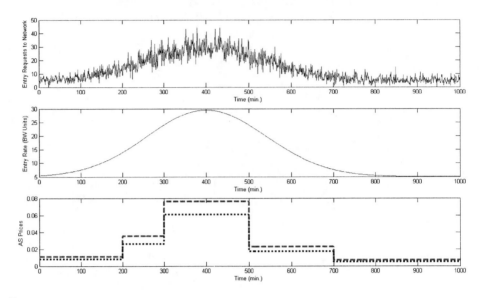

Note:

------ *price for high priority user profile*

...... *price for low priority user profile*

Literature has also addressed the dilemma of having a short-run congestion sensitive price mechanism versus the accounting complexity it might generate. A real-time price mechanism will effectively give the right price to pay at every moment of time, depending on current level of congestion, but would need a complex accounting and tracking system, on top of not being able to offer a reasonable horizon to consumer's planning (Falkner et al., 2000; Fulp & Reeves, 2004; Li et al., 2004). On the other hand, a mechanism based on long-term behavior or average figures will be easier to implement, but it will fail in timely response to congested periods of the network. Of course, both are extremes of what a real practical solution would be, which will depend on specific network traffic and architectural configurations.

Although our axiomatic allocation mechanism is derived using steady-state standard results from queuing theory, it allows enough flexibility to efficiently distribute congestion at shorter time frames. Let us consider an example where entry is characterized by a Poisson distribution with a varying entry rate. For the sake of clarity, we use model 1 and assume that $\lambda_1 = \lambda_2$, $\lambda(t) = \lambda_1 + \lambda_2 = 5 + (0.1)\exp(1.5 + 0.02t - 0.000025 * t^2)$, $\gamma_1 = 2$, $\gamma_2 = 1$. We calculate the AS prices and present the hypothetical example where the arrival rate changes in a time frame of 16 hours divided in minutes. We assume that the network bandthwidth is 40 units (e.g., 1 unit = 1 Mbps). If we divide the 16-hour time frame by the number M of time zones, we obtain a price per zone. Figure 5 shows AS prices as a function of time when M = 5.

It has been argued that congestion-based pricing does not strictly guarantee specific levels of QoS (Li et al., 2004). Fulp et al. (1998) argue that it is socially better to have fewer users receiving a good QoS than many users receiving poor QoS. In that sense, a system with blocking probabilities (up to the point where a new user is expected to be given a good QoS if he enters the system) might assure a given QoS. Axiomatic approaches that consider blocking probabilities under priority service have to be addressed by using computer simulation models. On the other hand, an approach in the spirit of O'Donnell and Sethu (2002, 2003), which achieves QoS guarantees under modifications of standard priority service models, is also an interesting way to explore the behavior of axiomatic mechanisms.

Acknowledgments

The authors are grateful to three anonymous reviewers, who call our attention to many points we have discussed in this work, and to the editor Jairo Gutiérrez for his valuable comments and insights.

References

Beltran, F., & Garcia-Diaz, C. (2005). The use of efficient cost allocation mechanisms for congestion pricing in data networks with priority service models. *International Journal of Business Data Communications and Networking, 1*(1), 33-49.

Billera, L., & Heath, D. (1982). Allocation of shared costs: A set of axioms yielding a unique procedure. *Mathematics of Operations Research, 7*(1), 32-49.

Chiu, D., & Jain, R. (1989). Analysis of the increase and decrease algorithms for congestion avoidance in computer networks. *Computer Networks and ISDN Systems, 17*(1), 1-14.

Courcoubetis, C., & Weber, R. (2003). *Pricing communication networks: Economics, technology and modelling.* West Sussex: John Wiley & Sons.

Crowcroft, J., & Oechslin, P. (1998). Differentiated end-to-end Internet services using a weighted proportionally fair sharing TCP. *ACM Computer Communications Review, 28*(3), 53-67.

Falkner, M., Devetsikiotis, M., & Lambadaris, I. (2000). An overview of pricing concepts for broadband IP networks. *The IEEE Communications Surveys & Tutorials, 3*(2).

Fulp, E., & Reeves, D. (2004). Bandwidth provisioning and pricing for networks with multiple classes of service. *Computer Networks Journal, 46*(1), 41-52.

Fulp, E., Ott, M., Reininger, D., & Reeves, D. (1998). Paying for QoS: An optimal distributed algorithm for pricing network resources. In *Proceedings of the IEEE Sixth International Workshop on Quality of Service* (pp. 75-84).

Garg, R., Kamra, A., & Khurana, V. (2002). A game-theoretic approach towards congestion control in communication networks. *ACM SIGCOMM Computer Communications Review, 32*(3), 47-61.

Gibbens, R., & Kelly, F. (1999). Resource pricing and the evolution of congestion control. *Automatica, 35*(12), 1969-1985.

Gupta, A., Stahl, D., & Whinston, A. (1998). Priority pricing of integrated services networks. In L. McKnight & J. Bailey (Eds.), *Internet economics* (pp. 323-352). Cambridge, MA: MIT Press.

Henriet, D., & Moulin, H. (1996). Traffic-based cost allocation in a network. *Rand Journal of Economics, 27*(2), 332-345.

Jin, N., & Jordan, S. (2004). The effect of bandwidth and buffer pricing on resource allocation and QoS. *Computer Networks Journal, 46*(1), 53-71.

Kelly, F. (1997). Charging and rate control for elastic traffic. *European Transactions on Telecommunications, 8*, 33-37.

Kelly, F., Maulloo, A., & Tan, D. (1998). Rate control in communication networks: shadow prices, proportional fairness and stability. *Journal of the Operational Research Society, 49*(3), 237-252.

Krishna, V. (2002). *Auction theory.* London: Academic Press.

Li, T., Iraqi, Y., & Boutaba, R. (2004). "Pricing and admission control for QoS-enabled Internet." *Computer Networks Journal, 46*(1), 87-110.

Mackie-Mason, J., & Varian, H. (1995a). Pricing the Internet. In B. Kahin & J. Keller (Eds.), *Public access to the Internet* (pp. 269-314). Cambridge, MA: MIT Press.

Mackie-Mason, J., & Varian, H. (1995b). Pricing congestible network resources. *IEEE Journal on Selected Areas in Communications, 13*(7), 1141-1149.

McLean, R., Pazgal, A., & Sharkey, W. (2004). Potential, consistency and cost allocation prices. *Mathematics of Operations Research, 29*(3), 602-623.

McLean, R., & Sharkey, W. (1994). An approach to the pricing of broadband telecommunications services. *Telecommunications Systems, 2*, 159-184.

McLean, R., & Sharkey, W. (1998). Alternative methods for cost allocation in stochastic service systems. *Brazilian Electronic Journal of Economics, 1*(1). Retrieved from www.beje.decon.ufpe.br

Mirman, L., & Tauman, Y. (1982). Demand compatible equitable cost sharing prices. *Mathematics of Operations Research, 7*(1), 40-56.

O'Donnell, A., & Sethu, H. (2002). A novel, practical pricing strategy for congestion control and differentiated services. In *Proceedings of the IEEE International Conference on Communications,* New York (Vol. 2, pp. 986-990).

O'Donnell, A., & Sethu, H. (2003). Congestion control, differentiated services, and efficient capacity management through a novel pricing strategy. *Computer Communications, 26*(13), 1457-1469.

Roberts, J. W. (2004). Internet traffic, QoS and pricing. In *Proceedings of the IEEE, 92*(9), 1389-1399.

Ros, D., & Tuffin, B. (2004). A mathematical model of the Paris metro pricing scheme for charging packet networks. *Computer Networks Journal, 46*(1), 73-85.

Semret, N. (1999). *Market mechanisms for network resource sharing.* PhD thesis, Columbia University.

Shenker, S. (1995). Service models and pricing policies for an integrated services Internet. In B. Kahin & J. Keller (Eds.), *Public access to the Internet* (pp. 315-337). Cambridge, MA: MIT Press.

Wang, X., & Schulzrinne, H. (2000). Performance study of congestion price based adaptive service. In *Proceedings of the International Workshop on Network and Operating System Support for Digital Audio and Video (NOSSDAV '00)*, Chapel Hill, NC (pp. 1-10).

Wolff, R. (1989). *Stochastic modeling and the theory of queues.* Englewood Cliffs, NJ: Prentice-Hall.

Yaïche, H., Mazumdar, R., & Rosenberg, C. (2000). A game theoretic framework for bandwidth allocation and pricing in broadband networks. *IEEE/ACM Transactions on Networking, 8*(5), 667-678.

Endnotes

[1]   In McLean and Sharkey's model (1994), such heterogeneity is represented by differences in consumer's information valuation, intensity of use of network services and average information size per request.

[2]   The reason we use the inverse of the service rate in the definition of AS-based two-part tariffs is, loosely speaking, the cost increases when α increases (the same as λ). This keeps consistency with the axioms presented for AS prices.

Appendix:
Summary of Price Calculations

A. Aumann-Shapley Prices

For model 1, the calculation of the Aumann-Shapley prices (AS prices) for user profile 1 takes the following form:

$$P_1^{AS}(F,\lambda) = \frac{\gamma_1}{\mu\rho_1}\left\{\frac{\rho}{(1-\rho_1)} + \left[\frac{\rho_2}{\rho_1}\right]\ln(1-\rho_1) - \rho_1\right\}$$

$$+\frac{\gamma_2}{\mu}\left\{\frac{A_2}{1-\rho_1} + \frac{A_4}{1-\rho} - \frac{A_1}{\rho_1}\ln(1-\rho_1) - \frac{A_3}{\rho}\ln(1-\rho)\right\} \tag{A.1}$$

where the Ai's are calculated using the following matrix expression:

$$\begin{bmatrix} 1 & 1 & 1 & 1 \\ -\rho_1\rho^2 & 0 & -\rho\rho_1^2 & 0 \\ \rho^2+2\rho\rho_1 & \rho^2 & \rho_1^2+2\rho\rho_1 & \rho_1^2 \\ -(2\rho+\rho_1) & -2\rho & -(2\rho_1+\rho) & -2\rho_1 \end{bmatrix}\begin{bmatrix} A_1 \\ A_2 \\ A_3 \\ A_4 \end{bmatrix} = \begin{bmatrix} 0 \\ -\rho_2\rho^2 \\ \rho_2^2 \\ \rho_2 \end{bmatrix} \tag{A.2}$$

For model 2, the price assigned to user profile 1 is obtained from the following expression:

$$P_1^{AS}(F,\lambda) = \frac{\gamma_1}{2}C_1(\lambda,\mu)\int_0^1\frac{t}{(1-\rho_1 t)}dt + \frac{\gamma_1}{2}\rho_1\lambda E(S^2)\int_0^1\frac{t^2}{(1-\rho_1 t)^2}dt$$

$$+\frac{\gamma_2}{2}C_2(\lambda,\mu)\int_0^1\frac{t}{(1-\rho_1 t)(1-\rho t)}dt - \frac{\gamma_2}{2}\frac{\lambda_2\lambda E(S^2)}{\mu_1}\int_0^1\frac{(\rho t+\rho_1 t-2)t^2}{(1-\rho_1 t)^2(1-\rho t)^2}dt \tag{A.3}$$

where:

$$C_1(\lambda, \mu) \equiv \frac{\partial[\lambda_1 \lambda E(S^2)]}{\partial \lambda_1} = (2\lambda_1 + \lambda_2)E(S^2) + \frac{2\lambda_1 \lambda_2}{\lambda_1 + \lambda_2}\left[\frac{1}{\mu_1^2} - \frac{1}{\mu_2^2}\right]$$

(A.4)

$$C_2(\lambda, \mu) \equiv \frac{\partial[\lambda_1 \lambda E(S^2)]}{\partial \lambda_1} = \lambda_2 E(S^2) + \frac{2\lambda_2^2}{\lambda_1 + \lambda_2}\left[\frac{1}{\mu_1^2} - \frac{1}{\mu_2^2}\right]$$

(A.5)

The price for user profile 2, in both model 1 and model 2, is calculated using the cost-sharing axiom:

$$P_2(F, \lambda) = \frac{1}{\lambda_2}\left[\sum_{i=1}^{r} \gamma_i \lambda_i d_i - \lambda_1 P_1^{AS}(F, \lambda)\right]$$

(A.6)

B. Shapley Value Prices (SV Prices)

Using the standard waiting time results for M/M/1 queues, we can show that the congestion cost function is $F(\gamma,\lambda,\mu) = \gamma\lambda[\rho/(\mu(1-\rho))] = \gamma\rho^2/(1-\rho)$, independently of the model to be used. Based on that, it is possible to construct an incremental cost table by user type according to each possible order (Table B.1).

The price calculations are made using weighted sums of the aggregate costs in table A.1, following the order probabilities presented. For model 1, these prices result in:

$$P_1^{SV}(F,\lambda) = \frac{1}{\lambda_1}\left\{\frac{1}{2}\left[\frac{\gamma_1\rho_1^2}{1-\rho_1}\right] + \frac{1}{2}\left[F(\gamma,\lambda,\mu) - \frac{\gamma_2\rho_2^2}{1-\rho_2}\right]\right\}$$

$$= \frac{1}{2\lambda_1}\left\{\frac{\gamma_1\rho_1}{1-\rho_1}[\rho_1 + \rho] + \gamma_2\rho_2\left[\frac{\rho}{(1-\rho_1)(1-\rho)} - \frac{\rho_2}{1-\rho_2}\right]\right\} \qquad (A.7)$$

$$P_2^{SV}(F,\lambda) = \frac{1}{2\lambda_2}\left\{\gamma_1\frac{\rho_1\rho}{(1-\rho_1)} + \gamma_2\frac{\rho_2\rho}{(1-\rho_1)(1-\rho)} - \frac{\gamma_1\rho_1^2}{1-\rho_1} + \frac{\gamma_2\rho_2^2}{1-\rho_2}\right\}$$

$$= \frac{1}{2\lambda_2}\left\{\frac{\gamma_1\rho_1\rho_2}{1-\rho_1} + \gamma_2\rho_2\left[\frac{\rho}{(1-\rho_1)(1-\rho)} + \frac{\rho_2}{1-\rho_2}\right]\right\} \qquad (A.8)$$

Table B.1. Aggregate costs by user profile to calculate the Shapley value

Arrival order	Order probability	Aggregate cost for user type 1	Aggregate cost for user profile 2
1,2	1/2	$\gamma_1\rho_1^2/(1-\rho_1)$	$F(\gamma,\lambda,\mu)-\gamma_1\rho_1^2/(1-\rho_1)$
2,1	1/2	$F(\gamma,\lambda,\mu)-\gamma_2\rho_2^2/(1-\rho_2)$	$\gamma_2\rho_2^2/(1-\rho_2)$

For model 2, the expressions that represent the prices take the following form:

$$P_1^{SV}(F,\lambda) = \frac{1}{2\lambda_1}\left\{\frac{\gamma_1\rho_1^2}{1-\rho_1} + \gamma_1\lambda_1\frac{\lambda\sum_{i=1}^{2}\frac{\lambda_i}{\lambda}\left[\frac{2}{\mu_i^2}\right]}{2(1-\rho_1)} + \gamma_2\lambda_2\frac{\lambda\sum_{i=1}^{2}\frac{\lambda_i}{\lambda}\left[\frac{2}{\mu_i^2}\right]}{2(1-\rho_1)(1-\rho)} - \frac{\gamma_2\rho_2^2}{1-\rho_2}\right\}$$

(A.8)

$$P_2^{SV}(F,\lambda) = \frac{1}{2\lambda_2}\left\{\gamma_1\lambda_1\frac{\lambda\sum_{i=1}^{2}\frac{\lambda_i}{\lambda}\left[\frac{2}{\mu_i^2}\right]}{2(1-\rho_1)} + \gamma_2\lambda_2\frac{\lambda\sum_{i=1}^{2}\frac{\lambda_i}{\lambda}\left[\frac{2}{\mu_i^2}\right]}{2(1-\rho_1)(1-\rho)} - \frac{\gamma_1\rho_1^2}{1-\rho_1} + \frac{\gamma_2\rho_2^2}{1-\rho_2}\right\}$$

(A.9)

It can be seen the realization of the additivity axiom, which leads to the recovery of conges-
tion costs: $\lambda_1 P_1^{SV}(F,\lambda) + \lambda_2 P_2^{SV}(F,\lambda) = (1/2)(\gamma_1\rho_1^2/(1-\rho_1)) + (1/2)F(\gamma,\lambda,\mu) - (1/2)(\gamma_2\rho_2^2/(1-\rho_2))$
$+ (1/2)F(\gamma,\lambda,\mu) - (1/2)(\gamma_1\rho_1^2/(1-\rho_1)) + (1/2)(\gamma_2\rho_2^2/(1-\rho_2)) = F(\gamma,\lambda,\mu)$.

C. AS Two-Part Tariffs for $\mu_1=\mu_2=1$ (Model 1)

$P_{\lambda 2}^{AS}$	$\gamma_1 \int_0^1 \dfrac{2\lambda_1 t^3 + \lambda_2 t^3 - \lambda_1^2 t^5}{\left(1-\lambda_1 t^2\right)}\,dt + \gamma_2 \int_0^1 \dfrac{\lambda_2 t^3 + \lambda_2^2 t^5 - \left(\lambda_1+\lambda_2\right)^2 \lambda_2 t^7}{\left(1-\lambda_1 t^2\right)^2 \left(1-\lambda_1 t^2 - \lambda_2 t^2\right)^2}\,dt$
$P_{\lambda 1}^{AS}$	$\gamma_1 \int_0^1 \lambda_1 \dfrac{t^3}{\left(1-\lambda_1 t^2\right)}\,dt + \gamma_2 \int_0^1 \dfrac{\left[\left(\lambda_1 t^2 + 2\lambda_2 t^2\right)\left(1-\lambda_1 t^2 - \lambda_2 t^2\right)+\lambda_2\left(\lambda_1+\lambda_2\right)t^4\right]}{\left(1-\lambda_1 t^2\right)\left(1-\lambda_1 t^2 - \lambda_2 t^2\right)^2}\,dt$
P_{α}^{AS}	$\gamma_1 \int_0^1 \lambda_1 \left(\lambda_1+\lambda_2\right)^2 \dfrac{\left[2t\left(1-\lambda_1 t^2\right)+\lambda_1 t^3\right]}{\left(1-\lambda_1 t^2\right)^2}\,dt +$ $\gamma_2 \int_0^1 \lambda_2 \left(\lambda_1+\lambda_2\right)^2 \dfrac{\left[2t\left(1-\lambda_1 t^2\right)\left(1-\lambda_1 t^2 - \lambda_2 t^2\right)+t^2\left(2\lambda_1 t + \lambda_2 t - 2\lambda_1^2 t^3 - 2\lambda_1 \lambda_2 t^3\right)\right]}{\left(1-\lambda_1 t^2\right)^2 \left(1-\lambda_1 t^2 - \lambda_2 t^2\right)^2}\,dt$

Section II:
Mobility

Chapter VI

Mobile Multimedia:
Communication Technologies, Business Drivers, Service and Applications

Ismail Khalil Ibrahim, Johannes Kepler University Linz, Austria

Ashraf Ahmad, National Chiao Tung University, Taiwan

David Taniar, Monash University, Australia

Abstract

Mobile multimedia, referring to multimedia information exchange over wireless networks or wireless Internet, is made possible due to the popularity and evolution of mobile computing devices, coupled with fast and affordable mobile networks. This chapter discusses various state-of-the-art communication technologies to support mobile multimedia. The range of complexity of applications and services provided to end-users also play an important part in the success of mobile multimedia.

Introduction

Number of subscribers for mobile communications has increased much faster than predicted, particularly for terrestrial use. In the year 2000, number of mobile subscribers was approximately 400 million worldwide, and in the year 2010 more than 1.8 billion mobile subscribers are estimated. An interesting fact was presented in a new report by Telecommunications Management Group, Inc. (TMG) (Wireless World Forum) providing the statistical basis to show the number of mobile multimedia users exceeding 100 million in 2004. This breathtaking fact inspires us to start researching the mobile multimedia in all possible related aspects. In order to provide experts and researcher in the field of mobile multimedia, a description of basic definition of mobile multimedia is introduced, and then essential business driver controlling the mobile multimedia is illustrated. A full and up-to-date description of technologies beneath the mobile multimedia is presented. In addition to the services and applications, a set of mobile multimedia is discussed thoroughly, as well as anticipating the future of mobile multimedia.

The demand for mobile access to data no matter where the data is stored, what is kind of data and where the user happens to be, in addition to the explosive growth of the Internet and the rising popularity of mobile devices are among the factors that have created a dynamic business environment, where both handset manufacturers and service provider operators companies are competing to provide customers access to information resources and services anytime, anywhere.

Advances in wireless networking, specifically the development of the IEEE 802.11 and IEEE 802.16 protocol family and the rapid deployment and growth of GSM (and GPRS, 3G, 3GPP), have enabled a broad spectrum of novel and out breaking solutions for new applications and services. Voice services are no longer sufficient to satisfy customers' business and personal requirements. More and more people and companies are demanding for mobile access to multimedia services. Mobile multimedia seems to be the next mass market in mobile communications following the success of GSM and SMS. It enables the industry to create products and services to meet the consumer needs better. However, an innovation itself does not guarantee a success; it is necessary to be able to predict the new technology adaptation behavior and to try to fulfill customer needs rather than to wait for a demand pattern to surface.

The major step from the second generation to third generation and further to fourth generation was the ability to support advanced and wideband multimedia services, including emails, file transfers, and distribution services like radio, TV, and software provisioning (e.g., software download). These multimedia services can be symmetrical and asymmetrical services, real-time, and non real-time services.

It is beyond all expectations that mobile multimedia will create significantly added values for costumers by providing mobile access to Internet-based multimedia services, video conferencing, and streaming. Mobile multimedia is one of the mainstream systems for the next generation mobile communications, featuring large voice capacity, multimedia applications and high-speed mobile data services (Bull, Canagarajah, & Nix, 1999). As for the technology, the trend in the radio frequency area is to shift from narrowband to wideband with a family of standards tailored to a variety of application needs. Many enabling technologies including WCDMA, software-defined radio, intelligent antennas, and digital processing devices are greatly improving the spectral efficiency of third generation systems. In the mobile network area, the trend is to move from traditional circuit-switched systems to packet-switched programmable networks that integrate both voice and packet services, and eventually evolve towards an all-IP network (Bi, Zysman, & Menkes, 2001).

While for the information explosion, the addition of mobility to data communications systems has enabled a new generation of services not meaningful in a fixed network, such as positioning-based services. However, the development of mobile multimedia services has only started and in the future we will see new application areas opening up (Bi, Zysman, & Menkes, 2001; Blair, Coulson, Davies, Robin, & Fitzpatrick, 1997; Brown & Syfrig, 1996; Bruno, Conti, & Gregori, 2001; Bull, Canagarajah, & Nix, 1999).

Research in mobile multimedia is typically focused on bridging the gap between the high resource demands of multimedia applications and the limited bandwidth and capabilities offered by state-of-the-art networking technologies and mobile devices.

Communication engineering approaches this problem by considering not only characteristics of the networks and devices used, but also on the tasks and objectives the user is pursuing when applying/demanding mobile multimedia services and exploit this information to better adapt those services to the users' needs. This method is referred to it as user centric multimedia processing approach.

Mobile Multimedia

External market studies have predicted that in Europe in the year 2010 more than 90 million mobile subscribers will use mobile multimedia services and will generate about 60% of the traffic in terms of transmitted bits. In China, the DGI predicted that there will be over 500 million mobile phones in China by year 2008, and over 150 million for multimedia applications. These results grab our attention how important it is to precisely define the mobile multimedia and its related terms.

Mobile multimedia can be defined as a set of protocols and standards for multimedia information exchange over wireless networks. It enables information systems to process and transmit multimedia data to provide end users with services from various areas, such as the mobile working place, mobile entertainment, mobile information retrieval, and context-based services.

Multimedia information as combined information presented by more than one media type (i.e. text, pictures, graphics, sounds, animations, videos) enriches the quality of the information and is a way to represent reality as adequately as possible. Multimedia allows users to enhance their understanding of the provided information and increases the potential of person to person and person to system communication.

Mobility as one of the key drivers of mobile multimedia can be decomposed into:

1.   **User mobility:** The user is forced to move from one location to location during fulfilling his activities. For the user, the access to information and computing resources is necessary regardless his actual position (e.g., terminal services, VPNs to company-intern information systems).

2. **Device mobility:** User activities require a device to fulfill his needs regardless of the location in a mobile environment (e.g., PDAs, notebooks, tablet pc, cell-phones, etc.).

3. **Service mobility:** The service itself is mobile and can be used in different systems and can be moved seamlessly among those systems (e.g., mobile agents).

The special requirements coming along with the mobility of users, devices, and services; and specifically the requirements of multimedia as traffic type; bring the need of new paradigms in software-engineering and system-development; but also in non-technical issues such as the emergence of new business models and concerns about privacy, security, or digital inclusion, to name a few.

For instance, in the context of mobile multimedia, 3G communication protocols have great deals. Even some mobile protocol experts tend to define 3G as a mobile multimedia, personal services, the convergence of digitalization, mobility, and the internet, new technologies based on global standards, the entire of the aforementioned terms. In 3G, the end user will be able to access the mobile internet at the bandwidth at various bit rates. This makes great challenges for handset device manufacturers and mobile network operators. In addition, a large number of application and related issues need to be addressed considering the heterogeneity nature of the Internet. Also, the various and rich content of the internet should be considered whenever one of the roles of 3G is being deployed.

In network traffic point of view, the majority of traffic is changing from speech-oriented communications to multimedia communications. It is also generally expected that due to the dominating role of mobile wireless access, the number of portable handsets will exceed the number of PCs connected to the Internet. Therefore, mobile terminals will be the major person-machine interface in the future instead of the PC. Due to the dominating role of IP-based data traffic in the future, the networks and systems have to be designed for economic packet data transfer. The expected new data services are highly bandwidth consuming. This results in higher data rate requirements for future systems.

Business Drivers

The key feature of mobile multimedia is reaching customers and partners, regardless of their locations and delivering multimedia content to the right place at the right time. Key drivers of this technology are on the one hand technical and on the other business drivers.

Evolutions in technology pushed the penetration of the mobile multimedia market and made services in this field feasible. The miniaturization of devices and the coverage of radio networks are the key technical drivers in the field of mobile multimedia.

1. **Miniaturization:** The first mobile phones had brick-like dimensions. Their limited battery capacity and transmission range restricted their usage in mobile environments. Actual mobile devices with multiple features fit into cases with minimal dimensions and can be (and are) carried by the user in every situation.

2. **Vehicle manufacturer:** Furthermore, mobility also calls for new types of services (and thus revenues). Vehicle manufacturers want to improve the ears' man-machine interface by using superior input/output devices. An open application platform would allow upgrading of multimedia equipment during the lifecycle of a vehicle, which is much longer than the lifetime of computing equipment. Safety equipment for automated emergency and breakdown calls brings positioning hardware into the car and thus enabling other location-aware services. But vehicle makers also seek an after-market relationship to their customers: Once having ears connected, they can offer ear-specific services, including direction-finding and safeguarding support.

3. **Radio networks:** Today's technology allows radio networks of every size for every application scenario. Nowadays public wireless wide-area networks cover the bulk of areas especially in congested areas. They enable (most of the time) adequate quality of service. They allow location-independent service provision and virtual private network access.

4. **Mobile terminal manufacturers:** Mobile terminal manufacturers serve individual people instead of households. Since there are more individuals than households, the market is naturally bigger then the home terminal market. Furthermore, there is a large potential for use and fashion-based diversification and innovation of terminals.

5. **Market evolution:** The market for mobile devices changed in the last years. Ten years ago the devices were not really mobile (short-time battery operation, heavy, and large devices) but therefore they have been expensive and affordable just for high-class business people. Shrinking devices and falling operation (network) costs made mobile devices to a mass-consumer-good available and affordable for everyone. The result is dramatic subscriber growth and therefore a new increasing market for mobile multimedia services.

6. **Subscribers:** Persons spend a good percentage of their lifetime traveling, either for business or leisure, while they want to stay connected in every respect. This desire is more than proven by the current sales figures for mobile phones and the emerging standards for mobile narrow-band data services.

7. **Service evolution:** The permanent increasing market brought more and more sophisticated services, starting in the field of telecommunication from poor quality speech-communication to real-time video conferencing. Meanwhile, mobile multimedia services provide rich media content and intelligent context-based services.

8. **Vehicle terminal manufacturers:** Vehicle terminal manufacturers currently suffer from vertical markets due to high customization efforts for OEM products. An open application platform would help them to reduce development time and costs. It is also a key driver for after market products. A wide range of services will increase the number of terminals sold.

9. **Ears:** For ear drivers, security and travel assistance are important aspects as well. They probably want to use the same services in the car they are used to at home and in the office. This is only possible with an open application platform.

Technology drives mobile multimedia with new means to communicate, cache, process, and display multimedia content:

- **Connectivity:** New means to communicate enable new services to be provided.

- **Memory and persistent storage:** Developing memory technology allows caching of more content and offline processing, thus creating the illusion of instant access to interactive remote content. For example, audio/video content and whole Websites may be downloaded in background and consumed offline. This is above all important for data broadcast services, which are transmitted in different fashions.

- **Processing:** More processing resources with less power consumption allow rendering of more complex multimedia content.

- **Display:** Visualizing multimedia content demands for cheap high resolution displays that comply to "handset" requirements "screen driver, pixel per bits, width, height."

The value chain of mobile multimedia services describes the players involved in the business with mobile multimedia. Every service in the field of mobile multimedia requires that their output and service fees must be divided to them considering interdependencies in the complete service life-cycle.

1. **Network operators:** They provide end-users with the infrastructure to access services mobile via wireless networks (e.g., via GSM/GPRS/UMTS). The network operators want to boost the sales of network bandwidth, by enabling new types of services with new network technologies. In many countries a close cooperation between the transmitter and cellular network operators has been established to be able to offer hybrid network capacity. Service and content providers see the opportunity to promote and sell their services to people everywhere and anytime, thus increasing the total usage of their services.

2. **Content provider:** Content provider and aggregators license content and prepare it for end-users. They collect information and services to provide customers with convenient service collection adapted for mobile use. In another hand, some national broadcasters are forced by law to provide nationwide TV coverage through terrestrial transmission. They are interested in digital TV, because, firstly, it strongly reduces their transmission costs per channel by high ratio and, secondly, they improve the attractiveness of terrestrial reception which decreased strongly since the beginning of cable and satellite services

3. **Fixed Internet company:** Those companies create the multimedia content. Usually they provide it already via the fixed Internet but are not specialized on mobile service provisioning. They handle the computing infrastructure and content creation.

4. **App developers and device manufacturers:** They deliver hard- and software for mobile multimedia services and are not involved with any type of content creation and delivering.

Communication Technologies

Wireless Wide Area Networks

After the first-generation analog mobile systems, the second-generation (2G) mobile digital systems were introduced around 1991 offering higher capacity and lower costs for network operators, while for the users, they offered short messages and low-rate data services added to speech services. Reader may refer to figure one as it holds general comparison among the first to four generation communication system. Presently, the 2G systems are GSM, TDMA, PDC, and cdmaOne. GSM is used in most parts of the world except in Japan, were PDC is the second-generation system used (Dixit, Guo, & Antoniou, 2001).

An important evolution of the 2G systems, sometimes known as 2.5G, is the ability to use packet-switched solution in GPRS (general packet radio system). The main investment for the operators lies in the new packet-switched core network, while the extensions in the radio access network mainly is software upgrades. For the users GPRS offers the possibility to always be online and only pay for the data actually transferred. Data rates of up to 20 kbps per used time slot will be offered, and with multiple time-slots per user in the downlink, attractive services can be offered (Stallings, 2001).

The shift to third-generation in the radio access networks is demanding a lot of efforts. The ITU efforts through IMT-2000 have led to a number of recommendations. These recommendations address areas such as user bandwidth, richness of service offerings (multimedia services), and flexibility (networks that can support small or large numbers of subscribers). The recommendations also specify that IMT-2000 should operate in the 2-GHz band. In general, however, the ITU recommendations are mainly a set of requirements and do not specify the detailed technical solutions to meet the requirements (UMTS Forum, 1998, 2000).

To address the technical solutions, the ITU has solicited technical proposals from interested organizations, and then selected/approved some of those proposals. In 1998, numerous air interface technical proposals were submitted. These were reviewed by the ITU, which in 1999 selected five technologies for terrestrial service (non-satellite based). The five technologies are (Collins & Smith, 2001):

- Wideband CDMA (WCDMA)
- CDMA 2000 (an evolution of IS-95 CDMA)
- TD-SCDMA (time division-synchronous CDMA)
- DECT
- UWC-136 (an evolution of IS-136)

Here is a brief description of each one of these selected technologies.

Figure 1. Comparison among the four generation communication system

1G	2G	3G	4G
Basic mobility	Advance mobility "roaming"	Seamless roaming	IP based mobility
Basic service	Various services "data exchange"	Service concept and model	Extremely high data rates
Incompatibility	Headed for global solution	Global solution	Perfect telecom, datacom convergence

Wideband CDMA (WCDMA)

The worldwide introduction of WCDMA took place in 2001 and 2002, starting in Japan and continuing to Europe. In the U.S, several 3G alternatives will be available. GSM and TDMA operators can evolve toward EDGE, with WCDMA as a possible step, while cdma-One operators can evolve toward cdma2000 systems.

WCDMA, as specified by the third-generation partnership project (3GPP), is a 3G system operating in 5 MHz of bandwidth. Variable spreading and multicode operation is used to support a multitude of different radio access bearers. Different service classes are supported by an advanced quality-of-service (QoS) support. Data rates of up to 384 kbps for wide area coverage are provided (Bi, Zysman, & Menkes, 2001; Stallings, 2001; Dixit et al., 2001).

EDGE is an evolution of GPRS with data rates of up to 60 kbps per time-slot together with improved spectrum efficiency. EDGE uses higher-order modulation together with link adaptation and incremental redundancy to optimize the radio bearer to the radio connection characteristics. Currently, additions in the form of a new set of radio access bearers to align EDGE toward WCDMA are being standardized within the R5 of the 3GPP standards. The same service classes as in the WCDMA and the same interface to the core network will be used (Dornan, 2000; Ephremides et al., 2000; Fabri, Worrall, & Kondoz, 2000; Fasbender & Reichert, 1999; Flament et al., 1999; Frodigh, Parkvall, Roobol, Johansson, & Larsson, 2001).

CDMA 2000 (Evolution of IS-95 CDMA)

cdmaOne has evolved into cdma2000 and is available in two flavors, 1x and 3x. The former uses the same 1.25 Mhz bandwidth as cdmaOne and supports up to approximately 600 kbps, while the latter is a multi-carrier system using 3.75 Mhz and supporting approximately 2 Mbps at the moment, the focus on 3x is very limited. As a complement to 1x, the 3GPP2 has recently specified 1xEV-DO (1x Evolution-Data Only). 1xEV-DO uses a separate 1.25 Mhz carrier and supports best-effort data traffic only, using a new air interface compared to cdma2000 carrier. The peak rate in the 1x EV-DO downlink is almost 2.5 Mbps, excluding overhead. Phase two of the 1x evolution, known as 1xEV-DV (1x Evolution-Data and

Voice), is currently being discussed within 3GPP2 and there are a number of proposals under consideration. The purpose is to specify an extension to cdma2000 1x in order to support high-rate data and voice on the same carrier (Bi, Zysman, & Menkes, 2001; Stallings, 2001; Dixit et al., 2001).

TD-SCDMA (Time Division-Synchronous CDMA)

UTRA TDD was developed to harmonize with the FDD component. This was achieved by harmonization of important parameters of the physical layer and a common set of protocols in the higher layers are specified for both FDD and TDD (Flament et al., 1999). TD-SCDMA has significant commonality with UTRA TDD. TD-SCDMA combines TDMA system with an adaptive CDMA component. TD-SCDMA eliminates the uplink/downlink interference, which affects other TDD methods by applying "terminal synchronization" techniques, so TD-SCDMA can support of all radio network scenarios (Wide Area - Macro, Local Area - Micro, Hot Spots - Pico and Corporate Networks) to provide full service coverage. In this way, TD-SCDMA stands alongside W-CDMA and CDMA2000 as a fully-fledged 3G standard (Wireless Ethernet Compatibility Alliance).

DECT

DECT (digital enhanced cordless telecommunications) (European Telecommunications Standards) is a common standard for cordless personal telephony established by ETSI. DECT is used for those cordless communication systems which supports only indoor and pedestrian environment, but it does not allow full network coverage so is not satisfied to all requirements of third generation system.

UWC-136 (Evolution of IS-136)

DECT is based on TDMA. Different from UWC-136 (also based on TDMA), which uses two separate bandwidths (200 kHz provides medium bit rates up to 384 Kb/s and 1.6 MHz provides highest bit rates up to 2 Mb/s), DECT uses only one carrier with 1.728 MHz bandwidth. Variable bit rates are achieved by allocating different numbers of basic channels to a user. TDMA is flexible for TDD with asymmetric services and the training sequence is optimized for high bit rate services (Veerakachen, Pongsanguansin, & Sanguanpong, 1999).

In the fourth generation mobile communication (4G mobile), the combination and convergence of the different world's information technology industry, media industry and telecommunications will incorporate communication with information technology. As a result, mobile communications together with information technology will penetrate into the various fields of the society. In the future, 4G mobile (global and ubiquitous) communications will make people free from spatial and temporal constraints. Versatile communication systems will also be required to realize customized services based on diverse individual needs. The user outlook are increasing with regard to a large variety of services and applications with diverse degree of quality of service (QoS), which is related to delay, data rate, and bit error requirements. Therefore, seamless services and applications via different access systems and technologies that take full advantage of the use of available spectrum will be the driving forces for future developments.

Wireless Local Area Networks

Wireless local area networks (WLANs) based on the different versions of IEEE 802.11 standard have been around for some years in the 2.4 GHz ISM licensed band. Data rates up to 11 Mbps (802.11b) with reasonable indoor coverage have been offered, another licensed band is the microwave ovens which operates on 2.45 GH.

The ISM band is used in:

- 802.11
- Bluetooth
- Spread spectrum cordless phone

In an attempt to attain higher data rates new standards were proposed to operate on 5 GHz band with a rate up to 54 Mbps. Products based on two different standards, HIPERLAN 2 (H2) and IEEE 802.11a, The physical layers of the two are more or less identical with some differences where hiperlan2 uses several types of preambles but only PLCP is used in 802.11a to maintain synchronization and in modulation schemes (hiperlan2 supports 7 modes while 80.11a supports 8), with a carrier spacing of 20 MHz, OFDM modulation, and data rates up to 54 Mbps. The difference is the MAC protocol, where Hiperlan 2 has a more advanced protocol supporting QoS and mobility in a consistent way (Bi, Zysman, & Menkes, 2001).

802.11g is proposed to support high rates too up to 54 Mbps, Networks employing 802.11g operate at radio frequencies between 2.400 GHz and 2.4835 GHz, the same band as 802.11b (11 Mbps). But the 802.11g specification employs orthogonal frequency division multiplexing (OFDM), the modulation scheme used in 802.11a, to obtain higher data speed.

IEEE 802.11x

The current IEEE 802.11 (IEEE, 1999) is known to lack a viable security mechanism. In order to address this issue, IEEE has proposed the robust security network (RSN). RSN approved the 802.1x standard to provide strong authentication, access control, and key management. In a wireless environment, there are no physical perimeters, thus, the network access authentication must be provided. In this case, RSN provides mechanisms to restrict network connectivity to authorized entities only via 802.1x.

802.1x also provides various authentication methods such as one-time password and smart-cards. It provides network access control for hybrid networking technologies (e.g., not only for wireless).

There are three entities specified in the IEEE 802.1x standard, including: supplicant, authenticator, and authentication server.

Wi-Fi

Wi-Fi (short for "wireless fidelity") is a term for certain types of wireless local area network (WLAN) that uses specifications in the 802.11 family (Vaughan-Nichols, 2003). The term Wi-Fi was created by an organization called the Wi-Fi Alliance, which oversees tests that certify product interoperability. A product that passes the alliance tests is given the label "Wi-Fi certified" (a registered trademark).

Originally, Wi-Fi certification was applicable only to products using the 802.11b standard (Ferro & Potorti, 2005). Today, Wi-Fi can apply to products that use any 802.11 standard. The 802.11 specifications are part of an evolving set of wireless network standards known as the 802.11 family. The particular specification under which a Wi-Fi network operates is called the "flavor" of the network. Wi-Fi has gained acceptance in many businesses, agencies, schools, and homes as an alternative to a wired LAN. Many airports, hotels, and fast-food facilities offer public access to Wi-Fi networks. These locations are known as hot spots. Many charge a daily or hourly rate for access, but some are free. An interconnected area of hot spots and network access points is known as a hot zone.

Unless adequately protected (Hole, Dyrnes, & Thorsheim, 2005), a Wi-Fi network can be susceptible to access by unauthorized users who use the access as a free Internet connection. The activity of locating and exploiting security-exposed wireless LANs is called war driving. An identifying iconography, called war chalking, has evolved. Any entity that has a wireless LAN should use security safeguards such as the wired equivalent privacy (WEP) encryption standard, the more recent Wi-Fi protected access (WPA), Internet protocol security (IPsec), or a virtual private network (VPN).

HiperLAN

It is a WLAN communication standard primarily used in European countries. There are two specifications: HiperLAN/1 and HiperLAN/2. Both have been adopted by the European Telecommunications Standards Institute (ETSI). The HiperLAN standards provide features and capabilities similar to 802.11. HiperLAN/1 provides communications at up to 20 Mbps in the 5-GHz range of the radio frequency (RF) spectrum. HiperLAN/ 2 is defined as a flexible Radio LAN standard designed to provide high speed access up to 54 Mbps to a variety of networks including 3G mobile core networks, ATM networks, and IP-based networks, and also for private use as a wireless LAN system. Basic applications include data, voice and video, with specific Quality of Service (QoS) parameters taken into account. HiperLAN/2 systems can be deployed in offices, classrooms, homes, factories, hot spot areas like exhibition halls, and more generally where radio transmission is an efficient alternative or a complement to wired technology. It is worth noting that HiperLAN/2 has been developed in conjunction with the Japanese standards body, the Association of Radio Industries and Broadcasting.

HiperLAN/2 offers a number of advantages over 802.11a in that it incorporates quality of service (QoS) features. However, there is a long tradition of Europe developing standards which are not adopted because the US does something different. Most observers suggest that HiperLAN/2 will loose out to 802.11a, but that some of the features developed by ETSI will be incorporated in revised versions of the 802.11a standard.

WiMAX

WiMAX (Ghosh et al., 2005; Vaughan-Nichols, 2004; Hamalainen et al., 2002; Giuliano & Mazzenga, 2005) is a wireless industry coalition whose members organized to advance IEEE 802.16 standards for broadband wireless access (BWA) networks. WiMAX 802.16 technology is expected to enable multimedia applications with wireless connection and, with a range of up to 30 miles, enable networks to have a wireless last mile solution.

WiMAX was formed in April 2001, in preparation for the original 802.16 specification published in December of that year. According to the WiMAX forum, the group's aim is to promote and certify compatibility and interoperability of devices based on the 802.16 specification, and to develop such devices for the marketplace. Members of the organization include Airspan, Alvarion, Analog Devices, Aperto Networks, Ensemble Communications, Fujitsu, Intel, Nokia, OFDM Forum, Proxim, and Wi-LAN

WiMAX is a wireless industry coalition whose members organized to advance IEEE 802.16 standards for broadband wireless access (BWA) networks. WiMAX 802.16 technology is expected to enable multimedia applications with wireless connection and, with a range of up to 30 miles, enable networks to have a wireless last mile solution (Giuliano & Mazzenga, 2005; Ghavami, Michael, & Kohno, 2005). For reader reference, we are attaching a general specifications Table 1 for WiMAX standard.

Wireless Personal Area Networks

A WPAN (wireless personal area network) is a personal area network—a network for interconnecting devices centered around an individual person's work space—in which the connections are wireless. Typically, a wireless personal area network uses some technology that permits communication within about 10 meters—in other words, a very short range. One such technology is Bluetooth, which was used as the basis for a new standard, IEEE 802.15.

Table 1. WiMax (IEEE 802.16) specifications

Frequency range	Modulation	Multiple access	Duplex	Channel bandwidth	Number of channels	Peak data rate
2 GHz to 66GHz in various bands	BPSK, QPSK, 16QAM, 64QAM, QFDM, SC	TDMA/ OFDMA	TDD/ FDD	In accordance with local radio regulations	79	15 Mbit/s (5MHz channel) to 134 Mbit/s (28 MHz channel)

A WPAN could serve to interconnect all the ordinary computing and communicating devices that many people have on their desk or carry with them today—or it could serve a more specialized purpose such as allowing the surgeon and other team members to communicate during an operation.

A key concept in WPAN technology is known as plugging in. In the ideal scenario, when any two WPAN-equipped devices come into close proximity (within several meters of each other) or within a few kilometers of a central server, they can communicate as if connected by a cable. Another important feature is the ability of each device to lock out other devices selectively, preventing needless interference or unauthorized access to information.

The technology for WPANs is in its infancy and is undergoing rapid development. Proposed operating frequencies are around 2.4 GHz in digital modes. The objective is to facilitate seamless operation among home or business devices and systems. Every device in a WPAN will be able to plug in to any other device in the same WPAN, provided they are within physical range of one another. In addition, WPANs worldwide will be interconnected. Thus, for example, an archeologist on site in Greece might use a PDA to directly access databases at the University of Minnesota in Minneapolis, and to transmit findings to that database.

Infrared IR

802.11 also includes a specification for a physical layer based on infrared (IR) that is low enough that IR ports are standard on practically every laptop. IR is extremely tolerant of radio frequency (RF) interference because radio IR is unregulated. Product developers do not need to investigate and comply with directives from several regulatory organizations throughout the world and unauthorized users connecting to a network. Light can be confined to concerns. This comes at a price. IR LANs rely on scattering light off the ceiling, so range is much shorter. This discussion is academic, however.

No products have been created based on developed by the Infrared Data Association (IrDA), not 802.11. Even if products were created around the IR PHY, the big drivers to adopt 802.11 are flexibly penetrating solid objects. Using infrared light instead of radio waves seems to have several advantages. IR ports are less expensive than radio transceivers—in fact, the cost waves operate at a totally different frequency. This leads to a second advantage: Security concerns regarding 802.11 are largely based on the threat of conference room or office by simply closing the door. IR-based LANs can offer some of the advantages of flexibility and mobility but with less security the IR PHY. The infrared ports on laptops comply with a set of standards and mobility, which are better achieved by radio's longer range.

IrDA

IrDA (Infrared Data Association) is an industry-sponsored organization set up in 1993 to create international standards for the hardware and software used in infrared communication links (Williams, 2000; Vitsas & Boucouvalas, 2003). In this special form of radio transmission, a focused ray of light in the infrared frequency spectrum, measured in terahertz, or trillions of hertz (cycles per second), is modulated with information and sent from a transmitter to a receiver over a relatively short distance. Infrared radiation (IR) is the same technology used to control a TV set with a remote control.

IrDA has a set of protocols covering all layers of data transfer and, in addition, has some network management and interoperability designs. IrDA protocols have IrDA DATA as the vehicle for data delivery and IrDA CONTROL for sending the control information. In general, IrDA is used to provide wireless connectivity technologies for devices that would normally use cables for connectivity (Robertson, Hansen, Sorensen, & Knutson, 2001).

IrDA is a point-to-point, narrow angle, ad-hoc data transmission standard designed to operate over a distance of 0 to 1 meter and at speeds of 9600 bps to 16 Mbps. Adapters now include the traditional upgrades to serial and parallel ports. In the IrDA-1.1 standard, the maximum data size that may be transmitted is 2048 bytes and the maximum transmission rate is 4 Mbps (Vitsas & Boucouvalas, 2002).

HomeRF

HomeRF (HomeRF) is a subset of the International Telecommunication Union (ITU) and primarily works on the development of a standard for inexpensive RF voice and data communication. The HomeRF Working Group has also developed the Shared Wireless Access Protocol (SWAP). SWAP is an industry specification that permits PCs, peripherals, cordless telephones and other devices to communicate voice and data without the usage of cables. It uses a dual protocol stack: DECT for voice, and 802.11 packets for data. It is robust, reliable, and minimizes the impact of radio interference. Its target applications are home networking, as well as remote control and automation.

Bluetooth

Bluetooth (Chiasserini, Marsan, Baralis, & Garza, 2003) is a high-speed, low-power microwave wireless link technology, designed to connect phones, laptops, PDAs and other portable equipment together with little or no work by the user. Unlike infrared, Bluetooth does not require line-of-sight positioning of connected units. The technology uses modifications of existing wireless LAN techniques but is most notable for its small size and low cost. Whenever any Bluetooth-enabled devices come within range of each other, they instantly transfer address information and establish small networks between each other, without the user being involved. To a large extent, Bluetooth have motivated the present WPAN attempts and conceptualizations; moreover, it constitutes the substance of the IEEE

Table 2. Bluetooth specifications

Frequency range	Modulation	Multiple access	Duplex	Channel bandwidth	Number of channels	Peak data rate
2402 MHz to 2480 MHz	GFSK	FHSS	TDD	1 MHz	79	723,2 kbit/s

802.15.1 WPAN standard. For reader reference, we are attaching general specifications in Table 2 for Bluetooth.

Bluetooth and 3G

Third-generation (3G) mobile telephony networks are also a familiar source of hype. They promise data rates of megabits per cell, as well as the "always on" connections that have proven to be quite valuable to DSL and cable modem customers. In spite of the hype and press from 3G equipment vendors, the rollout of commercial 3G services has been continually pushed back.

At the same time as 3G standards are being introduced, other air interfaces have been developed and standardized. First of all, Bluetooth is already available, enabling devices to communicate over short distances. The strength of Bluetooth is low power consumption and a design enabling low-cost implementations. Bluetooth was integrated into mobile phones, laptop computers, PDAs, and so forth. The first version of Bluetooth offers up to 700 kbps, but higher data rates, up to approximately 10 Mbps, are currently being standardized for later releases.

In contrast to Bluetooth and 3G, equipment based on the IEEE 802.11 standard has been an astounding success. While Bluetooth and 3G may be successful in the future, 802.11 is a success now. Apple initiated the pricing moves that caused the market for 802.11 equipment to explode in 1999. Price erosion made the equipment affordable and started the growth that continues today. IEEE

802.15 WPAN

802.15 is a communications specification that was approved in early 2002 by the Institute of Electrical and Electronics Engineers Standards Association (IEEE-SA) for wireless personal area networks (WPANs) (Chiasserini et al., 2003). The initial version, 802.15.1, was adapted from the Bluetooth specification and is fully compatible with Bluetooth 1.1.

The IEEE 802.15 Working Group proposes two general categories of 802.15, called TG4 (low rate) and TG3 (high rate). The TG4 version provides data speeds of 20 Kbps or 250 Kbps. The TG3 version supports data speeds ranging from 11 Mbps to 55 Mbps. Additional features include the use of up to 254 network devices, dynamic device addressing, support for devices in which latency is critical, full handshaking, security provisions, and power management. There will be 16 channels in the 2.4-GHz band, 10 channels in the 915-MHz band, and one channel in the 868-MHz band (HomeRF; Shiraishi, 1999).

The IEEE plans to refine the 802.15 specification to work with the specification and description language (SDL), particularly SDL-88, SDL-92, and SDL-2000 updates of the International Telecommunication Union (ITU) recommendation Z.100.

Figure 2. ZigBee standard stack definition

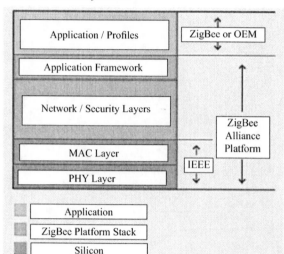

ZigBee

Wireless networks present colossal opportunities; at the same time, they are constrained by substantial development challenges. ZigBee™ provides standard-based solution for lightweight wireless networks based on the IEEE 802.15.4 (You, Park, Ju, Kwon, & Cho, 2001). Figure 2 provides clear elaboration for the ZigBee stack definition. While IEEE has defined the standards for MAC and PHY layers, the ZigBee™Alliance has added standards for network, security, and application layers.

Our readers may also refer to the general description Table 3 of ZigBee.

To conclude our section, a comparison in Table 4 among a set of frequently used personal wireless not working up to the standard is provided. This table states the standard bandwidth, power consumption, protocol stack size, stronghold, and finally draws preferred applications for each standard.

Applications and Services

Overview

The concept of mobile multimedia services was first introduced in 1992 when the ITU realized that mobile communications were playing an increasingly important role. It began

Table 3. ZigBee (IEEE 802.15.4) specifications

Frequency range	Modulation	Multiple access	Duplex	Channel bandwidth	Number of channels	Peak data rate
2.4 GHz to 2.4835 GHz (World) 902 MHz to 928 MHz (America) 868.3 MHz (Europe)	BPSK (868/915 MHz), OQPSK (2.4 GHz)	CSMA/ CA	TDD	5 MHz	1 (868 MHz) 10 (915 MHz) 16 (2.4 GHz)	20 kbit/s (868 MHz) 40 kbit/s (915 MHz) 250 kbit/s (2.4 GHz)

Table 4. Wireless technology comparison table

Standard	Bandwidth	Power Consumption	Protocol Stack Size	Stronghold	Applications
Wi-Fi	Up to 54Mbps	400+mA TX, standby 20mA	100+KB	High data rate	Internet browsing, PC networking, file transfers
Bluetooth	1Mbps	40mA TX, standby 0.2mA	~100+KB	Interoperability, cable replacement	Wireless USB, handset, headset
ZigBee	250kbps	30mA TX, standby 1uA	4"32KB	Long battery life, low cost	Remote control, battery-operated products, sensors

working on a project called *FPLMTS* (Future Public Land Mobile Telecommunications System) aiming to unite the world under a single standard.Given the fact, however, that this acronym is difficult to pronounce, it was subsequently renamed *International Mobile Telecommunications – 2000* (IMT-2000).

IMT-2000 is a single family of compatible standards defined by a set of ITU-R Recommendations. The main objectives for IMT-2000 are (UMTS Forum Report, 2000):

- high data rates, 144 Kbps/384 Kbps for high mobility users with full coverage and 2 Mbps for low mobility users with limited coverage,
- capability for multimedia application and all mobile applications,
- high spectrum efficiency compared to existing systems,
- high flexibility to introduce new services,
- high degree of commonality of design worldwide, and
- use of a small pocket terminal with seamless global roaming.

The main applications will not be on only traditional voice communications, but also on services such as e-mail, short messages, multimedia, simultaneous voice and data and the broadband integrated service digital network (B-ISDN) access (UMTS Forum Report, 2000). Although the PC has been the dominant Internet client, soon mobile phones and personal digital assistants (PDAs) will outnumber PCs and be the major source of Internet connections. With the third-generation (3G) network, mobile device users won't have to worry about bandwidth. People will access video on their phones as easily as they do on their PCs. In fact, the development of GSM Networks and terminals to support more advanced data bearer technologies has allowed the introduction of new exciting data services. These technologies allow a greater bandwidth and more capable execution environment permitting the development of mobile applications. The world has become increasingly computer centric, and computer applications are now used for a number of tasks such as communications, financial management, information retrieval, entertainment, and game playing.

It is a natural progression for the user to expect these applications to be available for them on their mobile terminal. The initial developments in mobile applications were basic, running on the GSM SIM Card using SIM toolkit interfacing through capable terminals and using SMS to communicate with the application infrastructure. These were followed by the introduction of browsers utilizing special mobile protocols (WAP, HDML, etc.) and the basic data capabilities of the GSM terminals of the time. These allow the user to use their mobile terminal to access basic text format content such as news, sport, entertainment, and information, among others.

The introduction of high bandwidth capability allows for richer applications, and the packet switched nature of GPRS networks allows for more efficient applications. They will smooth the progress of the introduction of true multimedia services such as multimedia messaging service (MMS) which will allow the user to send and receive messaging containing pictures, images, sound, and text. New network features, such as location servers, can allow the mobile applications to be improved to tailor the way they work, and improve the value to the user. Mobile commerce is the effective delivery of electronic commerce into the consumer's hand, anywhere, using wireless technology. This advance has the power to transform the mobile phone into a "mobile wallet." Already, major companies have begun to establish partnerships with banks, ticket agencies, and top brands to take benefit of the retail outlet in the consumer's hand.

Location based services provide personalized services to the subscriber based on their current position. Two categories of methods can be used to find the location of the subscriber: basic and advanced. Basic positioning methods are based on the information of the cell the subscriber is using (cell ID). This can be used alone, or together with other information available in the network such as timing advance and network measurement reports. This information is available for all handsets. Advanced techniques will be available in new handsets such as enhanced observed time difference and assisted GPS which uses the GSM network to help the reception of the freely available GPS system. The division of position technologies above is based on accuracy of the positioning method. Other factors also very important are for example complexity of the system, availability of the positioning technology in the network (e.g., assisted-GPS may not be available everywhere) and the investment needed on the network side and in handsets. Mobile video streaming is another application of whole big set of applications in field of mobile multimedia. The facts of high bit rate and smart phone availability will put a hundred of applications ongoing for mobile multimedia.

Last but not least, interesting new technology, the so-called mobile TV, has strongly emerged in the mobile multimedia field as taking breath and killer application. Interest in television services over cellular or broadband wireless networks is intensifying as operators seek a new and high margin application. Philips Semiconductors is predicting that, within a decade, the majority of its television chips will go into cell phones, not conventional television sets.

Classification of Services

Mobile multimedia services aim to combine the Internet, telephones, and broadcast media into a single device (UMTS Forum Report, 2000). To achieve this, IMT-2000 systems have been designed with six broad classes of service in mind. None of them are yet set in hardware but they are useful for regulators planning coverage and capacity, and perhaps for people buying terminals when they finally become available.

It's likely that 3G devices will be rated according to the types of service they can access, from a simple phone to a powerful computer. Three of the service classes are already present to some extent on 2G networks, while three more are new and involve mobile multimedia. In order of increasing data rate:

- **Voice:** Even in the age of high-speed data, this is still regarded as the "killer app" for the mobile market. 3G will offer call quality at least as good as the fixed telephone network, possibly with higher quality available at extra cost. Voicemail will also be standard and eventually integrated fully with email through computerized voice recognition and synthesis.

- **Messaging:** This is an extension of paging, combined with Internet e-mail. Unlike the text-only messaging services built into some 2G systems, 3G will allow email attachments. It can also be used for payment and electronic ticketing.

- **Switched data:** This includes faxing and dial-up access to corporate networks or the Internet. With always-on connections available, dial-up access ought to be obsolete, so this is mainly included to support legacy equipment. In 3G terms, legacy means any product that doesn't support a fully packet-switched network.

- **Medium multimedia:** This is likely to be the most popular 3G service. Its downstream data rate is ideal for Web surfing. Other applications include collaborative working, games, and location-based maps.

- **High multimedia:** This can be used for very high-speed Internet access, as well as for high-definition video and CD-quality audio on demand. Another possible application is online shopping for "intangible" products that can be delivered over the air; for example, music or a program for a mobile computer.

- **Interactive high multimedia:** This can be used for fairly high-quality videoconferencing or videophones, and for telepresence, a combination of videoconference and collaborative working.

The data rates of these services are shown in Table 1, together with their level of asymmetry and switching mode. These services refer to three basic levels by which these services are structured according to the dependencies among these services:

1. **Basic level services:** Those services form the building blocks of other more complex applications and services, such as voice messaging, data retrieval, video, and so forth, and can be used as stand-alone services or form the ingredients of higher level services and applications.

2. **Value added services:** Those services form the intermediate level services formed by one or more basic level services. VAS offer optimized functionality to suit the needs of diverse professional groups. Examples of such services are wireless home networking, high data rate PAN, high density networks, P2P communication collaboration, Internet/Intranet access, video conferencing, telemetry, location based services, payments, and UMS.

3. **High level applications:** Those address the specific requirements and interests of professional or consumer user groups. These are functionally stand-alone and serve the full range of user needs supporting services forms them. Examples can be business applications, transaction management, information applications, entertainment applications, telematics, construction, electronic healthcare, provision, e-government, e-learning, wireless home networking, and so on.

The above taxonomy refers to the functionality of the service and the group of users it targets. In the context of mobile multimedia, the basic level services refer to the collection, sharing and exchange of multimedia data, while the value added level refers to the provision and distribution of the multimedia information and the high level applications is concerned about the usage and consumption of the data.

The Future of Mobile Multimedia

Future generation mobile terminals will start to incorporate ubiquitous network functionality by efficiently dealing with a massive amount of communication modes and various multimedia applications. Further, these terminals will also need adaptive behavior to intelligently manage the computational resources that will be distributed and shared across the environing systems. Researchers should find integrated research platform aiming to resolve the fundamental technological issues for future mobile terminals allowing the true ubiquitous network environment to become a reality. Complexity, cost, power consumption, high throughput at low latency, and flexibility are the five primary hurdles in developing a mobile terminal.

In addition, many types of objects as well as people will have network functions and communicate with each other through networks. Therefore, different communication relationships such as person to person, machine to machine and mainly machine to person and vice versa, will determine mobile and wireless communications in the future.

Given the increasing demand for flexibility and individuality in society, the mean for the end-user might be assessed. Potentially, the value would be in the diversity of mobile applications, hidden from the complexity of the underlying communications schemes. This complexity would be absorbed into an intelligent personality management mechanism, which would learn and understand the needs of the user, and control the behavior of their reconfigurable and open wireless terminals accordingly in terms of application behavior and access to future support services.

In the future wireless service provision will be characterized by global mobile access (terminal and personal mobility), high quality of services (full coverage, intelligible, no drop and no/lower call blocking and latency), and easy and simple access to multimedia services for voice, data, messages, video, WWW, GPS, and so forth, via one user terminal.

End-to-end secured services will be fully coordinated via access control, authentic use of biometric sensors and/or smart card and mutual authentication, data integrity, and encryption. User added encryption feature for higher level of security will be part of the system.

Considering how second-generation systems have evolved by adding more and more system capabilities and enhancements to make them resemble the capabilities of 3G systems; it is possible that with third-generation systems there may be a continuum of enhancements that will render those systems practically indistinguishable from future generation systems. Indeed, it is expected that it will be more difficult to identify distinct generation gaps, and such a distinction may only be possible by looking back at some point in the future.

Progress has also been made in the development of other signal processing techniques and concepts for use in tomorrow's wireless systems. These include smart antennas and diversity techniques, better receivers, and hand over and power control algorithms with higher performance (Bi, Zysman, & Menkes, 2001).

Acknowledgments

The authors of this chapter would like to express their heartfelt thanks to Huang Hsin-Yi and Lin Yu-Hua (Monica) for their proofreading our chapter.

References

Bi, Q., Zysman, G.I., & Menkes, H. (2001). Wireless mobile communications at the start of the 21st century. *IEEE Communications Magazine,* 110-116.

Blair, G.S., Coulson, G., Davies, N., Robin, P., & Fitzpatrick, T. (1997). Adaptive middleware for mobile multimedia applications. In *Proceedings of the 7th International Conference on Network and Operating System Support for Digital Audio and Video (Nossdav '97),* St Louis, Missouri (pp. 259-273)

Brown, M.G., & Syfrig, H. (1996). Follow-me-video in a distributed computing environment. In the *Proceedings of the 3rd International Workshop on Mobile Multimedia Communications.* Princeton, NJ: Plenum Publishers.

Bruno, R., Conti, M., & Gregori, E. (2001). WLAN technologies for mobile ad hoc networks. In *Proceedings of the 34th Hawaii International Conference on System Sciences.*

Bull, D., Canagarajah, N., & Nix, A. (1999). *EEE Communications Magazine, 39*(2).

Chiasserini, C.F., Marsan, M.A., Baralis, E., & Garza, P. (2003). Towards feasible topology formation algorithms for Bluetooth-based WPAN's. In *Proceedings of the 36ᵗʰ Annual Hawaii International Conference on System Sciences.*

Collins, D., & Smith, C. (2001). *3G wireless networks.* McGraw-Hill Professional.

Dixit, S., Guo, Y., & Antoniou, Z. (2001). Resource management and quality of service in third generation wireless network. *IEEE Communication Magazine, 39*(2).

Dornan, A. (2000). *The essential guide to wireless communications applications: From cellular systems to WAP and m-commerce.* Prentice Hall PTR.

Ephremides, A., et al. (2000). *Wireless technologies and information networks.* International Technology Research Institute, World Technology (WTEC) Division, WTEC Panel Report.

Fabri, S.N., Worrall, S.T., & Kondoz, A.M. (2000). Video communications over mobile networks. *Communicate 2000*, Online Conference, London.

Fasbender, A., & Reichert, F. (1999). Any network, any terminal, anywhere. *IEEE Personal Communications*, 22-29.

Ferro, E., & Potorti, F. (2005). Bluetooth and Wi-Fi wireless protocols: A survey and a comparison. *Wireless Communications, 12*(1), 12-26.

Flament, M., et al. (1999). An approach to 4ᵗʰ generation wireless infrastructures: Scenarios and key research issues. *IEEE VTC 99*, Houston, TX.

Frodigh, M., Parkvall, S., Roobol, C., Johansson, P., & Larsson, P. (2001). Future generation wireless networks, *IEEE Personal Communications.*

Ghavami, M., Michael, L.B., & Kohno, R. (2005). Ultra wideband signals and systems in communications engineering, *Electronics Letters, 41*(25).

Ghosh, A., et al. (2005). Broadband wireless access with WiMax=802.16: Current performance benchmarks and future potential. *IEEE Commun.Mag., 43*(2), 129-136.

Giuliano, R., & Mazzenga, F. (2005). On the coexistence of power-controlled ultrawideband systems with UMTS, GPS, DCS 1800, and fixed wireless systems, *IEEE Trans. Veh. Technol., 54*(1), 62-81.

Hamalainen, M., et al. (2002). On the UWB system coexistence with GSM900, UMTS=WCDMA, and GPS, *IEEE J. Sel. Areas Commun., 20*(9), 1712-1721.

Hole, K.J., Dyrnes, E., & Thorsheim, P. (2005). Securing Wi-Fi networks. *Computer, 38*(7), 28-34.

IEEE 802.11 (1999). *Local and metropolitan area networks: Wireless LAN medium access control (MAC) and physical specifications.* ISO/IEC 8802-11:1999

Robertson, M.G., Hansen, S.V., Sorenson, F.E., & Knutson, C.D. (2001). Modeling IrDA performance: The effect of IrLAP negotiation parameters on throughput. *Proceedings of the 10ᵗʰ International Conference on Computer Communications and Networks* (pp. 122-127).

Shiraishi, Y. (1999). Communication network: Now and in future. *OKI Technical Review*, Issue 162, *65*(3).

Stallings, W. (2001). *Wireless communications and networks.* Prentice Hall.

UMTS Forum Report No. 10 (2000). *Shaping the mobile multimedia future.*

UMTS Forum Report No. 11 (2000). *Enabling UMTS Third Generation Services and Applications.*

UMTS Forum Report No. 3 (1998). *The impact of license cost levels on the UMTS business case.*

UMTS Forum Report No. 4 (1998). *Considerations of licensing conditions for UMTS network operations.*

UMTS Forum Report No. 9 (2000). *The UMTS third generation market: Structuring the service revenue opportunities.*

Vaughan-Nichols, S.J. (2003). The challenge of Wi-Fi roaming, *Computer, 36*(7), 17-19.

Vaughan-Nichols, S.J. (2004). Achieving wireless broadband with Wi-Max. *IEEE Computer, 37*(6), 10-13.

Veerakachen, W., Pongsanguansin, P., & Sanguanpong, K. (1999). Air interface schemes for IMT-2000. *NECTEC Technical Journal, 1*(1).

Vitsas, V., & Boucouvalas, A.C. (2002). IrDA IrLAP protocol performance and optimum link layer parameters for maximum throughput, *Global Telecommunications Conference, 2002. GLOBECOM'02, 3,* 2270-2275.

Vitsas, V., & Boucouvalas, A.C. (2003). Optimization of IrDA IrLAP link access protocol. *IEEE Transactions on Wireless Communications, 2*(5), 926-938.

Williams, S. (2000). IrDA: Past, present and future. *Personal Communications, 7*(1), 11-19.

You, Y.-H., Park, C.-H., Ju, M.-C., Kwon, K.-W. & Cho, J.-W. (2001). Adaptive frequency hopping scheme for interference-limited WPAN applications. *Electronics Letters, 37*(15), 976-978.

Chapter VII

Mobile Information Systems in a Hospital Organization Setting

Agustinus Borgy Waluyo, Monash University, Australia

David Taniar, Monash University, Australia

Bala Srinivasan, Monash University, Australia

Abstract

The emerging of wireless computing motivates radical changes of how information is obtained. Our paper discusses a practical realisation of an application using push and pull based mechanism in a wireless ad-hoc environment. We use a hospital information system as a case study scenario for our proposed application. The pull mechanism is initiated from doctors as mobile client to retrieve and update patient records in the central database server. The push mechanism is initiated from the server without a specific request from the doctors. The application of push mechanism includes sending a message from central server to a specific doctor, and multicasting a global message to all doctors connected to the server application. The global message can be disabled by each doctor to perform selective recipients.

Introduction

Recent advances in wireless technology have led to mobile computing, a new dimension in data communication and processing. Many predict a new emerging, gigantic market with millions of mobile users carrying a small, battery-powered terminal equipped with wireless connection (Acharya, Alonso, Franklin, & Zdonik, 1995; Barbara, 1999; Imielinski & Viswanathan, 1994). The main properties of mobile computing include mobility, severe power and storage restriction, frequency of disconnection is much greater than in a traditional network, bandwidth capacity, and asymmetric communications costs. Radio wireless transmission usually requires approximately 10 times more power as compared to the reception operation (Zaslavsky & Tari, 1998).

There are two ways of data delivery in wireless environment. One is called *pull* mechanism, and the other is *push* mechanism (Aksoy et al., 1999). In this paper, we apply these two mechanisms in a wireless ad-hoc environment. We use hospital information system as a case study scenario to show the effective uses of the mechanisms. The hospital information system relates to doctors as the principal clients to a server application. Pull mechanism refers to data delivery on a demand basis. In the hospital information system, we apply this mechanism for doctors to retrieve his/her patients. Once the patient has been diagnosed, doctors can update the record in the database. In push mechanism, the server initiates the delivery of data without a specific request from the client. We apply this mechanism to send a direct message to a specific doctor, and to distribute information to all or selective doctors such as news bulletin. The information or message is sent from central server.

Push mechanism can be categorized into 1-1 (unicast) and 1-N (multicast/broadcast) communication type. Unicast communication involves a server and a client, and the data is sent from the server to the client. 1-N communication can be either multicast or broadcast mode. In multicast mode, the recipients are known and the data are delivered only to those recipients, for example; the information is delivered to doctors and nurses that are registered in a specific domain. On the contrary, the broadcast mode simply sent the data without knowing the number of clients who might receive the data. This paper concerns with 1-N (multicast mode) communication type.

Push-based data dissemination approaches can be performed in aperiodic or periodic manner (Franklin & Zdonik, 1997). Aperiodic data dissemination is event-driven; whereas, periodic data dissemination adheres to a pre-defined schedule. An example of aperiodic push-based event is when the central administrator sends an urgent message to a specific doctor in the hospital. In contrast, periodic push-based transmission is managed by an automated server program transmitting data (or information) according to a pre-defined schedule such as, distribution of news bulletin to doctors in every hour or so.

The advantage of push mechanism over pull mechanism is that query performance is not overwhelmed by multiple client requests. Push mechanism avoid the possibility of congested channel bandwidth and server queue causes by increase of number of clients, request arrival rate, and overlap in user"s requests. The congested channel and server queue may severely affect the power consumption of mobile clients. Figure 1 illustrates the push and pull mechanism.

This application will demonstrate the usability of wireless networks, and improve the mobility of doctors through wireless data dissemination. The subsequent sections in this paper

Figure 1. The pull and push mechanism

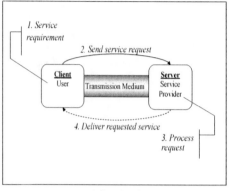 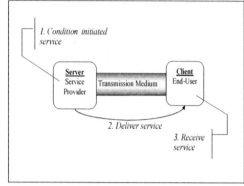

(a) Pull Mechanism   (b) Push Mechanism

are organized as follows. The following section provides the infrastructure of push and pull wireless information system. The next section describes the client and server processes in the system. It is then followed by the development of push and pull wireless information system in a hospital environment. Finally, the last section concludes the paper.

Push and Pull Mobile
Information Systems: Infrastructure

In this section, we describe the infrastructure of a push and pull wireless information system. We use the hospital information system scenario for implementation purposes. This section includes design overview, technology aspect, database aspect, server, and client model. The model is designed to realize and to demonstrate pull-based and push-based approaches for data dissemination.

Design Overview

The proposed model comprises of three specific components. The three components are: (1) a data source, (2) a server application, and (3) a client application. The data source component is a simple Microsoft Access® database. The proposed model intends to retrieve information from the database for pull-based and push-based communications. All pull-based and push-based communications are routed through a server component. The data source and server components are located on the same server device. The server component is an application that functions as a mediator between the data source and client application. The client application accepts push-based information from the server; or the client can create requests for processing (by the server application). The client component does not access

Figure 2. Proposed model

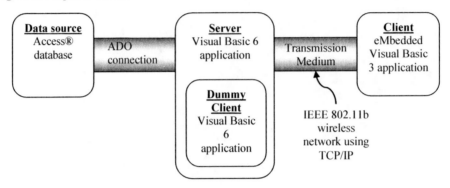

the data source directly. The diagram shown in Figure 2 illustrates the three components of the test application.

The client application is required to connect to the server application. This is a necessary requirement for two-way communication between the server and the client. Without an initial connection, communication between the server and client is impossible. The connection over the TCP/IP network is created via the Winsock controls on both the server and client application. The Winsock control allows for both pull-based and push-based communications. A dummy client application is located within the server application.

The dummy client application mimics the client component of the proposed model. The purpose of the dummy client is to enable multi-client experimentation. Since the client application is located on a Personal Digital Assistant, the dummy client application enables multi-client experimentation without the exorbitant cost of procuring multiple PDAs.

The database utilized by the application comprises of three related tables. The three tables are titled *Doctors*, *Patients*, and *Remote*. The Doctors table stores records of doctors employed by the hospital. The Patients table stores records of patient details; including the doctor assigned to care for the patient. Finally, the Remote table stores a list of IP addresses. Each IP address stored in the Remote table is assigned to a doctor. The diagram shown in Figure 3 depicts the relationship between the three tables.

It indicates that there is a one-to-many relationship between the records in the Doctors table and the records in the Patients table. This relationship implies that each record in the Patients table can have one associated doctor; but each record in the Doctors table can be assigned to several patient records. Basically, a patient can be cared by one doctor only; but a doctor can care for several patients.

Furthermore, it also indicates that there is a one-to-many relationship between the records in the Doctors table and the records in the Remote table. This relationship implies that each record in the Remote table can have one associated doctor; but each record in the Doctors table can be assigned to several records in the Remote table. However, assigning a doctor to multiple records in the Remote table is ill-advised. The purpose of the Remote table is to separate network-related information from the Doctors table. The desired relationship

Figure 3. Table relationships for hospital database

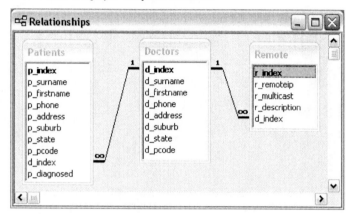

between the Doctors and Remote table is a one-to-one relationship. Hence, each doctor in the Doctors table is assigned one (and only one) IP address from the Remote table. Furthermore, the Remote table acts as a quasi-subscription table to track all remote client devices.

Technology

The hardware technology we use is a computer as the server side, and pocket PC-based personal digital assistant (PDA) as the client device. Hewlett Packard iPAQ™ H5450 Pocket PC is the type of PDA that we use. The PDA communicates with the server device over a wireless LAN. Since the transmission medium is wireless, the nominated wireless transmission standard is 802.11b. Figure 4 illustrates the communication architecture of client and server model.

As for the software technology, we utilize Microsoft® WindowsTM 2000 for operating system software for the server device, and Microsoft® Pocket PC 2002 for the client system software. Furthermore, Microsoft® Pocket PC 2002 also features a set of network-related services required by the proposed model. Two software development products that we employee are Microsoft® Visual Basic® 6.0 and Microsoft® eMbedded Visual Basic® 3.0.Microsoft® eMbedded Visual Basic® 3.0 is an object-oriented/event-driven high-level programming language. It is similar to Microsoft® Visual Basic® 6.0; except, it is a software component that enables Visual Basic® 6.0 applications to connect to various data sources such as a Microsoft® Access®2002 database to perform search and update functions.

The service device and the PDA both use 802.11b to create a wireless ad-hoc network (Blake, 2002). The TCP/IP protocols are used to manage the transmission of messages between the server device and client device over the 802.11b wireless network. TCP/IP is a necessity on the server device and client device because the two software development programs use a control called Winsock (Zak, 1999). The Winsock control is added to both the server application and client application at design time. This enables the server application and client application to communicate messages over a TCP/IP network.

Figure 4. Communication architecture

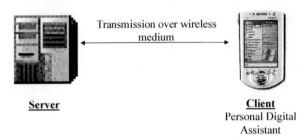

Server

Client
Personal Digital
Assistant

Figure 5. Push-based application: (a) Sending a message from server to client; (b) multi-casting information from server to client(s)

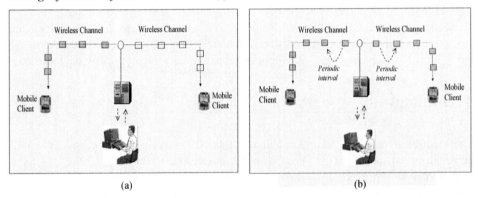

(a)   (b)

Server

The server is designed to perform push-based mechanism. We classify the application into two categories, one is sending a message from server to client, and second is multicasting information from server to client(s).

In Figure 5, we assume a database is attached in the central server. Figure 5 (a) illustrates a situation when a message is sent from server to a specific doctor in the network but first the central server needs to connect to the database and check the available doctors. Figure 5 (b) depicts a scenario when the message are multicast to all doctors in the network periodically. In this case, the server not only checks the doctors in the network but also checks whether the doctor is interested in receiving the global message, and selectively send the message to the interested recipient in the list.

Figure 6. Pull-based application

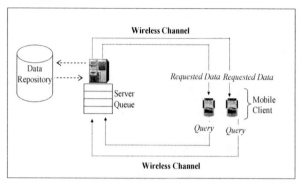

Client

Mobile client application is expected to perform pull-based mechanism. In this paper we designed the doctors as mobile client to be able to conduct conventional patient information retrieval via wireless channel as illustrated in Figure 6, as well as updating the content of the database.

Server and Client Processes in Push and Pull Mobile Information Systems

In this section, we describe the underlying concept of server and client processes in the wireless hospital information system. These processes explain the main functions for both server and client application in the system.

Server Processes

There are four important functions of the server application. The four functions cover: (1) how the server accept and close connection from client; (2) how the server processes messages sent by the client; (3) how the server retrieves information from the database; and (4) how the server handles client messages or requests.

Accepting and Closing Connections

Whenever a remote client requests a connection, the connection request event procedure of the Winsock control is executed. Firstly, the event procedure checks if the connection request

Figure 7. Connection identifier lngConnection

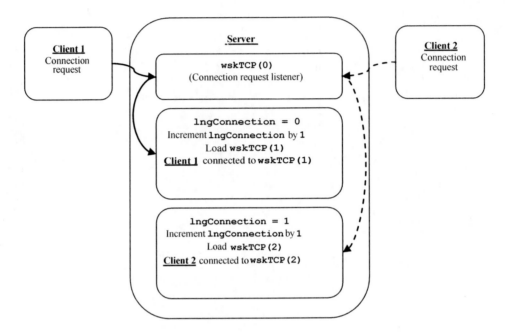

resulted from the Winsock listener control wskTCP(0). The event procedure then uses the form-level variables (declared in general declarations) to label the connection and to track the number of connections. With each incoming connection request, the counter lngCounter and connection identifier lngConnection are both incremented by the value of one. The new value of the connection identifier lngConnection is assigned to each new connection. A new Winsock control is created and loaded according to the connection identifier lngConnection. The following diagram shown in Figure 7 illustrates how the connection identifier is used to identify each new connection.

The connection request event procedure also resizes the arrays strRetrieveBuffer(), strData(), and strRemoteHostIP() to provide storage spaces for new connections. The first two arrays are used as storage spaces for incoming data received from pull-based interactions, whereas the last array is used to store the IP address of the remote client device. The size of the three arrays is determined by the value of lngConnection, which acts as a maxima value for the number of connections and hence the size of each array needs to be the sized (or resized). The following diagram shown in Figure 8 depicts the resizing of the three arrays.

Finally, the connection request event procedure checks if the value of lngCounter is greater than zero. If it is greater than zero, then the button that executes a Push-based data transmission is enabled.

When a remote client attempts to disconnect from the server application, the Winsock close event procedure is executed. The event procedure receives an Index value, which is the same as the connection identifier. By passing the connection identifier through the parameter

Figure 8. Re-sizing arrays strRetrieveBuffer(), strData(), and strRemoteHostIP()

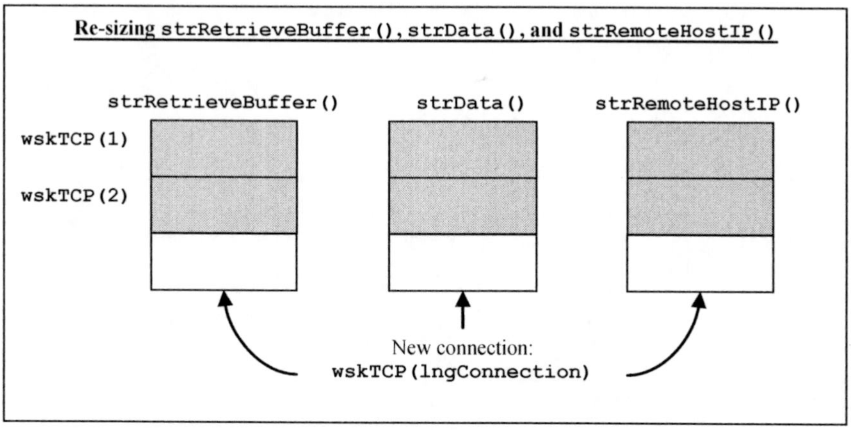

Index, the event procedure is able to discern which connection is being closed. When the connection is closed, the Winsock control is also unloaded.

The event procedure also checks the value of the form-level variable lngCounter to determine if there are any remaining connections. If lngCounter is zero, then the button that executes a push-based data transmission is disabled.

Processing a Message

A timer event periodically checks the strData() array for any unprocessed data. If the array is not empty, then the event procedure calls the processData() subroutine to process the array. A loop is employed to cycle through all clients connected to the server application. A second (nested) loop is used to process the contents of the array. Figure 9 depicts the logic used to determine whether the array is empty; or if any further processing is required.

The processData() subroutine processes the data in the array strData() based on the value passed by its parameter Index, which accepts a value from the connection identifier lngConnection. The subroutine uses the Index value to perform a search on the array.

The data extracted by the subroutine can be a SQL query string or a special keyword. Given that the extracted data is a SQL query string, the subroutine passes the data to another subroutine for further processing. The subroutine retrieveRecord() accepts a SQL query string. This subroutine uses the SQL query string to connect to the database, search the database to obtain relevant results, and to return the results to the client.

Finally, the extracted data is removed from the array and any remaining data is shifted to the start of the array. The unprocessed data in is left for future processing. Figure 10 illustrates the processData() subroutine as it processes data in strData()array.

Figure 9. Message array processing

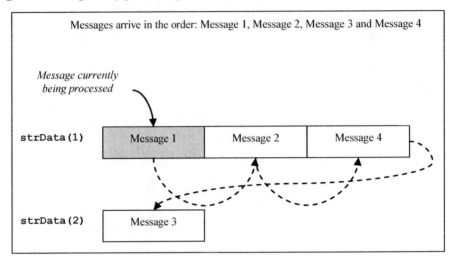

Figure 10. Example data processing subroutine

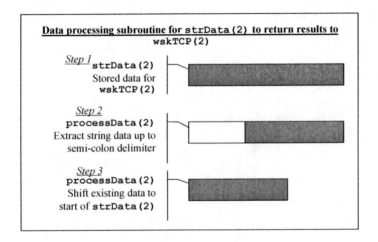

Retrieves Information from Database

The retrieval of records from the database is performed by the generic subroutine retrieveRecord(), which is executed by numerous event procedures in the server application. The subroutine accepts two parameters: SQLString and Index. The parameter SQLString passes a SQL query string that is used to search the database. The subroutine also creates a Recordset object by using the form-level connection string and the parameter SQLString to create a local copy of the records returned by the query in SQLString.

The subroutine first checks if the Recordset object returns any records. If no records are returned, the subroutine is terminated. Otherwise, the subroutine sends the message to the appropriate client based on the value of Index. Before the subroutine ends, a timer event is started for a brief period delay. This is a necessary step to allow the SendData method of the Winsock control to execute correctly. A peculiarity in the Winsock control necessitates a delay prior to the end of the subroutine.

Handles a Message or Request

The server application accommodates traditional pull-based interactions by accepting messages from remote client devices via the Winsock data arrival event procedure. The data arrival event procedure is only triggered when the data buffer is not empty. This condition is met when data arrives from any remote client. To determine which Winsock control triggered the data arrival event procedure, an Index value, which is representative of the connection identifier lngConnection is passed as a parameter in the wskTCP_DataArrival() event procedure. For example, an Index value of two refers to the connection assigned by lngConnection; and is the Winsock control wskTCP(2).

To retrieve the buffered data, the GetData method for the corresponding Winsock control is used to retrieve the buffered data. The buffered data is a string value, and is placed into temporary storage in the strRetrieveBuffer() array. The data is then immediately appended into the strData() array. This step is necessary because the GetData method does not append

Figure 11. Data buffering process

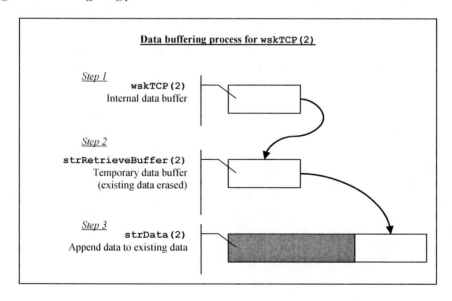

data, it instead overwrites the data in strRetrieveBuffer(). If the GetData method is executed for wskTCP(2), the buffered data is then placed into the array strRetrieveBuffer(2) in position 2. The data in strRetrieveBuffer(2) is subsequently appended into strData(2). Figure 11 illustrates the steps taken to transfer buffered data into strData().

The retrieval of the buffered data into the strData() essentially queues the data for processing. The queue size is finite at approximately two billion characters (the maximum allowable string length in the Microsoft® Visual Basic 6.0) (Zak, 1999). The size of the strData() array is determined by the highest value of connection identifier lngConnection. The wskTCP_ DataArrival() event procedure is triggered for any client sending a message to the server. To individualise each message for each connection, the two string arrays strRetrieveBufer() and strData() are used to store the messages received by the server. This ensures that a message sent by wskTCP(1) does not overwrite a message sent by wskTCP(2).

Client Processes

The tasks performed by client application include a situation when: (1) the client attempts to connect or disconnect from the server application; (2) the client attempts to send a message to the server application; and (3) the client application receives a message from the server. It is followed by brief description of using keywords and delimiters for data processing

Creating and Closing Connections

To connect to the server application, the client application provides a command button cmdConnect. The event procedure connects the Winsock CE control wskTCP. The Connect method uses the initialized Winsock properties in the form load event procedure (namely Protocol, RemoteHost and RemotePort) to connect to the server application.

Upon connection, the command button cmdConnect is disabled. This step is necessary to prevent the client from performing a second connection attempt while the first attempt is in progress. If the server application is terminated, then the connection to the client is also terminated. The Winsock CE control closes the connection when the server application closed. The client application uses the cmdDisconnect command button to close the connection, and to enable and disable appropriate buttons and controls.

Sending a Message

When the client application is connected to the server application, the client application can send data by using the SendData method of the Winsock CE control wskTCP. A command button is provided to generate a pull-based interaction with the server. A SQL query string is stored in a local variable strQuery. The contents of strQuery are sent to the server application by calling the SendData method of wskTCP. The server accepts the string for processing and returns relevant results.

Alternatively, the client can communicate with the server application by sending keywords to prompt the server to perform some form of maintenance action to the database. There is another event procedure prompts the server application to enable or disable the multicasting of data from the server.

Receiving a Message

When the client application receives data from the server, the Data Arrival event procedure of the Winsock CE control wskTCP is triggered. This may be the result of a pull-based or push-based interaction between the client and the server. The data received from the server is retrieved using the GetData method of the Winsock CE control wskTCP. The data is immediately assigned to the text box txtOutput for display on the client screen.

Using Keywords and Delimiters for Data Processing

Keywords are special words used to distinguish different messages sent between the server and client application. Keywords are amended to the beginning of every message. This is true for messages sent by the server application; and for messages sent by the client application. Therefore, the message construct is as follows: (1) the keyword is placed at the beginning of the message; followed by; (2) a colon delimiter value; then (3) the message contents; and finally (4) a semi-colon as the end-of-message delimiter. The following diagram shown in Figure 12 graphically demonstrates the message construct.

The algorithm employed by the data processing subroutines in both the server application and client application are identical. Each data processing subroutine retrieves and parses the message. The first step is to determine the nature of the message. This is achieved by inspecting the value of the keyword. By inspecting the value of the keyword, each data processing subroutine is then able to act appropriately on the message contents.

Figure 12. Message construct

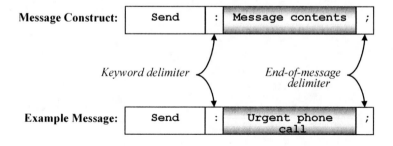

Push and Pull Mobile Information System in a Hospital Environment

In this section, the infrastructure and processes will be put to use in a wireless hospital information system. The system focuses on doctors as the principal clients to a server application. In terms of data dissemination, the application aims to demonstrate two uses of pull-based communications and two uses of push-based communications. The four techniques for demonstrating the dissemination of data are as follows: (1) a pull-based event to retrieve information from a database; (2) a pull-based event to update information in the database; (3) a push-based event to send a simple message to a client; and (4) a push-based event to multicast information to all clients, as well as to multicast information to selective clients.

Server

The server application form comprises of: a command button entitled "*Send Message*"; two text boxes; one list box; three timers; a Winsock control; a Common Dialog control; and a menu item "*New → Client*." The image shown in Figure 13 depicts the server form during design time. When the server application is executed, the image in Figure 14 is displayed.

The server application responds to four human-generated events: opening a dummy client, sending a message to a specific doctor, multicasting a global message to all doctors connected to the server application, and closing the server application. The command button "*Send Message*" is used to send a message to a specific doctor selected from the list box. The list box is populated when a doctor (or doctors) connects to server application.

Figure 13. Server form at design time

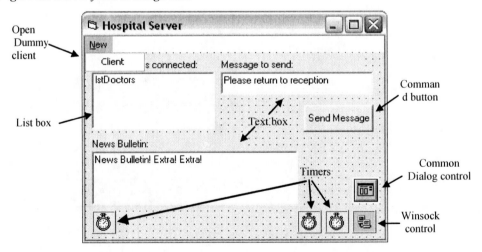

Figure 14. Server form at runtime

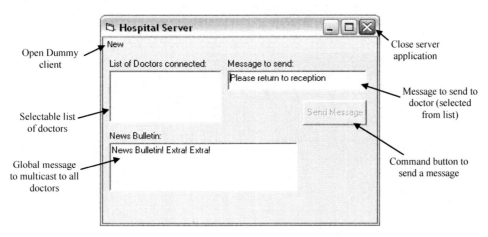

Open Dummy client

Selectable list of doctors

Global message to multicast to all doctors

Close server application

Message to send to doctor (selected from list)

Command button to send a message

The "*Send Message*" command button is only enabled when at least one doctor is connected to the server application. Finally, the text box labeled "*News Bulletin*" is used to multicast a global message to all doctors connected to the server application.

Although the server application form is visually sparse, the server application also performs several additional functions. Some functions require human intervention; while other functions do not require human intervention.

Sending a Message from Server to Client

Whenever a doctor connects to the server, a list of all doctors currently connected is displayed on the server application. This is shown in Figure 15. The list is created or updated whenever a doctor connects or disconnects from the server application. When a doctor attempts to connect the server, a connection request is sent via Winsock Connection Request. It will then create a connection for each connection request; and adds the details of the doctor to the list.

To send a message to the client, the server operator simply: selects the desired client from the list; types the desired message into the "*Message to send*" text box; and clicks "*Send Message.*" This is shown in Figure 16.

When the server operator clicks the "*Send Message*" button, the event procedure cmdSend-Message_Click() is triggered. The code segment for the cmdSendMessage_Click() event procedure is shown in Figure 17. The selected doctor in the list box is evaluated to determine the necessary connection identifier value required by the Winsock control wskTCP. The event procedure searches for a specific value—the delimiter value ":". The number preceding the delimiter is the connection identifier value required by the Winsock control wskTCP. Using Figure 16, the event procedure extracts the value of 1 from the selected doctor.

Figure 15. One client connected to the server

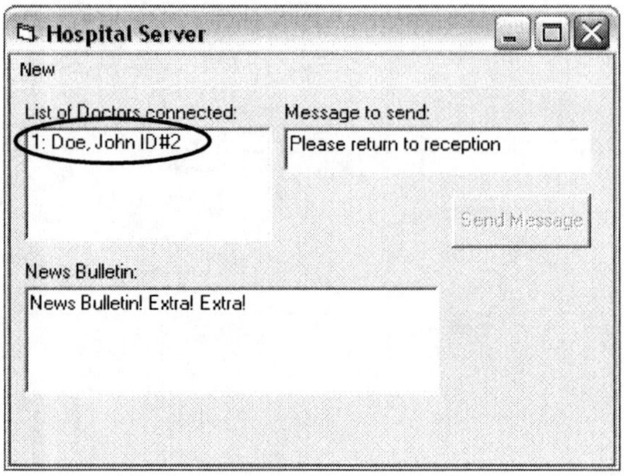

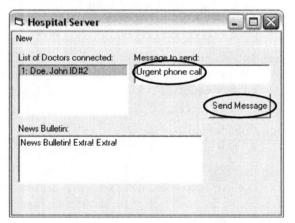

Figure 16. Sending a message from server to client

The Winsock control wskTCP uses the connection identifier value and the SendData method to send a message to the correct doctor. The cmdSendMessage_Click() event procedure retrieves the text message in the "*Message to send*" text box and amends prefix "Send:" keyword and an end-of-message delimiter ";".The complete message as shown in Figure 16 is: Send:Urgent phone call;. Therefore, the complete command to send a message to the selected doctor is: wskTCP(1).SendData "Send:Urgent phone call;". Since the message originates from the server application, the transmission is push-based.

When the client application receives a message, the entire message is processed to determine the nature of the message. The keyword Send is utilised by the client application to identify

Figure 17. The "Send Message" button event procedure

```
Private Sub cmdSendMessage_Click()

  '** Notes:
  '** - This buttons sends the contents of txtMessage to selected Doctor.
  '** - The message is appended to the keyword "Send:".
  '** - A semi-colon is used to mark the end of the message.

    'Declare local string variable for storing the Connection Identifier.
    Dim strIndex As String

    'Determine the Connection Identifier from the list.
    'The Connection Identifier is the numeric value preceding the colon.
    strIndex = Mid(lstDoctors.List(lstDoctors.ListIndex), 1, _
    InStr(lstDoctors.List(lstDoctors.ListIndex), ":") - 1)

    'Send the contents of txtMessage to the selected client.
    wskTCP(strIndex).SendData "Send:" & txtMessage.Text & ";"

End Sub
```

Figure 18.Result of sending message at client side

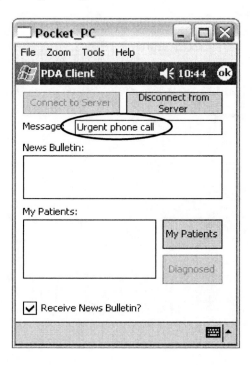

the nature of the message. The processData() subroutine in the client application searches for a keyword in the message and determines that Send is the keyword. The processData() subroutine extracts the message and displays it to the "*Message*" text box on the client application. The image shown in Figure 18 demonstrates the result of the server application sending a message to the client application.

Multicasting Information from Server to Client(s)

The server application automatically sends a news bulletin to each doctor connected to the server. The server application uses a timer to periodically send the news bulletin to each doctor every 25 seconds. Whenever a client connects to the server application, the IP address of the client is stored in a form-level string array on the server application. The server application determines which clients are the recipients of the news bulletin by comparing the values stored in strRemoteHostIP() to the r_remoteip field in the *Remote* table. Furthermore, the server application also determines if the doctor wishes to receive a copy of the news bulletin.

Figure 19. Remote table and the fields used for multicasting the news bulletin

r_index	r_remoteip	r_multicast	r_description	d_index
1	192.168.0.2	☑	HP iPaq	2
2	10.0.0.50	☑	PC	1
3	10.0.0.100	☑	Laptop	3
(AutoNumber)		▨		0

Record: ◄ ◄ 1 ► ►◄ ►* of 3

Figure 20. The "Send Bulletin" timer event procedure

```
Private Sub tmrSendBulletin_Timer()
On Error Resume Next

'** Notes:
'** - This timer event auto-sends the news bulletin to all clients
'**   that have 'r_multicast' field set to True in Remote table.
'** - The news bulletin is the contents of txtNewsBulletin.
'** - The message is appended to the keyword "NewsBulletin:".
'** - A semi-colon is used to mark the end of the message.
'** - The 'r_multicast' field from 'Remote' table is matched to a
'**   string array strRemoteHostIP()
'** - The string array strRemoteHostIP() stores the IP address of
'**   currently-connected clients.
'** - This is an automatic 'Push' event that triggers depending
'**   on the time interval set.
```

Figure 20. continued

```
'** - Interval currently set to 25 seconds.

'Declare local rst object for ADO Recordset and local variables.
 Dim rst As ADODB.Recordset
 Dim strQuery As String
 Dim i As Integer

 i = 0

'Set rst object variable as ADO.Recordset object
 Set rst = New ADODB.Recordset

'Retrieve records from the remote table.
 strQuery = "SELECT * FROM remote;"

'Open the Recordset based on strQuery using global Connection
'String cnn.
 rst.Open strQuery, cnn, adOpenStatic, adLockReadOnly

'Check to see if the RecordCount is 0.
 If rst.RecordCount = 0 Then
     'If it is 0, exit this subroutine.
     Exit Sub

 Else

     'Otherwise, move to the first record.
     rst.MoveFirst

     'Move through the Recordset rst from first record to last record.
     Do While Not rst.EOF

         'Send to all clients connected and when lngCounter > 0.
         For i = 1 To lngConnection And lngCounter > 0

             'On Error Resume Next used to avoid situations where
             'i for Connection Identifier is a non-existent value.
             'This may occur when a client manually disconnects.

             'Call retrieveRecord if the value of 'r_multicast'
             'matches the strRemoteHostIP for the value i.
             If rst!r_multicast = True And _
             rst!r_remoteip = strRemoteHostIP(i) Then

                 'Send the contents of txtNewsBulletin to the
                 'clients that require the News Bulletin.
                 wskTCP(i).SendData "NewsBulletin:" _
                 & txtNewsBulletin.Text & ";"

             End If
```

This is determined by the r_multicast field in the *Remote* table. If the checkbox field in r_multicast is checked, then the doctor requires a copy of the news bulletin. The image shown in Figure 19 depicts the table and fields used by the server application.

When the timer interval expires, the timer event procedure tmrSendBulletin_Timer() is triggered. Figure 20 depicts the event procedure that is executed every 25 seconds. The

Figure 21. Sending a news bulletin to doctors connected to the server application

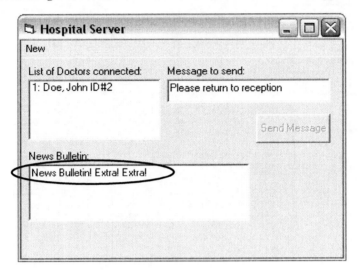

Figure 22. Result of sending the news bulletin

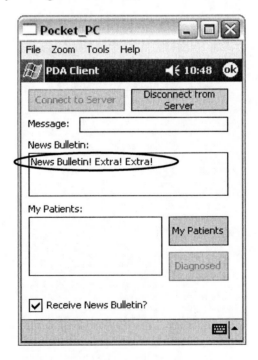

event procedure performs a check to determine which doctors require a copy of the news bulletin.

If a match is determined, the event procedure retrieves the text message in the "*News Bulletin*" text box. The text message is then amended with the prefix "NewsBulletin:" keyword and an end-of-message delimiter ";". Figure 21 shows an image when the server sends a news bulletin to doctors, complete message is: NewsBulletin:News Bulletin! Extra! Extra!;. The news bulletin is then sent to each client that requires a copy of the news bulletin.

To modify the contents of the news bulletin, the server operator simply changes the text in the "*News Bulletin*" text box. When the 25 second interval expires, the new contents of the "*News Bulletin*" text box are sent to each doctor who requires a copy of the news bulletin. When the client application receives a message, the entire message is processed to determine the nature of the message. The keyword NewsBulletin is utilised by the client application to identify the nature of the message. The processData() subroutine in the client application searches for a keyword in the message and determines that NewsBulletin is the keyword. The processData() subroutine extracts the message and displays it to the "*News Bulletin*" box on the client application. The image shown in Figure 22 demonstrates the result of the server application sending a message to the client application.

The client can enable or disable the automatic sending of the news bulletin by selecting or de-selecting the check box marked "*Receive News Bulletin?*" Figure 23 illustrates this feature. Once the record is located, the value is set to True or False for BulletinYes and BulletinNo respectively. The image shown in Figure 24 highlights the fields that is updated as a result of select or deselect the bulletin check box

Clicking the "*Receive News Bulletin*" check box triggers the chkSelectiveMulticast_Click() event procedure to send a message to the server application. The message contains a keyword. The keyword is either BulletinYes or BulletinNo. The keyword is amended with suffix ":;". The colon delimiter is used by the processData() subroutine on the server application to determine the nature of the message. The semi-colon delimiter is used to mark the end of the message. Figure 25 depicts the code segment of the client application used to send the keyword to enable or disable the sending of the news bulletin.

The server application receives the message from the client application. The processData() subroutine transfers the keyword to the sendBulletin() subroutine for additional processing. The code segment for sendBulletin() is shown in Figure 26 The sendBulletin() subroutine uses the connection identifier value associated with the (connected) client application and strRemoteHostIP() to locate the appropriate record in the *Remote* table. Once the record is located, the value of r_multicast is set to True or False for BulletinYes and BulletinNo respectively.

Since this function involves more than one client, dummy clients are used to represent multi users. The code segment in Figure 27 depicts the creation of a dummy client, which is the server-side version of the client application.

Client

Client application form comprises of: four command buttons; two text boxes; one list box; one check box; one timer; and a Winsock CE control. The image shown in Figure 28 depicts

Figure 23. Check box for receiving news bulletin

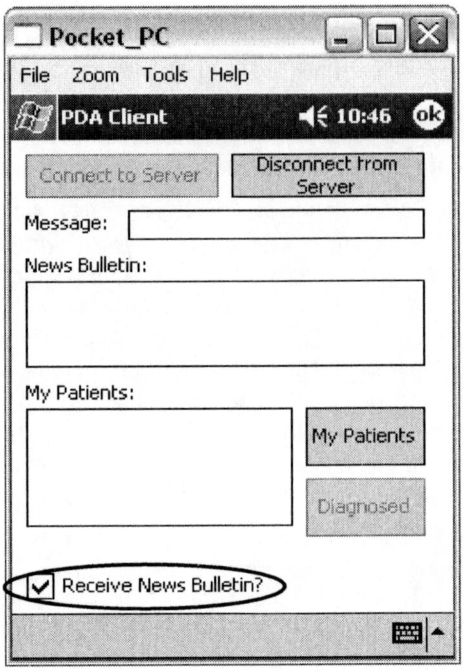

Figure 24. Remote table and the field affected by bulletin check box

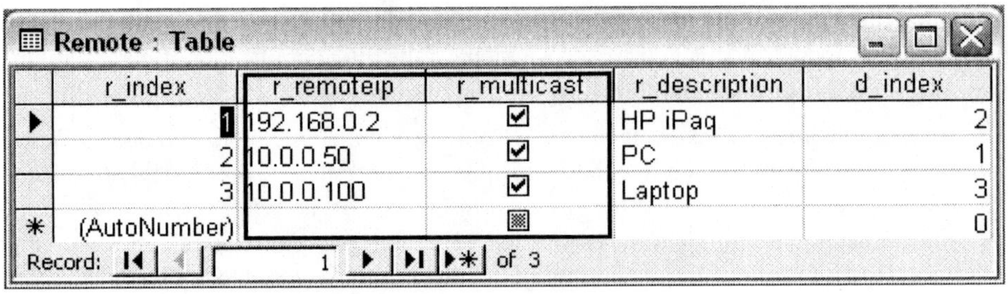

Remote : Table

	r_index	r_remoteip	r_multicast	r_description	d_index
▶	1	192.168.0.2	☑	HP iPaq	2
	2	10.0.0.50	☑	PC	1
	3	10.0.0.100	☑	Laptop	3
*	(AutoNumber)		☐		0

Record: 1 of 3

the client form at design time. When the client application is executed on the Personal Digital Assistant, the image in Figure 29 is displayed to the client. The client application responds to six human-generated events. The six events are as follows: clicking any of four command buttons, clicking the check box; and closing the client application.

When the doctor clicks the command button "*Connect to Server*," the application attempts to connect to the server. Once connected, the doctor can choose to retrieve relevant information about patients from the database (via the server application). This is achieved by clicking

Figure 25. The "Receive News Bulletin" check box event procedure

```
Private Sub chkSelectiveMulticast_Click()
    '** Notes:
    '** - Once connected to the server application, the user can elect
    '**    to enable or disable selective multicasting.
    '** - Sending the keyword 'BulletinYes' prompts the server
    '**    application to enable selective multicasting to this client.
    '** - Sending the keyword 'BulletinNo' turns off selective multicasting.

    'Check if the checkbox is checked.
    If Me.chkSelectiveMulticast.Value = 1 Then

        'If it is, send 'BulletinYes'
        wskTCP.SendData "BulletinYes:;"

    Else
        'Otherwise, send 'BulletinNo;'
        wskTCP.SendData "BulletinNo:;"
```

the "*My Patients.*" Once a list of patients is returned to the list box labeled "*My Patients,*" the doctor can choose to diagnose a patient. The doctor can diagnose a patient by: selecting the desired patient; and then clicking the "*Diagnosed*" button.

The client can also enable or disable the multicasting of a global news bulletin (sent by the server application). The doctor simply enables or disables the multicasting feature by selecting or deselecting the check box labeled "*Receive News Bulletin?*" The doctor can choose to disconnect from the server application by clicking the "*Disconnect from Server*" command button. Finally, clicking the "*OK*" button situated to the top right of the application window causes the client application to close.

The objective of client application is to display the results client-specific messages such as a global news bulletin, retrieving patient records, and diagnosing patients. The client-specific messages and the global news bulletin result from push-based communications. Retrieving patient records and diagnosing patients result from pull-based communications with the server application. Additionally, the client application also performs several additional functions. Some functions require human intervention; while other functions do not require human intervention.

Client Retrieving Data from the Database

When a doctor connects to the server application, the doctor may retrieve a list of patients from the database. The list of patients is displayed in the list box entitled "*My Patients.*" When a doctor creates a connection with the server application, a specific identity value is automatically sent by the server application to the client application. The specific identity value sent by the server application is the primary key value assigned to the doctor in the *Doctors* table.

The field in the *Doctors* table representing the primary key is the d_index field. The image shown in Figure 30 highlights the primary key field of the *Doctors* table. Using the specific

Figure 26. The sendBulletin() subroutine

```vb
Private Sub sendBulletin(Index As Integer, Multicast As String)
    '** Notes:
    '** - Modify the Remote table in the database to determine which
    '**    IP addresses (and hence, doctors) require the auto-sending
    '**    of the news bulletin.

    'Declare local rst object for ADO Recordset
    'and local string variable for SQL query.
    Dim rst As ADODB.Recordset
    Dim strQuery As String

    'Set rst object variable as ADO.Recordset object.
    Set rst = New ADODB.Recordset

    'Retrieve records from the remote table.
    strQuery = "SELECT * FROM remote;"

    'Open Recordset based on strQuery using global Connection String cnn.
    rst.Open strQuery, cnn, adOpenDynamic, adLockOptimistic

    'Check to see if the RecordCount is 0.
    If rst.RecordCount = 0 Then
        'If it is 0, exit this subroutine.
        Exit Sub
    Else
        'Otherwise, explicitly move to the first record.
        rst.MoveFirst

        'Find the record for r_remoteip equalled to
        'strRemoteHostIP(Index), e.g. r_remoteip = '192.168.0.2'.
        'The r_remoteip field in Remote table doesn't allow
        'duplicate values.
        rst.Find "r_remoteip = '" & strRemoteHostIP(Index) & "'"

        'If a match is found, change the value of r_multicast field
        'to True/False depending on the value of the Multicast parameter.
        If rst!r_remoteip = strRemoteHostIP(Index) Then

            'Multicast parameter is either 'BulletinYes' or 'BulletinNo'
            Select Case Multicast
                'BulletinYes: set r_multicast to True
                Case "BulletinYes"
                    rst.Fields("r_multicast") = True
                    rst.Update
                'BulletinNo: set r_multicast to False
                Case "BulletinNo"
                    rst.Fields("r_multicast") = False
                    rst.Update
            End Select
        End If
    End If

    'Close the Recordset object rst and set it to Nothing.
    rst.Close
    Set rst = Nothing
End Sub
```

Figure 27.   Create a dummy client event procedure

```
Private Sub Client_Click(Index As Integer)
    '** Notes:
    '** - Create 'Dummy' clients by creating newClient objects.
    '** - Connect to this application via Winsock to mimic behaviour of PDA.

    'Explicitly create newClient objects based on Form frmClient.
    Dim newClient As Form
    Set newClient = New frmClient

    'Use lngCounter form-level variable to display the Form based on
    'connection order.
    newClient.Caption = "Client " & Str(lngCounter + 1)

    'Load the newClient object and display it.
    Load newClient
    newClient.Show
```

Figure 28. Client form at design time

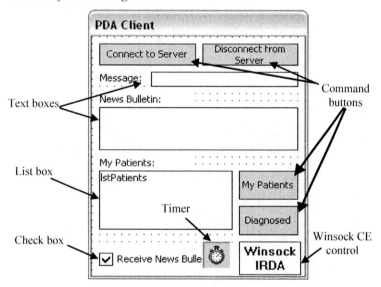

identity value stored in the d_index field enables a doctor to return information from the database that is relevant (or related) to the doctor. However, the *Doctors* table does not supply enough information to determine which identity value needs to be implicitly sent to the client application. Therefore, the server application uses the *Doctors* table in conjunction with the *Remote* table to determine the necessary identity value required by the client program. Figure 31 highlights the foreign key of the *Remote* table that relates to the *Doctors* table.

One of the event procedures uses the relationship between the *Doctors* and *Remote* table, in conjunction with the IP addresses stored in the r_remoteip field of the *Remote* table, to

Figure 29. Client form at runtime

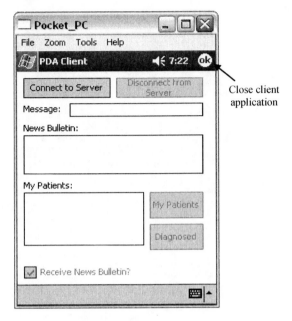

Close client
application

Figure 30. Doctors table and the identity field

		d_index	d_surname	d_firstname	d_phone	d_address	d_suburb	d_state	d_pcode
▶	+	1	Clark	John	9421 8844	P.O. Box 5087	Burnley	Victoria	3121
	+	2	Doe	John	9585 1544	33 Wangara Road	Cheltenham	Victoria	3192
	+	3	Hardy	Thomas	9464 7686	P.O. Box 41	Thomastown	Victoria	3074
	+	4	Moreno	Antonio	9740 8860	P.O. Box 351	Sunbury	Victoria	3429
	+	5	Smith	John	9697 8333	59 Fran Street	Glenroy	Victoria	3046
✳		oNumber)							

Record: I◀ ◀ [1] ▶ ▶I ▶✳ of 5

Doctors : Table

Figure 31. Remote table showing the identity field for doctors

Remote : Table

	r_index	r_remoteip	r_multicast	r_description	d_index
▶	1	192.168.0.2	☑	HP iPaq	2
	2	10.0.0.50	☑	PC	1
	3	10.0.0.100	☑	Laptop	3
✳	(AutoNumber)		▓		0

Record: I◀ ◀ [1] ▶ ▶I ▶✳ of 3

Figure 32. The "My Patients" button

determine the correct identity value to send to the client device. If a doctor wishes to retrieve a list of patients, the doctor simply clicks the "*My Patients*" button on the client application. The image shown in Figure 32 highlights the "My Patients" button on the client program.

The cmdMyPatients_Click() event procedure sends the identity value (supplied as a result of the initial connection request) to the server application. The code segment shown Figure 33 depicts the cmdMyPatients_Click()subroutine that is sent to the server.

The identity value is stored in form-level variable entitled strMyID. This value is available for use after the client application successfully connects to the server application. The cmdMyPatients_Click() event procedure utilizes the value stored in strMyID by amending the prefix "MyPatients:" keyword and an end-of-message delimiter ";" to create a complete message. Given that the value of strMyID is 2, then the complete message is: MyPatients:2;. The complete message is subsequently sent to the server application for processing. When the server application receives the complete message, a local subroutine processData()parses the complete message. The keyword MyPatients is utilised by the processData() subroutine to determine the nature of the message. The processData() subroutine determines the keyword by searching for the keyword delimiter ":". After determining the nature of the message from the keyword, the server application extracts the identity value from the message. The identity value is then transferred to a myPatients() subroutine on the server application. The code segment for the myPatients() subroutine is shown in Figure 34.

The myPatients() subroutine creates a query string which searches the *Patients* table for undiagnosed patients. Furthermore, the query string returns patient records relevant to the

Figure 33. The "My Patients" button event procedure

```
Private Sub cmdMyPatients_Click()
    '** Notes:
    '** - When the doctor connects to the server, the doctor's ID
    '**    d_index is automatically sent to the client device.
    '** - When the doctor wishes to retrieve the list of patients under
    '**    his/her care, the doctor clicks on the 'My Patients' button.
    '** - The button sends the keyword 'MyPatients' followed by the
    '**    doctor's ID to the server application.
    '** - The message is sent using the keyword followed by a colon
    '**    delimiter (to mark the end of the keyword), the ID of the doctor,
    '**    and a semi-colon delimiter to mark the end of the message.

    'Clear the list of patients if it is not already blank.
    lstPatients.Clear

    'Send request for service using keyword 'MyPatients' and strMyID.
    wskTCP.SendData "MyPatients:" & strMyID & ";"
End Sub
```

Figure 34. The myPatients() subroutine

```
Private Sub myPatients(myID As String, Index As Integer)

    '** Notes:
    '** - This subroutine is called when the client (doctor) requests
    '**    a list patients under his/her care.
    '** - It is called from two places:
    '**    1. processData() - The data processor; when requested by the
    '**       client.
    '**    2. patientDiagnosed - When a patient is diagnosed; the client
    '**       list is refreshed.
    '** - This subroutine expects the parameters myID and Index.
    '** - myID represents the ID of the doctor d_index.
    '** - Index represents the connection identifier of the doctor's
    '**    device.

    'Declare local string variable.
    Dim strQuery As String

    'Query string to be used to perform a search.
    'The Query string is built using the string value list lstDoctors.
    strQuery = "SELECT p_index, p_firstname, p_surname FROM patients " _
    & "WHERE p_diagnosed = False AND d_index = " & myID & ";"

    'Pass strQuery to retrieveRecord subroutine and send
    Call retrieveRecord(strQuery, Index)

End Sub
```

Figure 35. The retrieveRecord() subroutine

```
Private Sub retrieveRecord(ByVal SQLString As String, ByVal Index As Integer)
    '** Notes:
    '** - Generic procedure to return records from the database based
    '**   on SQLString parameter for the wskTCP control in question
    '**   (based on the Index).
    '** - This procedure is used extensively for all 'Pull' and 'Push'
    '**   events.
    'Declare local rst object for ADO Recordset.
    Dim rst As ADODB.Recordset

    'Set rst object variable as ADO.Recordset object
    Set rst = New ADODB.Recordset

    'Open the Recordset based on SQLString using global Connection
    'String cnn.
    rst.Open SQLString, cnn, adOpenStatic, adLockReadOnly
```

doctor. The query string is then utilized by another local subroutine on the server application entitled retrieveRecord(). The code segment for the retrieveRecord() subroutine is shown in Figure 35.

The query string utilised by retrieveRecord() is to search the *Patients* table and to return any patient records related to the identity value supplied by the doctor. The subroutine retrieves: the surname from p_surname; the first name from p_firstname; and patient identity value from p_index.

The image shown in Figure 37 highlights the targeted fields in the table. Given that p_index as 1 is the first record retrieved, then the complete message is: Results:Hsieh, Raymond, ID#1. The complete message is sent by the server application to the client application. The client application parses the complete message and processes the complete message for display. The client application updates the list box entitled "*My Patients*" by displaying the surname, first name and identity value of each patient. The following image shown in Figure 36 illustrates the client application displaying patient details.

Client Updating the Database

As an extension to retrieving patient information from the database, the client application also enables the doctor to diagnose a patient. Once a list of patients is retrieved from the server application, the doctor may click the "*Diagnosed*" button to remove a selected patient from the list of patients. The image shown in Figure 38 illustrates a selected patient and the relevant "*Diagnosed*" button.

The cmdDiagnosed_Click() event procedure creates a message by amending the prefix "Diagnosed:" keyword to the patient identity value. The patient identity value is succeeded by a special separator keyword "&" and the doctor identity value. The end-of-message delimiter ";" is then appended to the end of the message. The code segment shown Figure 39 depicts how cmdDiagnosed_Click() event procedure creates the complete message. Given that the

Figure 35. continued

```
        'Check to see if the RecordCount is 0.
        If Not rst.RecordCount = 0 Then

            'Otherwise, move to the first record in the Recordset
            rst.MoveFirst

            'SQLString returns only 1 record, but this is necessary
            'for correctness.
            Do While Not rst.EOF
                'Send requested data from nominated field (m_surname) to
                'client wskTCP of paramater Index.
                'This is somewhat less than ideal.
                'However, since the SQLString always contains a 'WHERE'
                'clause for the Identity (Primary) Key field of the table,
                'only 1 result is ever returned.

                Dim strSend As String

                strSend = "Results:" & rst!p_surname & ", " &
                          rst!p_firstname _& ", ID#" & rst!p_index & ";"
                          wskTCP(Index).SendData strSend

                'Use a delay timer tmrWait to send record(s) to all clients.
                'For some peculiar reason only the last connected client
                'receives any data. This deliberate pause ensures that all
                'clients receives data.
                'Even though this procedure is often called in a loop, the
                'error described still occurs.
                'It is assumed that the loop runs too fast...
                'Turn on the timer object tmrWait.
                tmrWait.Enabled = True

                'Force a loop while tmrWait is true (to delay the
                'processing). This avoids the error described above.
                Do While tmrWait.Enabled = True

                    'While forcing a delay (pause), let other events run their
                    'course.
                        DoEvents
                Loop
                'Move to the next record in rst.

                rst.MoveNext
            Loop
        End If
        'Close the Recordset object rst and set it to Nothing.
        rst.Close
        Set rst = Nothing
    End Sub
```

extracted patient identity value is 1 and the doctor identity value is 2, then the complete message is: Diagnosed:1&2;.

The complete message created by the cmdDiagnosed_Click() event procedure is sent by the client application to the server application. The server application receives the message and the message is parsed by the processData() subroutine. The keyword Diagnosed is utilised

Figure 36. Client details returned for display

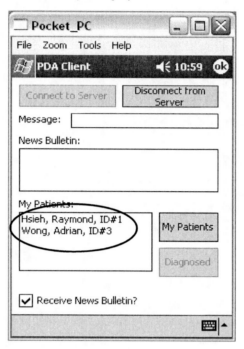

Figure 37. Patients table showing the identity value, surname and first name of each patient

p_index	p_surname	p_firstname	p_phone	p_address	p_suburb	p_state	p_pcode	d_index	p_diagnosed
1	Hsieh	Raymond	9560 5602	494 Springvale	Glen Waverl	Victoria	3150	2	☐
2	Hsieh	Kenneth	9560 5602	494 Springvale	Glen Waverl	Victoria	3150	3	☐
3	Wong	Adrian	9123 4567	P.O. Box 100	Wantirna	Victoria	3074	2	☐
6	De Silva	Rohan	9876 5432	P.O. Box 200	Glen Waverl	Victoria	3150	1	☐
＊ (Number)								0	▣

Record: I◀ ◀ | 1 ▶ ▶I ▶＊ | of 4

by the processData() subroutine to determine the nature of the message. The processData() subroutine determines the keyword by searching for the keyword delimiter ":". After determining the nature of the message from the keyword, the server application extracts the patient and doctor identity values from the message. The identity values are then transferred to a patientsDiagnosed() subroutine on the server application. The code segment for the patientsDiagnosed() subroutine is shown in Figure 40.

The patientDiagnosed() subroutine uses the patient identity value to update the relevant record in the *Patients* table. The patientDiagnosed() subroutine targets a specific field in the

Figure 38. Selected patient and "Diagnosed" button

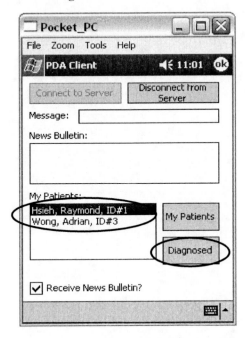

Figure 39. The "Diagnosed" button event procedure

```
Private Sub cmdDiagnosed_Click()

    '** Notes:
    '** - When the doctor completes a diagnosis on a patient, the
    '**   doctor selects the patient from the list and clicks the
    '**   Diagnosed button.
    '** - The button sends the keyword 'Diagnosed' followed by the
    '**   patients's ID to the server application.
    '** - The message is sent using the keyword followed by a colon
    '**   delimiter (to mark the end of the keyword), the ID of the
    '**   patient, and a semi-colon delimiter to mark the end of the
    '**   message.

    'Declare local variable to store the ID of the patient.
    Dim strPatientID As String

    'Strip out the ID of the patient from lstPatients as a string value.
    strPatientID = Right(lstPatients.List(lstPatients.ListIndex), _
    Len(lstPatients.List(lstPatients.ListIndex)) - _
    InStr(lstPatients.List(lstPatients.ListIndex), "#"))

    'Send request for service using keyword 'Diagnosed' and strPatientID.
    wskTCP.SendData "Diagnosed:" & strPatientID & "&" & strMyID & ";"

    'Clear the patients list (this will be filled after the list is
    'refreshed).
    lstPatients.Clear
```

Figure 40. The patientsDiagnosed() subroutine

```
Private Sub patientDiagnosed(PatientID As String, myID as String, Index As
Integer)
    '** Notes:
    '** - This subroutine is called when the client (doctor) has
    '**    completed diagnosing a patient.
    '** - It is called from processData() when requested by the
    '**    client.
    '** - This subroutine expects the parameters PatientID and Index.
    '** - PatientID represents the ID of the patient p_index.
    '** - myID represents the ID of the doctor d_index.
    '** - Index represents the connection identifier of the doctor's
    '**    device.
    '** - When the patient table is update, a call to myPatients()
    '**    subroutine is made to update the list of patients on the
    '**    client device.

    'Declare local rst object for ADO Recordset and local variables.
    Dim rst As ADODB.Recordset
    Dim strQuery As String

    'Set rst object variable as ADO.Recordset object
    Set rst = New ADODB.Recordset

    'Source string for Recordset rst.
    strQuery = "SELECT p_diagnosed FROM patients WHERE p_index = " _
    & PatientID & ";"

    'Open the Recordset based on strQuery using global Connection
    'String cnn.
    rst.Open strQuery, cnn, adOpenStatic, adLockOptimistic

    'Check if the query string returns any records.
    If rst.RecordCount = 0 Then

        'If it does not, exit this subroutine.
        Exit Sub

    Else

        'The query should return only 1 record.
        'Move to the first record.
        rst.MoveFirst

        'Update the record for field p_diagnosed
        rst.Fields("p_diagnosed") = True
        rst.Update

    End If

    'Close the Recordset object rst and set it to Nothing.
    rst.Close
    Set rst = Nothing

    'Update patient list on client device.
```

Figure 41. Patient removed from client display

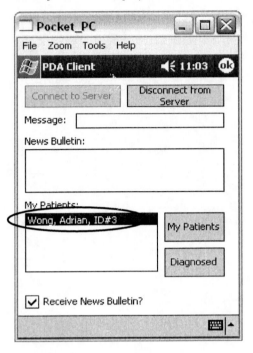

Figure 42. Patients table and the "Diagnosed" field for each patient

	p_index	p_surname	p_firstname	p_phone	p_address	p_suburb	p_state	p_pcode	d_index	p_diagnosed
✍	1	Hsieh	Raymond	9560 5602	494 Springvale	Glen Waverl	Victoria	3150	2	☑
	2	Hsieh	Kenneth	9560 5602	494 Springvale	Glen Waverl	Victoria	3150	3	☐
	3	Wong	Adrian	9123 4567	P.O. Box 100	Wantirna	Victoria	3074	2	☐
	6	De Silva	Rohan	9876 5432	P.O. Box 200	Glen Waverl	Victoria	3150	1	☐
✱	(Number)								0	▣

Record: ◄ ◄ [1   ] ► ►► ►✱ of 4

Patients table – namely the p_diagnosed field. The patientDiagnosed() subroutine updates the value of the p_diagnosed field from unchecked to checked. The image shown in Figure 42 highlights the p_diagnosed field and the status of the patient.

Once a patient is diagnosed, the list of patients on the client application is updated to reflect the changes made to the *Patients* table. The patientDiagnosed() subroutine ends by calling the myPatients() subroutine and passing the doctor identity value into the parameter myID. The myPatients() subroutine updates the client display accordingly. The image shown in Figure 41 illustrates the updated client display.

Conclusion and Future Work

A wireless network environment enables mobility. Personal Digital Assistants enable portability. Together, they provide a potentially useful tool for highly mobile users. However, traditional methods to data dissemination often involve the client requesting data or information from a server. This is practical if the client requires something specific from the server. However, this pull-based method does not cater to all scenarios.

In this paper, we present pull-based and push-based wireless information system. In order to demonstrate the effective uses of the application, we use hospital information system information system scenario. The hospital information system relates to doctors as the principal clients to a server application. The system demonstrates the use of the pull-based mechanism to retrieve specific information from the database. Furthermore, the information retrieved from the database can be acted upon by the client. In doing so, the database is updated by the client. This is demonstrated via the retrieval and updating of patient records by doctors.

The server application is also able to push information to the client application. The server application utilizes push-based mechanisms to send messages to specific doctor in the hospital. Furthermore, the server application is able to multicast a global message to all doctors connected to the server application. The global message can be disabled by each doctor; demonstrating a pull-based interaction with the server application.

For future work, we plan to incorporate a sensor positioning device e.g. global positioning system (GPS) used to detect the location of mobile users. This way enables us to push information based on the location of the user. With regard to hospital context, location based services will support doctors in diagnosing patients by disseminate relevant data whenever the doctor is about to diagnose a patient. This will enhance the flexibility and efficiency of the activity.

References

Acharya, S., Alonso, R., Franklin, M., & Zdonik, S. (1995). Broadcast disks: Data management for asymmetric communication environments. In *Proceedings of the ACM Sigmod* (pp. 199-210).

Aksoy, D., Altinel, M., Bose, R., Cetintemel, U., Franklin, M., Wang, J., & Zdonik, S. (1999). Research in data broadcast and dissemination. In *Proceedings of the AMCP* (LNCS 1554, pp. 194-207).

Barbara, D. (1999). Mobile computing and databases: A survey. *IEEE TKDE, 11*(1), 108-117.

Blake, R. (2002). *Electronic communication systems* (2nd ed.). New York: Thomson Learning.

Franklin, M., & Zdonik, S. (1997). A framework for scalable dissemination-based systems. In *Proceedings of the 12th ACM OOPSLA, 32* (pp. 94-105).

Housel, B. C., Samaras, G., & Lindquist, D.B. (1998). WebExpress: A client/intercept based system for optmising Web browsing in a wireless environment. *ACM/Baltzer MONET, 3*(4), 419- 431.

Imielinski, T., & Viswanathan, S. (1994). Adaptive wireless information systems. In *Proceedings of the SIGDBS* (pp. 19-41).

Imielinski, T., Viswanathan, S., & Badrinath, B. R. (1994). Energy efficient indexing on air. In *Proceedings of the ACM Sigmod* (pp. 25-36).

Kistler, J.J., & Satyanarayanan, M. (1992). Disconnected operation in the code file system. *ACM Trans. on Computer Systems, 10*(1), 213-225.

Leong, H. V., & Si, A. (1997). Database caching over the air-storage. *The Computer Journal, 40*(7), 401-415.

Satyanarayanan, M., Kistler, J.J., Kumar, P., Okasaki, M.E., Siegel, E.H., & Steere, D.C. (1990). Coda: A highly available file system for a distributed workstation environment. *IEEE Trans. on Computers, 39*(4), 447-459.

Si, A., & Leong, H. V. (1999). Query optimization for broadcast database. *DKE, 29*(3), 351-380.

Terry, D., Demers, A. J., Peterson, K., Spreitzer, M.J., Theimer, M.M., & Welch, B. (1994). Session guarantees for weakly consistent replicated data. In *Proceedings PDIS* (pp. 140-149).

Terry, D., Theimer, M.M., Peterson, K., Demers, A. J., Spreitzer, M.J., & Hauser, C.H. (1995). Managing update conflicts in Bayou: A weakly connected replicated storage system. In *Proceedings of the ACM Symposium on OS* (pp. 172-183).

Zak, D. (1999). *Programming with Microsoft Visual Basic 6.0.* Thomson Publishing.

Zaslavsky, A., & Tari, S. (1998). Mobile computing: Overview and current status. *Australian Computer Journal, 30*(2), 42-52.

Chapter VIII

Data Caching in a Mobile Database Environment

Say Ying Lim, Monash University, Australia

David Taniar, Monash University, Australia

Bala Srinivasan, Monash University, Australia

Abstract

In this chapter, we present an extensive study of the available types of data caching in a mobile database environment. We explore the different types of possible cache management strategy that can be adopted in a mobile environment. Generally, it is important to be able to cache frequent access data items because very often mobile users may require to downloading the same data over again. And by having the ability to cache the data, would helps avoid having to re-download the same data again. We include some discussions regarding the issues that arise from cache management strategy as well as include investigation on using cache management strategy involving location dependent data.

Introduction

With the rapid development as well as recent advances in wireless network technologies have led to the development of the concept mobile computing. Mobile computing environment enables mobile users query databases from their mobile devices over the wireless communication channels (Cai & Tan, 1999). The potential market for mobile computing applications is projected to increase overtime by the currently increasingly mobile world which enables user to satisfy their need by having the ability to access information anywhere, anytime. However, the typical nature of a mobile environment would include low bandwidth and low reliability of wireless channels which causes frequent disconnection to the mobile users. Often, mobile devices are associated with low memory storage and low power computation and with a limited power supply (Imielinski & Badrinath, 1994). Thus, for mobile computing to be widely deployed, it is important to cope with the current limitation of power conservation and low bandwidth of the wireless channel. These two issues create a great challenge for fellow researchers in the area of mobile computing.

By introducing data caching into the mobile database environment, it is believe to be a very useful and effective method in conserving bandwidth and power consumptions. This is because when the data items are cached, the mobile user can avoid requesting for the same data if the data are valid. And this would lead to reduce transmission which implies better utilization of the nature of the wireless channel of limited bandwidth. The cached data are able to support disconnected or intermitted connected operations as well. In addition, this also leads to cost reduction if the billed is per KB data transfer (Papadopuli & Issarnyy, 2001). Caching has emerged as a fundamental technique especially in distributed systems as it not only helps reduce communication costs but also off loads shared database servers. Generally, caching in mobile environment is complicated by the fact that the caches need to be kept consistent at all time.

In this chapter, we would concentrate on several types of caching management particularly semantic and cooperative caching as well as cache invalidation strategy. Each of these different types of cache management will be further explored in the subsequent sections.

Background and Preliminaries

The effect of having the ability to cache data is of great importance especially in the mobile computing environment than in other computing environment. This is due to the reason that contacting the remote servers for data is expensive in the wireless environment and with the vulnerable to frequent disconnection can further increase the communication costs (Leong & Si, 1997). We would first introduce the mobile computing environment, followed by traditional mobile query processing, then overview of cache management and then discussions on the issues of caching.

Mobile Computing Environment

Generally, mobile users with their mobile devices and servers that store data are involved in a typical mobile environment (Hurson & Jiao, 2005). Each of these mobile users communicates with a single server or multiple servers that may or may not be collaborative with one another. However communication between mobile users and servers are required in order to carry out any transaction and information retrieval. Basically the servers are more or less static and do not move, whereas the mobile users can move from one place to another and are therefore dynamic. Nevertheless, mobile users have to be within specific region to be able to received signal in order to connect to the servers (Seydim, Dunham, & Kumar, 2001). Figure 1 illustrates a scenario of a mobile database environment.

It can be seen from Figure 1 that mobile user 1 when within a specific location is able to access servers 1 and 2. By downloading from both servers, the data will be stored in the mobile device which can be manipulated later locally. And if mobile user 1 moves to a different location, the server to access maybe the same but the list downloaded would be different since this mobile client is located in a different location now. The user might also be able to access to a different server that is not available in his pervious location before he moves. This introduces the concept of location dependent queries.

> **Example 1:** *A property investor while driving his car downloads a list of nearby apartments for sale from a real-estate agent. As he moves, he downloads the requested information again from the same real-estate agent. Because his position has changed since he first enquires, the two lists of apartments for sale would be different due to the relative location when this investor was inquiring the information. Based on these two lists, the investor would probably like to perform an operation on his mobile device to show only those apartments exist in the latest list, and not in the first list.*

Figure 1. A mobile database environment

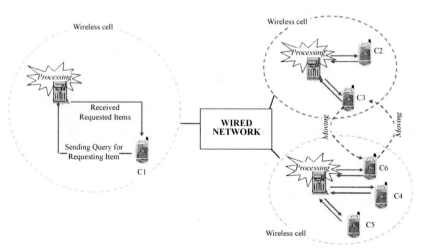

Due to the dynamic nature of this mobile environment, mobile devices face several limitations (Paulson, 2003; Trivedi, Dharmaraja, & Ma, 2002). These include limited processing capacity as well as storage capacity. Moreover, limited bandwidth is an issue because this wireless bandwidth is smaller compared with the fixed network. This leads to poor connection and frequent disconnection. Therefore, it is important to comprehensively study the available cache management that can be carried out locally on mobile devices. Also, by caching the frequently accessed data in the mobile devices will help reduce tune in time and power consumption because requested data can be fetched for the cache without tuning into the communication channel for retrieval (Lee, Leong, & Si, 1999). Caching has also been proved as a significant technique in improving the performance of data retrieval in peer to peer network in helping to save bandwidth for each data retrieval that are made by the mobile clients (Joseph, Kumar, Shen, & Das, 2005). The cached data are meant to support disconnected or intermitted connected operations. Further discussions regarding the types of cache management that can be adhered in a mobile environment will be discussed in the later sections.

Traditional Mobile Query Processing

Generally, the aim of query processing is to transform a query in a high level declarative language such as SQL into a correct and efficient execution strategy (Elmasri & Navathe, 2003). Therefore query optimization comes into discussion. There are many ways to produce the same result in the real world. However sometimes, one way would out perform another way. Therefore, to find the most efficient way to process user query is to find out which way is the best in certain situation. This is known as query optimization which is to optimize the way the query is process.

> **Example 2:** *A mobile user ask a server a question by writing the question in a language the server can understand, and the user has to send the question to the server. The server break the question down into parts and process each part, and then assemble the results and send back to the user. Figure 2 shows an example of a typical simple query processing.*

Database queries in a mobile environment frequently raise several complexities that cannot be found in traditional database systems. As a result of the desire to process queries between servers that might not be collaborative, traditional join query techniques might not be applicable (Lo, Mamoulis, Cheung, Ho, & Kalnis, 2003). One of the main issues that make query processing in a mobile environment differs from traditional database systems are the location dependent queries which has created a new perspective of query operation. An example query might be "to find the nearest petrol kiosk" or "to find the three nearest vegetarian restaurants" queries that are issued from mobile users as they moves around.

In the context of location dependent processing, whenever mobile users move from one location to another location, the downloaded data would be different even though the query is direct to similar source. And because of this, whenever the downloaded data differ as the

Figure 2. An illustration of a simple query processing

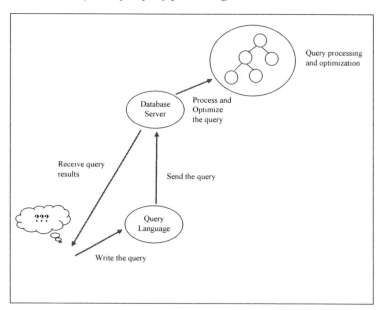

users move to a new location, the database server must be intelligent enough to inform that existing list contains different information and prompt if user wants to download a new list. This leads to the term *Location Dependent Query*. Generally, for location dependent query, the change of the results is dependent on the location of the issuer. This means that if a user sends a query and then changes his/her location, the answer of that query has to be based on the location of the user issuing the query (Seydim, Dunham, & Kumar, 2001).

From the query processing perspective, the most important element is to help reduce the communication cost, which occurs due to data transfer between to and from the servers and mobile devices (Xu et al., 2003). The need for collecting information from multiple remote databases and processing locally becomes apparent especially when mobile users collect information from several non-collaborative remote databases. Therefore, it is of great magnitude to investigating the optimization of database processing on mobile devices, because it helps addresses issue of communication cost. It would also be of a great interest to be able to work on optimizing processing of the database operations to make the processing more efficient and cost effective.

Caching Overview

Caching at the mobile client helps in relieving the low bandwidth constraints imposed in the mobile environment (Kara & Edwards, 2003). Without the ability to cache data, there will be increase communication in the remote servers for data and this eventually leads to increase cost and with the nature of the environment that is vulnerable to frequent disconnection may also lead to higher costs (Xu et al., 2005). Caching has also been proved as a significant technique in improving the performance of data retrieval in peer to peer network in helping to save bandwidth for each data retrieval that are made by the mobile clients (Joseph et al., 2005). The cached data are meant to support disconnected or intermitted connected operations. There are many different types of caching strategy which serve the purpose to improve query response time and to reduce contention on narrow bandwidth (Yajima et al., 2004).

Regardless of which caching strategy one chooses, they have their own advantages and disadvantages in some way. In principle, caching can improve system performance in two ways: (a) It can eliminate multiple requests for the same data and (b) improve performance is by off-loading the work. The first way can be achieved by allowing mobile clients to share data among each other by allowing them to access each other cache within a reasonably boundary between them. The second way however can be demonstrated as in an example of a mobile user who is interested in keeping stock prices and cache them into his mobile device. And by having copies in his own mobile device, he can perform his own data analysis based on the cached data without communicating directly to the server over the wireless channel.

However, the frequent disconnection and the mobility of clients complicate the issue of keeping the cache consistent with those that are stored in the servers (Persone & Grassi, 2004). Thus, when caching is used, ensuring data consistency is an important issue that needs considerably attention at all times (Papadopuli & Issarnyy, 2001). This is because the data that has been cached may have been out dated and no longer valid in comparison to the data from the corresponding servers or broadcast channel.

Due to the limitation such as cache space, cache replacement, cache granularity, as well as cache coherence are the three main issues that characterize caching mechanism. This will be further explained next.

Issues of Cache Management

In traditional cache replacement, the most important factor affecting cache performance is the access probability. Due to limited memory capacity, cache replacement arises in investigation. The replacement policy discards old cache data items that are no longer relevant or is out of date and replaced them with the newly obtained data items (Chan, Si, & Leong, 1998; Xu, Hu, Lee, & Lee, 2000; Xu et al., 2005). The issue that needs to be addressed in respective to this policy is to determine what data items that are no longer needed and that are to be replaced. This has to be address carefully because if a bad replacement policy are being used, then it may results in waste of energy as well as memory space since the mobile user may not be able to use the cache data but still have to send a query to obtain the desired data items. Thus, the more effective a caching replacement will affect the performance of the queries whereby if an effective cache replacement is use, the better a query will performed as well as more queries cold be served especially during disconnection situation. Most of the replacement policies investigated on involves utilizing access probability as the primary factor in determining which data items to be replaced. This refers to replacing the data with the least access probability to free up more cache space for the new data. There is a large variety of caching replacement policies and most of them utilize access probability as the primary factor in determining which data items are to be replaced.

Cache granularity relates to determining a physical form of cached data items. It appears to be one of the key issues in caching management systems. There are three different level of caching granularities in an object-oriented database which includes (a) attribute caching, (b) object caching, and (c) hybrid caching (Chan, Si, & Leong, 1998). Attribute caching refers to frequently accessed attributes that are stored in the client's local storage. As for object caching, instead of the attributes itself being cache, the object is cached. In attribute caching, it creates undesirable overheads due to the large number of independent cache attributes. Thus, for hybrid caching which appear to be a better approach, which comprises of the combinations of both granularities.

Cache coherence or known as invalidation strategy involves cache invalidation and update schemes to invalidate and update out-dated or non-valid cached item (Chan, Si, & Leong, 1998; Cao, 2003). After a certain period, a cached data may appear as no longer valid and therefore mobile users should obtain a newer cache before retrieving the data (Chand, Joshi, & Misra, 1996; Tan, Chai, & Ooi, 2001). There are several techniques that have been proposed to overcome this issue. These include (a) stateful server, (b) stateless server, (Barbara & Imielinski, 1994) and (c) leases file caching mechanism (Lee, Leong, & Si, 2001). Stateful server refers to the server having obligation to its clients which means the server has the responsibility in notifying the users about changes if there is any. In contrast, stateless server refers to the server not aware for its clients whereby the server broadcast a report which contains the updated item either asynchronously or synchronously. The leases files mechanism which is also known as lazy invalidation approach assigns each mobile user to be responsible for invalidating its cached items.

Consequently, a good caching management strategy is needed to deal with the critical caching issues such as caching replacement, caching granularity and caching coherence.

Types of Cache Management

In this section, we would focus one two types of cache management that has been studied in the existing work mainly on semantic caching and cooperative caching. Each of this cache management strategy has its own advantages and disadvantages in use with conjunction of a typical mobile environment.

Semantic Caching in Mobile Environment

A better way of query processing specifically for use in mobile environment is by allowing the users to specify precisely what data items are missing from its local storage to server the query. This could be achieved by having the previously evaluated query results being cached (Dar, Franklin, Jonsson, Srivastava, & Tab, 1996; Lee, Leong, & Si, 2000). Semantic caching which is basically a type of caching strategy that is content based reasoning ability with the ability to in addition of caching query results, it also remembers the queries that generated these results. Semantic caching provides accurate, semantic description of the content of the cache.

A semantic cache is defined to be consisting of a set of distinct semantic segments which can be decomposed into separate components or come together as a whole of the query results. A semantic segment can be specified by having the base relation of relation and attributes in the creation of the semantic segment, followed by the criteria that satisfy and the actual content represented by pages (Ren, Dunham, & Kumar, 2003). Semantic caching stores semantic descriptions and associated answers of the previous queries in the mobile client (Dar et al., 1996). The main feature of semantic caching is the content based reasoning ability as well as the fact that only the required data as opposed to a file or pages of data is transmitted over the wireless channel.

When a new query exists, the mobile client can determine whether should it be totally answered, by how much can it be answered and what data are missing. With these ability, the wireless traffic can be greatly reduces because only the needed data are transferred. This helps with disconnection too since total or partial results may be obtained even when the server is unreachable (Lee, Heong, & Si, 1999). As a result, if a query can be partially answered from the cache, the volume of missing data requested from the server as well as the wireless bandwidth consumed can be reduced. And if the query could be answered completely based on the cache, then no communication between the client and the server is required at all. This ability is of particular significance during disconnection which is the main constraints the mobile environment is currently facing. This also leads to reduction of overhead due to redundant computation as the amount of data transferred over the wireless channel can be substantially reduced.

> **Example 3:** *Suppose a mobile user who is traveling from one location to another location suddenly wished to find a nearby rest place. So the user issue a query while he is in Location A and the server returns the nearest rest place which is P1, P2, P3, P4, and P5. But the user is not satisfied with the results. So he re-issued another query while he is moving towards Location B. And the query returns another set of results which may contain some overlapping results such as P5 same as the user previously received. Hence, the cached results are immediately returned since it has been previously cached. Thus, the user actually only need to submit the complement of the new query in order to obtain only results that are not the same as the one previously obtained. This example can be illustrated as in Figure 3. This shows that semantic caching not only saves the wireless bandwidth due to less re transmission but also reduces the query response time since some cached results can be immediately returned.*

There are several advantages that can be gained by using semantic caching with the main reason that only required data are being transferred communication cost between the client and the servers would be reduced. Moreover, cache space overhead is low for semantic caching since only the data that satisfy previous queries are being stored. With the ability of semantic caching that keeps semantic information enables missing data to be exactly determined which causes easy parallel query processing. Hence, semantic caching is very

Figure 3. Overlapping results from two queries issued

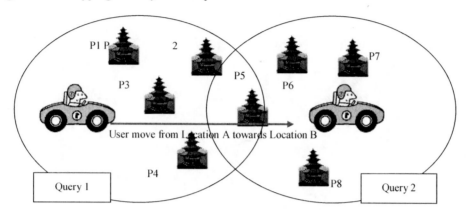

efficient to be use in the mobile environment since more autonomy is given to the clients and partial results can be derived when disconnections from the wireless channels occur (Ren, Dunham, & Kumar, 2003).

Besides all the benefits semantic caching brings in, there are also limitations and drawbacks that semantic caching brings. Generally, semantic caching captures the semantics of the queries only, and ignores the semantics of the cached objects. Therefore, the granularity is at a query level that helps answering similar queries faster, but cached objects from different types of queries become difficult. (Ren, Dunham, & Kumar, 2003) In addition, the types of spatial queries supported by semantic caching are rather limited to simple range query and nearest neighbor (NN) query (Ren & Dunham, 2000). It is difficult to support complex queries such as k-nearest-neighbor (kNN). Besides that, it also demonstrates complicated cache management. For example, when a new query to be cached overlaps some cached query, a decision has to be made for whether to bring these two queries or to trim either of them. When the cache size grows the all these drawbacks are would become more remarkable.

Example 4: *The same scenario as describe in Example 3, instead of the user issuing a query 2 in a new location after the query 1 which has been sent, he would like to issue query 2 which comprises of 3 nearest neighbor (3NN) query. Due to the limitation of semantic caching that is not able to trim a 3NN query from the first query, the user would have to sent a full complete query 2 to the server even though the results data P1, P3, P4 has been cached as a result of the first query that has been issued earlier on. They are actually partial results of the new query and should have been returned immediately to the user but are not able to do so. This example can be illustrated as in Figure 4. The retransmission of this result to the mobile users has wasted the wireless bandwidth as well as unnecessary transfer and has prolonged the response time (Ren, Dunham, & Kumar, 2003).*

Figure 4. Issuing a 3NN query

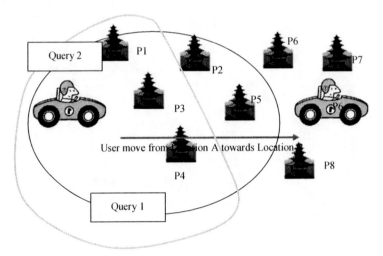

In order to process a query from a semantic cache, first of all we would check whether the query can be answered locally by the cache. If the answer can be obtained from the cache, the results are locally processed from the cache in the mobile device. However, in cases where the answered are not fully obtainable from the cache but can only be partially answered, we will trim the original query by either removing or annotating those parts that are answered and send it over the wireless channel to the server for further processing (Godfrey & Gryz, 1999). In other words, if the answer can be totally answered from the cache, a probe query is being issued whereas a remainder query is being issued to the server when only partial answers are obtainable. Figure 5 shows the semantic caching query processing mechanisms (Waluyo, Srinivasan, & Taniar, 2005).

> **Example 5:** *Consider a mobile user who previously issued queries in getting movie information. This information has been cached into his local memory storage previously. Now he would like to send another query in obtaining another list of movie information. So, it first processed locally via the semantic cache and determined if any of the semantic segments contributes to the query results from the cache index. If the result can be partially answer by the semantic segment then a probe query will retrieve the results that can be obtained locally and a remainder query will be issued to the server for evaluation to define the other partial results. And then the result for the query is obtained by integrating all the partial results into a single result which may consist of the results from probe query and remainder query.*

Due to the fact that mobile users in a typical mobile environment that moves around frequently by changing location has opens up a new challenge of answering queries that is dependent on the current geographical coordinates of the users (Barbara, 1999). An example

Figure 5. Semantic caching query processing mechanisms

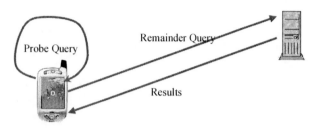

of a location dependent query can be "Find the nearest restaurants from where I am standing now." This is an example of static object whereby restaurants are not moving. An example of a dynamic object would be "What is the nearest taxi that will pass by me."

Queries should be processed in a way that minimizes the consumption of bandwidth and battery power. The problem is challenging because the user location is changing and the results would also change accordingly (Ren & Dunham, 2000). And with the keep on changing location that causes changing results to be downloaded would cost high communication cost if excessive communication is needed to and from the server several times (Seydim, Dunham, & Kumar, 2001). Hence, caching plays a role in location dependent query processing. This allows the queries to be answered without connecting to the server.

In summary, there are a series of steps that can be carried out in answering a query. First of all, the when a query has been issued, the local cache is checked to see whether the results can be obtainable locally or not. If there are no suitable answer to the queries that is issued that correspond to location of the user in cases of location dependent, then the information of the location of the user will be transmitted to the server to answer the query and returned back to the user. Otherwise if there is some related data from the cache itself, then the data can be retrieved directly from the cache and the answer to the query has been completed. For location dependent situation, by giving the current location of the user as well as the speed, the time when this user will moves to another location be computed and determined. However before the whole answering process ends, after getting the results from the server, a new cache is inserted into the local cache memory for future use (Ren & Dunham, 2000).

Cooperative Caching in Mobile Environment

Another type of cache management strategy that works well in a mobile environment that is investigated in this chapter would be cooperative caching. There are times when the data that are required by the user can be obtained from other clients. Hence, the cooperative caching is a kind of information sharing that was developed by the heavy influence and emergence of the robust yet reliable *peer to peer* (*P2P*) technologies which allows mobile client (Kortuem et al., 2001). With this type of information sharing among clients in a mobile environment has generally allow the clients to directly communication among themselves by being able to share cached information through accessing data items from the cache in

Figure 6. An overview of cooperative caching architecture

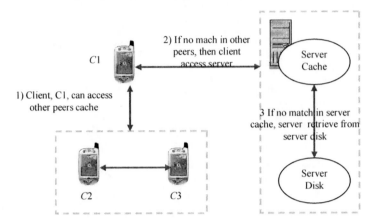

their neighboring peers rather than having to rely on their communication to the server for each query request (Chow, Leong, & Chan, 2004).

There are several distinctive and significance benefits that cooperative caching brings to a mobile computing environment. These include improving access latency, reducing server workload and alleviating point-to-point channel congestion. Though the benefits outdo the drawbacks, there is still a main concern that cooperative caching may produce. This refer to the possibility of increase in the communication overheads among mobile clients (Roy et al., 2005; Sailhan & Issarny, 2003, Shen et al., 2004)

Several clients and servers are connected together within a wireless channel in a mobile environment. Basically, the clients which denotes the mobile hosts are connected to each other wirelessly within a certain boundary among each other and they can exchange information by allowing each other in accessing the other peers cache (Shen et al., 2005)

Figure 6 illustrate an example of the framework architecture design of the cooperative caching which provides the ability for mobile clients to communicate among each other. If the clients encounters a *local cache miss*, it will sends query to request from its neighboring peers to obtain a communication and the desired data from its peers cache, otherwise it will be known as a *local cache hit* if the desired data exist in its local cache. As for trying to obtain data from its peers, if the desired data is available from its neighboring peers or if the other peers can turn in the requested data before it is being broadcast on the channel, then it is known as a *global cache hit*, otherwise it is called a *global cache miss* and the client would have to wait for the desired data to arrive in the broadcast channel or access the server cache and if that fails, then the server would retrieves the desired data from the disk. (Cortes, Girona, & Labarta, 1997; Hara, 2002; Chow, Leong, & Chan, 2005).

As a summary, a mobile client can choose to either (*a*) retrieve data from the server directly by having a direct communication through issuing query (Sailhan & Issarny, 2003) or (*b*) capturing the data from a scalable broadcast channels (Prabhajara, Hua, & Oh, 2005). These are known as pull base and push base mechanism respectively. Further investigation on pull- and push-based environment are being made on the subsequent sub sections.

Figure 7. Example of an on demand environment system (pull based system)

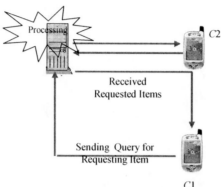

Cooperative caching can be use in either on-demand environment or broadcast environment. An on-demand or also known as a pull-based environment refers to relating the use of traditional point-to-point scenario similar to client-server communication directly. It can also be known as on-demand query or server strategy whereby processing can be done on the server upon request sent by the mobile clients. Figure 7 illustrate example of the architecture of a pull based environment system. It can be seen that the mobile client issue direct query to the server over a dedicated channel to be process. Processing would takes place in the server and once the requested data items have been obtained, it will returned back to the client directly.

The main advantages of this system is that client can issue query directly to the server and wait for the server to process and return the results accordingly to the query being issued. Also it is appropriate in situations where privacy is a major concern. On the other hand, the limitation is that this is not desirable in a mobile environment where there are limited resources to satisfy each individual client directly. Thus, this shows limitation when it comes to large scale systems.

Example 6: *Looking at Figure 8 suppose a shopper in a shopping complex wants to know which shops to visit by wishing to obtain information from the store directories. Imagine that this client is denoted as C2 in Figure 8. If this shopper, C2, finds the target shop in its local cache as she has previously visited this shopping complex and has cache the store directories in her mobile device. If this is the case, then she can just merely obtain the information from the cache. If not, then it will send request to its neighboring peers which in this example are C1 and C3 since the boundary of the wireless transmission for C2 covers clients C1 and C3. So C2 can obtain the desired data from either C1 or C3. Assuming C3 has the data that C2 wanted, so this means C2 can obtain the data from the cache in his peer, in this example is C3. Otherwise, C2 would have to obtain it from the server directly.*

Figure 8. Using cooperative caching in on demand environment

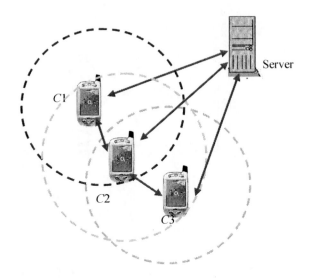

Now we would look at using cooperating caching in a broadcast environment which can sometimes be referred to as a push-based system or also known as on-air strategy. In a broadcast environment, a mobile client is able to tune into the broadcast channel to retrieve the data that they want by having the server to broadcast the data items into the air for the user to tune into (Waluyo, Srinivasan, & Taniar, 2005). Thus, each client can access a piece of data by waiting for its data to arrive. Figure 9 depicts an example of a broadcast environment. The main advantages of this broadcast environment in terms of its delivery mechanism is its higher throughput for data access for a larger number of clients because with the absence of the communication contention between the clients requesting data would means they are able to share the bandwidth more efficiently (Hara, 2002). Information broadcast appears to be an essential method for information dissemination for mobiles user since it is able to broadcast to and arbitrary number of mobile users (Lee & Lee, 1999).

There are advantages and disadvantages of the broadcast environment. The strength would be its ability to disseminate data to an immense number of mobile clients. However, the greatest disadvantage lies in the way in which the data item are broadcast in a sequential way. This will leads to longer access latency if there is a substantial increase in the number of data items being broadcast. Also by broadcasting the data item on the air, this means the mobile clients have to consume considerable amount of power to listen to the broadcast channel until the target data items reaches its turn and appears in the broadcast channel.

In this section, we would like to illustrate the use of cooperative caching in the broadcast environment. It is always a benefit to allow client to have access to more data in the mobile

Figure 9. Example of a broadcast environment system (push based system)

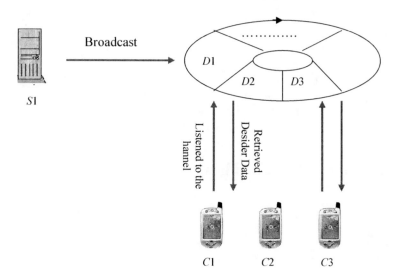

environment by improving the data availability and data accessibility (Shen et al., 2005). By having the clients to share bandwidth together in the wireless channels, it is believed that cooperative caching is able to further save bandwidth for each data retrieval (Joseph et al., 2005). An example of application utilizing this push base mechanism can be a situation where, in the airport, up-to-date schedules could be broadcast and passengers with their mobile devices are able to receive and store the information.

Generally, there are also a series of steps that are involved in cooperative caching in a broadcast environment. Basically, when a client issue a request to a particular data item on the broadcast channel, the issued request client would first checks whether the desired data has been previously cached. If it has, then the answer would be immediately returned and succeeds at once. However, if it does not, then it will secondly check to see if the response time in accessing the desired item that is cached by the neighboring peers is shorter than to wait for the item to appear on the broadcast channel. If it is, then it will obtain from it peers, otherwise it may be easier just to obtain from the broadcast channel if it appears to be faster. Otherwise, it received a reply from other neighboring peers that cached the desired data item and the request would be completed and succeeded when the transmission of the item is completed. However in case of situation where no neighboring peers obtain the desired data then the client would have to wait for the next broadcast period for the desired data item to appear (Hara, 2002).

In the next section, we would look at another different type of cache strategy, which is known as cache invalidation.

Cache Invalidation in a Mobile Environment

Due to the important issue in mobile environment which is the ability to maintain data consistency, cache invalidation strategy is utmost significance to ensure that the data items cached in the mobile client are consistent with those that are stored on the server. In order to ensure that data that are about to use is consistent, a client must validate its cache prior to using any data from it. This section would be divided into two sub sections which is the first section we would talk about an overview of a cache invalidation strategy and then followed y the using cache invalidation involving location dependent data.

Overview of Cache Invalidation

There are several distinctive and significance benefits that cache invalidation brings to a mobile computing environment. If cache data are not validated to check for consistency, it will become useless and out of date. However if one can utilize the cache data then the benefits it may brings include energy savings that is by reducing the amount of data transfer and in return results in cost savings.

Very often, we would use cache invalidation strategy in a broadcast environment. This is because by using broadcast environment, the server can broadcast a series of invalidation report which states what data items has been made changes on to a large amount of users simultaneously. And this can be done by using broadcasting concept in communicating cache validation information to mobile clients. The server broadcast the cache information which is known as cache invalidation report (IR) periodically on air to help clients validate their cache to ensure they are still consistent and can be used. It appears that broadcast mechanism is more appropriate for the mobile environment due to their characteristic of salability which allows it to broadcast data to an arbitrary number of clients who can listen to the broadcast channel anytime (Papadopuli & Issarnyy, 2001). By using the broadcasting approach whereby the server periodically broadcast the IR to indicate the change data items, it eliminates the need to querying directly to the server for a validation cache copies. The mobile clients would be able to listen to the broadcast channel on the IR and use them to validate their local cache respectively (Cao, 2002).

Although cache invalidation strategy is important in a mobile environment, it will be vulnerable to disconnection and the mobility of the clients. One of the main reasons that cause mobile clients to frequent disconnection is the limited battery power and that is why mobile clients often disconnect to conserve battery power. It may appear to be very expensive at times to validate the cache for clients that experience frequent disconnection especially with narrow wireless links. Other drawbacks would include long query latency which is associated with the need of the mobile client to listen to the channel for the next IR first before he is able to conclude whether the cache is valid or not before answering a query. Another major drawback is the unnecessary data items in the IR that the server keeps. This refers to data items that are not cached by any mobile clients. This thereby wastes a significant amount of wireless bandwidth.

Example 7: *A mobile client in a shopping complex wanted to know which store to visit by obtaining store directories. The client has previously visited this store and already has a copy of the result in his cache. In order to answer a query, the client will listen to the IR that are broadcasted and use it for validation against its local cache to see if it is valid or not. If there is a valid cached copy that can be used in answering the query which is getting the store directories then the result will be returned immediately. Otherwise if the shop directories has changed and now contained new shops, then the invalid caches have to be refreshed via sending a query to the server (Elmagarmid, Jing, Helal, & Lee, 2003). The server would keep track of the recently updated data and broadcast the up to date IR every now and then for the clients to tune in. This can be done either by sending a request directly to the server (pull-based system) or tune into the broadcast channel (push-based system). Figure 10 illustrate an example of a push based system involving cache invalidation mechanism.*

In this location dependent query, the server would produce answer to a query based on location of the mobile client issuing the query. Thus, different location may sometimes yield a different result even though the query is taken from similar source.

Figure 10. Using cache invalidation in a mobile environment location dependent cache invalidation

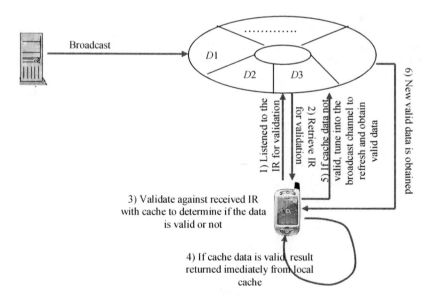

Figure 11. Architecture of location dependent query processing

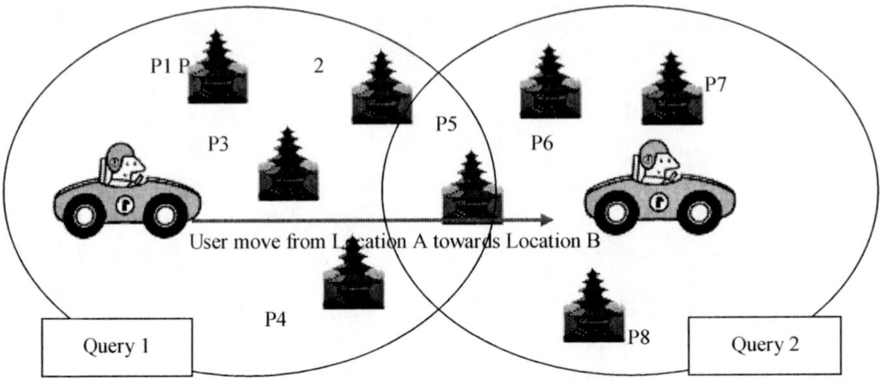

Figure 11 depicts an illustration of a location dependent query processing. This shows that when the mobile client in Location *A*, the query would return a set of results and when the mobile client move towards a new Location *B*, another set of results will be returned. However there are cases of results overlapping between nearby locations. An example of a location dependent query can be "Find the nearest restaurants from where I am standing now." This is an example of static object whereby restaurants are not moving. An example of a dynamic object would be "What is the nearest taxi that will pass by me" (Lee, Leong, & Si, 2002).

With the frequent movement of mobile users, very often the mobile clients would query the same server to obtain results or with the frequent movement of mobile users from location to location, very often the mobile clients would suffer from scarce bandwidth and frequent disconnection especially when suddenly move towards a secluded area (Seydim, Dunham, & Kumar, 2001). Hence, is essential to have data caching which can cope with cases of frequent disconnections. And often data may have become invalid after a certain point of time especially in the area of location dependent.

> **Example 8:** *A mobile user who is in Location A, cached result of the nearby vegetarian restaurants in Location A. As he moves to Location B, he would like another list of nearby vegetarian restaurants. The user are sending query to the same source but results returned are different due to location dependent data. And because there are data previously cached, this data which is the result obtained when he is in Location A would become invalid since he has now moves to Location B.*

Hence, location dependent cache invalidation serves the purpose of maintaining the validity of the cached data when the mobile client moves from one location to another location

(Zheng, Xu, & Lee, 2002). The emergence of this location dependent cache invalidation is due to mobile clients' movement and thus the data value for a data item is actually dependent on the geographical location. Hence, traditional caching that do not consider geographical location are inefficient for location dependent data.

There are both advantages and disadvantages of location dependent cache invalidation. The major benefit that the attached invalidation information provided is that it provides a way for the client to be able to check for validity of cached data in respect to a certain location. These are necessary especially in cases of when the mobile clients wishes to issue the same query later when he/she moves to a new location. Another situation for the importance in checking the validity of the cached data is that because mobile clients keep on moving even right after he has submit a query and would have arrived to a new location when the results are returned. This may occur if there is a long delay in accessing data. Thus, if these two situations occur, then it is significant to validate the cached data because it may have become invalid (Zheng et al., 2002).

Future Trend

There have been several researches done in the area of exploring semantic, cooperative and cache invalidation in mobile environment. The usage of these different types of cache management strategy has obviously provoked extensive complicated issues. There are still many limitations of the nature of the mobile environment as well as mobility of the users that generates a lot of attention from researching in finding a good cache strategy that can cope well with frequent disconnection and low power consumption.

In the future, it is critical to design algorithms for using semantic caching to cope with the low bandwidth of the wireless channel as well as the vulnerable disconnection problem. Applying semantic caching to several different scenarios of location dependent queries, including in a multiple cell environment and a cooperative strategy between multiple clients, is also beneficial. Caching management strategies which focus on semantic mechanism that are designed for real mobile queries that will utilize space more efficiently, is also needed in the future.

It is also advantageous to look further into incorporation of an effective replication scheme that may increase data availability and accessibility as well as improve the average query latency. It would be useful to always take into account in reducing number of server requests, power consumption as well as shortening the access latency as more neighboring peers increase. As far as most situations explain in this chapter, the focus does not take into location dependency queries. Thus, it can be a good idea to consider location dependent queries as well as accessing multiple non-collaborative servers instead of just obtaining data from a single server.

Besides these, further investigation as well as to build an analytical model to get a better understanding of how cache invalidation works and how well it can cope in the mobile environment is desirable. By developing caching strategies that support cache invalidation for multiple channel environments is also desirable whereby a mixture of broadcast and point-to-point channels are being used. By including a dynamic clustering is also beneficial in order to allow the server to group data items together as their update changes. Besides these, further investigation on other cache replacement policies as well as granularities issue is also beneficial.

Due to the nonstop moving clients, further research on adapting cache invalidation into location dependent data is favorable. Another possible issue that could open up for future work may involve minimizing the waiting time for the mobile client in acquiring the IR. Since the mobile client has to obtain an IR prior to their cache being validated. Thus, it is essential to be able to reduce waiting time. Another aspect is due to wireless channel that are often error prone due to its instability bandwidth and so on. Thereby, having techniques to handle errors in a mobile environment is definitely helpful. Last but not least, by having further study on integrating several different strategies to obtain a more optimal solution in coping with mobile environment is advantageous.

Conclusion

Although there are significant increase in the popularity of mobile computing, there are still several limitations that are inherent be it the mobile devices it self or the environment itself. These include limited battery power, storage, communication cost, and bandwidth problem. All these have become present challenges for researchers to address. Caching appears to be a key factor in helping to improve performance of answering queries in mobile environment.

In this chapter, we have described the pros and cons of adopting the different types of cache management strategy in a mobile environment. We include adapting semantic caching in both location and non-location dependent queries as well as explored on the new state of the art information sharing known as cooperative caching allows mobile clients an alternative way to obtain desired data items. Clients can now have the ability to access data items from the cache in their neighboring peers with the implementation of cooperative caching. We also include adapting cache invalidation strategy in both location and non-location dependent queries and discussions regarding the issue that arises when choosing a good cache management strategy.

This chapter serves as a valuable starting point for those who wish to gain some introductory knowledge about the usefulness of the different types of cache management strategy that can be use in a typical mobile database environment.

References

Barbara, D. (1999). Mobile computing and databases: A survey. *IEEE Transactions on Knowledge and Data Engineering, 1*(1), 108-117.

Barbara, D., & Imielinski, T. (1994). Sleepers and workaholics: Caching strategies in mobile environments. *MOBIDATA: An Interactive Journal of Mobile Computing, 1*(1).

Cai, J., & Tan, K.L. (1999). Energy efficient selective cache invalidation. *Wireless Networks, 5*(6), 489-502.

Cao, G. (2003). A scalable low-latency cache invalidation strategy for mobile environment. *IEEE Transaction on Knowledge and Data Engineering (TKDE), 15*(2), 1251-1265.

Cao, G. (2002). On improving the performance of cache invalidation in mobile environment. *Mobile Networks and Applications, 7*(4), 291-303.

Chan, B. Y., Si, A., & Leong, H. V. (1998). Cache management for mobile databases: Design and evaluation. In *Proceedings of the International Conference on Data Engineering (ICDE)* (pp. 54-63).

Chand, N., Joshi, R., & Misra, M. (1996). Energy efficient cache invalidation in a disconnected mobile environment. In *Proceedings of the Twelfth International Conference on Data Engineering* (pp. 336-343).

Chow, C. Y., Leong, H.V., & Chan, A.T.S. (2005). Distributed group-based cooperative caching in a mobile environment. In *Proceedings of the 6th international conference on Mobile Data Management (MDM)* (pp. 97-106).

Chow, C.Y., Leong, H.V., & Chan, A.T.S. (2004). Group-based cooperative cache management for mobile clients in a mobile environment. In *Proceedings of the 33rd International Conference on Parallel Processing (ICPP)* (pp. 83-90).

Chow, C. Y., Leong, H.V., & Chan, A.T.S. (2004). Peer-to-peer cooperative caching in a hybrid data delivery environment. In *Proceedings of the 2004 International Symposium on Parallel Architectures, Algorithms and Networks (ISPAN2004)*.

Chow, C. Y., Leong, H.V., & Chan, A.T.S. (2004). Cache signatures for peer-to-peer cooperative caching in mobile environments. In *Proceedings of 2004 International Conference on Advanced Information Networking and Applications*.

Cortés, T., Girona, S., & Labarta, J. (1997). Dessign issues of a cooperative cache with no coherence problems. In *Fifth Workshop on I/O in Parallel and Distributed Systems (IOPADS'97)* (pp. 37-46).

Dar, S., Franklin, M., Jonsson, B., Srivastava, D., & Tab, M. (1996). Semantic data caching and replacement. In *Proceedings of 22nd International Conference on Very Large Data Bases* (pp. 330-341).

Elmagarmid, A., Jing, J., Helal, A., & Lee, C. (2003). Scalable cache invalidation algorithms for mobile data access. *IEEE Transaction on Knowledge and Data Engineering (TKDE), 15*(6), 1498-1511.

Elmasri, R., & Navathe, S. B. (2003). *Fundamentals of database systems* (4th ed.). Addison Wesley.

Godfrey, P., & Gryz, J. (1999). Answering queries by semantic caches. In *Proceedings of Database and Expert Systems Applications (DEXA)* (pp. 485-498).

Hara, T. (2002). Cooperative caching by mobile clients in push-based information systems. In *Proceedings. of ACM International Conference on Information and Knowledge Management (ACM CIKM'02)* (pp. 186-193).

Hu, Q., & Lee, D. (1998). Cache algorithms based on adaptive invalidation reports for mobile environment. *Cluster Computing*, 39-48.

Hurson, A.R., & Jiao, Y. (2005). Data broadcasting in mobile environment. In D. Katsaros, A. Nanopoulos, & Y. Manolopoulos (Eds.), *Wireless information highways*. Hershey, PA: IRM Press.

Imielinski, T., & Badrinath, B. (1994). Mobile wireless computing: Challenges in data management. *Communications of the ACM, 37*(10), 18-28.

Joseph, M.S., Kumar, M., Shen, H., & Das, S.K. (2005). Energy efficient data retrieval and caching in mobile peer-to-peer networks. In *Proceedings of the 2nd Workshop on Mobile Peer-to-Peer Networks (MP2P)* (pp. 50-54).

Kara, H., & Edwards, C. (2003). A caching architecture for content delivery to mobile devices. In *Proceedings of the 29th EUROMICRO Conference: New Waves in System Architecture (EUROMICRO'03)*.

Kortuem, G., Schneider, J., Preuitt, D., Thompson, C., Fickas, S., & Segall, Z. (2001). When peer to peer comes face to face: Collaborative peer to peer computing in mobile ad hoc networks. In *Proceedings of the First International Conference on Peer to Peer Computing*.

Lee, K. C. K., Leong, H. V., & Si, A. (2000). A semantic broadcast scheme for a mobile environment based on dynamic chunking. In *Proceedings of the IEEE International Conference on Distributed Computing Systems (ICDCS)* (pp. 522-529).

Lee, C. K. K., Leong, H. V., & Si, A. (2001). Adaptive semantic data broadcast in a mobile environment. In *Proceedings of the 2001 ACM Symposium on Applied Computing* (pp. 393-400).

Lee, K. C. K., Leong, H. V., & Si, A. (2002). Semantic data access in an asymmetric mobile environment. In *Proceedings of the 3rd Mobile Data Management* (pp. 94-101).

Lee, K. C. K., Leong, H. V., & Si, A. (1999). Semantic query caching in a mobile environment. *ACM Mobile Computing and Communications Review, 3*(2), 28-36.

Lo, E., Mamoulis, N., Cheung, D. W., Ho, W. S., & Kalnis, P. (2003). *Processing ad-hoc joins on mobile devices* (Tech. Rep.). The University of Hong Kong. Retrieved from http://www.csis.hku.hk/~dbgroup.techreport

Papadopouli, M., & Issarny, V. (2001). Effects of power conservation: Wireless coverage and cooperation on data dissemination among mobile devices. In *Proceedings. of the 2nd ACM International Symposium on Mobile Ad HOC Networking and Computing (MobiHoc)* (pp. 117-127).

Prabhajara, K., Hua, K.A., & Oh, J.H. (2000). Multi-level, multi-channel air cache designs for broadcasting in a mobile environment. In *Proceedings of the 16th International Conference on Data Engineering* (pp. 167-186).

Persone, V., & Grassi, V. (2003). Performance analysis of caching and prefetching strategies for palmtop-based navigational tools. *IEEE Transactions on Intelligent Transportation System, 4*(1), 23-32.

Ren, Q., & Dunham, M. H. (2000). Using semantic caching to manage location dependent data in mobile computing. In *Proceedings of the 6th International Conference on Mobile Computing and Networking* (pp. 210-221).

Ren, Q., Dunham, M. H., & Kumar, V. (2003). Semantic caching and query processing. *IEEE Transactions on Knowledge and Data Engineering, 15*(1), 192-210.

Roy, N., Roy, A., Basu, K., & Das, S.K. (2005). A cooperative learning framework for mobility-aware resource management in multi-inhabitant smart homes. In *Proceedings of 2nd Annual IEEE International Conference on Mobile and Ubiquitous Systems: Networking and Services* (pp. 393-403).

Sailhan, F., & Issarny, V. (2003). Cooperative caching in ad hoc network. In *Proceedings. of the 4th International Conference on Mobile Data Management (MDM)* (pp. 13-28).

Sarkar, P., & Hartman, J.H. (2000). Hint-based cooperative caching. *ACM Transactions on Computer Systems, 18*(4), 387-419.

Seydim, A. Y., Dunham, M. H., & Kumar, V. (2001). Location-dependent query processing. In *Proceedings of the Second International Workshop on Data Engineering on Mobile and Wireless Access (MobiDE'01)* (pp. 47-53).

Shen, H., Joseph, M.S., Kumar, M., & Das, S.K. (2005). PReCinCt: An energy efficient data retrieval scheme for mobile peer-to-peer networks. In *Proceedings of 19th IEEE International Parallel and Distributed Processing Symposium (IPDPS)*.

Shen, H., Joseph, M.S., Kumar, M., & Das, S.K. (2004). Cooperative caching with optimal radius in hybrid wireless networks. In *Proceedings of Third IFIP-TC6 Networking Conference* (LNCS. 3042, pp. 841-853).

Tan, K.L., Cai, J., & Ooi, B.C. (2001). An evaluation of cache invalidation strategies in wireless environment. *IEEE Transactions on Parallel and Distributed Systems, 12*(8), 789-807.

Waluyo, A.B., Srinivasan, B., & Taniar, D. (2005). Indexing schemes for multi channel data broadcasting in mobile databases. *International Journal of Wireless and Mobile Computing, 1*(6).

Waluyo, A.B., Srinivasan, B., & Taniar, D. (2005). Research in mobile database query optimization and processing. *Mobile Information Systems, 1*(4).

Xu, J., Hu, Q., Tang, X., & Zheng, B. (2005). Mobile cache management. In D. Katsaros et al. (Eds.), *Wireless information highways* (pp. 32-59). Hershey, PA: IRM Press..

Xu, J., Hu, Q., Lee, D. L., & Lee, W.-C. (2000). SAIU: An efficient cache replacement policy for wireless on-demand broadcasts. In *Proceedings of the 9th International Conference on Information and Knowledge Management* (pp. 46-53).

Xu, J., Hu, Q., Lee, W.-C., & Lee, D. L. (2004). Performance evaluation of an optimal cache replacement policy for wireless data dissemination. *IEEE Transaction on Knowledge and Data Engineering (TKDE)*, *16*(1), 125-139.

Xu, J., Zheng, B., Lee, W.-C., & Lee, D. L. (2003). Energy efficient index for querying location-dependent data in mobile broadcast environments. In *Proceedings of the 19th IEEE International Conference on Data Engineering (ICDE '03)* (pp. 239-250).

Yajima, E., Hara, T., Tsukamoto, M., & Nishio, S. (2001). Scheduling and caching strategies for correlated data in push-based information system. *ACM SIGAPP Applied Computing Review*, *9*(1), 22-28.

Zheng, B., Xu, J., & Lee, D.L. (2002). Cache invalidation and replacement strategies for location-dependent data in mobile environments. *IEEE Transactions on Computers*, *51*(10), 1141-1153.

Chapter IX

Mining Walking Pattern from Mobile Users

John Goh, Monash University, Australia

David Taniar, Monash University, Australia

Abstract

Mining walking pattern from mobile users represents an interesting research area in the field of data mining which is about extracting patterns and knowledge out from a given dataset. There are a number of related works in knowledge extraction from mobile users, but none have previously examined the situation of how mobile users walks from one location of interest to another location of interest in the mobile environment. Walking pattern is the proposed method where it examines from the source data in order to find out the two-step, three-step and four-step walking patterns that are performed by mobile users significantly and strongly through location movement database using measure of support and confidence. Performance evaluation shows the tendency for the increased number of candidate walking patterns with the increase in location of interest and steps. Walking pattern has proven itself to be a suitable method in finding knowledge from mobile users.

Introduction

With the advances of information technology, data processing and memory capacity are becoming more advanced and more accessible. The same processing power and memory capacity would not be affordable or accessible 10 years ago. Information technologies have been adopted by the economy in many aspects. As information technologies have the capability to record a massive amount of data and also to process these data in a remarkable speed, one of such application is to record the activities carried out by a subject matter in order for further analysis (Tjioe & Taniar, 2005; Roddick & Lees, 2001; Roddick & Spiliopoulou, 2002).

Subject matter can be anything from mobile users, customers, weather balloon, motor vehicles, and so forth. With information technologies, these subjects can be identified quickly and efficient, and their dealings or activities could be tracked and recorded in a storage capacity which is available in vast amount of size at an affordable cost. Mobile users are one of such subjects that are used for recording of activities and then further analysis. The process of recording vast amount of data and later for analysis is also known as knowledge extraction or data mining (Han & Plank, 1996; Han, Dong, & Yin, 1999; Han, Pei, & Yin, 2000; Jayaputera & Taniar, 2005).

Mobile users are a promising candidate for knowledge extraction because mobile devices, especially mobile phones are increasingly capable in terms of processing capacity, network bandwidth, and also storage capacity. Mobile devices are not limited to mobile phones, but also devices such as personal digital assistant (*PDA*), laptop computer, and other potentially newly developed mobile devices as long as it serves the mobile users on the move and have the ability to communicate to a server and be able to be queried by server.

New generation of mobile phones (Varshey, Vetter, & Kalakota, 2000; Reed Electronics, 2002) have capability of downloading movies on the move, and playing back the movie to mobile users (Tse, Lam, Ng, & Chan, 2005). Such operation would take a great deal of processing power, memory and also bandwidth. As mobile devices are carried by mobile users at most of the times, and with the advent of technologies such as global positioning system (*GPS*) (Song, Kang, & Park, 2005; Zarchan,1996) or other location identification technologies (Hofmann-Wellenhof, Lichtenegger, & Collins, 1994; Häkkilä & Mäntyjärvi, 2005) incorporated into mobile devices, mobile devices now can be queried (Lee, Zhu, & Hu, 2005) and detail of mobile users such as their name, age, address, date/time, and current location on earth can be gathered.

As the goal of knowledge extraction (Chen & Loi, 2005) is to find useful knowledge out from the subject (Koperski & Han, 1995; Forlizzi, Guting, Nardelli, & Schneider, 2000; Cho, Pei, Wang, & Wang, 2005), such as how the mobile users behaves by looking at who the mobile users interacts with (*person*), when the mobile users interacts (*timing*), how the mobile users interacts (*method*), what the mobile users interacts with (*objects*), where the mobile users interacts with (*location*). This is done by analyzing the source dataset in order to detect patterns or trends or any other useful information in which it could make sense. A piece of information that makes good deal of sense describing how mobile users behave is a piece of knowledge and thus knowledge extraction (Chakrabarti, Sarawagi, & Dom, 1998; Chen & Loi, 2005). Depending on the application domain and data collected such as temporal data (Chakrabarti et al., 1998; Wang, Yang, & Yu, 2002), and different data structure (Xiao, Yao, & Yang, 2005) different approach of knowledge extraction is taken. This chapter is all about applying the proposed method walking pattern in order to make sense out of data collected from mobile users.

Privacy will certainly be an issue that needs to be addressed for such knowledge extraction operation, especially when it involves human beings who deserves a certain degree of privacy. Privacy preserving issues remains a future work for this research area of extracting knowledge from mobile users. Issues such as how to collect the information of where the mobile users have visited, how to collect personal information from mobile users, how to perform analysis and yet preserving the privacy of personal details of mobile users are issues that needs to be addressed in the future. For the scope of this chapter, proposed method of walking pattern is provided but privacy issues will be addressed in the future.

The rest of this chapter is organized as follows. Background section provides background of knowledge that is required before one can understand the proposed method walking pattern clearly. Walking pattern section provides the proposed method including description on the knowledge extraction process, and also relevant definition and algorithms. Case study provides the case study for the proposed method using walkthrough from a small sample user movement database. Performance evaluation section provides the performance evaluation of the proposed method. Conclusion section provides the conclusion of this chapter, and also provides some brief overview of potential future works that can be done in this area.

Background

Data concerning mobile users are stored in a database. This database is usually large in terms of size, and complex in terms of data structure. For this chapter, the database is a static relational database. Static database refers to database which data stored previously into the database is no longer being updated. In this case, the database used throughout the knowledge extraction process is not updated, or changed. In another words, after the knowledge extraction process is started, the database no longer being updated and their subsequent values does not change.

Relational database is a database where each table in the database is represented by two dimensional table showing rows and columns. The database can be normalized in order connect one table to another, such as the mobile user identification number being the primary key and refers to another table via a foreign key or primary key in another table, such as the family background of the mobile users. Relational database is commonly used method to store data collected.

Due to the fact that knowledge extraction had to collect data from mobile devices which can range from different architecture, it is important that the database be as simple as possible so that all architectures can support the database. In this chapter, user movement database (UMD) is used which is a database that stores the location coordinates (x, y) of mobile users. It is very much possible that mobile devices can be configured to store summarized location data, such as providing the exact location attributes, such as the name of the library that the mobile user is currently located. It has been decided that it is not the best way to approach the data mining problem, because not all mobile devices can perform so, and also there many be many totally different ways the knowledge extraction process can gather data from different sources.

User movement database is there represented in the following way: Figure 1 represents a user movement database (*UMD*). It consists of rows which are representing time and columns each representing individual mobile users. Each cell represents a (x, y) coordinate which are the coordinates recorded by the location tracking system in the mobile environment. The coordinates (x, y) maps directly to the mobile environment in a two dimensional space, where x represents the horizontal axis, and y represents the vertical axis. Throughout the location tracking process, (x, y) are represented as a non negative integer number. As mobile users moves along places in mobile environment of limited mobile services, and therefore, the location data is sometimes unavailable and is not recorded in the user movement database. This can happen when the mobile users went into an underground subway station, or inside an underground building.

Location of interest (*LOI*) is interesting locations in the mobile environment worthwhile for the knowledge extraction process. Example of location of interest is the *coffee shop*, *library*, *shopping centre*, *cinema*, *classroom*, *gym*, *bookstore, and so on.* Each location of interest is not general, as it does not represent bookstore in general but it represent a specific bookshop on a particular street. This is known as physical representation whereas the method

Figure 1. User movement database

Time	User 1	User 2	User 3	User 4	User 5	User 6
1	(1, 1)	(2, 1)	(3, 1)	(20, 1)	-	(1, 1)
2	(1, 2)	(2, 2)	(3, 2)	(20, 2)	-	(1, 2)
3	(1, 3)	(2, 3)	(3, 3)	(20, 3)	-	(1, 3)
4	(1, 4)	(2, 4)	(3, 4)	(20, 4)	-	(1, 4)
5	(1, 5)	(2, 5)	(3, 5)	(70, 1)	(70, 1)	(1, 5)
6	-	(1, 1)	(3, 5)	(70, 2)	(70, 2)	-
7	-	(1, 2)	(3, 5)	(70, 3)	(70, 3)	-
8	-	(1, 3)	(3, 5)	(70, 4)	(70, 4)	-
9	-	(1, 4)	(3, 5)	-	(20, 1)	-
10	-	(1, 5)	(3, 5)	-	(20, 2)	-
11	(20, 1)	(20, 1)	(3, 5)	-	(20, 3)	(70, 1)
12	(20, 2)	(20, 2)	(3, 5)	-	(20, 4)	(70, 2)
13	(20, 3)	(20, 3)	(3, 5)	-	(20, 1)	(70, 3)
14	(20, 4)	(20, 4)	-	(1, 1)	(20, 2)	(70, 4)
15	(20, 5)	(70, 1)	-	(10, 1)	(20, 3)	(20, 1)
16	(70, 1)	(70, 2)	-	(20, 1)	(20, 4)	(20, 2)
17	(70, 2)	(70, 3)	-	(30, 1)	-	(20, 3)

Figure 1. continued

18	(70, 3)	(70, 4)	-	(40, 1)	-	(20, 4)
19	-	(70, 5)	-	(50, 1)	-	(2, 1)
20	-	-	(20, 1)	(60, 1)	(70, 1)	(2, 2)
21	-	-	(20, 2)	(1, 1)	(70, 2)	(2, 3)
22	-	-	(20, 3)	(1, 2)	(70, 3)	(2, 4)
23	-	-	(20, 4)	(1, 3)	(70, 4)	(2, 5)
24	(1, 1)	-	(70, 1)	(1, 4)	(2, 1)	-
25	(10, 1)	-	(70, 2)	(1, 5)	(2, 2)	-
26	(20, 1)	(1, 1)	(70, 3)	(1, 6)	(2, 3)	(1, 1)
27	(30, 1)	(1, 2)	(70, 4)	-	(2, 4)	(1, 2)
28	(40, 1)	(1, 3)	(70, 5)	-	(2, 5)	(1, 3)
29	(50, 1)	(1, 4)	(70, 6)	-	-	(1, 4)
30	(60, 1)	(1, 5)	(70, 7)	-	-	(1, 5)

of representing a non specific bookstore is known as logical representation. In this chapter, physical representation is used. The following represents a location of interest database.

Figure 2 shows the location of interest database. It represents all location of interest in the knowledge extraction process, and thus these locations of interests have to be identified before the mining process and their subsequent zones also are determined. There are altogether 15 locations of interest in the database above, ranging from coffee shops to post offices. Each *LOI* have start and finish coordinates. The start coordinate represents the bottom left hand corner and finish coordinate represents the top right hand corner of a rectangle which will represents the zone of the location of interest. Note that both start and finish coordinates must be available.

Location of interests can overlap and they may overlap in two cases. First, it may overlap with each other by being a subset of another location of interest. For instance, in a library, there is a coffee shop around the corner, and therefore, the coffee shop is zoned as coffee shop and also library, but the remaining area of the library remains the library zone. Second, it may overlap with each other by intersection. For instance, there are coffee shop and post office neighboring each other. The zones for post office and coffee shop can be slightly more than the actual physical boundary, as mobile users standing near to the coffee shop may be drinking coffee and looking at stamps to buy. Therefore, in between coffee shop and post office, the middle boundary is the intersection where it belongs to coffee shop and post office, but the rest belongs to coffee shop or post office individually.

The term patterns and rules will be used interchangeably though this chapter. They both have been used for the same meaning for repeated occurrence of a specific trends, or phenomenon. For example, it was found that mobile users tend to travel from $a \rightarrow b \rightarrow c$, and then it is known as a pattern or rule. A group of useful pattern or rules forms a body of knowledge.

Figure 2. Location of interest database

ID	Location of Interest (LOI)	Start	Finish
I1	coffee1	(1, 1)	(10, 10)
I2	coffee2	(7, 7)	(25, 25)
I3	coffee3	(30, 30)	(50, 50)
I4	library1	(70, 70)	(80, 80)
I5	library2	(10, 10)	(14, 14)
I6	library3	(80, 1)	(80, 10)
I7	cinema1	(20, 20)	(30, 30)
I8	cinema2	(70, 10)	(70, 20)
I9	cinema3	(20, 30)	(20, 40)
I10	shop1	(90, 1)	(90, 10)
I11	shop2	(90, 11)	(90, 20)
I12	shop3	(90, 21)	(90, 30)
I13	post1	(80, 1)	(80, 5)
I14	post2	(10, 15)	(20, 15)
I15	post3	(30, 30)	(40, 30)

The term data mining and knowledge extraction is also being used interchangeably, as both of them are used for the process of analyzing large databases in order to determine all the patterns and rules within the database. It thus extracts knowledge or mines out knowledge from databases.

Related Work

There are a few related works in the field of knowledge extraction from mobile users. Yida Wang et al. developed group pattern whereby it is designed to analyze user movement database in order to determine the mobile users that frequently meets with each other throughout the mining horizon. This piece of work looks at another type of knowledge from mobile users, which is about the mobile users who have physical distance among each other lesser than max-distance threshold, and for a duration greater than min-duration, and finally occurs frequently enough such that weight greater than min-weight. The result of group pattern is a list of mobile users that meets frequently, as such given input of min-duration, max-distance and min-weight, the knowledge extraction process will output, where each group represents a group of mobile users that satisfies the three thresholds.

2 valid group pattern:

$\{u_1, u_2\}, \{u_1, u_3\}, \{u_1, u_5\}, \{u_1, u_6\}$

3 valid group pattern:

$\{u_1, u_2, u_3\}, \{u_2, u_3, u_4\}, \{u_4, u_5, u_6\}$

4 valid group pattern:

$\{u_1, u_2, u_3, u_4\}$

Agrawal et al. (1994, 1995) developed the association rule and sequential pattern. Although these are applied to market basket analysis in retail database transactions, and they are not strictly related to mobile users, the concept do have contribution towards the motivation in the development of methods and techniques for mining from mobile users. Association rules and sequential pattern both uses support measurement for statistical significance, and association rules uses confidence measurement for the strength of rules. For association rules, each rule have a antecedent and consequent, as such $A \rightarrow B$ means if A occurs then B will also occur, which have a meaning of if-then situation.

The process of association rules is to find the list of items which are frequent enough to satisfy statistical significance. Items that are not statistically significant are discarded for the rest of the data mining process. Once the lists of items that are statistically significant are found, the set of items is used to generate candidate rules and measurement is performed on the rules in order to find out the confidence of the rule. The confidence of the rule is calculated by support (A and B occurs) / support (only A occurs). In another words, it is a measurement of given A occurs, out of how many times B also occurs given A also occurs.

Forsyth (1999) and Wang, Lim, and Hwang (2003, 2004) developed an enhancement of group pattern called summarized location sphere by providing location summarization. It is a performance enhancement drive in order to reduce the performance bottlenecks occurred at generating two-candidate groups. It is the process that consumes the most processing power and memory. This is due to the algorithm requiring comparing the distance and duration thresholds for each and every two-candidate group. As always, it occurs that two-candidate group generates the most number of groups, thus leading to a large amount of comparisons and testing to be done. It tries to resolve the problem by dividing the user movement database into multiple windows, each window represents a predefined duration, and is constant throughout the database. If the window size is five and there are 30 time in the series, then six windows will be produced. Each window is summarized by using a formula and a centre point and radius is determined. Each window is now having a summarized reference point as the center and the radius, thus the word sphere. The result of this method is lesser calculation performed.

Hwang, Loi, Chiu, and Lim (2005) developed a trajectory method in user movement database in order to take into account situation whereby the data in the database may become unavailable or delayed due to unavailability of mobile devices or delay in transmission or record of data from mobile devices to the server. It tries to solve the problem by using linear trajectories and regression. Given a set of time points for a mobile users, it is assumed that the mobile users generally moves from source to destination in a relatively straight line, the algorithm uses linear regression to return a linear function to represent the movement. Therefore, for the duration of linear regression, say every 5 minutes, any location of the time point is predicted by substituting the desired time point into the formula in order to get the predicted (x, y) values for the mobile users.

Sequential pattern (Agrawal & Srikat, 1995) however, given a database first sorts the database, and tries to find a list of frequently occurring combination. It uses database join and pruning method in order to find the list of candidate sequences. Each candidate sequences are measured against the original database in order to determine the level of support. This process is continued until the maximal sequence is found with a support greater than min-support. In sequential pattern, confidence measurement is not used, as there is no if-then situation occurring, rather than pattern of sequence occurring.

Finally, after describing others related work in knowledge extraction from mobile users, we have developed a variety of methods in finding interesting knowledge from mobile users. They are namely, frequency pattern (Goh & Taniar, 2004), static group pattern mining (*SGPM*) (Goh & Taniar, 2006), mobile user database static object mining (*MUDSOM*) (Goh & Taniar, 2005), location dependent mobile data mining (Goh & Taniar, 2004), and parallel pattern (Goh & Taniar, 2004). Only recent works of frequent pattern, *MUDSOM* and *SGPM* will be described here in order to preserve valuable space for proposed method.

Frequency pattern (Goh & Taniar, 2004) is a method in which it looks at how mobile users communicate with each other. This is done by analyzing the communication log among mobile users. It is determined that mobile users who communicates frequently enough with other mobile users is deemed to have some relationship among them. It can be colleague, student, family, close friends, employer-employee, social work relationships, and so forth. By analyzing the frequency of communication among mobile users coupled with the timing of communication giving the weight of communication at different time, provides an output of the group of mobile users that are close. For example, mobile users that talk to each other during afternoon are likely to be talking with fellow colleagues for lunch breaks, and so on. The result of frequency pattern is such as $\{u_1, u_2, u_3\}$ represents a group of close friends that frequently communicates with each during Monday evening 7pm.

Static group pattern mining (*SGPM*) (Goh & Taniar, 2005) is an improvement from group pattern in which it not only tells the occurrence of group of mobile users that are close together long and frequently enough, but it also tells the specific location where the group of mobile users meets. This is performed by the technique of first replacing the values of user movement database with a set of pre-defined locations of interests. Location of interests is pre-defined zones in the mobile environment where the location presents some interesting feature in which is useful for knowledge extraction. For example, the neighborhood library would be a very good candidate of location of interest. The result of *SGPM* is as such: $\{u_1, u_2, u_3, u_4\}$ is a group of mobile users that frequently spends time together at the coffee shop in Blackburn road. It provides specific location of group pattern occurring.

Mobile user database static object mining (*MUDSOM*) (Goh & Taniar, 2005) is a method in which it takes into consideration of static barriers in the mobile environment. Quite often in the mobile environment there will be static barriers, such as walls, doors, glass windows in which it separates the relationships among mobile users. Although the location tracking device can determine the current location by pinpointing the exact location that mobile users are currently located, if they are separated by a wall, glass window or a door, or river, it would be obvious that although they are spending time together, physically near to each other, and satisfying the measurement requirements of group pattern, it will certainly have no relationship among them at all. *MUDSOM* defines a set of static barriers in the mobile environment, and provides algorithm in order to track and detect the presence of static barriers through source to destination walking process. If static barrier is detect that separates two mobile users, the distance measurement between the two mobile users is disregarded even if the distance is lesser than max-distance. The result of *MUDSOM* is a more accurate result of group pattern.

These related works tackles at different problems found in the knowledge extraction from mobile users. Each of them has room for improvement, and some works well only at some situation and some works badly in other situations. Situations in mobile environment can vary from lots of mobile users, long duration of time, complexity in movement, availability of tracking technologies, and availability of storage and recording facilities, among others. The ongoing objective of knowledge extraction from mobile users remains to enhance the accuracy of the knowledge found, and then improving the performance of the algorithm.

Walking Pattern

Walking pattern is about finding how mobile users walks from one location to another location. For all movement, there is a source and destination. In the mobile environment, records of mobile users movement are recorded at all times. A mobile user can move from location to another to transit from the source to destination, or simply staying within a location in order to interact with that location. The pattern of how mobile users represent a piece of useful knowledge because it can provide the knowledge on the walking trends and behaviors of mobile users.

If a mobile user desires to move from a source to a destination. It may walk from A to B directly, A being the source and B being the destination. However, a mobile user may also walk from $A \rightarrow B$ via other intermediate locations, such as I_1, I_2 such as $A \rightarrow I_1 \rightarrow B$, or $A \rightarrow I_1 \rightarrow I_2 \rightarrow B$. A two step walking pattern is the walking pattern in which mobile user moves from A directly to B as such $A \rightarrow B$. A three step walking pattern is the walking pattern in which mobile users moves from A to B via an intermediate location, as such $A \rightarrow I_1 \rightarrow B$. A four step walking pattern is the walking pattern in which mobile users moves from A to B via two intermediate locations, as such $A \rightarrow I_1 \rightarrow I_2 \rightarrow B$.

> **Definition 1:** *Given mobile environment, mobile user U is represented as such U = {u1, u2, u3, ..., un} such that un represents an individual mobile user. Individual mobile user also represents the individual mobile device.*

> **Definition 2:** *For each mobile user un, and for each of the given time point T = {t₁, t₂, t₃, ..., tₙ}, a (x, y) coordinate is given for each time point in which x represents the x axis coordinate and y represents the y axis coordinate of the*

current location of mobile user at time t_n, in a two dimensional geographical space. It is possible to have an empty coordinate.

Definition 3: *Given user movement database, (x, y) coordinates given may be converted into a location label if there exist location (x, y) in location of interest database whereby (x, y) is within start(x, y) and finish(x, y) of any of the location of interest. Not all (x, y) will be converted into location label.*

Definition 4: *Location of interest is defined by start(x, y) and finish(x, y) in which start(x, y) represents the bottom left hand corner of a rectangle which defines the start of location of interest, and finish(x, y) represents the top right hand corner of a rectangle which defines the end of location of interest.*

Definition 5: *For all location of interest L = {l_1, l_2, l_3, ..., l_n}, there may exist where $\exists: l_i \cap l_j \neq 0$.*

Definition 6: *For a given valid segment, the valid segment must come from the same mobile user u_i whereby there is a continuous occurrence where $u_i[t]$, $u_i[t+1]$, $u_i[t+2]$, $u_i[t+n] = l_j$. Valid segment occurs when within the same mobile user, there exist a situation where location of interest remains constant over the min-duration of time whereby n = min-duration.*

Definition 7: *A valid segment is represented by the common location of interest l_i. The immediate next valid segment is also represented by the common location of interest l_j. In order to represent a walking process, they are both represented as ($l_i \rightarrow l_j$). Duration between l_i and l_j is not taken into consideration in this mining process.*

Definition 8: *A valid movement is represented by the continuous set of movement. For example, a valid movement of ($l_1 \rightarrow l_2$, $l_2 \rightarrow l_3$) is represented by the occurrence of ($l_1 \rightarrow l_2$) first and then ($l_2 \rightarrow l_3$) next.*

Definition 9: *Given (l_1, $l_2 \rightarrow l_3$, l_4), the resulting movements in sequence include ($l_1 \rightarrow l_3$), ($l_1 \rightarrow l_4$), ($l_2 \rightarrow l_3$), ($l_2 \rightarrow l_4$).*

Definition 10: *Given ($l_i \rightarrow l_j$), the support for this rule is the number of occurrence of ($l_i \rightarrow l_j$) within the database. Given ($l_i \rightarrow l_j \rightarrow l_k$), the support for this rule is the number of occurrence of ($l_i \rightarrow l_j$, $l_j \rightarrow l_k$). Given ($l_i \rightarrow l_j \rightarrow l_k \rightarrow l_l$), the support for this rule is the number of occurrence of ($l_i \rightarrow l_j$, $l_j \rightarrow l_k$, $l_k \rightarrow l_l$).*

Definition 11: *Given* $(l_i \rightarrow l_j)$ *the confidence of this rule is calculated by*

$\dfrac{\sup port(l_i, l_j)}{\sup port(l_i)}$. *Given* $(l_i \rightarrow l_j \rightarrow l_k)$, *the confidence of this rule is calculated by*

$\dfrac{\sup port(l_i, l_j, l_k)}{\sup port(l_i, l_k)}$. *Given* $(l_i \rightarrow l_j \rightarrow l_k \rightarrow l_l)$, *the confidence of this rule is calcu-*

lated by $\dfrac{\sup port(l_i, l_j, l_k, l_l)}{\sup port(l_i, l_l)}$.

The walking pattern mining process starts by the given user movement database (UMD).

- **Step 1. Sorting and cleaning user movement database phase:** User movement database is sorted in order to ensure that each row represents coordinates for each given time unit, each unit is of equal duration to the next unit. User movement database is checked to ensure that all (x, y) coordinates are within the limit such as $x < x\text{-}max$, and $y < y\text{-}max$.

- **Step 2. Transformation phase:** For each (x, y) coordinate in the user movement database, it is transformed into location of interest if there exist a location of interest in the location of interest database. For each coordinate, it is matched against the location of interest, and if found that a location of interest where $start(x, y) \leq (x, y)$ and $finish(x, y) \geq (x, y)$ then the location of interest l_i is recorded for the mobile user. If further location of interest is found, both location of interest will be recorded such as (l_i, l_j).

Figure 3 shows a transformed user movement database. In this database, all the coordinates with a valid location of interest is transformed and renamed using their subsequent location of interest. Note that for cases such as (90, 20) and (90, 30), there is no match to any location of interest, and therefore, the (x, y) coordinates remains unchanged. If the cell is null previously, it will certainly not match to any location of interest and thus null remains. Certain cells may match to more than 1 location of interest, an example would be a cell having $\{l_1, l_2\}$ or $\{l_3, l_4\}$.

- **Step 3. Location of interest database building phase:** Significant location of interest has to be found. A significant location of interest is where one which have continuously occurred for duration of n amount of time. If $n = 3$, Figure 4 will shows all the significant location of interest where the exact same location of interest have occurred for more than n amount of duration continuously. Each of the significant location of interest is summarized into an individual location of interest and placed in a new database. The following shows the new database known as location movement database (*LMD*).

- **Step 4. Location movement database conversion phase:** Location movement database (*LMD*) is converted into movements. This means that for each of the significant location of interest, it's subsequent location of interest is the place where the mobile

Figure 3. Transformed user movement database

User 1	User 2	User 3	User 4	User 5	User 6
l_1	l_1	l_1, l_2	l_1	-	l_1
l_1	l_1	l_1, l_2	l_2	-	l_1
l_1	l_1	l_1, l_2	l_1	-	l_1
l_2	l_2	l_3, l_4	l_2	-	l_3
l_2	l_2	l_3, l_4	l_1	l_1	l_3
l_2	l_2	l_3, l_4	l_2	l_1	l_3
l_3	l_3	l_1	l_1	l_1	-
l_3	l_3	l_1	l_2	l_3	-
l_3	l_3	l_1	-	l_3	-
l_4	l_4	l_1	-	l_3	-
l_4	l_4	l_1	-	l_4	l_4
l_4	l_4	l_1	-	l_4	l_4
l_5	l_1	l_1	-	l_4	l_4
l_5	l_2	-	l_1	l_2	l_2
l_5	l_3	-	l_1	l_2	l_2
l_6	l_4	-	l_1	l_2	l_2
l_6	l_5	-	l_3	-	l_1
l_6	l_6	-	l_3	-	l_1
-	(90, 10)	-	l_3	-	l_1
-	-	l_2	l_2	l_1	l_3
-	-	l_2	l_2	l_1	l_3
-	-	l_2	l_2	l_1	l_3
-	-	l_2	l_2	l_3	l_4
l_1	-	l_2	l_2	l_3	l_4
l_1	-	l_2	l_2	l_3	l_4
l_1	l_1	l_2	l_2	l_4	l_2
l_2	l_1	l_2	-	l_4	l_2
l_2	l_1	l_2	-	l_4	l_2
l_2	(90, 20)	l_2	-	-	l_2
l_3	(90, 30)	l_2	-	-	l_2

user have visited, it is then converted into movement representation as such $\{l_1, l_2\}$ will be converted into $\{l_1 \rightarrow l_2\}$ as shown in Figure 5.

- **Step 5. Generate frequent walking sequence phase:** This step finds the frequent walking sequence. In order to generate all candidates walking sequence, the total number of location of interest has to be found. In this case, location of interest consists of $\{l_1, l_2, l_3, l_4, l_5, l_6\}$. Depending on whether the desired walking pattern is a two-step, three-step, or four-step walking pattern, different algorithms are applied. A frequent walking sequence is a walking sequence where the support for corresponding *source* $\geq$ *min-support*. A *support* $\geq$ *min-support* represents that the walking sequence have a statistical significance that is frequent enough and worthwhile for further investigation.

- **Step 6. Generate strong walking pattern phase:** This step finds out all the possible intermediate location of interest between the source and destination in order to find out the strength of the walking pattern. Depending on whether the desired walking pattern is two-step, three-step, or four-step walking pattern, different algorithms are applied. The strength of the walking pattern is determined by measuring the *confidence* of the walking pattern. A walking pattern is strong enough if *confidence* $\geq$ *min-confidence*. A *confidence* $\geq$ *min-support* means that the walking pattern is strong enough to be represented as knowledge. Given $A \rightarrow B$ representing walking pattern of location of interest A to location of interest, confidence measures the number of chances that mobile users moves from A to anywhere else to the ratio of chances mobile users moves from A to B directly. In other words, it is a measurement of given the antecedent, how much percentage of chances that the consequent will also occur.

Two-Step Walking Pattern

A two-step walking pattern is a walking pattern where it takes two steps to walk from source to destination.

Figure 6 shows a graphical illustration of two-step walking pattern. Source is represented by *src* and destination is represented by *dst*. Each node represents a location of interest, and the edge represents the direction of movement. The two nodes are related via a single direction and single movement to reach from source to destination. In the two-step walking pattern, it provides the knowledge of frequent direct visits among mobile users from *src* to *dst* in two steps without any intermediate nodes.

Figure 7 shows a graphical illustration of two-step walking pattern with possible paths. Given *src* being the source location, for all movement out from *src*, there are potentially movement to *dst*, or other locations marked by the question mark "?". This gives a representation where mobile users moves from one location to another, there is a need to trace the destination of the mobile user in order to determine the strength of the walking pattern. It is also not possible to walk from *src* back to *src* immediately because this situation is encapsulated into a single valid section.

Figure 4. Location movement database (LMD)

User 1	User 2	User 3	User 4	User 5	User 6
l_1	l_1	l_1, l_2	l_1	l_1	l_1
l_2	l_2	l_3, l_4	l_3	l_3	l_3
l_3	l_3	l_1	l_2	l_4	l_4
l_4	l_4	l_2		l_2	l_2
l_5	l_1			l_1	l_1
l_6				l_3	l_3
l_1				l_4	l_4
l_2					l_2

Figure 5. Converted location movement database

User 1	User 2	User 3	User 4	User 5	User 6
$l_1 \rightarrow l_2$	$l_1 \rightarrow l_2$	$l_1 \rightarrow l_3$	$l_1 \rightarrow l_3$	$l_1 \rightarrow l_3$	$l_1 \rightarrow l_3$
$l_2 \rightarrow l_3$	$l_2 \rightarrow l_3$	$l_1 \rightarrow l_4$	$l_3 \rightarrow l_2$	$l_3 \rightarrow l_4$	$l_3 \rightarrow l_4$
$l_3 \rightarrow l_4$	$l_3 \rightarrow l_4$	$l_2 \rightarrow l_3$		$l_4 \rightarrow l_2$	$l_4 \rightarrow l_2$
$l_4 \rightarrow l_5$	$l_4 \rightarrow l_1$	$l_2 \rightarrow l_4$		$l_2 \rightarrow l_1$	$l_2 \rightarrow l_1$
$l_5 \rightarrow l_6$		$l_3 \rightarrow l_1$		$l_1 \rightarrow l_3$	$l_1 \rightarrow l_3$
$l_6 \rightarrow l_1$		$l_4 \rightarrow l_1$		$l_3 \rightarrow l_4$	$l_3 \rightarrow l_4$
$l_1 \rightarrow l_2$		$l_1 \rightarrow l_2$			$l_4 \rightarrow l_2$

An example of possible result from the two-step walking pattern is the knowledge that mobile users appears significantly to walk from bookstores to coffee shops. The support and confidence for the two-step walking pattern can be measured by:

support = count (src)

confidence = supprt (src • dst) / support (src)

The support represents the significance of the pattern. Unless the occurrence of mobile users walking out from *src* such as bookstore to any other destinations, there is insufficient statistical significance to indicate that *src* is worthwhile for pattern generation. However, if *src* have a strong support, such as occurrence of mobile users walking out from *src* is frequently enough throughout the database, it provides a statistical significance worthy for further investigation. Until this point, the *dst* of the pattern is not yet examined.

Figure 6. Two-step walking pattern

Figure 7. Two-step walking pattern with possible paths

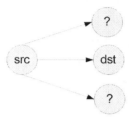

The confidence represents the strength of the pattern. The denominator is the *support* of the antecedent, which is *src*, and the nominator is the support of antecedent and consequent occurring together. In another words, given all the mobile users who moves out from *src* to any other location is used as the denominator, and for the nominator, the support of the number of occurrences where mobile users chooses to visit the *dst* in question instead of any other *dst* location. Therefore confidence tells given all the chances that mobile users can move from *src* out to any other location of interest, there were confidence percentage chance that the mobile user will move from *src* to *dst* instead of any other potential locations of interests.

Figure 8 shows the algorithm for mining the two-step walking pattern. The algorithm uses a graph data structure in order to solve the problem of mining the two-step walking pattern. The algorithm first determines the total number of unique location of interest in the user location database. Once this is determined, the algorithm generates a set of empty nodes in the graph data structure, in order to represent each location of interest to each generated nodes. These generated nodes are subsequently named with the same name of as identification number of each location of interest. The algorithm then traverses the location movement database in order to store all movement data into the graph data structure. If *A* moves to *B*, then node *A* will have a stored link to *B* and subsequently the occurrence of such event is recorded and stored in *A* under the edge to *B* section. Finally, the algorithm outputs all the walking patterns where they are walking sequences which *support ≥ min-support* and *confidence ≥ min-confidence*.

Three-Step Walking Pattern

A three step walking pattern is a walking pattern where it takes three steps to walk from source to destination via 1 intermediate location of interest.

Figure 8. Algorithm for mining two-step walking pattern

```
Algorithm
Input: location-movement-database, min-support, min-confidence
Output: set of significant and strong 2 step walking patterns
Procedure: 2-step-walking-pattern
01   lmd = location-movement-database;
02   n-locations = count-total-locations(lmd);
03   graph = generate-nodes(n-locations);
04   for i = 1 to n-locations do {
05       graph[i].node-name = l_i;
06   } // initialize graph
07   for each of movement m in lmd do {
08       src = lmd.current-movement.source();
09       dst = lmd.current-movement.destination();
10       graph[src].[dst] = graph[src].[dst] + 1;
11       next m;
12   } // map the movements into graphs
13   for each node n in graph do {
14       for each links l in node do {
15           if graph[n].l.count() ≥ min-support then {
16               confidence = graph[n].lcount() / graph[n].countall();
17               if confidence ≥ min-confidence then {
18                   display(n → n.l, support, confidence);
19                   } // display valid walking pattern
20               }
21           }
22   graph.display();
23   }
```

Figure 9 shows a graphical illustration of a three-step walking pattern. Each node represents a location of interest and each edge represents a movement. The source location is indicated by *src* and the destination location is indicated by *dst*. The source reaches the destination via an intermediate node int_1. All three-step walking pattern involves walking from a source to destination via an intermediate node. The movement is singular in nature whereby the movement moves from source to intermediate *node* 1 and then the immediate next movement is from intermediate *node* 1 to destination node.

Figure 10 shows the three-step walking pattern and the potential paths. Each node represents the location of interest and each edge represents a movement. The source *src* have the objective to move to destination *dst*. There is more than one option to move from *source* to *destination* via an intermediate node in steps. Mobile users can move from {*src* → int_1 → *dst*} or {*src* → int_2 → *dst*} or {*src* → int_3 → *dst*}.

For example, in a valid three-step walking pattern, mobile users moves from library to coffee shop, and then from coffee shop back to library, OR mobile users moves from library to coffee shop and then from coffee shop to classroom. Note that in a three-step walking pattern, the source and be the same as destination, in which the mobile users moves to another intermediate node and then arrives back to the source node as the intended destination, or it can arrive to another totally different destination node.

support = *count* (*src*)

confidence = *supprt* (*src* • *int1* • *dst*) / *support* (*src* • *x* • *dst*)

where *x* is any intermediate node,

and int_1 is the intermediate node in question.

In a valid three-step walking pattern, the source *src* will be significant enough whereby many mobile users have moved into and out of location *src*. However, in order to move out of location *src*, mobile users can choose int_1, int_2, int_3. After this movement, mobile users can

Figure 9. Three-step walking pattern via intermediate node

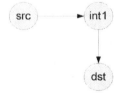

Figure 10. Three-step walking pattern possible paths

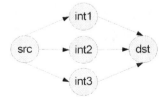

choose to move to any other destinations, or to the question destination *dst*. The statistical significance of a three-step walking pattern is determined by the support for *src* in terms of total number of mobile users who visited *src* and moved out from *src*.

The confidence represents the strength of the walking pattern. In a three-step walking pattern, the strength of the walking pattern is given by the ratio of the walking pattern happening *source* → intermediate node in question → *destination* to all possible occurrences from the *source* → any intermediate node → *destination*. If there are 100 occurrences of mobile users traveling from *source* → any intermediate node → *destination*, and there are 50 occurrences of mobile users traveling from *source* → intermediate node in question → *destination*, then the *confidence* is 50/100 = 0.5 or 50%.

Figure 11 shows the algorithm for a three-step walking pattern. The algorithm first initialize a graph as it will use the graph data structure to represent walking structure for display at the end of the algorithm. The algorithm then generates a set of potential candidate three-step walking patterns. Candidate three-step walking pattern are all the combinations of location of interest in the manner of *src* → int_1 → *dst*. A candidate three-step walking pattern will not have *src* = int_1 or int_1 = *dst*. For each candidate three-step walking pattern, it is stored in a database represented with a table, a column for three-step walking pattern, a column for support, a column for confidence and a column for validity. For each of row of the database, it will represent a candidate three-step walking pattern. Each of this will be tested against the location movement database for the occurrences of *src* → *X* where *X* is any location of interest. If this is greater than min-support, then *src* is statistically significant enough for the second part of the mining process.

The second part of the mining process involves examining the strength of the three-step walking pattern. It first defines the valid movement, such as *src* → *X* → *dst* where *X* can be any location of interest. It counts the occurrence of this in location movement database. Lets call this *p*. It then counts the valid movement in question, such as *src* → int_1 → *dst* in which it is the current three-step candidate walking pattern in question. Let's call this *q*. The ratio of *q* to *p*, such as *q/p* is the *confidence*, in which given that all possible occurrences of three-step walking pattern from source to any intermediate node to destination, there are confidence percentage of mobile users who travels from *source* to intermediate node in question then to the *destination*. If *confidence* ≥ *min-confidence*, then the algorithm will output the result. At the end of the mining process, the graph is displayed which shows all the possible walking patterns mobile users have taken.

Four-Step Walking Pattern

A four-step walking pattern is a walking pattern where it takes four steps to walk from source to destination via two intermediate locations of interest.

Figure 12 shows a graphical illustration of a four-step walking pattern. Source is represented by *src*, destination is represented by *dst*, and intermediate node 1 and intermediate node 2 are represented by int_1 and int_2 respectively. Each node represents a location of interest, and each edge represents a single directional movement. A four-step walking pattern is defined by the walking pattern where mobile users take from source to destination via two intermediate nodes. For example, mobile users can travel from *library* → *coffee* → *newsagent*

Figure 11. Algorithm for three-step walking pattern

Input: *location-movement-database, min-support, min-confidence*

Output: set of significant and strong 3 step walking patterns

Procedure: 3-step-walking-pattern

```
01   lmd = location-movement-database;
02   n-locations = count-total-locations(lmd);
03   graph = generate-nodes(n-locations);
04   for i = 1 to n-locations do {
05      graph[i].node-name = l_i;
06   } // initialize graph
07   for src = 1 to n-locations do {
08      for dst = 1 to n-locations do {
09         for int_1 = 1 to n-locations do {
10            if src ≠ int_1 ∩ dst ≠ int_1 then {
11               generate-candidate-3-walking-pattern(data, src-int_1-dst);
12            } // only generate if src ≠ int_1 and dst ≠ int
13         }
14      }
15   }
16   for each data d do {
17      valid-movement = (d.src, d.int_1, d.dst);
18      support = calculate-support(lmd, d.src);
19      // returns support which is the occurrence of movement in d.src
20      if support ≥ min-support then {
21         confidence = calculate-confidence(lmd, d.src, d.int_1, d.dst);
22         // returns confidence which is the ratio of
23         // (d.src → d.int_1 → d.dst) to (d.src → x → d.dst)
24         if confidence ≥ min-confidence then {
25            display(d.src, d.int_1, d.dst, support, confidence);
26            // output valid strong 3 step walking pattern
27               graph.update(d.src, d.int_1, d.dst);
28         }
29      }
30   graph.display(); // display the overall walking structure of mobile users
31   }
```

→ *classroom*, or *library* → *coffee* → *sports* → *library*. Mobile users may travel end up with the source and destination being the same for a four-step walking pattern. However, the current *location of interest* and the immediate next location of interest cannot be the same. For example *library* → *library* is not acceptable and is not possible if the database has been cleaned and sorted.

Figure 13 shows the four-step walking pattern and the possible paths to reach from source to destination via two intermediate nodes. From source to destination, all candidate walking patterns must take two intermediate nodes to reach the destination. If there are *m* intermediate node 1 and *n* intermediate node 2, the total number of possible paths to be taken is = *m* * *n*. One of the possible candidate walking pattern here is *src* → int_1 → int_4 → *dst*. It is possible for the location of interest being the same for *src* and *dst* for a four-step walking pattern. In this graph, there are altogether nine possible paths from source to destination.

In order for the four-step walking pattern to be significant, the source must have a high level of *support*, which means there are many mobile users that travels into the *location of interest* at source, and also travels out of source to any other *location of interest*. The *support* is satisfied when *support* ≥ *min-support*. The *support* is measured by the total number of counts for source being the source of any movements. A movement is from *A* → *B*, and therefore, as long as *A* is equal to source, it is counted as one occurrence of *support*.

support = count (src)

confidence = supprt (src • int1 • int2 • dst) / support (src • x • y • dst),

where *x* and *y* are any intermediate node,

and int_1 and int_2 are the intermediate node in question,

and *y* occurs after *x*, int_2 occurs after int_1.

The support is to measure the statistical significance of the walking pattern. For example, if there are many mobile users that moves into the library and later moves to any other place, this have raised a significance flag in which it represented that a potential pattern or

Figure 12. Four-step walking pattern via intermediate nodes

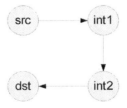

Figure 13. Four-step walking pattern possible paths

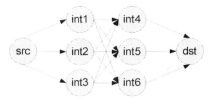

phenomenon may occur, because it has repeated many times, and not by random chance. Once this is qualified by *support ≥ min-support*, the second part of the mining process is to find out the strength of the walking pattern, measured by *confidence*. In another words, how much *confidence* we have to say that this walking pattern holds true.

The *confidence* measure is performed by measuring the ratio of all the occurrences where mobile users have moved from *source* to *destination* via two intermediate nodes in four steps. This can be represented by a template of (*source* → X → Y →*destination*) where X and Y can be any location of interest and X ≠ *source* and Y ≠ X and *destination* ≠ Y. For example, mobile users may go from *library* to *classroom* through a *coffee shop* and *newsagent* on the way, before reaching the ultimate destination. Therefore, it is measured by the denominator of given all the occurrences found in *location movement database* where (*source* → X → Y → *destination*) is satisfied, and the nominator as the candidate walking pattern in question, such that there are in the nominator amount of occurrences where (*source* → *intermediate location* 1 → *intermediate location* 2 → *destination*) is satisfied, where *intermediate location* 1 and *intermediate location* 2 are the int_1 and int_2 of the current candidate walking pattern in question.

Figure 14 shows the algorithm for mining valid four-step walking pattern. The algorithm first receives the location movement database, which have been sorted, cleaned, location identified and movement formed. The total number of unique location of interest is then calculated. The algorithm then defines and names each of the unique *location of movement* in a graph data structure where each node represents a unique *location of interest*, and each edge represents a movement. The algorithm then generates a list of candidate walking pattern fitting into the template of (*source* → int_1 → int_2 → *destination*), as such int_1 ≠ *source* ∩ int_2 ≠ int_1 ∩ *destination* ≠ int_2. This is stored in a database. Then, for each row of the database, the algorithm proceeds to find out the support of each of the candidate walking pattern. If the candidate walking pattern satisfies the *support*, the *confidence* is determined by measuring the strength of the walking pattern through the ratio of (*source* → int_1 → int_2 → *destination*) to (*source* → X → Y → *destination*). If *confidence ≥ min-confidence*, this candidate walking pattern becomes a valid 4 step walking pattern and result is then displayed.

Figure 14. Algorithm for mining four-step walking pattern

Input: *location-movement-database, min-support, min-confidence*

Output: set of significant and strong 3 step walking patterns

Procedure: 4-step-walking-pattern

```
01   lmd = location-movement-database;
02   n-locations = count-total-locations(lmd);
03   graph = generate-nodes(n-locations);
04   for i = 1 to n-locations do {
05     graph[i].node-name = l_i;
06   } // initialize graph
07   for src = 1 to n-locations do {
08     for dst = 1 to n-locations do {
09       for int_1 = 1 to n-locations do {
10         for int_2 = 1 to n-locations do {
11           if src ≠ int_1 ∩ int_2 ≠ int_1 ∩ dst ≠ int_2 then {
12               generate-candidate-3-walking-pattern(data, src-int1-dst);
13               } // only generate if src ≠ int_1 and int_2 ≠ int_1 and int_2 ≠ dst
14           }
15         }
16       }
17   }
18   for each data d do {
19     valid-movement = (d.src, d.int_1, d.int_2, d.dst);
20     support = calculate-support(lmd, d.src);
21     // returns support which is the occurrence of movement in d.src
22     if support ≥ min-support then {
23       confidence = calculate-confidence(lmd, d.src, d.int_1, d.int_2, d.dst);
24       // returns confidence which is the ratio of
25       // (d.src → d.int_1 → d.int_2 → d.dst) to (d.src → x → y → d.dst)
26       // where x and y are any intermediate nodes x ≠ y
27       if confidence ≥ min-confidence then {
28           display(d.src, d.int_1, d.int_2, d.dst, support, confidence);
29           // output valid strong 4 step walking pattern
30             graph.update(d.src, d.int_1, d.int_2, d.dst);
31       }
32     }
33   graph.display(); // display the overall walking structure of mobile users
34   }
```

Figure 15. Location movement database

$(l_1 \rightarrow l_2)$	$(l_1 \rightarrow l_4)$	$(l_2 \rightarrow l_3)$	$(l_5 \rightarrow l_1)$
$(l_2 \rightarrow l_3)$	$(l_1 \rightarrow l_4)$	$(l_3 \rightarrow l_4)$	$(l_5 \rightarrow l_2)$
$(l_3 \rightarrow l_4)$	$(l_1 \rightarrow l_2)$	$(l_2 \rightarrow l_5)$	$(l_2 \rightarrow l_3)$
$(l_4 \rightarrow l_5)$	$(l_1 \rightarrow l_2)$	$(l_2 \rightarrow l_5)$	$(l_2 \rightarrow l_4)$
$(l_5 \rightarrow l_1)$	$(l_1 \rightarrow l_5)$	$(l_3 \rightarrow l_4)$	$(l_2 \rightarrow l_3)$
$(l_1 \rightarrow l_2)$	$(l_1 \rightarrow l_2)$	$(l_3 \rightarrow l_1)$	$(l_2 \rightarrow l_5)$
$(l_1 \rightarrow l_2)$	$(l_1 \rightarrow l_2)$	$(l_4 \rightarrow l_1)$	$(l_3 \rightarrow l_1)$
$(l_1 \rightarrow l_2)$	$(l_1 \rightarrow l_2)$	$(l_4 \rightarrow l_2)$	$(l_4 \rightarrow l_1)$
$(l_1 \rightarrow l_3)$	$(l_1 \rightarrow l_3)$	$(l_1 \rightarrow l_4)$	$(l_5 \rightarrow l_2)$
$(l_1 \rightarrow l_3)$	$(l_1 \rightarrow l_3)$	$(l_1 \rightarrow l_5)$	$(l_3 \rightarrow l_4)$

Note:

Let min-support = 5

Let min-confidence = 0.5

Case Study

Case study is provided in order to enhance the understanding of how the walking pattern mining process works. The case study will be provided in the following structure. The location movement database (*LMD*) is first provided for each mining process. It consists of all the movements and is derived from user movement database, cleaned, sorted, and locations identified, and movements formed. The case study will then show how the walking patterns are formed, such as how candidate walking patterns and their subsequent support and confidence are calculated.

Two-Step Walking Pattern

Given the following set of movements in location movement database as shown in Figure 15.

- **Step 1. Count the occurrences of each location of interest:** An occurrence for l_1 is where $(l_1 \rightarrow X)$ where X can be any other location of interest.

$l_1 = 18$

$l_2 = 8$

$l_3 = 6$

$l_4 = 4$

$l_5 = 4$

Since *min-support* = 5, only l_1, l_2, l_3 are significant enough for rule generation.

- **Step 2. Generate candidate 2 step walking patterns:** In this step, each of the frequent location sets, in this case l_1, l_2, l_3 are further investigated by generating all possible candidate 2 step walking patterns.

Figure 16 shows how each of the frequent location of interest are further generated into candidate walking pattern. It is a permutation in the format of $(l_x \rightarrow l_y)$ where $x \neq y$. The generated candidate walking patterns are then recounted from location movement database. Besides each candidate two-step walking pattern, the total count of each is derived from location movement database, and is displayed on the right hand side. For instance, $(l_1 \rightarrow l_2)$ = 9 represents that there are altogether nine occurrences in location movement database where $(l_1 \rightarrow l_2)$.

The total support for l_1 = 18, l_2 = 8, l_3 =6. The total support is calculated by all the occurrences where the $(X \rightarrow Y)$ where X represents the source in question, and Y can represent any location of interest such that $Y \neq X$. Since *min-support* = 5, support count for l_1, l_2, l_3 all met min-support requirement as such *support* ≥ *min-support*. The *support* values are stored as it is required for confidence calculation in order to measure the strength of the walking pattern.

Confidence for $(l_1 \rightarrow l_2)$ is found by the ratio of the support for l_1 which is the antecedent as the denominator, and the nominator as the count number of occurrence where $(l_1 \rightarrow l_2)$. In other words, *confidence* is the measure of out of 18 times of 11 occurrences; there are altogether nine occurrences where l_1 actually moves to l_2. It gives a comparison among all possible outcomes to the candidate outcome. If *confidence* > *min-confidence*, in this case 0.5 ≥ 0.5, this qualifies as a valid two-step walking pattern. The remainder of the mining process have found $(l_1 \rightarrow l_2)$, $(l_2 \rightarrow l_3)$, $(l_3 \rightarrow l_4)$ as valid two-step walking pattern, and it satisfies the requirement of *support* ≥ *min-support* and *confidence* ≥ *min-confidence*.

Figure 16. Two- step walking pattern mining process

For l_1	For l_2	For l_3
$(l_1 \rightarrow l_2) = 9$	$(l_2 \rightarrow l_1) = 0$	$(l_3 \rightarrow l_1) = 2$
$(l_1 \rightarrow l_3) = 4$	$(l_2 \rightarrow l_3) = 4$	$(l_3 \rightarrow l_2) = 0$
$(l_1 \rightarrow l_4) = 3$	$(l_2 \rightarrow l_4) = 1$	$(l_3 \rightarrow l_4) = 4$
$(l_1 \rightarrow l_5) = 2$	$(l_2 \rightarrow l_5) = 3$	$(l_3 \rightarrow l_5) = 0$
Support(l_1) = 18	Support(l_2) = 8	Support(l_3) = 6
Confidence for	Confidence for	Confidence for
$(l_1 \rightarrow l_2) = 9/18 = 0.5$	$(l_2 \rightarrow l_1) = 0/8 = 0$	$(l_3 \rightarrow l_1) = 2/6 = 0.33$
$(l_1 \rightarrow l_3) = 4/18 = 0.22$	$(l_2 \rightarrow l_3) = 4/8 = 0.5$	$(l_3 \rightarrow l_2) = 0/6 = 0$
$(l_1 \rightarrow l_4) = 3/18 = 0.16$	$(l_2 \rightarrow l_4) = 1/8 = 0.125$	$(l_3 \rightarrow l_4) = 4/6 = 0.66$
$(l_1 \rightarrow l_5) = 2/18 = 0.11$	$(l_2 \rightarrow l_5) = 3/8 = 0.375$	$(l_3 \rightarrow l_5) = 0/6 = 0$
Valid 2 step walking pattern	Valid 2 step walking pattern	Valid 2 step walking pattern
$= (l_1 \rightarrow l_2)$	$= (l_2 \rightarrow l_3)$	$= (l_3 \rightarrow l_4)$

Three-Step Walking Pattern

Given the following set of movements in location movement database as shown in Figure 17.

- **Step 1. Count the occurrences of each location of interest:** An occurrence for l_1 is where $(l_1 \rightarrow X)$ where X can be any other location of interest.

  $l_1 = 14$
  $l_2 = 11$
  $l_3 = 6$
  $l_4 = 5$
  $l_5 = 4$

  Since *support* = 10, therefore, l_1, l_2 are significant enough for further investigation and rule generation.

- **Step 2. Generate candidate 3 step walking patterns:** In this step, each of the frequent location sets, in this case l_1, l_2 are further investigated by generating all possible candidate 3 step walking patterns.

Figure 18 shows the processes of mining a three-step walking pattern. For each of the location of interest that has *support* ≥ *min-support*, in this case l_1 and l_2, each are permutated using the following template of $(l_1 \rightarrow X \rightarrow Y)$ and $(l_2 \rightarrow X \rightarrow Y)$ such that $X \neq l_1 \cap X \neq l_2 \cap Y \neq X$. For each of the generated candidate 3 step walking pattern, the location movement database is visited and counted against total occurrence. Each occurrence is supported by a valid movement. A valid movement is such as $(l_1 \rightarrow l_2 \rightarrow l_3)$, which can be broken down into a sequence of $\{(l_1 \rightarrow l_2), (l_2 \rightarrow l_3)\}$. The occurrence of $(l_2 \rightarrow l_3)$ must occur after $(l_1 \rightarrow l_2)$, but the duration in between the occurrence of these two sub movements is not taken into consideration.

The total count for l1 represents the total count of occurrence where $l_1 \rightarrow X \rightarrow Y$ where X and Y represents any location of interest and $X \neq l_1 \cap Y \neq X$. For l_1, the total count is 10, and for l_2, the total count is two. The next step is to test the *confidence* of each candidate three-step walking patterns. Since there are many candidate valid three-step patterns with a count of zero, it will return zero and they are not illustrated in the interest of space. Only *counts* ≠ 0 are illustrated. In this case, $(l_1 \rightarrow l_2 \rightarrow l_3)$ have a total occurrence of six out of 10 occurrences of $(l_1 \rightarrow X \rightarrow Y)$. Therefore, *confidence* = 6 / 10 = 0.6. Since *confidence* 0.6 is ≥ *min-confidence* of 0.5, the strength of this candidate three-step walking pattern is satisfied and it becomes a valid three-step walking pattern.

Figure 17. Location movement database

$$
\begin{array}{llll}
(l_1 \to l_2) & (l_1 \to l_2) & (l_1 \to l_3) & (l_5 \to l_1) \\
(l_2 \to l_3) & (l_2 \to l_3) & (l_3 \to l_4) & (l_5 \to l_2) \\
(l_1 \to l_2) & (l_1 \to l_2) & (l_2 \to l_5) & (l_2 \to l_3) \\
(l_2 \to l_3) & (l_2 \to l_3) & (l_2 \to l_5) & (l_1 \to l_2) \\
(l_5 \to l_1) & (l_1 \to l_5) & (l_3 \to l_4) & (l_2 \to l_3) \\
(l_1 \to l_2) & (l_1 \to l_2) & (l_3 \to l_1) & (l_1 \to l_2) \\
(l_2 \to l_4) & (l_1 \to l_3) & (l_4 \to l_1) & (l_2 \to l_3) \\
(l_4 \to l_5) & (l_3 \to l_1) & (l_4 \to l_2) & (l_4 \to l_1) \\
(l_2 \to l_4) & (l_1 \to l_3) & (l_1 \to l_4) & (l_5 \to l_2) \\
(l_4 \to l_5) & (l_3 \to l_1) & (l_1 \to l_5) & (l_3 \to l_4) \\
\end{array}
$$

Note:

Let min-support = 10

Let min-confidence = 0.5

Four-Step Walking Pattern

Given the following set of movements in *location movement database* as shown in Figure 19.

- **Step 1. Count the occurrences of each location of interest:** An occurrence for l_1 is where $(l_1 \to X \to Y \to Z)$ where X, Y, Z can be any other location of interest, and $X \neq l_1 \cap Y \neq X \cap Z \neq Y$.

  $l_1 = 13$

  $l_2 = 11$

  $l_3 = 8$

  $l_4 = 4$

  $l_5 = 4$

  Since *support* = 10, therefore, l_1, l_2 are significant enough for further investigation and rule generation.

- **Step 2. Generate candidate 4 step walking patterns:** In this step, each of the frequent location sets, in this case l_1, l_2 are further investigated by generating all possible candidate 4 step walking patterns. Due to incredibly long permutations for 4 step walking pattern, there are $5 * 4 * 4 * 4 = 320$ permutations for each l_1 and l_2. Most of the resulting permutation candidate 4 step walking patterns has 0 count from *location movement database*. In order to conserve space, only candidate 4 step walking pattern with *count* $\neq$ 0 will be illustrated.

Figure 18. Three-step walking pattern mining process

For l_1

$(l_1 \rightarrow l_2 \rightarrow l_1) = 0$
$(l_1 \rightarrow l_2 \rightarrow l_3) = 6$
$(l_1 \rightarrow l_2 \rightarrow l_4) = 1$
$(l_1 \rightarrow l_2 \rightarrow l_5) = 0$
$(l_1 \rightarrow l_3 \rightarrow l_1) = 2$
$(l_1 \rightarrow l_3 \rightarrow l_2) = 0$
$(l_1 \rightarrow l_3 \rightarrow l_4) = 1$
$(l_1 \rightarrow l_3 \rightarrow l_5) = 0$
$(l_1 \rightarrow l_4 \rightarrow l_1) = 0$
$(l_1 \rightarrow l_4 \rightarrow l_2) = 0$
$(l_1 \rightarrow l_4 \rightarrow l_3) = 0$
$(l_1 \rightarrow l_4 \rightarrow l_5) = 0$
$(l_1 \rightarrow l_5 \rightarrow l_1) = 0$
$(l_1 \rightarrow l_5 \rightarrow l_2) = 0$
$(l_1 \rightarrow l_5 \rightarrow l_3) = 0$
$(l_1 \rightarrow l_5 \rightarrow l_4) = 0$

Total count for $(l_1 \rightarrow X \rightarrow Y) = 10$

Confidence for:
$(l_1 \rightarrow l_2 \rightarrow l_3) = 6/10 = 0.6$
$(l_1 \rightarrow l_2 \rightarrow l_4) = 1/10 = 0.1$
$(l_1 \rightarrow l_3 \rightarrow l_1) = 2/10 = 0.2$
$(l_1 \rightarrow l_3 \rightarrow l_4) = 1/10 = 0.1$

Valid 3 step walking pattern:
$(l_1 \rightarrow l_2 \rightarrow l_3)$

For l_2

$(l_2 \rightarrow l_1 \rightarrow l_2) = 0$
$(l_2 \rightarrow l_1 \rightarrow l_3) = 0$
$(l_2 \rightarrow l_1 \rightarrow l_4) = 0$
$(l_2 \rightarrow l_1 \rightarrow l_5) = 0$
$(l_2 \rightarrow l_3 \rightarrow l_1) = 0$
$(l_2 \rightarrow l_3 \rightarrow l_2) = 0$
$(l_2 \rightarrow l_3 \rightarrow l_4) = 0$
$(l_2 \rightarrow l_3 \rightarrow l_5) = 0$
$(l_2 \rightarrow l_4 \rightarrow l_1) = 0$
$(l_2 \rightarrow l_4 \rightarrow l_2) = 0$
$(l_2 \rightarrow l_4 \rightarrow l_3) = 0$
$(l_2 \rightarrow l_4 \rightarrow l_5) = 2$
$(l_2 \rightarrow l_5 \rightarrow l_1) = 0$
$(l_2 \rightarrow l_5 \rightarrow l_2) = 0$
$(l_2 \rightarrow l_5 \rightarrow l_3) = 0$
$(l_2 \rightarrow l_5 \rightarrow l_4) = 0$

Total count for $(l_2 \rightarrow X \rightarrow Y) = 2$

Confidence for:
$(l_2 \rightarrow l_4 \rightarrow l_5) = 2/2 = 1.0$

Valid 3 step walking pattern:
$(l_2 \rightarrow l_4 \rightarrow l_5)$

Figure 20 shows the simplified four-step walking pattern mining process. Due to the long permutation for l_1 and l_2 for candidate four-step walking pattern, only four-step candidate walking patterns where *count* $\neq 0$ are illustrated. In this case, there are four counts of $(l_1 \rightarrow l_2 \rightarrow l_3 \rightarrow l_4)$, which can be broken down into continuous occurrence of $\{(l_1 \rightarrow l_2), (l_2 \rightarrow l_3), (l_3 \rightarrow l_4)\}$. For l_2, there is only one count of $(l_2 \rightarrow l_3 \rightarrow l_4 \rightarrow 1)$ which can be broken down into continuous occurrence of $\{(l_1 \rightarrow l_2), (l_2 \rightarrow l_3), (l_3 \rightarrow l_4)\}$. Confidence for $(l_1 \rightarrow l_2 \rightarrow l_3 \rightarrow l_4)$ is therefore 4/4 = 1.0 or 100%, and *confidence* for $(l_2 \rightarrow l_3 \rightarrow l_4 \rightarrow l_1)$ is therefore 1/1 = 1.0 or 100%. The final two sets of valid four-step walking patterns are: $(l_1 \rightarrow l_2 \rightarrow l_3 \rightarrow l_4)$ and $(l_2 \rightarrow l_3 \rightarrow l_4 \rightarrow l_1)$. This is because both satisfies *min-support*, *min-confidence* and $(A \rightarrow B \rightarrow C \rightarrow D)$ such that $B \neq A \cap C \neq B \cap D \neq C$.

Figure 19. Location movement database

$(l_1 \to l_2)$	$(l_1 \to l_2)$	$(l_1 \to l_3)$	$(l_5 \to l_1)$
$(l_2 \to l_3)$	$(l_2 \to l_3)$	$(l_3 \to l_4)$	$(l_5 \to l_2)$
$(l_3 \to l_4)$	$(l_1 \to l_2)$	$(l_2 \to l_3)$	$(l_2 \to l_3)$
$(l_2 \to l_3)$	$(l_2 \to l_3)$	$(l_1 \to l_2)$	$(l_1 \to l_2)$
$(l_5 \to l_1)$	$(l_1 \to l_5)$	$(l_2 \to l_3)$	$(l_2 \to l_3)$
$(l_1 \to l_2)$	$(l_1 \to l_2)$	$(l_3 \to l_4)$	$(l_3 \to l_4)$
$(l_2 \to l_3)$	$(l_1 \to l_3)$	$(l_4 \to l_1)$	$(l_2 \to l_3)$
$(l_3 \to l_4)$	$(l_3 \to l_1)$	$(l_4 \to l_2)$	$(l_4 \to l_1)$
$(l_2 \to l_4)$	$(l_1 \to l_3)$	$(l_1 \to l_4)$	$(l_5 \to l_2)$
$(l_4 \to l_5)$	$(l_3 \to l_1)$	$(l_1 \to l_5)$	$(l_3 \to l_4)$

Note:

Let min-support = 10

Let min-confidence = 0.5

Figure 20. Four-step walking pattern mining process

For l_1 $(l_1 \to l_2 \to l_3 \to l_4) = 4$	For l_2 $(l_2 \to l_3 \to l_4 \to l_1) = 1$
Total count for $(l_1 \to X \to Y \to Z) = 4$	Total count for $(l_2 \to X \to Y) = 1$
Confidence for: $(l_1 \to l_2 \to l_3 \to l_4) = 4/4 = 1.0$	Confidence for: $(l_2 \to l_3 \to l_4 \to l_1) = 1/1 = 1.0$
Valid 4 step walking pattern: $(l_1 \to l_2 \to l_3 \to l_4)$	Valid 4 step walking pattern: $(l_2 \to l_3 \to l_4 \to l_1)$

Performance Evaluation

Performance is performed on Pentium IV laptop equipped with 384MB of main memory. A few attributes are used in performance evaluation and they are described as below. There are three datasets involved, namely *DBI*, *DBII*, and *DBIII*.

Figure 21 shows the performance attributes designed to evaluate the proposed method. The main attributes of measurement are the total number of location of interest, the candidate two- step, three-step, and four-step walking patterns, and the total valid two-step, three-step, and four-step walking patterns. *DB-I*, *DB-II* and *DB-III* are three synthetically generated dataset with a varying database generation seed of 0.2, 0.4, and 0.6 respectively. This generation seed represents the probability of a valid walking pattern be generated.

Figure 22 shows the total number of valid walking patterns found, and unique candidate movements in two-step, three–step, and four-step walking patterns. The first diagram gives

Figure 21. Performance evaluation attributes

Attribute	Description
m	*Number of mobile users*
n	*Number of location of interest (LOI)*
2-WP	*Number of valid 2 step walking pattern*
3-WP	*Number of valid 3 step walking pattern*
4-WP	*Number of valid 4 step walking pattern*
DB-I	*Synthetic DB Seed = 0.2*
DB-II	*Synthetic DB Seed = 0.4*
DB-III	*Synthetic DB Seed = 0.6*

Figure 22. Valid walking patterns found and unique candidate movements

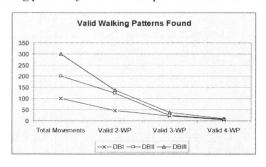

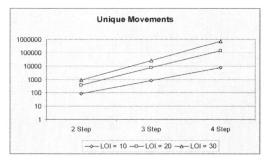

a comparison for the total number of walking patterns that can be found for *DBI*, *DBII* and *DBIII*. Each line represents *DBI*, *DBII*, or *DBIII*. It is observed that the total number of valid walking patterns found is reduced at a varying rate as the desired steps of valid walking pattern increases. As the desired steps of valid walking pattern increases, the chances of meeting the valid movement criteria is greatly reduced, and thus resulting in total number of walking patterns found. The second diagram gives a comparison between two-step, three-step, and four-step candidate walking patterns. The y axis is scaled to logarithmic scale. It can be observed that the total unique movements is increased at a very rapid rate from a two-step walking pattern to a three-step walking pattern, and from a three-step walking pattern to a four-step walking pattern. The second observation is that the total unique movement through increase in *LOI* also increased at a rate that is high but not as high as increase in steps in walking pattern.

Conclusion and Future Work

In conclusion, walking pattern is a representation of knowledge which can be extracted from movement data collected from mobile users. In a typical data mining exercise, the user movement database is gathered from mobile users, which contains information on the locations that mobile users have been to during each time over the mining horizon. Location of interest can be defined in order to define a boundary in the two-dimensional geographical area to represent the core values in each of the *location of interests*.

Through finding out how mobile users moves from one location of interest to another, which has been proven possible, there are opportunities to find two-step, three-step, and four-step walking patterns. These walking patterns helps decision maker in terms of better understanding of movement patterns of mobile users, and can also be helpful for geographical planning purposes.

Future work in this area include improving the algorithm and mining methods to incorporate the capability to find out maximal walking patterns if there is one present in the location movement database. Walking pattern can further be developed to find out different types of movement behavior regarding mobile users that are endless as behavior of mobile users evolves over time.

Reference

Agrawal, R., & Srikat, R. (1994). Fast algorithms for mining association rules In *Proceedings of the 20ᵗʰ VLDB* (pp. 487-499).

Agrawal, R., & Srikat, R. (1995). Mining sequential patterns. In *Proceedings of 11ᵗʰ ICDE* (pp. 3-14).

Chakrabarti, S., Sarawagi, S., & Dom, B. (1998). Mining surprising patterns using temporal description length In *Proceedings of 24ᵗʰ VLDB* (pp. 606-617).

Chen, S. Y., & Loi, X. (2005). Data mining from 1994 to 2004: An application-oriented review. *International Journal of Business Intelligence and Data Mining, 1*(1), 4-21.

Cho, M., Pei, J., Wang, H., & Wang, W. (2005). Preference-based frequent pattern mining. *International Journal of Data Warehousing and Mining, 1*(4), 56-77.

Forlizzi, L., Guting, R. H., Nardelli, E., & Schneider, M. (2000). A data model and data structures for moving objects databases. *ACM SIGMOD Record, 260,* 319-330.

Forsyth, D.R. (1999). *Group dynamics.* Belmont, CA: Wadsworth.

Goh, J., & Taniar, D. (n.d.). Mobile user data static object mining (MUDSOM). *The IEEE 20ᵗʰ International Conference on Advanced Information Networking and Applications.* (Submitted)

Goh, J., & Taniar, D. (n.d.). Static group pattern mining (SGPM). *The 10ᵗʰ Pacific Asia Conference on Knowledge Discovery and Data Mining PAKDD 2006.* (Submitted)

Goh, J., & Taniar, D. (2004). Mining frequency pattern from mobile users. *Knowledge Based Intelligent Information & Engineering and Systems* (LNCS Part III, 3215, pp. 795-801). Springer-Verlag.

Goh, J., & Taniar, D. (2005). Mining parallel pattern from mobile users. *International Journal of Business Data Communications and Networking, 1*(1), 50-76.

Goh, J., & Taniar, D. (2004). Mobile user data mining by location dependncies. In *5ᵗʰ International Conference on Intelligent Data Engineering and Automated Learning* (LNCS 3177, pp. 225-231). Springer-Verlag.

Häkkilä, J., & Mäntyjärvi, J. (2005). Combining location-aware mobile phone applications and multimedia messaging. *Journal of Mobile Multimedia, 1*(1), 18-32.

Han, J., & Plank, A. W. (1996). Background for association rules and cost estimate of selected mining algorithms. In *Proceedings of the 5ᵗʰ CIKM* (pp. 73-80).

Han, J., Dong, G., & Yin, Y. (1999). Efficient mining of partial periodic patterns in time series database. In *Proceedings of the 15ᵗʰ ICDE* (pp. 106-115).

Han, J., Pei, J., & Yin, Y. (2000). Mining frequent patterns without candidate generation. In *Proceedings of the ACM SIGMOD* (pp. 1-12).

Hofmann-Wellenhof, B., Lichtenegger, H., & Collins, J. (1994). *Global positioning system: Theory and practice* (3ʳᵈ rev. ed.). New York: Springer-Verlag Wien.

Hwang, S.-Y., Loi, Y.-H., Chiu, J.-K., & Lim, E.-P. (2005). Mining mobile group patterns: A trajectory-based approach. In *Proceedings of the 9ᵗʰ Pacific Asia Conference of Knowledge Discovery and Data Mining PAKDD 2005* (LNCS 3518, pp. 713-718). Springer-Verlag.

Jayaputera, J., & Taniar, D. (2005). Data retrieval for location-dependent queries in a multi-cell wireless environment. *Mobile Information Systems, 1*(2), 91-108.

Koperski, K., & Han, J. (1995). Discovery of spatial association rules in geographical information databases. In *Proceedings of 4ᵗʰ Internationl Symposium on Advances in Spatial Databases, 951,* 47-66.

Lee, D. L., Zhu, M., & Hu, H. (2005). When location based services meet databases. *Mobile Information Systems, 1*(2), 81-90.

Reed Electronics Research RER. (2002, October). *The mobile phone industry: A strategic overview.*

Roddick, J. F., & Lees, B. G. (2001). Paradigms for spatial and spatio-temporal data mining. In H. Miller & J. Han (Eds.), *Research monographs in geographical information systems* (pp. 1-14).

Roddick, J. F., & Spiliopoulou, M. (2002). A survey of temporal knowledge discovery paradigms and methods. *IEEE Trans. on Knowledge and Data Engineering, 14*(4), 750-767.

Song, M.-B., Kang, S.-W., & Park, K.-J. (2005). On the design of energy-efficient location tracking mechanism in location-aware computing. *Mobile Information Systems: An International Journal, 1*(2), 109-127.

Tjioe, H. C., & Taniar, D. (2005). Mining association rules in data warehouses. *International Journal of Data Warehousing and Mining, 1*(3).

Tse, P. K. C., Lam, W. K., Ng, K. W., & Chan, C. (2005). An implementation of location-aware multimedia information download to mobile system. *Journal of Mobile Multimedia, 1*(1), 33-46.

Varshney, U., Vetter, R., & Kalakota, R. (2000). Mobile commerce: A new frontier. *IEEE Computer: Special Issue on E-Commerce*, 32-38.

Wang, W., Yang, J., & Yu, P. S. (2002). InfoMiner+: Mining partial periodic patterns in time series data. In the *2nd IEEE International Conference on Data Mining ICDM 2002* (p. 725).

Wang, Y., Lim, E.-P., & Hwang, S.-Y. (2004). Efficient group pattern mining using data summarization. In *Proceedings of the 15th International Conference on Database and Expert Systems Applications DEXA 2004* (LNCS 2973, pp. 895-907). Springer-Verlag.

Wang, Y., Lim, E.-P., & Hwang, S.-Y. (2003). On mining group patterns from mobile users. In *Proceedings of the 14th International Conference on Database and Expert Systems Applications DEXA 2003* (LNCS 2736, pp. 287-296). Springer-Verlag

Xiao, Y., Yao, J. F., & Yang, G. (2005). Discovering frequent embedded subtree patterns from large databases of unordered labeled trees. *International Journal of Data Warehousing and Mining, 1*(2), 70-92.

Zarchan, P. (1996). *Global positioning system: Theory and applications* (Vol I). American Institute of Aeronautics and Astronautics.

Section III:

Wireless Deployment and Applications

Chapter X

Wi-Fi Deployment in Large New Zealand Organizations:
A Survey

Bryan Houliston, Auckland University of Technology, New Zealand

Nurul Sarkar, Auckland University of Technology, New Zealand

Abstract

Wi-Fi (also known as IEEE 802.11b) networks are gaining widespread popularity as wireless local area networks (WLANs) due to their simplicity in operation, robustness, low cost, and user mobility offered by the technology. It is a viable technology for wireless local area networking applications in both business and home environments. This chapter reports on a survey of large New Zealand organizations focusing on the level of Wi-Fi deployment, reasons for non-deployment, the scope of deployment, investment in deployment, problems encountered, and future plans. Our findings show that most organizations have at least considered the technology, though a much smaller proportion has deployed it on any significant scale. A follow up review of the latest published case studies and surveys suggests that while Wi-Fi networks are consolidating, interest is growing in wider area wireless networks.

Introduction and Motivation

Wi-Fi (short for wireless fidelity) is one of the popular technologies that has been standardised by the IEEE committee as 11 Mbps WLANs. In the generally flat hi-tech landscape of the last few years, Wi-Fi stands out as one technology that still attracts a good deal of interest (Broatch, 2003). There has been a significant growth in Wi-Fi networking in recent years, both in applications and as the subject of academic research papers, articles in the IT press and research house reports. However, the vast majority of these research papers about Wi-Fi technology are based on North American and European experience. Therefore, the question arises how much of this material is relevant to the New Zealand context.

New Zealanders have generally been early, and keen, adopters of technology. As Myers points out (Myers, 1996), New Zealanders have developed innovative IT applications to improve the competitiveness of many sectors of the economy. Wireless technology appears to be no different. According to a recent New Zealand Trade and Enterprise (NZTE) report, New Zealand is a "beacon for advanced wireless innovation" and amongst the global "leadership in the fixed and mobile wireless space" (MediaLab South Pacific, 2003). The major national telecommunications provider reports that New Zealanders have been quicker than most to access mobile Internet services (Telecom, 2003).

Based on the above discussion one can believe that New Zealand's experience with wireless technology may differ from that documented in overseas research. However, there is a dearth of published research focusing on New Zealand experiences. The most comprehensive survey in recent times is the NZTE report on New Zealand's fixed and mobile wireless sector (MediaLab South Pacific, 2003). Most of the previous studies have considered both users and vendors. In terms of the end-user experience, some case studies of individual organizations have been conducted (Jackson, 2003; Smith, 2003), and a small number of questions on wireless have been included in surveys on general IT issues (Bland, O'Neill, & Bell, 2003; Hind, 2003, 2004, 2005).

In this chapter, we report on a survey of Wi-Fi technology in New Zealand's largest IT end user organizations. The survey, conducted in the second half of 2003, seeks to gauge the current level of Wi-Fi deployment in these organizations and some details about the deployment process and related issues. To gain insights, we compared our survey results with those of similar surveys conducted overseas. We found that most large New Zealand organizations have at least considered Wi-Fi technology, although a much smaller proportion has actually deployed it on any significant scale. At the end of 2005 we carried out a further review of the latest published case studies and surveys relating to the use of Wi-Fi technology in large New Zealand organizations. The review suggests that the growth of Wi-Fi WLANs has slowed while existing WLANs are upgraded. But there is a rapidly growing interest in wide area wireless networks.

The chapter is organised as follows. We first summarize the previous work highlighting the growth of Wi-Fi in New Zealand. We then briefly describe the development of the survey, the target sample, and how it was administered. The survey results are next analyzed and interpreted. The findings of the follow-up literature review are then presented, along with discussion and a conclusion.

Background and Literature Review

In this section, we summarize the previous work highlighting Wi-Fi's position in the wireless networking environment, its rapid growth, the benefits and limitations of Wi-Fi in general, and the current state of Wi-Fi technology in New Zealand.

Wi-Fi Networks

The IEEE 802.11b is only one of numerous wireless networking standards. McFarland and Wong (2003) provide a very good introduction to the IEEE's 802.11 family of standards. One of these is 802.11g, which is compatible with 802.11b but uses a different radio signal modulation technique to increase throughput up to 54 Mbps. Another is IEEE 802.11a, which also increases throughput to 54 Mbps, but by operating over a larger radio frequency range which makes it incompatible with IEEE 802.11b. In addition to the IEEE, other bodies have defined wireless networking standards for particular geographic regions. For instance, the European Telecommunications Standards Institute (ETSI) has defined the High Performance Radio LAN standards, HiperLAN and HiperLAN2, similar to the 802.11b and 802.11a standards, respectively.

The IEEE 802.11b/a/g and HiperLAN standards are generally considered as most suitable for WLANs. As Varshney and Vetter (2000) point out, there are other technologies better suited to larger wireless metropolitan area networks (MANs) and wide area networks (WANs). For instance, cellular networks provide much greater range than WLANs, but at significantly reduced throughput. Networks based on wireless asynchronous transfer mode (Wireless ATM) and satellites can provide still greater range and throughput comparable to 802.11b, but are far more costly to set up. The IEEE 802.16 standard, popularly known as WiMax, is also emerging in this field. It offers a potential throughput of 70 Mbps over distances of up to 50 kilometers (or 30 miles) (Marks, Chang, & McCabe, 2002).

Malladi and Agrawal (2002) extend the comparison further, including technologies for smaller wireless networks such as sensor networks or personal area networks (PANs). The most common PAN technology, Bluetooth, has a significantly shorter range than the IEEE 802.11b, to reduce the risks of interference with other wireless networks, and a comparable setup cost. However, it also has lower throughput.

Growth of Wi-Fi

The rapid growth of Wi-Fi in the U.S. is clearly illustrated by two surveys. A 2001 survey commissioned by Cisco found that 10% of US organizations were using Wi-Fi (NOP World – Technology, 2001). A 2003 survey commissioned by AirMagnet reports that Wi-Fi is used by 57% of enterprises, suggesting a growth rate of 470% in two years (Ask, 2003). Growth in Europe has been much slower, due to competition from the high performance radio LAN (HiperLAN) standard (Collins, 2002). Recent research from Instat/MDR reports that in 2002 the Asia-Pacific region had the fastest growth in the use of Wi-Fi, driven largely by the rapid uptake in Japan and Korea (Collins, 2002; Griffith, 2002).

Benefits of Wi-Fi

Why has the growth in Wi-Fi been so rapid? Gartner Research has identified two potential benefits of Wi-Fi technology, namely cost reductions and improved productivity (Redman, 2003). Some of the cost savings offered by Wi-Fi are illustrated in a case study of McDonalds New Zealand (Smith, 2003). For example, a reduced need to lay network and telephone cables, or re-lay them when the office is re-arranged; a reduced need for printing, as staff can access their documents from anywhere in the office; and no need to maintain redundant networks for disaster recovery purposes. In a similar vein, Otago University has reduced their need to outfit additional dedicated computer labs by setting up WLANs in the library and other study areas to which students can connect their own notebook PCS (Brislen, 2004b).

The savings on cabling are offset by additional costs for wireless network interface cards (NICs) and access points (APs), but these costs are decreasing. While an 802.11b WLAN requires all APs to be connected with LAN cable, the emerging 802.11n standard allows for 'mesh' networking (Wexler, 2004). This will further reduce cabling costs by requiring only one AP in the network to be wired, with wireless communication between it and the other APs. NIC costs should also continue to fall, with Gartner Research predicting that by 2005 80% of all notebook computers will have built-in NICs (Simpson, Milanesi, & Keene, 2003). In 2001, the Cisco survey reported that only 18% of respondents considered Wi-Fi to have lower costs than wired LANs (NOP World – Technology, 2001). In 2003, the AirMagnet study reports that 42% of respondents believe Wi-Fi is the cost-effective alternative (Ask, 2003).

In the Cisco survey, anytime/anywhere access was rated an "important" benefit by 80% of respondents (NOP World – Technology, 2001). The AirMagnet survey reports that 59% of respondents believe that Wi-Fi improves the productivity of office employees, while 49% believe the same for mobile employees (Ask, 2003). In New Zealand case studies, Dunedin and Waikato hospitals are currently using trolley-mounted Wi-Fi clinical workstations on which doctors can easily access and update patient information (Jackson, 2003). Auckland Hospital recently trialled a similar system, equipping doctors with Wi-Fi enabled tablet PCs and personal digital assistants (PDAs) (Brislen, 2004a).

Limitations of Wi-Fi

The surveys identify the following limitations of Wi-Fi technology: weak security, uncertainty over standards, lack of expertise, inconsistent performance and business value.

Security is consistently one of the main challenges in Wi-Fi technology. For example, it is ranked in the top three by 54% of respondents to the AirMagnet survey (Ask, 2003) and in the top two by 63% of respondents to a survey commissioned by Bridgewater Systems (Telechoice, 2003). The security defined in the IEEE 802.11b standard is wired equivalent privacy (WEP), and it has widely acknowledged weaknesses (Cam-Winget, Housley, Wagner, & Walker, 2003; Housley & Arbaugh, 2003; Ryan, 2003). More recent standards address these weaknesses. For instance, the 802.11i standard supports much stronger encryption and the 802.1x standard provides improved authentication. However implementing these may require existing APs and NICs to be upgraded or replaced (Fogarty, 2005) and may adversely impact on network performance. A further security concern was recently highlighted by Australian researchers, who found that an effective denial-of-service (DoS) attack could be made on an 802.11b WLAN even by a "semi-skilled attacker" with a "low-powered, portable device" (Australian Computer Emergency ResponseTeam, 2004).

In the AirMagnet survey, uncertainty in Wi-Fi standards was identified as a problem by 20% of respondents, and risk of technology obsolescence by 19% (Ask, 2003). This reflects the range of emerging WLAN technologies that threaten to make 802.11b obsolete, such as the other 802.11 and 802.16 standards mentioned above.

While creating a small Wi-Fi network is relatively simple, setting up a large scale Wi-Fi network requires some expertise that wired network engineers are not likely to possess. Having data carried by radio signals requires attention to be paid to antenna design, power management and shielding to reduce signal leakage, and placement of access points to reduce disruption from structural features (Jackson, 2003; Watson, 2003e). To gain the anytime/anywhere access benefits of Wi-Fi, end users and IT support staff will also need to be familiar with mobile devices, such as laptop computers, tablet PCs and personal digital assistants, particularly the stylus-driven interface (Bolles, 2003). In the AirMagnet survey, 16% of respondents saw a lack of internal technical expertise in Wi-Fi as a problem (Ask, 2003).

The bandwidth of a wired LAN is typically 100 Mbps. In comparison, the theoretical bandwidth of an 802.11b WLAN is 11 Mbps; but in practice, the achievable throughput is around 4 to 6 Mbps (Know & Fang, 2003). Recent research suggests that a Wi-Fi WLAN's throughput is adversely affected by even a single device with a slow connection (Knight, 2003). In 2001, the Cisco survey reported that low throughput was a problem for 20% of respondents (NOP World – Technology, 2001). As mentioned above, IEEE 802.11a and g offer up to 5 times this throughput. Another emerging standard, IEEE 802.11n, is expected to have a maximum throughput of around 500 Mbps. However, the bandwidth of wired LANs also continues to increase, with the emergence of 1 Gbps and even 10 Gbps standards.

Other performance problems noted in the Cisco survey included limited range (16%), interference (11%), building deadspots (10%), and low reliability (5%) (NOP World – Technology, 2001). Although these problems still existed at the time of the AirMagnet survey, it finds that inconsistent performance is regarded as a problem by only 12% of respondents (Ask, 2003).

A larger problem, according to that survey, is establishing a business case: 29% of respondents had not allocated any budget for Wi-Fi, and 14% saw no need in their organisation (Ask, 2003). The NZTE report suggests that New Zealand organizations are reluctant or unable to invest in wireless technology generally (MediaLab South Pacific, 2003).

Wi-Fi in New Zealand

In discussing Wi-Fi technology, the NZTE report suggests that WLANs are becoming increasingly common in small businesses and private homes, although no evidence is given for this (MediaLab South Pacific, 2003). The largest Wi-Fi in New Zealand in terms of the number of users supported is generally considered to be at St Kentigern College, which has 1600 students with notebook PCs of which 900 may be on the network at any one time (Hill, 2004).

Wi-Fi technology is being used to create metropolitan area networks (MANs) in urban areas, such as Queenstown, Auckland and Wellington (Watson, 2003a, , 2003b, 2003f). It also forms the basis of some wide area networks (WANs) in provincial areas, delivering broadband Internet access as part of the government's Project PROBE (Watson, 2003d). Wi-Fi technology has been used to provide public wireless hotspots in Auckland airport, hotels, restaurants and service stations (Watson, 2003c). Auckland is also the base of the New Zealand Wireless Data Forum (NZWDF), established in 1999. The NZWDF was setup initially to educate New Zealand's organizations in wireless data solutions, but it has recently adopted a more commercial focus, aiming to enable the wireless economy.

The NZTE report surveys 105 vendors of wireless technology in New Zealand, with 28% identifying Wi-Fi as their "base product" (MediaLab South Pacific, 2003). In terms of a market for Wi-Fi, a survey of Australian and New Zealand organizations by CIO Magazine reports that 20% were using Wi-Fi at the end of 2001 (Hind, 2003). This increased to 38% at the end of 2002, indicating a growth rate of 90% for the year. An IDC survey of New Zealand organizations reports that 9% were using Wi-Fi in 2001 (Broatch, 2003). This increased to 20% in 2002, indicating a growth rate of 122%.

In these surveys, Wi-Fi was the subject of just a few questions, amongst many issues that respondents were asked about. For more detail on how Wi-Fi is being deployed and used in New Zealand, one must turn to case studies of individual organizations, some examples of which have been referenced in this section. To the best of our knowledge, there are no New Zealand surveys dealing specifically with Wi-Fi, in the manner of the Cisco, AirMagnet and Bridgewater surveys of US organizations referenced above. This chapter is a first step in filling that gap. In the following two sections we report on the detailed survey of Wi-Fi in New Zealand.

Survey

In this section, we briefly describe the development of the survey, the target sample, and how it was administered.

Choice of WLAN Technology

We considered the possibility of making this survey about generic WLANs, rather than Wi-Fi technology in particular. However, as mentioned earlier, different WLAN technologies have different profiles of range, performance, cost, security, and other features. To produce meaningful conclusions we felt it necessary to either focus on a particular technology, or analyze data separately for each technology. We decided against the latter course as we weren't confident of getting sufficient responses for all technologies from our relatively small sample.

Having chosen to focus on a single technology, Wi-Fi seemed the obvious choice. Where other surveys mentioned a particular technology, it was always Wi-Fi. As mentioned earlier, more vendors are selling Wi-Fi than any other WLAN technology, suggesting a similar pattern among purchasers. We believe our choice was justified by a survey published just after we had completed our analysis. Wexler and Taylor (2004) found that 802.11b was the most widespread WLAN technology, used by 67% of organizations with WLANs. The other IEEE standards, 802.11g and 802.11a, were used by 40% and 22% of organizations respectively. HiperLAN and Bluetooth were both used by around 5% of organizations.

Purpose and Structure

The survey questionnaire used in this study consists of three sections with a total of 14 questions (see Appendix). It was designed to serve three purposes. The primary purpose of the survey was to determine the level of, and problems encountered during, deployment of Wi-Fi technology in large New Zealand organizations and to compare it with results obtained from overseas. This was supported by asking about the current deployment level, in question 1; and the problems encountered, in questions 9 to 13. The survey's second purpose was to test the NZTE survey's finding that New Zealand organizations are unaware of the value and potential of wireless technology (MediaLab South Pacific, 2003). This was supported by asking about why Wi-Fi is not being used, in question 2; how Wi-Fi is being used, in questions 3 to 5; and how Wi-Fi will be used in the future, in question 14. The survey's third purpose was to test the NZTE survey's finding that New Zealand organizations are unable or reluctant to invest in wireless technology (MediaLab South Pacific, 2003). This was supported by asking about the investment of money, time and staff resources, in questions 6 to 8.

Figure 1. Organizations by number of screens

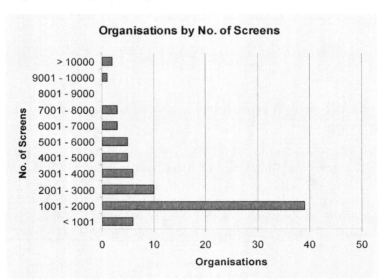

Figure 2. Organizations by industry

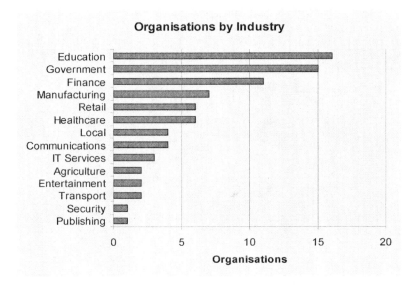

Target Sample

The target sample consisted of 80 organizations. They were selected from amongst the largest end users of IT in New Zealand, as these were considered to be the most likely market for the wireless vendors surveyed in the NZTE report (MediaLab South Pacific, 2003). The number of end users in an organisation was approximated by the number of screens, consistent with the approach of MIS magazine (Bell, 2003). Figure 1 shows a breakdown of organizations by number of screens. The organizations were from a range of industries, with most classified as Education providers and Government departments. No more than 20% were from any one industry. A breakdown of organizations by industry is shown in Figure 2.

Administering the Survey

A hardcopy of the survey questionnaire and a covering letter was sent to each organisation in the target sample in July 2003. A reply-paid envelope was included for the return of the completed survey. We opted for a postal survey instead of email or Internet based survey, because of the rash of viruses that was afflicting the Internet at the time.

Over the course of six weeks, 34 responses were received. This response rate of 42.5% was considered acceptable.

Figure 3. Current deployment

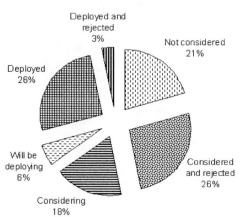

Findings

In this section we present the key results of the Wi-Fi survey. The results are presented in six themes: level of deployment, reasons for non-deployment, scope of deployment, investment in deployment, problems, and future plans.

Level of Wi-Fi Deployment

Question 1 asked all respondents for the current state of deployment of Wi-Fi in their organisation. The results are summarised in Figure 3.

We found that about 79% of organizations have at least considered deploying Wi-Fi. Of these organizations, there is an almost equal split between those that have or will be deploying Wi-Fi (32%), and those that have rejected them (29%), with 18% still considering.

Reasons for Non-Deployment of Wi-Fi

Question 2 asked those respondents who have not considered deploying, or had rejected Wi-Fi, the reason for this decision.

As seen in Figure 4, security is the overwhelming concern, accounting for almost half these responses. Lack of a business case and expense are a problem for 25%, performance ("Too

Figure 4. Reasons for non-consideration/non-deployment

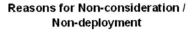

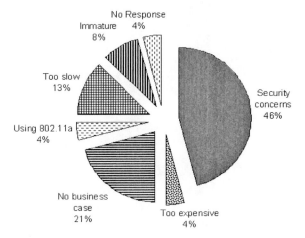

Reasons for Non-consideration /
Non-deployment

slow" and "Using 802.11a") for 17%, and uncertainty over standards ("Immature") for 8%. "Lack of expertise" was not mentioned even though "Too complicated" was a specific option given in the survey (see Appendix, Question 2).

Scope of Wi-Fi Deployment

We asked questions regarding Wi-Fi deployment to those respondents who are considering, will be deploying, or have deployed, Wi-Fi.

Question 3 asked whether Wi-Fi was used in infrastructure or ad-hoc mode. As can be seen in Figure 5, 83% of respondents are using infrastructure WLANs, whereas 28% are using ad-hoc networks.

Question 4 asked about the year in which the organizations first deployed, or plan to deploy, Wi-Fi. As can be seen in Figure 6, 2001 was the first year Wi-Fi was deployed by large New Zealand organizations two years after the IEEE 802.11b standard was approved. Approximately 9% of all respondents had deployed Wi-Fi by the end of 2001, and 24% by the end of 2002. We might expect 35% of respondents to have deployed by the end of 2003, and up to 53% by the end of 2004.

Question 5 asked for a breakdown of devices that are, or will be, Wi-Fi enabled. The results, in Figure 7, show that desktop PCs make up almost half the devices being attached to Wi-Fi networking. In comparison, the AirMagnet survey reports approximately the same propor-

Figure 5. Infrastructure or ad-hoc

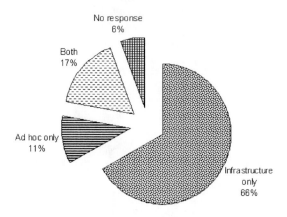

Figure 6. Year of first deployment

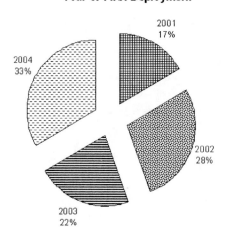

tions for tablets and PDAs, but much lower for 'other' devices (2%) and for desktops (16%), and much higher for laptops (71%) (Ask, 2003).

The device breakdown for the individual respondents that completed this question is shown in Table 1. It shows that the high proportion of desktops in Figure 7 is concentrated in two respondents. The support for laptops and PDAs is more widespread. Table 1 also suggests that most organizations are deploying Wi-Fi on a relatively small scale. The organizations sampled had an average of approximately 2100 desktop PCs and 270 laptops, tablets, and PDAs. Yet half of the respondents are using fewer than 100 Wi-Fi enabled devices.

Figure 7. Wi-Fi enabled devices

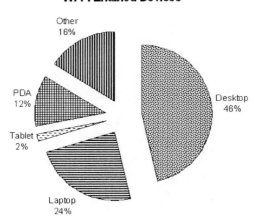

Wi-Fi Enabled Devices

Table 1. Wi-Fi enabled devices by respondent

Respondent	Desktop	Laptop	Tablet	PDA	Other
1	1000				
4		600			400
8		10		20	
9		100	10	10	
11					350
12	150	70		10	
14		10			
15	1000	100	50		
18		4			
19		10			
20		100	10	100	
22	10	2			
23				400	
24		50		20	
32		60			

Figure 8. Deployment cost

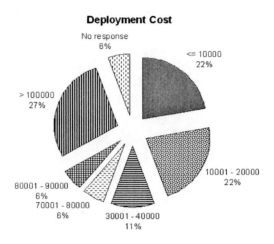

Figure 9. Responsible for deployment

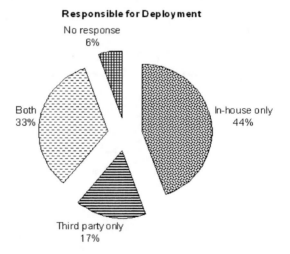

Figure 10. Deployment time

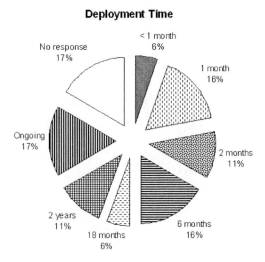

Deployment Time

Investment in Wi-Fi Deployment

The questions in this section were asked to those respondents who are considering, will be deploying, or have deployed, Wi-Fi.

Question 6 asked for the amount spent on deploying Wi-Fi. The results are shown in Figure 8. We found that the median cost (in NZ$) of deploying Wi-Fi is in the range $30,001 - $40,000. However, the distribution is skewed to the extremes, with the two largest proportions spending less than $20,000 and more than $100,000.

Question 7 asked who performed the Wi-Fi deployment. The results are summarized in Figure 9. We found that nearly half of respondents deployed Wi-Fi using only in-house staff, while just 17% required full service from a third party.

Question 8 asked for the total time taken for Wi-Fi deployment. As seen in Figure 10, 49% of the respondents took six months or less to deploy their Wi-Fi, with 17% making it an ongoing task.

Table 2 shows the combined data for the number of Wi-Fi enabled devices deployed, year of first deployment, deployment cost, responsibility, and deployment time for each respondent. We found very little correlation between the number of devices and cost. For example, respondent 20 deployed 210 Wi-Fi enabled laptops, tablets and PDAs for $10,001-$20,000, while respondent 18 required $30,001-$40,000 to deploy four Wi-Fi enabled laptops.

As seen in Table 2, there is a strong correlation between deployment cost and responsibility for deployment. Of the respondents using only in-house staff, only 12.5% spent more than $20,000. Of the respondents using a third party, only 11% spent less than $20,000.

Table 2.Devices, first deployment and investment in Wi-Fi by respondent

Resp.	Desktop	Mobile*	Year	Cost	Responsibility	Time
1	1000		2001	80,0001 – 90,000	Both	Ongoing
7			2004	> 100,000	Both	
8		30	2002	< 10,001	Both	2 months
9		120	2002	10,001 – 20,000	In-house only	Ongoing
11		350	2004	> 100,000	Third party only	18 months
12	150	80	2004	> 100,000	In-house only	Ongoing
13			2003	< 10,001	In-house only	
14		10	2002	10,001 – 20,000	In-house only	1 month
15	1000	150	2004	> 100,000	Third party only	Ongoing
18		4	2003	30,001 – 40,000	Third party only	1 month
19		10	2003	< 10,001	In-house only	2 months
20		210	2002	10,001 – 20,000	In-house only	2 years
22	10	2	2002	10,001 – 20,000	In-house only	
23		400	2003	> 100,000	Both	2 years
24			2004	30,001 – 40,000	Both	
26		70	2003	70,001 – 80,000	Both	6 months
32		60	2001	< 10,001	In-house only	< 1 month

*Note: *Total of Laptops, Tablet, PDA and Other*

One can see that there is a strong correlation between the year of first deployment and deployment cost. For example, of the respondents first deploying in 2001/2002, only 14% spent more than $20,000. Of the respondents first deploying in 2003/2004, only 20% spent $20,000 or less. This is initially surprising as it might be expected that early deployers would have deployed more devices over time, and purchased devices at a time when they were more expensive. However, closer examination suggests two reasons for the difference in spending. The respondents first deploying in 2001/2002 have deployed fewer devices (1010 desktops, 432 mobile) than the respondents first deploying in 2003/2004 (1150 desktops, 1064 mobile). The difference in the relatively more expensive mobile devices is particularly noticeable. In addition, respondents first deploying in 2001/2002 have made less use of third parties for deployment (29%) than respondents first deploying in 2003/2004 (70%).

We also found that there is a correlation between the number of Wi-Fi enabled devices deployed and deployment time. All respondents that deployed less than 100 Wi-Fi enabled devices took six months or less. All respondents that deployed more than 100 Wi-Fi enabled devices took more than six months.

Limitations of Wi-Fi

Question 9 asked the 53% of respondents that are considering, will be deploying, or have deployed, Wi-Fi what problems they did, or expect to, encounter during deployment. Questions 10 to 13 asked the 29% of respondents that had deployed Wi-Fi what ongoing problems they had experienced. The results are shown in Figures 11 to 15.

The most interesting aspect of these five questions is the number of respondents specifically stating "No issues," or making no response. Although these two possibilities have been shown separately in Figures 11 to 15, the wording of the questions is such that no response can be taken to mean that no issues were encountered (see Appendix, questions 9 through 13).

Figure 11. Issues in deployment

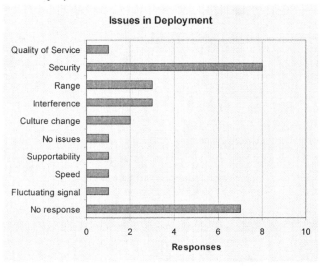

Figure 12. User support issues

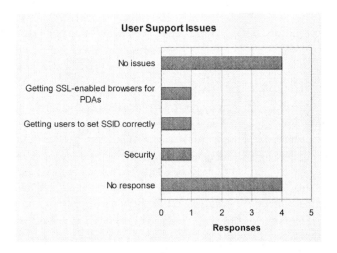

Figure 13. Network performance issues

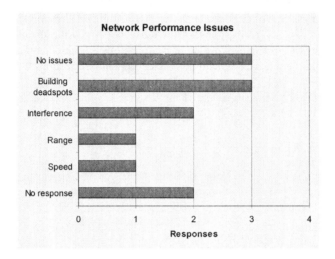

Figure 14. Network management issues

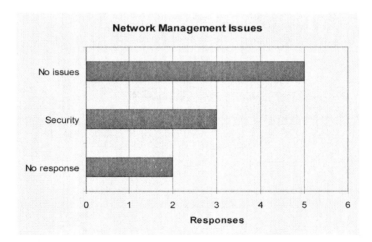

Mirroring the reasons for not deploying Wi-Fi, the most prevalent concern is security. However, the responses give little insight into organizations' specific security concerns. Most respondents simply used the word "security." Only two gave specific concerns, such as end users installing their own APs and finding SSL enabled browsers for PDAs. In contrast, respondents gave a number of specific concerns relating to inconsistent performance —quality of service, range, interference, speed, fluctuating signals, and building deadspots. Less prevalent issues mentioned are related to the inexperience of end users, including culture change and getting users to set SSIDs, and uncertain standards, including finding SSL enabled browsers for PDAs.

Figure 15. Other issues

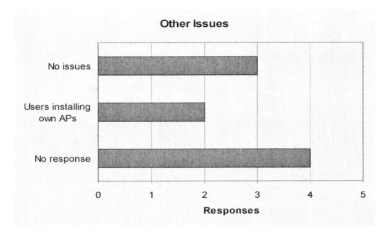

Future Plans for Wi-Fi

Question 14 asked the 26% of respondents who had Wi-Fi WLANs currently deployed about plans for future uses of Wi-Fi. The results are shown in Figure 16.

Given the relatively low level of issues raised in questions 9 to 13, it is not surprising to see that most respondents were expecting to increase the use and coverage of Wi-Fi WLANs within their organisation. However, it is interesting to note that those organizations nominating an upgrade path have preferred IEEE 802.11g over Gartner Research's (Dulaney, 2002) and Forrester Research's (Dolinov, 2003) recommendations for 802.11a. Given the widespread

Figure 16. Future deployments

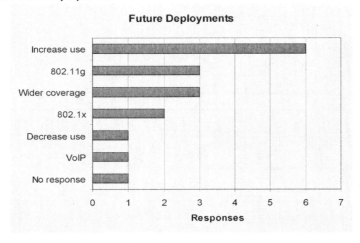

concern about security, it also is surprising that only two respondents have specifically referred to adopting the IEEE 802.1x standard, or some other means of improving it.

The mention of voice-over-IP (VoIP) is somewhat surprising. While the idea of voice-over-WLAN (VoWLAN) is not new, 802.11b, a and g are generally regarded as unsuitable. A timing-sensitive application such as VoWLAN ideally requires a standard with Quality of Service (QoS) features, allowing different types of network traffic to be given different priorities. The emerging standards that provide QoS features are 802.16 and 802.11e.

Table 3 shows the combined data for number of Wi-Fi enabled devices deployed, year of first deployment, responsibility for deployment, problems encountered and future plans for each respondent.

This shows very little correlation between the year of first deployment and problems encountered, or between responsibility for deployment and problems encountered.

Table 3. Devices, first deployment, responsibility, problems, and future plans for Wi-Fi (by respondent)

Resp.	Desktop	Mobile*	Year	Responsibility	Problems**	Plans***
1	1000		2001	Both		I
7			2004	Both		
8		30	2002	Both	Sc, P	I
9		120	2002	In-house only	Sp, P	I
11		350	2004	Third party only	Sc, P	I
12	150	80	2004	In-house only		
13			2003	In-house only	Sc, P	D
14		10	2002	In-house only	Sc, P	G, X
15	1000	150	2004	Third party only		
18		4	2003	Third party only	Sc	G, X
19		10	2003	In-house only	Sc, P	I
20		210	2002	In-house only	Sc, P	I
22	10	2	2002	In-house only		I
23		400	2003	Both	Sc, P	
24			2004	Both	Sc, C	
26		70	2003	Both	Sc, Sp, C	
32		60	2001	In-house only		I, G, V

Note:
*Total of Laptop, Tablet, PDA and Other
**Sc = Security, C = Culture, Sp = Support, P = Performance (Range, Speed, Interference, etc.)
***I = Increase use / Wider coverage, D = Decrease use, G = 802.11g, X = 802.1x, V = VoIP

Analysis

This section compares large New Zealand organizations' experience with Wi-Fi, as suggested by the survey results, with the international experience found in the literature review. It also discusses whether survey results support the findings of the NZTE survey (MediaLab South Pacific, 2003). In the process, a number of opportunities for further research are identified.

Growth of Wi-Fi

It would appear that Wi-Fi is one technology that large New Zealand organizations have not adopted particularly early or quickly, in comparison to other countries. Figure 6 suggests that Wi-Fi was not deployed in New Zealand until 2001. This is two years after the IEEE 802.11b standard was finalised, the Wi-Fi Alliance began certifying Wi-Fi products, and the NZWDF was founded. Figure 3 indicates that 26% of large New Zealand organizations are currently using Wi-Fi, with 6% planning to do so. This is approximately half the level of large US organizations, according to the AirMagnet survey (Ask, 2003). It is also well below the CIO magazine's survey showing the usage for combined Australian and New Zealand organizations at 38% at the end of 2002 (Hind, 2003). This suggests that, considering Australian organizations alone, somewhat more than 38% have deployed Wi-Fi.

It should be noted that the results of this survey may have been different had the sample included organizations from different industries or of smaller size. The Cisco survey suggests that organizations in different industries have different levels of Wi-Fi usage (NOP World - Technology, 2001). In particular, the average US educational institution is two-and-a-half times more likely to use Wi-Fi than the average US organisation. Although educational institutions make up 20% of the target sample for this survey, it is not known what proportion of respondents they represent. The AirMagnet survey suggests that small organizations are more likely than large organizations to deploy Wi-Fi, whereas this survey has focused on large organizations (Ask, 2003).

Benefits of Wi-Fi

It seems that large New Zealand organizations are more interested in the potential productivity benefits of Wi-Fi than in the cost reduction benefits. Table 1 shows that 11 out of 15 respondents (73%) are using Wi-Fi only with mobile devices, suggesting that they are hoping to increase productivity through anytime/anywhere access. The remaining 27% of organizations are using Wi-Fi primarily for desktops, suggesting that they are focusing on reducing cabling costs. In addition, Table 2 suggests that the difference will grow, with organizations new to Wi-Fi making more use of mobile devices than organizations that first deployed them in 2001/2002.

It also seems that many large New Zealand organizations that are using Wi-Fi are doing so on a small scale or perhaps a trial basis. Table 1 suggests that one-third of respondents have less than 10% of their devices Wi-Fi enabled, and around half have less than 100 devices

Wi-Fi enabled. This may in fact result in a reduction in the level of Wi-Fi usage as trials are completed. As Intel report, making trials too small results in less obvious cost reduction and productivity benefits (Intel, 2002).

Problems with Wi-Fi

It seems that the problems experienced with Wi-Fi by large New Zealand organizations generally mirror problems reported overseas. Figure 4 and Figures 11 to 15 are dominated by security. The respondents' comments for question 2 suggest that the issue is in meeting security requirements, rather than actual security breaches. For instance:

> *[security concerns] led us to implement only techniques which can be configured at appropriate levels to be able to meet evolving standards.*
>
> *"security protection requirements make it unattractive"*

This may also go some way to explaining the lack of specific security concerns given in responses to questions 9 to 13. It is possible that security is a concern because of the effort involved in developing and enforcing security policies, assuring senior management that WLANs are secure, and other administrative overhead. Another possibility is that organizations are reluctant to discuss security problems in too much detail. This would not be unusual, but clearly poses a challenge to identifying and resolving them.

For all the concern about security, Figure 16 suggests that few organizations are planning to address them. This may, again, reflect organizations' reluctance to discuss their security precautions. It may also indicate that organizations are familiar with the well-publicised shortcomings of Wi-Fi security, but less knowledgeable about the solutions available. Rapidly evolving standards mean that organizations may be unaware of developments such as the IEEE's 802.1x and 802.11i, and Wireless Protected Access (WPA). It has already been noted that implementing these standards may require significant upgrades or replacement of existing WLAN infrastructure. These organizations may be following some overseas who have chosen to manage the security risk until their infrastructure is due for replacement (Brewin, 2004; Fogarty, 2005). While organizations haven't placed a lack of RF expertise as a major issue, it does mean that they may not be aware of possible security improvements based on the physical layout of WLANs. For instance, APs may be shielded or use directional antennas to reduce signal leakage.

Figure 4 and Figures 11 through 15 also suggest that concerns over inconsistent performance are comparable with overseas findings. However, New Zealand organizations seem to perceive uncertainty over standards and lack of expertise as lesser problems. Figure 4 shows that making a business case for Wi-Fi is a problem for only about 13% of large New Zealand organizations, which is noticeably less than the AirMagnet survey of US organizations (Ask, 2003). This calls into question the NZTE survey's finding that New Zealand organizations are unaware of the value and potential of wireless technology (MediaLab South Pacific, 2003).

On the other hand, the NZTE finding that New Zealand organizations are unable or reluctant to invest in wireless technology seems justified. As seen in Figure 8, about 44% of respondents spent $20,000 or less deploying their Wi-Fi. However, Table 2 suggests that organizations new to Wi-Fi are spending more and making more use of vendors than are organizations that first deployed in 2001/2002. For a vendor who is prepared to invest in understanding organizations' security and business requirements, and how to maximise Wi-Fi performance, Figure 3 suggests that there is a market in 50% of New Zealand's large organizations.

Survey Limitations

We could not pilot test this survey because of time constraints. It is apparent from some responses that certain questions could have been worded more clearly. For instance, different respondents seem to have taken different interpretations of "spending" on Wi-Fi deployment, with some counting only wireless cards while others have included the entire cost of a Wi-Fi enabled laptop. The sample size is small, due to the desire to sample only large organizations. Anonymity was promised to respondents, to encourage participation. The combination of these two factors has, to some extent, restricted the results that can be included here.

Wi-Fi in 2005

While we have not conducted any further surveys, a number of those already mentioned have proceeded on an annual basis. The surveys of New Zealand organizations by CIO magazine (Hind, 2004, 2005) and MIS magazine (Paredes, 2005) suggest that the growth in deployment of Wi-Fi WLANs has slowed. Of the 100 organizations surveyed by MIS, only eight specifically mentioned "wireless networks" in their key projects for 2004 and 2005. Usage rates for WLANs were missing from the CIO survey results, which show only the ten technologies with the highest growth rates.

The apparent deceleration in growth is not surprising. As a greater proportion of organizations deploy WLANs, the room for growth naturally decreases. This is reflected in the US experience. A survey by Forrester Research found that 60% of enterprises were expecting to deploy or upgrade WLANs in 2005 (Computerworld Executive Briefings, 2005), up only slightly from 57% in the 2003 AirMagnet survey (Ask, 2003). The fact that New Zealand organizations appear to have reached this point at a significantly lower usage rate tends to support the conclusion that they have not been early or quick adopters of WLAN technology.

The CIO surveys do show that spending on wireless networks has risen slightly over 2004 and 2005, suggesting that New Zealand organizations with WLANs have been upgrading them. That is consistent with the responses to this survey's question on future plans.

While the growth in deployment of WLANs may have slowed, the CIO surveys show a very high rate of growth in fixed broadband wireless. While the survey doesn't explicitly define this term, it is generally used to describe a fixed infrastructure wireless MAN or WAN providing broadband Internet or telephony functions (Cunliffe, 2004). Examples of fixed broadband wireless include the world's first commercial wireless VoIP service (Palmer, 2005), and a WiMax network trial to provide high-speed Internet to a rural area (Saarinen, 2005). The major national telecommunications provider is also taking steps to introduce Wi-Fi and WiMax services (Brislen, 2005a, 2005b). Such technologies were used by 6.6% of New Zealand organizations in 2004, by 11.3% in 2005, and are expected to be used by 52.6% in 2006.

Future Work

Further research on the role that an organisation's industry and size plays in their Wi-Fi usage is suggested. A survey with a larger number of smaller organizations seems like the next logical step. Repeating this survey on a regular basis, perhaps annually, would also be of some benefit, allowing a picture to be built up of how large New Zealand organizations' use of Wi-Fi changes over time.

A case study of Wi-Fi technology adoption in specific settings, such as the hospital environment, is also suggested for future work. Such studies might collect more detailed data about the specific applications running on WLANs, and their particular implications for security and performance. They might also contribute to the growing body of research on mobility patterns (Balazinska & Castro, 2003; Henderson, Kotz, & Abyzov, 2004), or the business cases for, and benefits realised through, the use of Wi-Fi (Intel, 2002).

Concluding Remarks

We have surveyed 80 large New Zealand organizations about their level of Wi-Fi deployment, their reasons for non-deployment, the scope of their deployment, their investment in Wi-Fi deployment, the problems they have encountered, and their future plans for Wi-Fi. Our findings show that Wi-Fi has not been adopted quickly or widely, compared to other countries. Though large New Zealand organizations seem to be aware of the potential benefits of the technology, many organizations chose not to deploy Wi-Fi, or to deploy it on a small scale. They are particularly concerned about security and performance issues. Other issues identified in overseas research, such as difficulties making a business case, uncertainty over standards, and a lack of expertise, do not appear to be so pronounced in large New Zealand organizations. More recent surveys suggest that growth in Wi-Fi WLANs has slowed while existing WLANs are upgraded. They have also shown a rapidly growing interest in fixed wireless broadband technologies, such as WiMax.

We believe that this report will prove to be of value to New Zealand's large IT end-user organizations and wireless vendors. End-user organizations may reflect on the scope, investment, and issues experienced in previous deployments of Wi-Fi in planning their own. Wireless vendors may find the data on the level of deployment, investments, and future plans useful in formulating their future products and services.

This chapter also contributes to filling a research gap in how New Zealand organizations use Wi-Fi technology. As such, it may be a useful resource for both teachers and students interested in carrying out further research in the areas of wireless and mobile networking.

References

Ask, J. (2003). *Wi-Fi deployments: Are enterprises ready despite evolving security and standards?* Retrieved October 27, 2003, from www.jupiterresearch.com

Australian Computer Emergency ResponseTeam. (2004). *Denial of service vulnerability in IEEE 802.11 wireless devices.* Retrieved November 20, 2005, from www.auscert. org.au

Balazinska, M., & Castro, P. (2003). *Characterizing mobility and network usage in a corporate wireless local-area network.* Paper presented at the First ACM International Conference on Mobile Systems, Applications and Services, San Francisco.

Bell, C. (2003). *Is it the right way? MIS, 6,* 6.

Bland, V., O'Neill, R., & Bell, C. (2003). 10 top trends 2003. *MIS, 6,* 13.

Bolles, G. A. (2003). *Is the pen mightier?* Retrieved August 14, from www.cioinsight. com

Brewin, B. (2004). *Managers ready defenses against flaw in wireless LANs.* Retrieved November 20, 2005, from www.computerworld.com

Brislen, P. (2004a). Life support. *CIO, 51,* 48-49.

Brislen, P. (2004b). Why go wireless? *CIO, 51,* 53.

Brislen, P. (2005a). *Telecom gets serious about wireless.* Retrieved October 30, 2005, from www.computerworld.co.nz

Brislen, P. (2005b). *Telecom seeks to buy wired country spectrum.* Retrieved November 20, 2005, from www.computerworld.co.nz

Broatch, M. (2003, November 8). Stats watch: Wi-Fi shows its charms. *NZ Computer-World.*

Cam-Winget, N., Housley, R., Wagner, D., & Walker, J. (2003). Security flaws in 802.11 data link protocols. *Communications of the ACM, 46*(5), 35-39.

Collins, J. (2002). *Europe drags feet on 802.11b.* Retrieved October 28, 2003, from www. itweek.co.uk

Computerworld Executive Briefings. (2005). *Riding the wireless wave.* Retrieved November 10, 2005, from www.computerworld.com

Cunliffe, D. (2004). *Government announces allocation plan for wireless broadband spectrum.* Retrieved November 20, 2005, from www.med.govt.nz

Dolinov, M. (2003). *What to do about Wi-Fi.* Forrester Research.

Dulaney, K. (2002). *The wireless and mobile market starts to mature.* Gartner Research.

Fogarty, K. (2005). *Issues slow adoption of 802.11i standard*. Retrieved November 20, 2005, from www.computerworld.com

Griffith, E. (2002). *Where's the money?* Retrieved September 21, 2003, from www.wi-fi-planet.com

Henderson, T., Kotz, D., & Abyzov, I. (2004). *The changing usage of a mature campus-wide wireless network*. Paper presented at the 10th Annual International Conference on Mobile Computing and Networking, Philadelphia.

Hill, D. (2004). Brave New World. *CIO*, 14-19.

Hind, P. (2003). Forecast for Management 2003. *CIO, 46*, 16-27.

Hind, P. (2004). Forecast for Management 2004. *CIO, 55*, 24-32.

Hind, P. (2005). Forecast for Management 2005. *CIO, 68*, 14-23.

Housley, R., & Arbaugh, W. (2003). Security problems in 802.11-based networks. *Communications of the ACM, 46*(5), 31-34.

Intel. (2002). *Wireless LANs: Linking productivity gains to return on investment*. Retrieved October 10, 2003, from www.intel.com

Jackson, R. (2003). Wireless takes off. *CIO, 43*, 30-33.

Knight, W. (2003). *Single slow user can throttle wi-fi network*. Retrieved August 14, 2003, from www.newscientist.com

Know, Y., & Fang, Y. (2003). *A novel MAC protocol with fast collision resolution for wireless LANs*. Paper presented at the 22nd Annual Joint Conference of IEEE Computer and Communications Societies, San Francisco.

Malladi, R., & Agrawal, D. P. (2002). Current and future applications of mobile and wireless networks. *Communications of the ACM, 45*(10), 144-146.

Marks, R., Chang, D., & McCabe, K. (2002). *Broadband wireless access: An introduction to the technology behind the IEEE 802.16 WirelessMAN standard*. Retrieved November 20, 2005, from www.ieee.org

McFarland, B., & Wong, M. (2003). The family dynamics of 802.11. *Queue, 1*(3), 28-38.

MediaLab South Pacific. (2003). *No Wires - No Limits*. Retrieved from www.wirelessdataforum.co.nz

Myers, M. (1996). Can kiwis fly? Computing in New Zealand. *Communications of the ACM, 39*(4), 11-15.

NOP World – Technology. (2001). *Wireless LAN benefits study*. Retrieved October 10, 2003, from www.cisco.com

Palmer, K. (2005). *New Zealand hosts global wireless broadband summit*. Retrieved November 28, 2005, from www.computerworld.co.nz

Paredes, D. (2005). 100 biggest users of IT. *MIS*, 8.

Redman, P. (2003). *How to build a communications network that suits your needs*. Gartner Research.

Ryan, V. (2003). *Are wireless networks secure yet?* Retrieved April 10, from www.newsfactor.com

Saarinen, J. (2005). *Callplus trials WiMax.* Retrieved November 20, 2005, from www.computerworld.co.nz

Simpson, R., Milanesi, C., & Keene, I. (2003). *WLAN is ready, Bluetooth isn't.* Retrieved June 12, from www.zdnet.com

Smith, P. (2003). Freedom of information. *CIO, 45,* 16-19.

Telechoice. (2003). *Managed wireless LAN services: A User Perspective.* Bridgewater Systems.

Telecom. (2003). *Kiwis embrace advanced mobile phone services.* Retrieved June 12, from www.telecom-media.co.nz

Varshney, U., & Vetter, R. (2000). Emerging mobile and wireless networks. *Communications of the ACM, 43*(6), 73-81.

Watson, D. (2003a, November 11). Another wireless LAN for Queenstown. *NZ ComputerWorld.*

Watson, D. (2003b, November 11). Auckland wireless net lures Asians. *NZ ComputerWorld.*

Watson, D. (2003c, November 8). Walker delays hotspots for roaming ability. *NZ ComputerWorld.*

Watson, D. (2003d, November 8). Wi-Fi link tipped for Waikato school. *NZ ComputerWorld.*

Watson, D. (2003e, November 8). Wi-Fi threatened by sloppy users. *NZ ComputerWorld.*

Watson, D. (2003f, November 8). Wireless net spreads wider. *NZ ComputerWorld.*

Wexler, J. (2004). *Mesh moves into the wireless office.* Retrieved November 20, 2005, from www.computerworld.com

Wexler, J., & Taylor, S. (2004). *2004 wireless LAN state of the market report.* Retrieved May 20, 2004, from www.webtorials.com

Appendix:
Survey Questionnaire

Section 1: Awareness of Wi-Fi (IEEE 802.11b) Technology

All respondents complete this section.

1.   What is the current state of deployment of Wi-Fi in your organisation? (Tick one)
- ❑   We have not considered deploying it.
- ❑   We have considered deploying it, but decided against it.

- ❑ We are currently considering deploying it.
- ❑ We will be deploying it in the future.
- ❑ We have deployed it.
- ❑ We have deployed it, but are no longer using it.

2. If your organisation has not considered deploying Wi-Fi, or has decided against it, why is this? (Tick all that apply)

- ❑ Unaware of it.
- ❑ Consider it too expensive.
- ❑ Consider it too complicated.
- ❑ Consider it to lack sufficient security features.
- ❑ Other _____

Section 2: Deployment of Wi-Fi Technology

Only respondents that are considering deployment, will be deploying, or have deployed 802.11b complete this section.

3. How does, or will, your organisation utilise Wi-Fi? (Tick all that apply)

- ❑ Infrastructure Networks.
- ❑ Ad-hoc Networks.
- ❑ Other _____

4. In what year did, or will, your organisation first deploy Wi-Fi?

5. How many devices in your organisation do, or will, utilise 802.11b?

- ❑ Desktop PCs_____
- ❑ Laptop PCs_____
- ❑ Tablet PCs_____
- ❑ Pocket PCs/PDAs_____
- ❑ Other_____

6. How much did, or will, your organisation spend on deploying Wi-Fi? (Tick one)

❑ < $10,000	❑$40,001-$50,000	❑$80,001 - $90,000
❑$10,001 - $20,000	❑$50,001-$60,000	❑$90,001 - $100,000
❑$20,001 - $30,000	❑$60,001-$70,000	❑> $100,000
❑$30,001 - $40,000	❑$70,001-$80,000	

7. How did, or will, your organisation deploy Wi-Fi? (Tick all that apply)

- ❑ In-house staff.
- ❑ Third-party vendor.
- ❑ Other _____

8.   How long did, or will, your organisation take to deploy Wi-Fi?

9.   What problems did, or will, your organisation encounter in deploying Wi-Fi, if any?

Section 3: Experiences with Wi-Fi Technology

Only respondents that have deployed Wi-Fi complete this section.

10.   What issues has your organisation encountered with providing support to users of Wi-Fi, if any? (For example: Greater demand for support? Extra support staff or additional training? Has vendor support met expectations?)

11.   What issues has your organisation encountered with the network performance of Wi-Fi, if any? (For example: Has performance met expectations? Has interference been an issue? Have office layouts been an issue?)

12.   What issues has your organisation encountered with the network management of Wi-Fi, if any? (For example: Has it required new monitoring tools or techniques? Has it required more network staff? Is it more difficult to manage than wired networks?)

13.   What other issues has your organisation encountered with Wi-Fi, if any?

14.   What plans does your organisation have for Wi-Fi in the future, if any? (For example: Increase or decrease use? Upgrade to IEEE 802.11a or IEEE 802.11g?)

Chapter XI

Applications and Future Trends in Mobile Ad Hoc Networks

Subhankar Dhar, San Jose University, USA

Abstract

This chapter presents the current state of the art of mobile ad hoc network and some important problems and challenges related to routing, power management, location management, security as well as multimedia over ad hoc networks. A mobile ad hoc network (MANET) is a temporary, self-organizing network of wireless mobile nodes without the support of any existing infrastructure that may be readily available on the conventional networks. Since there is no fixed infrastructure available for MANET with nodes being mobile, routing becomes a very important issue. In addition, we also explain the various emerging applications and future trends of MANET.

Introduction

A mobile ad hoc network (MANET) is a temporary, self-organizing network of wireless mobile nodes without the support of any existing infrastructure that may be readily available on the conventional networks. It allows various devices to form a network in areas where no communication infrastructure exists. Although there are many problems and challenges that need to be solved before a large-scale deployment of a MANET, small- and medium-sized MANETs can be easily deployed.

As the number of applications of wireless ad hoc network grows, the size of the network varies greatly from a network of several mobile computers in a classroom, to a network of hundreds of mobile units deployed in a battlefield, for example. The variability in the network size is also true for a particular network over the course of time; a network of a thousand nodes may be split into a number of smaller networks of a few hundred nodes or vice versa, as the nodes dynamically move around a deployed area.

Ad hoc networks not only have the traditional problems of wireless communications like power management, security, and bandwidth optimization, but also the lack of any fixed infrastructure and their multi-hop nature poses new research problems. For example, routing, topology maintenance, location management, and device discovery, to name a few, are important problems and still active areas of research (Carson, Macker, & Cirincione, 1999, Chlamtac, Conti, & Liu, 2003, Liu & Chlamtac, 2004, Wu & Stojmenovic, 2004).

Wireless networks can be classified into three major categories: wireless personal area networks (WPAN), wireless local area networks (WLAN) and wireless wide area networks (WWAN) as shown in Figure 1. Current deployment of ad hoc networks is confined to wireless personal area networks and wireless local area networks. Of the shelf technologies for WPAN and WLAN are enablers of ad hoc networks. In future wide area ad hoc networks will be a reality.

Since there is no fixed infrastructure available for MANET and due to dynamic nature of the nodes, routing becomes an extremely important issue. Moreover, scarcity of resources like energy and limited bandwidth of the wireless links make the transmission problematic. In this chapter, we discuss the current state of the art of mobile ad hoc network and some important problems and challenges related to routing, power management, location management, security, and multimedia over ad hoc networks. In addition, we also explain the various emerging applications and future trends of MANET.

Figure 2 represents a MANET formed by various heterogeneous devices and heterogeneous networks. The Piconets are formed by Bluetooth enabled devices and the WLAN is formed by IEEE 802.11 enabled devices. All these devices form an ad hoc network when they are within proximity to each other, in other words, they are within their transmission radius.

Some Applications of MANET

An *ad hoc application* is a self-organizing application consisting of mobile devices forming a *peer-to-peer* network where communications are possible because of proximity of the

Figure 1. The entire wireless landscape

Table 1. Characteristics of MANETs

Mobile	The nodes may not be static in space and time resulting in a dynamic network topology. Nodes can move freely and independently. Also some new nodes can join the network and some nodes may leave the network.
Wireless	MANET uses wireless medium (radio, infrared, etc.) to transmit and receive data. Nodes share the same media.
Self-organizing, distributed and infrastructure-less	They are self-organizing in nature. There is no centralized control which implies that network management will have to be distributed across various nodes. This makes fault detection and management quite difficult.
Multi-hop	A message from source node to destination node goes through multiple nodes because of limited transmission radius. Every node acts as a router and forwards packets from other nodes to facilitate multi-hop routing.
Scarce resources	The wireless links have limited bandwidth and variable capacity. They are also error prone. In addition, the mobile nodes have limited battery power along with limited processing power. So energy is a scare resource.
Temporary and rapidly deployable	These networks are temporary in nature. There is no base station. Whenever the nodes are within their transmission radius, they form an ad hoc network. Hence they are rapidly deployable.
Neighborhood awareness	Host connections in MANET are based on geographical distance.

Figure 2. An ad hoc network

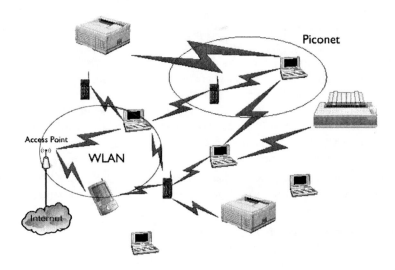

devices within a physical distance. MANET can be used to form the basic infrastructure for ad hoc applications.

Some typical applications are as follows.

a. **Mobile conferencing:** Ad hoc networks enable mobile conferencing for business users who need to collaborate outside their office where no network infrastructure is available. There is a growing need for mobile computing environment where different members of a project need to collaborate on design and development. The users need to share documents, upload and download files and exchange ideas.

b. **Personal area and home networking:** Ad hoc networks are quite suitable for home as well as personal area networking applications. Mobile devices with Bluetooth or WLAN cards can be easily configured to form an ad hoc network. With the Internet connectivity at home, these devices can easily be connected to Internet. Hence, the use of these kinds of ad hoc networks has practical applications and usability.

c. **Emergency services:** When the existing network infrastructure ceased to operate or damaged due to some kind of disaster like earthquakes, hurricanes, fire, and so on, ad hoc networks can be easily deployed to provide solutions to emergency services. These networks can also be used for search and rescue operations, retrieval of patient data remotely from hospital and many other useful services.

d. **Public hotspots:** In places like airports, train stations, coffee shops, and pubs, football ground, malls, ad hoc networks provide users to create their own network and communicate with each other instantly. Ad hoc networks can also be used for entertainment purposes like providing instant connectivity for multi-user games. In addition, household Internet connectivity can be provided by a community hotspot.

e. **Military applications:** In battlefield, MANET can be deployed for communications among the soldiers in the field. Different military units are expected to communicate, cooperate with each other and within a specified area. In these kinds of low mobility environments, MANET is used for communications where virtually no network infrastructure is available. For example, *mesh network* is an ad hoc peer-to-peer multi-hop network with no infrastructure. The important features are it is low in cost, with nodes being mobile, self-organized, self-balancing and self-healing. It is easy to scale. A good example is *SLICE* (soldier level integrated communications environment); a research project sponsored by DARPA in this area for this need. The idea is that every soldier is equipped with a mobile PC with headset and a microphone. SLICE is supposed to create mesh networks that handle voice communications while mapping whereabouts of soldiers and their companions.

f. **Mobile commerce:** Ad hoc networks can be used to make electronic payments anytime, anywhere. Business users can retrieve customer/sales related information dynamically and can build reports on the fly.

g. **Ubiquitous and embedded computing applications:** With the emergence of new generations of intelligent portable mobile devices, ubiquitous computing is becoming a reality. As predicted by some researchers (Weiser, 1993), ubiquitous computers will be around us, always doing some tasks for us without our conscious effort. These machines will also react to changing environment and work accordingly. These mobile devices will form an ad hoc network and, gather various localized information and sometimes inform the users automatically.

h. **Location-based services:** MANET when integrated with location-based information provides useful services. GPS (global positioning system), a satellite-based radio navigation system, is a very effective tool to determine the physical location of a device. A mobile host in a MANET when connected to a GPS receiver will be able to determine its current physical location. Another good example will be a group of tourists using PDAs with wireless LAN cards installed in them along with GPS connectivity. These mobile devices can be configured to form a MANET. These tourists can then exchange messages and locate each other using this MANET. Again consider the following scenario. Vehicles on highway can form an ad hoc network to exchange traffic information. In addition, location-based information services can be delivered by MANETs. For example, one can advertise location specific information like restaurants, shopping mall (*push*) and retrieve location-dependant information like travel guide, movie theatre, drug store, and so forth (*pull*).

MAC-Layer Protocols for MANET

An ad hoc network can be implemented very easily using the IEEE 802.11 standard for WLAN. Since the mobile nodes in WLAN use a common transmission medium, the transmissions of the nodes have to be coordinated by the MAC protocol. So we summarize the MAC layer protocols. The most important issues in the MAC layer are the hidden-terminal and the exposed terminal problems. The hidden-terminal problem arises when two or more terminals cannot detect each other's transmissions (because of the fact that they are outside each other's transmission radius) and their transmission radius are not disjoint. In this case, there may be a collision, which may be undetected. The exposed-terminal problem occurs when the transmission from a sender to another node has to be delayed due to another transmission between two other nodes within the sender's transmission radius.

- **Carrier sense multiple access (CSMA):** Carrier sense multiple access (CSMA) protocols were proposed in 1970's and have been used in a number of packet-radio networks in the past. These protocols attempt to prevent a station from transmitting simultaneously with other stations within its transmitting range by requiring each station to listen to the channel before transmitting. Because of radio hardware characteristics, a station cannot transmit and listen to the channel simultaneously. This is why more improved protocols such as CSMA/CD cannot be used in single channel radio networks. However, CSMA performs reasonably well except for some circumstances where multiple stations that are within range of the same receivers cannot detect one another's transmissions. This problem is generally called a "hidden terminal problem" which degrade the performance of CSMA significantly, as collision cannot be avoided in this case making the protocol behave like the pure ALOHA protocol (Fullmer & Garcia-Luna-Aceves, 1995).

- **Multiple access with collision avoidance (MACA):** Phil Karn proposed MACA to address the hidden terminal problem (Karn, 1992). This protocol was based on the protocol used in Apple Localtalk networks and request to send (RTS) and clear to send (CTS) control signals are used to explicitly indicate the intention of transmitting data onto the channel before actually transmitting the data. This ensures whoever that can hear these control signals postpone their transmission for the duration of current transmission, which is indicated in RTS or CTS packets. Most hidden node problems are solved by this approach and collisions are avoided.

- **Multiple access with collision avoidance for wireless LANs (MACAW):** Since not every hidden terminal problem is solved by MACA protocol, collisions do happen from time to time, especially when control messages collide with each other. MACA leaves the retransmission to the higher layer protocols such as transport protocols, which is not very efficient. A group of researchers, in 1994, proposed MACAW to improve the efficiency of MACA by adding retransmission mechanism to the MAC layer (Bharghavan, Demers, Shenker, & Zhang, 1994). In this improved version, an RTS-CTS handshake and subsequent data transmission is followed by an explicit acknowledgement from the receiver. When the sender does not receive the acknowledgement within some timeout period, it considers the data transmission to have failed and attempts to retransmit.

- **Floor acquisition multiple access (FAMA):** A general problem of MACA-based protocols was the collision of control packets at the beginning of each transmission as all terminals intending to transmit sends out RTS signals. In 1995, another protocol called FAMA was proposed which combined CSMA and MACA into one protocol where each terminal senses the channel for given waiting period before transmitting control signals (Fullmer et al., 1995). The objective of FAMA is for a station that has data to send to acquire control of the channel (which the authors of the protocol called the "floor") before sending any packet. Also, a waiting period after a transmission is enforced to all the neighbors of the transmitter-receiver pair so as to ensure collision-free delivery of the acknowledgement packet. FAMA is later incorporated into IEEE 802.11 MAC specification, which was finalized in 1997.

- **Multiple access with collision avoidance by invitation (MACA-BI):** This protocol was proposed in 1997, to reduce the turn around time, time taken to switch modes from TX to RX or RX to TX, which is up to 25 μs (Talucci & Gerla, 1997). A node that is ready to transmit, instead of "acquiring" the floor, waits for a "prepared" floor. That is, it waits for an "invitation" by the intended receiver in the form of a Ready To Receive (RTR) control packet. For example, when node A wants to send data to node B, node A asks for the floor by sending RTS and node B replies with CTS notifying that node A has acquired the floor in MACA. This is "driven by the transmitter," that is, node A decides when to start. However, in MACA-BI, the same effect is achieved with "receiver driven" schedule. Instead of node A sending RTS first, node B issues CTS packets, which were later renamed to RTR packets, at a rate matching the incoming traffic rate, inviting node A to transmit. In this case, RTS packets are omitted. As a result, RTS-CTS-Data-ACK sequence with three TX-RX turn-arounds becomes RTR-Data-ACK sequence that has only two TX-RX turn-arounds.

- **Dual busy tone multiple access (DBTMA):** Another significant cause of collision in MACA-based protocols is collision between control packets and data transmission. This problem can be solved by introducing separate channel for control messages, which was proposed in DBTMA protocol published in 1998 (Haas & Deng, 1998). Hidden node problems are solved by RTS-CTS handshake, and his protocol also introduces dual busy tones to eliminate exposed terminal problems as well. Exposed terminal problems occur when a node (node A) is not able to transmit while one of its neighbors (node B) is transmitting data to a node (node C) that is outside the range of node A (see Figure 3). If node A wants to transmit to a node (node D) that is outside the range of node B, the transmission between node A and node D does not affect the transmission between node B and node C. Exposed node problem in MACA such as this reduces the capacity of the network by suppressing harmless parallel transmissions.

In DBTMA, data transmission from node B to node C is protected by receiving busy tone (BTr) that is generated by the receiver, node C. All neighbors of node C, when they want to transmit data, sense the BTr and wait until the end of transmission. However, if there are no other nodes transmitting, node A will not hear BTr and thus it can transmit. Now node B generates transmit-busy tone (BTt) to warn its neighbors about its transmission. So if node A wants to *receive* data, it needs to check whether there is BTt in the control channel before it can send CTS. In this example, node A can transmit (absence of BTr) but cannot receive (presence of BTt). Likewise node D does not hear the BTt generated by node B so it can receive data. Therefore, transmission between node A to node D, in parallel with that between node B and node C, is possible. If only one busy tone was used, node A hears that busy tone but cannot distinguish whether node B is transmitting or receiving. So node A needs to sense the data channel as well to figure out that node A is transmitting and not receiving. Having to listen to both control channel and data channel is not desirable since it requires two independent receivers in the hardware. This is why two busy tones are used in this protocol so that having one receiver circuitry is enough to carry out this protocol.

Routing in MANET

A Classification of Routing Protocols

Routing issues for ad hoc networks with different devices having variable parameters leads to many interesting problems, as evidenced in the research literature (Rieck, Pai, & Dhar, 2005; Toh, 2002; Iwata, Chiang, Pei, Gerla, & Chen, 1999; Perkins & Royer, 1999; Ramanathan & Streenstrup, 1998). This is also validated by industry as well as government efforts such as DoD-sponsored MANET work (Freebersyser & Leiner, 2001). A good network routing protocol may be one that yields the best throughput and response time. Accordingly, an efficient ad hoc routing protocol should also be scalable and reliable. Various routing algorithms and protocols have been introduced in the recent years.

Routing protocols can broadly be classified into several major categories: *proactive routing, reactive routing, hierarchical cluster-based routing* (Belding-Royer, 2004, McDonald & Znati, 1999), *hybrid routing* (Haas & Pearlman, 2000; Basagni, Chlamtac, Syrotiuk, & Woodword, 1998). Proactive routing protocols propagate routing information throughout the network at regular time intervals. This routing information is used to determine paths to all possible destinations. This approach generally demands considerable overhead-message traffic as well as routing information maintenance. *Reactive routing* maintains path information on a demand-basis by utilizing a query-response technique. In this case, the total number of destinations to be maintained for routing information is considerably less than flooding and hence the network traffic is also reduced. In *hierarchical cluster-based routing*, the network is partitioned into several clusters and from each cluster; certain nodes are elected to be clusterheads. These clusterheads are responsible for maintaining the knowledge of the topology of the network. As it has already been said, clustering may be invoked in a

Figure 3. Exposed terminal problem

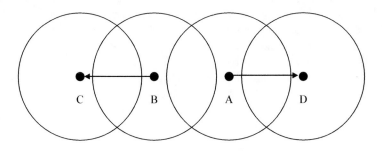

hierarchical fashion. In *hybrid routing*, both the features of reactive and proactive routing are integrated in a single protocol. In addition to these approaches, there are some protocols that utilizes geographical location information and some protocols that are based on intrusion detection and authentication techniques to make the routing secure.

Some of the specific approaches that have gained prominence in recent years are as follows: dynamic destination-sequenced distance-vector (DSDV) routing protocol (Johnson & Maltz, 1999), wireless routing protocol (WRP) (Murthy & Garcia-Luna-Aceves, 1996), cluster switch gateway routing (CSGR) (Chiang, Wu, & Gerla, 1997), source tree adaptive routing (STAR) (Garcia-Luna-Aceves & Spohn, 1999), fisheye state routing (FSR) (Pei, Gerla, & Chen, 2000), optimized link state routing (OLSR) (Jacquet et al., 2000), topology broadcast based on reverse path forwarding (TBRPF) (Ogier, Templin, Bellur, & Lewis, 2002) are all examples of proactive routing while ad hoc on-demand distance vector routing (AODV) (Perkins & Royer, 1999), dynamic source routing (DSR) (Broch, Johnson, & Maltz, 1999), temporally ordered routing algorithm (TORA) (Park & Corson, 1997), relative distance microdiversity routing (RDMAR) (Aggelou & Tafazolli, 1999), signal stability routing (SSR) (Ramanathan & Streenstrup, 1998) are examples of reactive routing. Zone routing protocol (ZRP) (Haas & Pearlman, 2000) is a hybrid protocol, which has the features of reactive and proactive protocols. Hierarchical state routing (Pei, Gerla, & Hong, 1999) and landmark ad hoc routing protocol (LANMAR) (Pei, Gerla, & Hong, 2000) are examples of dynamic hierarchical cluster-based routing. In Table 2, we summarize the main categories of the routing protocols and list examples from each category.

In the recent years, dominating set-based routing has gained popularity and a few papers have been written in this area. So we discuss them separately in the next section. Energy efficient routing protocols are also an active area of research and will be discussed in a later section. Location based routing protocols are discussed in the section following.

Dominating Set-Based Routing

Hierarchical routing schemes can be divided into two groups; one that is based on clustering and the other based on *virtual backbone* construction. Both the set of clusters and the set of backbone nodes form a second-level subnetwork. However, in the clustering schemes, the second-level nodes, i.e., the cluster heads) do not have to be connected—in fact, it is more desirable to have the cluster heads spread out—whereas in the backbone-based routing schemes the second-level nodes need to be connected to form the backbone.

Ad hoc wireless networks are typically represented by a connected graph where all the links are bi-directional. Several researchers have used minimum connected dominating sets to induce a virtual backbone in ad hoc wireless networks (Amis, Prakash, Vuong, & Huynh, 2000; Das & Bharghavan, 1997; Wu & Li, 2001). A subset D of nodes of a graph G is a dominating set if every node not in D is adjacent to at least one node in G. Minimum connected dominating set (*CDS*) problem is described as follows. Find a smallest subset D of nodes, such that them subgraph induced by D is connected and D forms a dominating set. Since *CDS* is an NP complete problem, several approximation algorithms have been proposed in this regard (Guha & Khuller, 1998).

CEDAR (Sivakumar, Sinha, & Bharghavan, 1999) is another distributed routing algorithm for ad hoc networks, which dynamically establishes a core network. This core network is a dominating set and this set is constructed by a core computation algorithm that approximates the minimum dominating set for the nodes. Hence the size of the core network is minimal.

Wu and Li (2001) proposed a heuristic for selecting dominating set-based on local neighborhood information and two rules that eliminate redundant nodes in the dominating set that result in a very small dominating set. It is worth mentioning that applying rules 1 and 2 reduces the size of the dominating set at the cost of incurring more communication.

In another paper, Wu and Li (2001) extended their dominating set-based protocol so that its routing maximizes the lifetime of the network by periodically re-elect dominating nodes, based on the residual energy level. This can be achieved by replacing the ID's (used in rule 1 and 2) by the residual energy. ID's are only used as a tiebreaker.

One advantage of clustering-based hierarchy over backbone-based hierarchy is that clustering usually results in a smaller set of second-level nodes and communication path between second-level nodes are not fixed, otherwise known as can take any route, which gives it more flexibility. In recent studies, it has been shown that *CDS* problem can be also used to find cluster-like hierarchical structure by extending the problem to finding minimum k-hop connected, k-dominating set (k-CDS) problem. In this structure (for $k>1$), the dominating nodes, together with their k-hop neighbors, form *virtual clusters* instead of a virtual backbone, as the dominating nodes are no longer directly connected (k-hop connected).

In an attempt to find structure using a simple localized algorithm, Rieck and a group of researchers have extended Wu and Li's algorithm to solve the k-CDS problem (Dhar, Rieck, & Pai, 2003; Rieck et al., 2005). However, the route through the dominating nodes does not always provide the shortest path and several algorithms have been proposed (called k-SPR-I and k-SPR-C algorithms) that produce a clustering-like structure based on k-CDS, which also guarantees that the route through the dominating nodes does always provide the shortest path (k-SPR property) (Dhar, Rieck, Pai, & Kim, 2004).

Energy-Efficiency in MANET

Wireless devices are often powered by batteries that have a finite amount of energy. In some ad hoc networks, it may not be always possible to change a battery once it runs out of energy. As a consequence, the conservation of energy is of foremost concern for those networks. A good ad hoc routing protocol should therefore be *energy-efficient*.

Lack of infrastructure, cost of using shared, wireless medium and the dynamic nature of ad hoc networks also entail significant amount of overhead when routing data in ad hoc networks and maintaining the route information. A good ad hoc routing protocol should contain *minimal overhead*. For large networks, minimizing the overhead is closely related to the scalability requirement, as the communication overhead often grows significantly with increasing number of nodes in a network.

Table 2. Summary of routing protocols

Routing Category	Main Features	Example
Proactive Routing (Table Driven)	Propagate routing information throughout the network at regular time intervals. This routing information is used to determine paths to all possible destinations. This approach generally demands considerable overhead-message traffic as well as routing information maintenance.	*Topology Broadcast based on Reverse Path Forwarding (TBRPF) (Ogier et al., 2002)*, Fisheye State Routing *(FSR) (Pei, Gerla, & Chen, 2000)*, Optimized Link State Routing *(OLSR) (Jacquet et al., 2000)*, Dynamic Destination-Sequenced Distance-Vector Protocol *(DSDV)* (Johnson & Maltz, 1999), *Source Tree Adaptive Routing (STAR)* (Garcia-Luna-Aceves & Spohn, 1999), Cluster Switch Gateway Routing *(CSGR)* (Chiang et al., 1997), Wireless Routing Protocol *(WRP)* (Murthy & Garcia-Luna-Aceves, 1996)
Reactive Routing (On-Demand)	Maintains path information on a demand-basis by utilizing a query-response technique. In this case, the total number of destinations to be maintained for routing information is considerably less than flooding and hence the network traffic is also reduced.	*Ad Hoc On-Demand Distance Vector Routing (AODV)* (Perkins & Royer, 1999), *Dynamic Source Routing (DSR)* (Broch, Johnson, & Maltz, 1999), *Relative Distance Microdiversity Routing (RDMAR)* (Aggelou & Tafazolli, 1999), *Signal Stability Routing (SSR)* (Ramanathan & Streenstrup, 1998), *Temporally Ordered Routing Algorithm (TORA)* (Park and Corson, 1997)
Hierarchical Routing	Hierarchical cluster-based structures provide efficient routing of messages in large dynamic networks. With this approach, the network is divided into several interconnected clusters of nodes, which might or might not overlap. This approach is good for scalability.	*Landmark Ad Hoc Routing Protocol (LANMAR) (Pei, Gerla, & Hong, 2000), Hierarchical State Routing (HSR) (Pei et al., 1999)*
Hybrid Routing	Integrate both proactive and reactive routing into a single protocol. Exhibits proactive behavior under a given set of circumstances and reactive behavior under a different set of circumstances.	*Zone Routing Protocol (ZRP)* (Haas & Pearlman, 2000), *Distance Effect Algorithm for Mobility (DREAM)* (Basagni et al., 1998)
Secure Routing	Secure routing using intrusion detection and authentication techniques.	*Authenticated Routing for Ad Hoc Networks (ARAN) (Sanzgiri et al., 2002), Secure Aware Routing (SAR) (Yi et al., 2002), Secure Routing Protocol (SRP) (Papadimitratos & Haas, 2000)*

Attempting to meet some of the requirements, copious volumes of papers have been published for mobile ad hoc networks in the last decade and researches in this area have gone through a number of phases over the years.

The first generation protocols developed for mobile ad hoc networks were table-driven routing protocols such as DSDV, which attempt to maintain up-to-date routing information stored in one or more tables. Paths towards all destinations are periodically refreshed even if not used. Normally, these protocols require nodes to broadcast information about their neighbors, and, based on this information, each node in the network computes the minimum path to every possible destination. The main objective of these protocols is to maximize the *throughput* and minimize the *response time*.

It was soon apparent to some researchers that it is not always necessary for *every node* to maintain routing information for all destinations. Especially for a large ad hoc network consisting of hundreds or thousands of nodes, the amount of routing information stored in each node grows proportionally. Periodical update messages will eventually consume all the resources leaving the network unusable. To improve the *scalability* of ad hoc routing protocols, hierarchical routing protocols have been proposed. A flat routing protocol is one that distributes information as needed to any router that can be reached or receive information. No effort is made to organize the network, only to discover the best route to a destination. On the contrary, a hierarchical protocol consists of clusters and network of cluster heads. The main advantage of hierarchical schemes is that only a small number of nodes have *complete (or global) view* of the network while the other nodes only need to maintain their *local view*.

A different solution to the scalability problem of table-driven protocols appeared soon after, as they noticed that it is not always necessary to maintain routing information for *all destinations*. Thus the second generation of ad hoc routing protocols was born, namely, the source-initiated on-demand protocols. In these reactive routing protocols such as DSR or AODV, the path to reach a destination is discovered only when needed by means of a procedure called route discovery. With this procedure, the source finds more than one path and selects the shortest (usually in terms of number of hops). Note that routing algorithms need to know the network topology, so a given amount of control traffic overhead is always present and should be minimized in order to increase the useful data throughput and to decrease the packet delivery time and the energy consumption.

Both table-driven and source-initiated protocols attempt to improve the throughput and latency; thus, most of these proposals are based on the intuitive goal of choosing the shortest paths, in other words, minimizing the number of hops. Third generation of ad hoc routing protocols have recently appeared, in which various routing strategies are compared in terms of energy consumption, such as based on the amount of energy that is spent in correctly delivering a packet to its final destination. The authors of PAMAS, Singh and Raghavendra proposed new metrics to evaluate the performance of routing algorithms (Singh & Ragavendra, 1998). Those metrics are power-aware, that is their target is to maximize energy efficiency (e.g., by finding the lowest energy routing path) and/or the lifetime of the whole network (e.g., by balancing traffic). New path cost for a static network is proposed by several authors, which can be used with any existing algorithm. The objective is to find the link cost function that will lead to the maximization of the system lifetime.

Many issues need to be addressed in ad hoc networking, one of the most relevant being the packet route selection. In proactive routing protocols such as OLSR or DSDV, paths towards all destinations are periodically refreshed even if not used. Normally, these protocols require nodes to broadcast information about their neighbors, and, based on this information, each node in the network computes the minimum path to every possible destination. In reactive routing protocols such as DSR or AODV, the path to reach a destination is discovered only when needed by means of a procedure called route discovery. With this procedure, the source finds more than one path and selects the "shortest" (usually in terms of number of hops). Note that routing algorithms need to know the network topology, so a given amount of control

Table 3. Taxonomy of energy efficient routing protocols

Protocol	Approach	Goal
Flow Argumentation Routing (FAR) (Chang and Tassiulas, 2000) Online Max-Min (OMM) (Li et al., 2001) Power Aware Localized Routing (PLR) (Stojmenovic and Lin, 2001) Minimum Energy Routing (MER) (Doshi et al., 2002)	Minimize active communication energy	Minimize the total transmission energy but avoid low energy nodes
Retransmission-energy Aware Routing (RAR) (Banerjee and Misra, 2002) Smallest Common Power (COMPOW) (Narayanaswamy et al., 2002)	Minimize active communication energy	Minimize the total transmission energy while considering retransmission overhead or bi-directional requirement
Localized Energy-aware Routing (LEAR) (Woo et al., 2001) Conditional Max-Min Battery Power Routing (CMMBCR) (Toh, 2001)	Minimize active communication energy	Distribute load to energy rich energy nodes
SPAN (Chen et al., 2001) Geographic Adaptive Fidelity (GAF) (Xu et al., 2001) PAMAS (Singh and Raghavendra, 1998), Prototype Embedded Network (PEN) (Girling et al., 1997)	Minimize inactive energy	Minimize energy consumption during inactivity using sleep/power down mode

traffic overhead is always present and should be minimized in order to increase the useful data throughput and to decrease the packet delivery time and the energy consumption.

In Table 3, we present the taxonomy of various energy-efficient routing protocols that have gained popularity in the recent years.

There are several challenges that arise in designing energy-efficient systems for ad hoc networks which we summarize in the following section.

Challenges of Designing Energy-Efficient Protocols

a. **End-to-end delay:** Shortest path routing reduces delay, but may increase power consumption due to increased distance between two adjacent nodes in the path, since transmit power is proportional to some power of distance as mentioned in the previous section. Increased delay also means increased number of packets in the system and this could become a problem in terms of network capacity.

b. **Packet loss rate:** Low transmit power reduces power consumption, but may increase the packet loss rate due to weaker signal strength. When packet loss rate increases, it results in retransmissions of the packets, again increasing total number of packets in the system.

c. **Network capacity:** Low transmit power also decreases the range of the transmitting node, which may result in less number of connections to neighboring nodes. Reduced number of links per node could also reduce the traffic carrying capacity of the network;

worse, it can even break the network connectivity and leave the network into disjoint sub-networks.

d.   **Relaying overhead:** Routing in MANET results in multi-hop transmissions because of low transmits power of the nodes require having more intermediate nodes from source to destination. Multi-hop routing adds relaying overhead to each node in the routing path, as each node in the path needs to receive the packet from physical layer, figure out the next hop and retransmit through the network stack. But multi-hop routing in some cases consumes less power than single-hop routing.

e.   **Interference:** High power transmission also induces greater interference to neighboring nodes. Interference also results in unnecessary power consumption in the neighboring nodes, as they have to receive the signal even when the signal is not destined for them. Stronger interferences could cause increased number of collisions, thus increasing the power consumption even more.

f.   **Battery life:** In minimum transmitted power routing, several other nodes for routing packets can use the same route. When this keeps happening over a period of time, the battery power on those nodes that are on the routing path will run out, thus reducing the network lifetime.

g.   **Connectivity:** Sleep mode reduces power consumption by an order of magnitude. But when a number of nodes go into the sleep mode to save power, without coordination, it may disrupt network connectivity.

A Classification of Energy-Efficient Protocols

The energy-efficient protocols for ad hoc networks can be classified into the following four major categories: *minimum transmits power protocols*; *transmit power control protocols*, *maximum lifetime protocols*, and *power save protocols*. This classification roughly follows the chronological order of energy-aware protocol development.

- **Minimum transmit power protocols:** Some of the earliest power-aware routing protocols are *minimum transmit power protocols*, which incorporate power consumption in link cost calculation and thus finding a path that consumes the least power for the end-to-end transmission of a packet. These protocols inherently presume the use of a *variable transmit power system* which is discussed next in more detail; if a common transmit power level is used for every transmission regardless of the distance to the receiver, the energy cost for a route will be proportional to the number of links in the route, in which case the minimum transmit power protocols will degenerate into shortest path routing. One problem often associated with the minimum transmit power protocols is that they tends to use the same route over and over, eventually draining the battery power of those nodes prematurely, which was later addressed by *maximum lifetime protocols*.

- **Transmit power control protocols:** Another approach is to use a power control scheme which suitably varies transmit power to reduce energy consumption, depending on the distance to the receiver. To do this, a node needs to know (or estimate) the distance to each neighbor and calculate the minimum transmit power level required to ensure good reception by the receiver, both of which are not so easy to achieve. Varying transmit power level has other consequences too. For example, virtual collision avoidance using RTS-CTS exchange may not work correctly under variable transmit power scheme. Low power transmissions cannot be sensed by distant nodes, which may then initiate transmissions using sufficient power to disrupt ongoing transmissions (Feeney, 2002). Two papers by Jung and Vaidya (2002) are proposed to solve this problem. Also several researchers (Narayansawamy, Kawadia, Sreenivas, & Kumar, 2002) try to combine power control scheme with clustering where clusters are determined whether they are reachable at a given power level. In addition to providing energy saving, power control can potentially be used to improve spatial reuse of the wireless channel.

- **Maximum lifetime protocols:** As pointed out before, the main disadvantage of the *minimum transmit power protocol* is that it always selects the least-energy cost routes and as a result, nodes along these routes tend to die soon because of the battery energy exhaustion. This is doubly harmful since the nodes that die early are precisely the ones that are needed most to maintain the network connectivity (and hence useful service life). Therefore, it is better to use a higher energy cost route (e.g., a multi-hop route) if it avoids using nodes that have a small amount of remaining battery energy (also called the *residual energy*). This gave rise to another family of power-aware routing protocols, which try to maximize network lifetime.

- **Power save protocols:** More recently, a number of papers found that the energy savings achieved by reducing the energy used in transmitting or receiving packets are significantly smaller than those achieved by taking advantage of low power mode (or *sleep* mode) of the physical interface. Power-saving mechanisms allow a node to enter a doze state or sleep state by powering off its wireless network interface when deemed reasonable. Singh and Raghavendra produced some pioneering works on power-saving mechanism in their power-aware multi-access protocol with signaling (PAMAS) (Singh & Raghavendra, 1998). The main challenge of utilizing the power save mode is that if nodes go in and out of the sleep mode without coordination, the throughput of the network drops significantly as each transmitter has to wait until the receiver is awake to receive the data. This is done in the MAC layer as opposed to the network layer.

IEEE 802.11 Power Save Mode

As pointed out by a number of authors (Chen, Jamieson, Balakrishnan, & Morris, 2001), (Sheu, Liu, Wu, & Tseng, 2004), IEEE 802.11 distributed coordination function (DCF) in power save mode (PSM) only works for fully connected network. Before going on to more detailed description of current proposals in the area of energy-efficient ad hoc networks, we introduce power saving mechanisms in the IEEE 802.11 standard. Due to the widespread availability of inexpensive hardware and its relatively stable and complete protocol definition, the IEEE 802.11 standard is a common choice for use in ad hoc networking research. The standard includes power save mechanisms for use in both infrastructure (BSS) and infrastructure-less (IBSS) operating modes. Obviously IBSS power save is the only alternative for ad hoc networking, although there are differences between a multi-hop wireless network and an IBSS, where each station explicitly discovers and synchronizes itself to a *single, connected* IBSS.

A synchronized beacon interval is established by the station that initiates the IBSS and is maintained in a distributed fashion. In addition to the beacon interval, the IBSS also defines a fixed length ATIM window, which occurs at the beginning of each beacon interval. All stations in the IBSS wake up at the beginning of the beacon interval and remain awake until the end of the ATIM window. At the beginning of the beacon interval, stations contend, using random backoff, to transmit the synchronization beacon. Once the synchronization beacon has been transmitted, each station sends an ATIM message to every other station for which it has pending unicast traffic. Each station that receives such an ATIM responds with an acknowledgment. Announcements of broadcast and multicast traffic indication messages (DTIM) are sent to the appropriate broadcast or multicast address, but are not acknowledged. Only beacons, ATIM's/DTIM's and ATIM acknowledgments are sent during the ATIM window. At the end of the ATIM window, stations that have not sent or received ATIM announcements go back to sleep. All other stations remain awake throughout the remainder of the beacon interval. Traffic which is not transmitted (e.g. due to lack of time in the ATIM window or beacon interval) is announced in successive beacon intervals until it is eventually discarded (Feeney, 2002).

Problems in Designing Power-Saving Protocols for IEEE 802.11-Based MANET

Major Challenges

Two major challenges that one would encounter when designing power-saving protocols are: clock synchronization and the neighbor discovery. Clock synchronization in a multi-hop MANET is difficult since there is no central control and packet delays may vary due to unpredictable mobility and radio interference. Without precise clocks, a host may not be able to know when other PS hosts will wake up to receive packets.

In ad hoc network, hosts wake up periodically by a short interval called the ad hoc traffic identification map (ATIM) window, which connects and synchronizes all hosts. Mobile host contends to send a beacon frame that serves the purpose of synchronizing mobile hosts' clocks, also inhibits other hosts from sending their beacons to avoid collisions.

Three important problems related to power save mode:

Tseng et al. (2002) pointed out problems of IEEE 802.11 power save mode when applied to ad hoc networks. The PS mode of IEEE 802.11 is designed for a single-hop (or fully connected) ad hoc network. When applied to a multi-hop ad hoc network, three problems may arise. All these will pose a demand of redesigning the PS mode for multi-hop MANET.

a. **Clock synchronization:** In a multi-hop MANET clock synchronization is difficult since there is no central control, packet delays and radio interference and mobility are all unpredictable, especially when the network scale is large. Also with synchronization two sub-networks may independently enter PS mode and thus have different ATIM timing. With the clock-drifting problem, the ATIM windows of Different hosts are not guaranteed to be synchronous. Thus, the ATIM window has to be re-designed.

b. **Neighbor discovery:** A host can only be aware by other hosts if it transmits a signal that is heard by the others, so a host must compete with other hosts to transmit its beacon. A host will cancel its beacon frame once it hears other's beacon frame. This may run into a dilemma that hosts are likely to have inaccurate neighborhood information when there are PS hosts.

c. **Network partitioning:** Inaccurate neighbor information creates packet delays or even network partitioning problem. PS hosts with unsynchronized ATIM windows may wake up at different times and may be partitioned into several groups. Thus, many existing routing protocols may fail to work in their route discovery process unless all hosts are wake up at the time of the searching process.

Span: An Energy-Efficient Coordination Protocol

Introduction

Span (Chen et al., 2001) is one of several ad hoc networking protocols based on the notion of a dominating set. In Span, "coordinators"—a group of nodes that form a connected dominating set over the network—do not sleep. Non-coordinator nodes follow a synchronized sleep/wake cycle, exchanging traffic using an algorithm based on the beaconing and traffic announcement methods of IEEE 802.11 IBSS power save. The routing protocol is integrated with the coordinator mechanism so that only coordinators forward packets, acting as a low latency routing backbone for network. Span is intended to maximize the amount of time nodes spend in the sleep state, while minimizing the impact of energy management on latency and capacity.

Protocol

The set of coordinators is determined using a localized algorithm intended to approximate a minimal, capacity preserving set of coordinators. Nodes periodically wake up and exchange neighbor information, then schedule a coordinator announcement, using an adaptive backoff algorithm. Nodes with high connectivity and energy reserves announce themselves more quickly than less effective ones, which volunteer later and only if they are still needed to obtain the dominating set. Rotating the coordinator role in this way tends to balance nodes' energy reserves, even in the case of initially unequal reserves.

Results

Simulation using *ns-2* suggests that Span provides about 50% energy saving, with little impact on throughput, latency and packet loss. Rotation of the coordinator role equalizes energy consumption and the time to first node failure increases 50% and the network half-life doubles. The results also support the informal calculation in section II. Even when Span is used to limit idle energy consumption, sending and receiving traffic accounts for well under 10% of the total energy consumed.

Limitations

The synchronized nature of the Span protocol reveals a major limitation of this approach. Both the beaconing in the underlying 802.11 power save protocol and the coordinator election require synchronization. Coordinator election is based on knowledge of the local topology, based on periodic broadcast neighbor discovery. The coordinators cannot mediate this because nodes have to be awake simultaneously to determine their connectivity.

Span's global heartbeat requires two kinds of synchronization. The first ensures that the stations' oscillators tick at the same rate. (The IEEE 802.11 standard specifies hardware tolerance of 10^{-4}.) This is fairly straightforward. The second ensures that the stations are synchronized in phase. This is a challenge because the choice of phase is completely arbitrary.

The IEEE 802.11 IBSS solves this problem in a centralized way. The "first" station initializes the beacon interval for the IBSS and "subsequent" stations explicitly associate themselves with exactly one IBSS and synchronize themselves to it. This kind of approach can lead to the "parking lot problem"; problematic race conditions that occur among a group of devices are turned on (more or less) simultaneously. Nevertheless, this method works well for scenarios in which a master station for the network can be conveniently designated and all the other stations can be configured to recognize that master. In effect, it requires that all nodes must be initialized together within the same well-connected cloud or that there is some mechanism for identifying the "right" cloud for a node to associate with.

This limitation is especially unfortunate because the ad hoc networking model is specifically intended to support more flexible methods of creating a network. In particular, consider the case of two separate task groups, such as military units on patrol, each of which has formed an ad hoc network. When the two groups meet, their networks should merge seamlessly together. In order to merge two (or more) networks having different phases, some mechanism must be developed which allows the networks to discover and synchronize with each other. Though solvable, this kind of distributed consensus problem is nontrivial.

Location Management in MANET

Since there is no fixed infrastructure available for MANET with nodes being mobile in the three-dimensional space, location management becomes a very important issue. For example, *route discovery* and *route maintenance* are some of the challenges in designing routing protocols. In addition, finding the position of a node at a given time is an important problem. This led to the development of *location-aware* routing, which means that a node will be able to know its current position. A great deal of work has been done using GPS to determine the position of a node at particular instance of time.

A useful application of location based service for MANET will be in the area of navigation. When devices are equipped with wireless connectivity along with location based information integrated with navigation systems, users can communicate with each other forming an ad hoc network. Location-based emergency services are also potential applications of these systems. Another important application area is geocast, which means sending messages to all the hosts in a particular geographic region. Geocasting will be a very useful application when someone wants to send some messages to people in a particular region. This is particularly important in situations when there is a disaster or emergency.

There are quite a few protocols that have been proposed in the recent years specifically for location management. They can be classified into two major categories, *location-assisted* and *zone-based* protocols. Location-assisted protocols take advantage of local information of hosts. In zone-based routing, the network is divided into several non-overlapping regions (zones) and each node belongs to a certain zone based on its physicals location. *Location-aided routing (LAR)* (Ko & Vaidya, 1998), *greedy perimeter stateless routing (GPSR)* (Karp and Kung, 2000), *geographical routing algorithm (GRA)* (Jain et al., 2001), *geographic distance routing (GEDIR)* (Lin & Stomenovic, 1999) are examples of location-assisted routing protocols. *Zone-based routing protocol* (Joa-Ng & Lu, 1999) and *GRID* (Liao et al., 2001) are examples of zone-based routing protocols.

Multimedia Over MANET

In the recent years, we have witnessed a tremendous growth in the multimedia applications and hence multimedia traffic over wired and wireless networks. With the growing demand for services that support multimedia traffic, it is expected that ad hoc networks will have the capability to deliver multimedia traffic with reasonable quality. However, due to the very nature of ad hoc networks and the constraints described earlier, this is going to be a difficult task.

Let us first summarize the problems for delivering real-time multimedia. The need for more bandwidth, less delay and minimum packet loss are some of the criteria for high quality transmission. However, the current best-effort network architecture does not offer any quality of service (QoS). It is well known that TCP is mainly designed for reliable data traffic. It is not suitable for real-time multimedia traffic as the delay and jitter caused by TCP retransmissions may be intolerable, the slow-start and congestion avoidance are not suitable for real-time multimedia transport. In addition, TCP does not support multicast. The UDP is typically used in almost all real-time multimedia applications. It extends the best-effort, host-to-host IP service to process-to-process level. When congestion occurs, an unlimited amount of UDP datagrams may be dropped since UDP is non adaptive. Hence real-time multimedia applications must implement additional rate control and error control techniques in order to cope with network congestion.

In ad hoc networks, wireless link have high transmission error rate because of fading, path loss and interference. An end-to-end path found in ad hoc networks has an even higher error rate since it is composed of multiple links. The frequent link failures (some nodes moves away out of the transmission range due to mobility) and route changes cause packet losses and reduce the received video quality. In order to maintain a good quality of video in ad hoc network, there should be effective error control to reduce packet losses to a certain level. Traditional error control techniques including forward error control (FEC) and automatic repeat request (ARQ) have been adapted to take link failures into consideration (REF).

Recent research efforts try to address the delivery of real-time multimedia over ad hoc networks. Y. Li and a group of researchers (Li, Mao, & Panwar, 2004) use mulitpath transport for real-time multimedia to reduce congestion and other problems in the network. Wei and Zakhor have proposed a robust multipath source routing protocol for both interactive and video-on-demand application for unicast transmissions (Wei & Zakhor, 2004). S. Mao and group of researchers have proposed a multiple description video multicast scheme for ad hoc networks, which is both error resilient and scalable (Mao, Cheng, Hou, & Sherali, 2004). Their simulation results show that the video quality has been enhanced by their approach. For the case of multicasting, they also propose a distributed multicast routing protocol called Serial MDTMR. These protocols enhance the quality of the video applications over wireless links in ad hoc networks. There has been some work to support multimedia traffic for asynchronous ad hoc networks by modifying the existing asynchronous MAC protocols like RTMAC (Reddy, Manoj, & Murthy, 2004). The proposed protocol by Reddy, Manoj, and Murthy efficiently utilize available bandwidth for carrying multimedia traffic and best effort traffic and improves packet delivery ratio and end-to-end delay.

Security in Mobile Ad Hoc Networks

In addition to the major security concerns about wireless networks, security for MANETs poses a great challenge as there is no central authority to manage the network. We first describe various potential attacks and then discuss various protocols developed for security.

Potential Attacks

The attacks can be classified into two types namely, external versus internal attacks. There are several external attacks that can happen to a MANET because the attacker is in the proximity of the network and is not a trusted node belonging to that network. In the case of internal attacks, the nodes belong to the network but act as malicious participant.

There are several types of attacks as noted in the literature (Papadimitratos & Haas, 2000; Hu, Johnson, & Perrig, 2002; Hu et al, 2003; Sanzgiri, Dahill, Levine, & Shields, 2002) which are summarized as follows:

- Pretend to be another node of the network to route message to a different destination for malicious purpose
- Broadcast a route metric in a deceptive manner so that other node misinterpret the network topology

- Flooding routers with packets creating denial of service

- Provide falsified information for route messages

- Creating bogus route error to break down a working route and suppress route error to mislead others

- Two malicious nodes collaborate together and create a tunnel (virtual link) between them to misrepresent hop-count metric. This is known as *wormhole attack*.

Protocols Based on Security

A considerable research effort has been made for prevention of attacks in MANETs. To prevent attacks, authentication, encryption, key management are among several techniques that have been deployed or proposed. However, key generation, distribution and management in MANET have become very challenging tasks because of a lack of central management authority.

In the recent years, several routing protocols have been proposed for MANETs to address security. Current secure routing protocols are mainly based on reactive on-demand strategy such as DSR and AODV. The SRP, (Secure Routing Protocol) proposed by Papadimitratos and Haas prevents attacks from the route discovery process; it also ensures that correct topological information is preserved (Papadimitratos & Haas, 2000). ARIADNE is another on-demand secure routing protocol (Hu, Perrig, & Johnson, 2003). It is based on DSR and uses symmetric key cryptography. The ARAN is another on-demand secure routing protocol which guard an ad hoc network against malicious attacks carried out by third parties and peers (Sanzgiri et al., 2002). The SAODV (Secure AODV) protocol has been proposed to have security features to AODV by using public key cryptography (Zapata & Asokan, 2002). SEAD (secure efficient ad hoc distance vector) is a proactive secure routing protocol based on DSDV (Hu, Johnson, & Perrig, 2002).

Issues, Challenges and Future Trends

Although a great deal of work has been done, there are still many important challenges and problems that need to be addressed. We summarize the important problems here.

The problems that arise in the network layer of an ad hoc network can be broadly classified into the following three categories: topology control, data communication and service access (Wu & Stojmenovic, 2004). Topology control problems are discovering neighbors, determining the transmission radius, location identification, link establishment to neighbors, scheduling the node-awake and sleep time, cluster formation and maintenance, and so on. Data communication problems are as follows.

a. **Routing:** Find the best strategy to send a packet from source to destination under certain constraints and parameters.

b. **Location updating:** How does a node in the network maintain accurate information about the location of the other nodes while the nodes are moving?

Table 4. Comparison of location-aware routing protocols (Adapted from Table 18.1, Tseng & Hsu, 2003)

Scheme	Routing Strategy	Required Information
LAR (Ko and Vaidya, 1998)	Discover route by flooding request packets in request zone	Destination's location and roaming speed
GPSR (Karp and Kung, 2000)	Greedy forwarding (distance-based) and perimeter forwarding	Destination's location and all neighbors' locations
GRA (Jain et al., 2001)	Greedy forwarding (distance-based) and flooding	Destination's location and some neighbors' locations
GEDIR (Lin and Stojmenovic, 1999)	Greedy forwarding (distance- or direction-based) and flooding	Destination's location and all neighbors' locations
Zone-Based (Joa-Ng and Lu, 1999)	Intra-zone: table-driven Inter-zone, zone by zone, table driven	Intra-zone, inter-zone routing tables
GRID (Liao et al., 2001)	Intra-grid: direct transmission Inter-grid: grid-by-grid, on-demand	Destination's grid ID

c. **Broadcasting:** How to send a message from a source node to all other nodes in the network?

d. **Multicasting:** How to send a message from a source node to a set of specific nodes in the network efficiently?

e. **Geocasting:** How to send a message from a source node to all the nodes inside a geographic region efficiently?

Service access problems typically deals with cellular network access, Internet access, IP addressing in merge or split network scenarios, data or service replication upon detection or expectation of network partition.

In order for large scale deployment of MANETs in the future, there are some major technical issues that the research community has to be resolved. Here we list them all.

a. **Security:** Ad hoc networks use wireless links to transmit data. This makes MANET very vulnerable to attack. Although there is some work done on the security issues of MANET, many important problems and challenges still need to be addressed. With the lack of any centralized architecture or authority, it is always a difficult to provide security because key management becomes a difficult problem (Perkins, 2001). A centralized security control is almost impossible to deploy. It is also not easy to detect a malicious node in a multi-hop ad hoc network and implement denial of service properly. In addition, in a multicasting scenario, traffic may pass through unprotected routers which can easily get unauthorized access to sensitive information (as in the case with military applications). So special efforts need to be done to provide secure as well as reliable communication. Some of the most important issues related to security are access control, data integrity, denial of service to malicious nodes and eavesdropping by unauthorized nodes.

b.   **Reliability:** Reliable data communications to a group of mobile nodes that continuously change their locations is extremely important particularly in emergency situations. The wireless links between nodes are very unreliable because of variable capacity, limited bandwidth and prone to error. In addition, most of the modes have limited battery power. So some nodes may run out of energy and hence some of the links may no longer work. So these nodes will not be able to transmit data. This makes communications very unreliable.

c.   **Scalability:** Most of the routing algorithms are designed for relative small wireless ad hoc networks. However, there are some ad hoc applications that may require thousands of nodes. For example, there are some applications of sensor networks and tactical networks (Freebersyser & Leiner, 2001), which require deployment of large number of nodes. Scalability becomes a difficult problem because of the random movement of the nodes along with limited transmission radius and energy constraints of each node.

d.   **Quality of service:** Certain applications require QoS without which communication will be meaningless. Incorporating QoS in MANET is a non trivial problem because of the limited bandwidth and energy constraints. Designing protocols that support multi-class traffic and allows preemption, mobile nodes position identification, packet prioritization are some of the open areas of research. In order to provide end-to-end QoS guarantee, a coordinated effort is required for multi-layer integration of QoS provisioning. The success and future application of MANET will depend on how QoS will be guaranteed in the future.

e.   **Power management:** Portable hand-held devices have limited battery power. These devices often participate as nodes in a MANET and deliver and route packets. Whenever the power of a node is depleted, the MANET may cease to operate or may not function efficiently. An important problem is to maximize the lifetime of the network and efficiently route packets.

f.   **Interoperability:** Integrating MANETs with heterogeneous networks (fixed wireless, wired networks, Internet, etc.) seamlessly is a very important issue. Hosts should be able to migrate from one network to other seamlessly and make pervasive computing a reality.

g.   **Group membership:** In a MANET, sometimes a new node can join the network and sometimes some existing nodes may leave the network. This poses a significant challenge in designing efficient routing protocols.

h.   **Mobility:** In MANETs, all the nodes are mobile. Multicasting becomes a difficult problem because mobility of nodes creates inefficient multicast trees and inaccurate configuration of network topology. In addition, modeling mobility patterns is also an interesting issue. Several researchers have been quite actively investigating this area and this is still a wide open area of research.

i.   **Support for multimedia:** With the growing number of various portable mobile devices with increase in computing power and multimedia capabilities, increase in bandwidth of wireless links, it is expected that multimedia service over ad hoc networks will be a reality. However, there are some challenges and problems that need to be solved before real-time multimedia can be delivered over wireless links in ad hoc networks. The need for more bandwidth, less delay and minimum packet loss are some of the criteria for high quality transmission. However, the current best-effort network architecture does not offer any quality of service (QoS). Hence, in order to support multimedia traffic, efforts must be made to improve QoS parameters like end-to-end delay, packet loss ratio, and jitter.

Conclusion

The growing importance of ad hoc wireless networks can hardly be exaggerated, as portable wireless devices are now ubiquitous and continue to grow in popularity and in capabilities. In such networks, all of the nodes are mobile and so the infrastructure for message routing must be *self-organizing* and *adaptive*. In these networks routing is an important issue because there is no base station that can be used for broadcasting. Although, a great deal of work has been done on routing protocols, current technologies still do not properly integrate physical and MAC layers with datalink and network layers of the TCP/IP hierarchy (Page 47, Perkins, 2001). Design and implementation techniques of ad hoc networks are still a wide-open area of research.

MANET will continue to grow in terms of capabilities and applications in consumer as well as commercial markets. Currently, it is not just an area of academic research, but also plays an important role in business applications for the future. As we have already seen that in military there are quite useful applications of MANET. This trend will continue in the future.

The usefulness of MANET also lies on how this technology will be integrated with Internet and other wireless technologies like Bluetooth, WLAN and cellular networks. MANET when integrated with GPS have lot of potential in future location based applications and services. So the future of MANET and its growth looks very promising along with its practical applications.

Current and future research will not only address the issues described earlier but will also try to find new applications of MANET. So far the research community has been unable to find the "killer app" using MANET other than military applications. Having said this, there are more and more new applications in the commercial sector that are using MANET recently. So the success of this technology will largely depend on how it will be integrated with Internet, personal area network (PAN) and wireless LAN. MANET will also play an important role in ubiquitous computing when it will be able to seamlessly integrate with heterogeneous networks and devices, provide various services on demand, and offer secure and reliable communications.

References

Aggelou, G., & Tafazolli, R. (1999). RDMAR: A bandwidth-efficient routing protocol for mobile ad hoc networks. In *Proceedings of the Second ACM International Workshop on Wireless Mobile Multimedia (WoWMoM)*, Seattle, WA.

Amis, A.D., Prakash, R., Vuong, T.H.P., & Huynh, D.T. (2000). Max-min D-cluster formation in wireless ad hoc networks. In *Proceedings of IEEE INFOCOM*, Tel Aviv.

Bannerjee, S., & Khuller, S. (2001). A clustering scheme for hierarchical control in multi-hop wireless networks. *IEEE Infocom*, Anchorage, AK.

Banerjee, S., & Misra, A. (2002). Minimum energy paths for reliable communication in multi-hop wireless networks. In *Proceedings of Annual Workshop on Mobile Ad Hoc Networking & Computing (MobiHOC 2002)* (pp. 146-156).

Basagni, S., Chlamtac, I., Syrotiuk, V., & Woodword, B. (1998). A distace routing effect algorithm for mobility (DREAM). In *Proceedings of the 4th Annual ACM/IEEE International Conference on Mobile Computing and Networking (MobiCom)*, Dallas, TX (pp. 76-84).

Belding-Royer, E.M. (2004). Routing approaches in mobile ad hoc networks. In S. Bagagni et al. (Eds.), *Mobile ad hoc networking* (pp. 275-300). IEEE Press.

Bharghavan, V., Demers, A., Shenker, S., & Zhang, L. (1994). MACAW: A medium access protocol for wireless LANs. In *Proceedings of the ACM SIGCOMM*.

Broch, J., Johnson, D., & Maltz, D. (1999). *The dynamic source routing protocol for mobile ad hoc networks* (Internet draft 03). IETF, MANET Working Group.

Carson, M.S., Macker, J.P., & Cirincione, G.H. (1999). Internet-based mobile ad hoc networking. *IEEE Internet Computing, 3*(4).

Chen, T-W., & Gerla, M. (1998). Global state routing: A new routing scheme for ad-hoc wireless networks. In *Proceedings IEEE ICC*.

Chang, J-H., & Tassiulas, L. (2000). Energy conserving routing in wireless ad hoc networks. In *Proceedings of IEEE Infocom*.

Chen, B., Jamieson, K., Balakrishnan, H., & Morris, R. (2001). Span: An energy-efficient coordination algorithm for topology maintenance in ad hoc wireless networks. In *Proceedings Mobicom* (pp. 85-96).

Chiang, C-C., & Gerla, M. (1997). Routing and multicast in multihop mobile wireless networks,. In *Proceedings of IEEE ICUPC'97*, San Diego, CA.

Chiang, C.C., Wu, H.K., & Gerla, M. (1997). Routing in clustered multihop mobile wireless networks with fading channel. In *Proceedings of IEEE Singapore International Conference on Networks*.

Chlamtac, I., Conti, M., & Liu, J. (2003). Mobile ad hoc networking: Imperatives and challenges. *Ad Hoc Networks Journal, 1*.

Das, B., & Bharghavan, V. (1997). Routing in ad-hoc networks using minimum connected dominating sets. In *Proceedings of the IEEE Int'l Conf. Communications* (pp. 376-380).

Dhar, S., Rieck, M.Q., & Pai, S. (2003). On shortest path routing schemes for wireless ad-hoc networks. In *Proceedings of the 10ᵗʰ Int'l Conf. High Performance Computing (HiPC'03) (LNCS 2918)* (pp. 130-141). Springer-Verlag.

Dhar, M., Rieck, Q., Pai, S., & Kim, E. J. (2004). Distributed routing schemes for ad hoc networks using d-SPR sets. *J. Microprocessors and Microsystems.*

Doshi, S., Bhandare, & Brown, T.X. (2002). An on-demand minimum energy routing protocol for a wireless ad hoc network. *Mobile Computing and Communications Review, 6*(2), 50-66.

Feeney, L.M. (2002). A QoS aware power save protocol for wireless ad hoc networks. *Med-Hoc-Net2002,* Sardegna, Italy.

Freebersyser, J., & Leiner, B. (2001). A DoD perspective on mobile ad hoc networks. In C. Perkins (Ed.), *Ad hoc networking.* Addison Wesley.

Fullmer, C., & Garcia-Luna-Aceves, J.J. (1995). Floor acquisition multiple access (FAMA) for packet radio networks. *Computer Communication Review, 25*(4).

Garcia-Luna-Aceves, J.J., & Spohn, M. (1999). Source tree adaptive routing in wireless networks. In *Proceedings of IEEE ICNP.*

Girling, G.,Wa, J., Osborn, P., & Stefanova, R. (1997). The design and implementation of a low power ad hoc protocol stack. *IEEE Personal Communications, 4*(5), 8-15.

Guha, S., & Khuller, S. (1998). Approximation algorithms for connected dominating sets. *Algorithmica, 20,* 1998.

Haas, Z., & Deng, J. (1998). Dual busy tone multiple access (DBTMA): A new medium access control for packet radio networks. *IEEE International Conference on Universal Personal Communications,* Florence, Italy.

Haas, Z.J., & Liang, B. (1999). Ad hoc location management using quorum systems. *ACM/ IEEE Transactions on Networking.*

Haas, A., & Pearlman, M. (2000). *The zone routing protocol (ZRP) for ad hoc network* (Internet draft 03). IETF, MANET Working Group.

Hu, Y., Johnson, D., & Perrig, A. (2002). SEAD: Secure efficient distance vector routing for mobile wireless ad hoc networks. *Ad Hoc Networks, 1*(1), 175-192.

Hu, Y., Perrig, A., & Johnson, D. (2003). Ariadne: A secure on-demand routing protocol for ad hoc networks. *In Proceedings of ACM MOBICOM.*

Iwata, A., Chiang, C.-C., Pei, G., Gerla, M., & Chen, T.-W. (1999). Scalable routing strategies for ad hoc wireless networks. *IEEE Journal on Selected Areas in Communications, Special Issue on Ad-Hoc Networks,* 1369-79.

Jacquet, P., Muhlethaler, P., Qayyum, A., Laouiti, A., Viennot, L., & Clausen, T. (2000). *Optimized link state routing protocol* (Internet draft). IETF MANET Working Group. Retrieved from http://www.ietf.org/internet-drafts/draft-ietf-manet-olsr-05.txt

Jain, R., Puri, A., & Sengupta, R. (2001). Geographical routing using partial information for wireless ad hoc networks. *Personal Communications,* 48-57.

Joa-Ng, M., & Lu, I.T. (1999). A peer-to-peer zone-based two-level link state routing for mobile ad hoc networks. *IEEE Journal on Selected Areas in Communications, 17,* 1415-1425.

Johnson, D.B., & Maltz, D.A. (1999). *The dynamic source routing protocol for mobile ad hoc networks* (IETF draft). Retrieved from http://www.ietf.org/internet-drafts/draft-ietf-manet-dsr-03.txt

Jung, E-S., & Vaidya, N.H. (2002). A power control MAC protocol for ad-hoc networks. *ACM MOBICOM*.

Karn, P. (1992). MACA: A new channel access method for packet radio. In *Proceedings of the 9th ARRL/CRRL Amateur Radio Computer Networking Conference*.

Karp, B., & Kung, H.T. (2000). *GPSR: Greedy perimeter stateless routing for wireless networks*. Mobicom, Boston (pp. 243-254).

Ko, Y.B., & Vaidya, N.H. (1998). *Location-aided routing (LAR) in mobile ad hoc networks*. Mobicom, Dallas, TX.

Li, Q., Aslam, J., & Rus, D. (2001). Online power-aware routing in wireless ad hoc networks. In *Proceedings of MobiCom 2001*.

Li, Y., Mao, S., & Panwar, S.S. (2004). The case for multipath multimedia transport over wireless ad hoc networks. In *Proceedings of First Annual Conference on Broadband Networks (BroadNets)*, San Jose.

Liang, B., & Haas, Z.J. (2000). Virtual backbone generation and maintenance in ad hoc network mobility management. In *Proceedings of IEEE Infocom '00*, Tel Aviv (Vol. 5, pp. 1293-1302).

Liao, W.H., Tseng, Y.C., & Sheu, J.P. (2001). GRID: A fully location-aware routing protocol for mobile ad hoc networks. *Telecommunication Systems, 18*, 61-84.

Lin, X., & Stojmenovic, I. (1999). GEDIR: Loop-free location based routing in wireless networks. In *Proceedings of IASTED International Conference on parallel and Distributed Computing and Systems* (pp. 1025-1028).

Liu, J.J-N., & Chlamtac, I. (2004). Mobile ad hoc networking with a view of 4G wireless: Imperatives and challenges. In S. Bagagni et al. (Eds.), *Mobile ad hoc networking* (pp. 1-45). IEEE Press.

Mao, S., Cheng, X., Hou, Y.T., & Sherali, H.D. (2004, October). Multiple description video multicast in wireless ad hoc networks. In *Proceedings of First Annual Conference on Broadband Networks (BroadNets)*, San Jose.

McDonald, A.B., & Taieb Znati. (1999). A mobility-based framework for adaptive clustering in wireless ad-hoc networks. *IEEE Journal on Selected Areas in Communication, 17*(8).

Murthy, S., & Garcia-Luna-Aceves, J.J. (1996). An efficient routing protocol for wireless networks. *ACM Mobile Networks and App. J., Special Issue on Routing in Mobile Communication Networks*, 183-97.

Narayanaswamy, S., Kawadia, V., Sreenivas, R.S., & Kumar, P.R. (2002). *Power control in ad-hoc networks: Theory, architecture, algorithm and implementation of the COMPOW protocol*. European Wireless Conference.

Ogier, R.G., Templin, F.L., Bellur, B., & Lewis, M.G. (2002). *Topology broadcast based on reverse-path forwarding (TBRPF)* (Internet draft). MANET Working Group. Retrieved from http://www.ietf.org/internet-drafts/draft-ietf-manet-tbrpf-05.txt

Papadimitratos, P., & Haas, Z. (2000). Secure routing for mobile ad hoc networks. In *Proceedings of the SCS Communication Networks and Distributed Systems Modeling and Simulation Conference*, San Antonio, TX.

Park, V.D., & Corson, M.S. (1997). A highly adaptive distributed routing algorithm for mobile wireless networks. In *Proceedings of INFOCOM*.

Pei, G., Gerla, M., & Chen, T.-W. (2000). Fisheye state routing: A routing scheme for ad hoc wireless networks. In *Proceedings of ICC 2000*, New Orleans.

Pei, G., Gerla, M., & Hong, X. (2000). LANMAR: Landmark routing for large scale wireless ad hoc networks with group mobility. In *Proceedings of IEEE/ACM MobiHOC 2000* (pp. 11-18).

Pei, G., Gerla, M., Hong, X., & Chiang, C.-C. (1999). A wireless hierarchical routing protocol with group mobility. In *Proceedings of IEEE ICCCN '99*, Boston.

Perkins, C. (2001). *Ad hoc networking*. Prentice Hall.

Perkins, C., & Royer, E. (1999). Multicast operation of the ad-hoc on-demand distance vector routing protocol. In *Proceedings of MobiCom*, Seattle, WA (pp. 207-218).

Perkins, C.E., Royer, E., & Das, S.R. (n.d.). *Ad hoc on-demand distance vector routing* (IETF draft). Retrieved from http://www.ietf.org/internet-drafts/draft-ietf-manet-aodv-04.txt

Ramanathan, R., & Streenstrup, M. (1998). Hierarchically organized, multi-hop mobile wireless networks for quality-of-service support. *Mobile Networks and Applications, 3*, 101-119.

Reddy, T.B., Manoj, B. S., & Murthy, C.S.R. (2004, October). Multimedia traffic support for asynchronous ad hoc wireless networks. In *Proceedings of First Annual Conference on Broadband Networks (BroadNets)*, San Jose.

Rieck, M.Q., Pai, S., & Dhar, S. (2005). Distributed routing algorithms for multi-hop ad hoc networks using d-hop connected d-dominating sets. *Computer Networks Journal (COMNET), 47*(6), 785-799.

Sanzgiri, K., Dahill, B., Levine, B.N., Shields, C., & Belding-Royer, E. M. (2002). A secure routing protocol for ad hoc networks. In *Proceedings of the 10th IEEE International Conference on Network Protocols (ICNP)*, Paris.

Singh, S.R., & Raghavendra, C.S. (1998). PAMAS: Power aware multi-access protocol with signaling for ad-hoc networks. *ACM Computer Communication Review, 28*, 5-26.

Singh, S., Woo, M., & Raghavendra, C.S. (1998). Power-aware routing in mobile ad hoc networks. In *Proceedings of ACM/IEEE Mobicom '98 Conference*.

Sivakumar, R., Sinha, P., & Bharghavan, V. (1999). CEDAR: A core-extraction distributed ad hoc routing algorithm. *IEEE Journal of Selected Areas of Communications, 17*(8).

Sheu, J., Liu, C.H., Wu, S.-L., & Tseng, Y.-C. (2004). A priority MAC protocol to support real-time traffic in ad hoc networks. *Wireless Network, 10*(1), 61-69.

Stojmenovic, I., & Lin, X. (2001). Power-aware localized routing in wireless networks. *IEEE Transaction on Parallel and Distributed Systems, 12*(11), 1122-1133.

Talucci, F., & Gerla, M. (1997). MACA-BI (MACA By Invitation): A wireless MAC protocol for high speed ad hoc networking. In *Proceedings of ICUPC '97*.

Toh, C-K. (2002). *Ad hoc wireless mobile networks*. Upper Saddle River, NJ: Prentice Hall.

Toh, C-K. (2001). Maximum battery life routing to support ubiquitous mobile computing in wireless ad hoc networks. *IEEE Communications, 39*(6), 138-147.

Tseng, Y. C., & Hsu, C. S. (2003). Location-aware routing and applications of mobile ad-hoc networks. In M. Illyas (Ed.), *The handbook of ad hoc wireless networks*. CRC Press.

Tseng, Y.C., Hsu, C.S., & Hsieh, T.Y. (2002). Power-saving protocols for IEEE 802.11-nased multi-hop ad hoc networks. *IEEE Infocom*, New York.

Wei, W., & Zakhor, A. (2004). Multipath unicast and multicast video communication over wireless ad hoc networks. In *Proceedings of First Annual Conference on Broadband Networks (BroadNets)*, San Jose.

Wu, J. (2002). Extended dominating-set-based routing in ad hoc wireless networks with unidirectional links. *IEEE Trans. Parallel and Distributed Systems, 13*(9).

Wu, F., Dai, Gao, & Stojmenovic, I. (2002). On calculating power-aware connected dominating sets for efficient routing in ad hoc wireless networks. *IEEE/KICS J. Communication Networks, 4*(1), 59-70.

Wu, J., & Li, H. (2001). A dominating-set-based routing scheme in ad hoc wireless networks. *Telecommunication Systems, 18*(1-3), 13-36.

Wu, J., & Stojmenovic, I. (2004). Ad hoc networks. *IEEE Computer,* 29-31.

Weiser, M. (1993). Some computer sciences issues in ubiquitous computing. *Communications of the ACM, 36*(7).

Woo, K., Yu, C., Youn, H.Y., & Lee, B. (2001). Non-blocking, localized routing algorithm for balanced energy consumption in mobile ad hoc network. In *Proceedings of Intl. Symposium on Modeling, Analysis and Simulation of Computer and Telecommunication Systems (MASCOTS 2001)* (pp. 117-124).

Xu, Y., Heidemann, J., & Estrin, D. (2001). Geography-informed energy conservation for ad hoc routing. In *Proceedings of International Conference on Mobile Computing and Networking (MobiCom2001)* (pp. 70-84).

Ye, F., Luo, H., Cheng, J., Zhang, L., & Lu, S. (2002). A two-tier data dissemination model for large-scale wireless sensor networks. In *Proceedings of Mobicom '02* (pp. 148-159).

Yi, S., Naldurg, P., & Kravets, R. (2002). A security aware routing protocol for wireless ad hoc networks. In *Proceedings of the 6th World Multi-Conference on Systemics, Cybernetics and Informatics (SCI)* (pp. 286-292).

Zapata, M., & Asokan, N. (2002). Securing ad hoc routing protocols. In *Proceedings of the ACM Workshop on Wireless Security (WiSe 2002)*, Atlanta, GA.

Section IV:

Network Security

Chapter XII

Addressing WiFi Security Concerns

Kevin Curran, University of Ulster at Magee, UK

Elaine Smyth, University of Ulster at Magee, UK

Abstract

Signal leakage means that wireless network communications can be picked up outside the physical boundaries of the building in which they are being operated, meaning a hacker can operate from the street outside. In addition to signal leakage—the wired equivalent privacy protocol is inherently weak and there are various other attacks that can be initiated against WLAN's. This research commences by conducting a war driving expedition to ascertain the number of unprotected WLAN devices in use in a one small town. We conclude by making recommendations for three groups of user; home user, small office/home office (SOHO) and medium to large organisations. Home users should implement all the security measures their hardware offers them, to include WEP at the longest key length permitted and implement firewalls on all connected PCs changing their WEP key on a weekly basis. The small office group should implement WPA-SPK; and the medium to large organisations should implement one or more of either WPA enterprise with a RADIUS server, VPN software, IDSs, and provide documented policies in relation to WLANs and their use.

Introduction

Radio devices utilized within WLANs operate in the 2.4-2.4845GHz range of the unlicensed industrial scientific and medical (ISM) frequency band, using either frequency hopping spread spectrum (FHSS) or direct sequence spread spectrum (DSSS), which are special modulation techniques used for spreading data over a wide band of frequencies sacrificing bandwidth to gain signal-to-noise (S/N) performance (Harte, Kellog, Dreher, & Schaffinit, 2000). Wireless devices have the option of participating in two type of networks: ad hoc and infrastructure. An ad hoc (also known as peer-to-peer) network is the simplest form of WLAN. It is composed of two or more nodes communicating without any bridging or forwarding capability; all nodes are of equal importance and may join and leave the network at any time, each device also has equal right to the medium. Access points (APs) are not necessary. For this to work, the devices wishing to participate in an Ad Hoc network must be within transmission range of each other, when a nodes goes out of range it will lose connection with the rest of the devices. The range of this type of network is referred to as a "single cell" and is called an independent basic service set (IBSS) (Tourrilhes, 2000).

In an infrastructure network communications take place through an AP, in a many-to-one configuration, with the AP at the single end. In its simplest form it consists of one AP and a group of wireless clients/devices, which must be within transmission range of the AP, and be properly configured to communicate with the AP. This type of network is called a basic service set (BSS) (Sikora, 2003). If two or more BSSes are operated in the same network, by linking the APs via a background network, this is then called an extended service set (ESS). Such a configuration can cover larger, multi-floor, buildings. However, support is required for 'roaming' between different APs on the network, that is the hand-off between a device leaving one APs range and going into the range of another AP (Geier, 1999).

APs can be overlapped if they are each given a different channel, within the 2.4-2.4835GHz, range to communicate on. There are eleven overlapping frequencies specified in IEEE 802.11, which means that with careful planning multiple networks can coexist in the same physical space without interfering with each other (Tourrilhes, 2000). APs must also be configured with a service set identifier (SSID), also known as the network name. It is a simple 1-32 byte alphanumeric string given to each ESS that identifies the wireless network and allows stations to connect to one desired network when multiple independent networks operate in the same physical area. It also provides a very basic way of preventing unauthorised users from joining your network, as all devices in an ESS must have the same ESSID to participate.

Most APs can provide additional, basic, security features, such as WEP and MAC address filtering. WEP, an abbreviation for Wired Equivalent Protocol, is a protocol designed specifically for use on wireless networks and is supposed to provide the security equivalent of the cable in a wired network through the use of encryption. Communicating devices must use the same WEP key in order to communicate. MAC address filtering provides a basis for screening users wanting to connect to a network; for a client device to be able to successfully communicate with the AP, its name must appear on an access control list of MAC addresses held by that AP. However, both these methods have been proven weak in their ability to secure wireless networks; both can be easily broken.

Security in Wireless Networks

Wired networks have always presented their own security issues, but wireless networks introduce a whole new set of rules with their own unique security vulnerabilities. Most wired security measures are just not appropriate for application within a WLAN environment; this is mostly due to the complete change in transmission medium. However, some of the security implementations developed specifically for WLANs are also not terribly strong. Indeed, this aspect could be viewed as a "work-in-progress"; new vulnerabilities are being discovered just as quickly as security measures are being released. Perhaps the issue that has received the most publicity is the major weaknesses in WEP, and more particularly the use of the RC4 algorithm and relatively short initialisation vectors (IVs). WLANs suffer from all the security risks associated with their wired counterparts; however, they also introduce some unique risks of their own. The main issue with radio-based wireless networks is signal leakage. Due to the properties of radio transmissions it is impossible to contain signals within one clearly defined area. In addition, because data is not enclosed within cable it makes it very easy to intercept without being physically connected to the network. This puts it outside the limits of what a user can physically control; signals can be received outside the building and even from streets away. Signal leakage may not be a huge priority when organisations are implementing their WLAN, but it can present a significant security issue, as demonstrated below. The same signals that are transmitting data around an organisation's office are the same signals that can also be picked up from streets away by an unknown third party. This is what makes WLANs so vulnerable. Before WLAN's became common, someone wishing to gain unauthorised access to a wired network had to physically attach themselves to a cable within the building. This is why wiring closets should be kept locked and secured. Any potential hacker had to take great risks to penetrate a wired network. Today potential hackers do not have to use extreme measures, there's no need to smuggle equipment on site when it can be done from two streets away. It is not difficult for someone to obtain the necessary equipment; access can be gained in a very discrete manner from a distance.

Wired Equivalent Protocol (WEP)

To go some way towards providing the same level of security the cable provides in wired networks, the Wired Equivalent Protocol (WEP) was developed. IEEE 802.11 defined three basic security services for the WLAN environment (Karygiannis & Owens, 2003):

- Authentication (a primary goal of WEP)
- Confidentiality (privacy – a second goal of WEP)
- Integrity (another goal of WEP)

WEP was designed to provide the security of a wired LAN by encryption through use of the RC4 (Rivest Code 4) algorithm. It's primary function was to safeguard against eavesdropping ("sniffing"), by making the data that is transmitted unreadable by a third party who does not have the correct WEP key to decrypt the data. RC4 is not specific to WEP, it is a random generator, also known as a keystream generator or a stream cipher, and was developed in RSA Laboratories by Ron Rivest in 1987 (hence the name Rivest code (RC)). It takes a relatively short input and produces a somewhat longer output, called a pseudo-random key stream. This key stream is simply added modulo two that is exclusive ORed (XOR), with the data to be transmitted, to generate what is known as ciphertext. WEP is applied to all data above the 802.11b WLAN layers (physical and data link layers, the first two layers of the OSI reference model) to protect traffic such as transmission control protocol/Internet protocol (TCP/IP), Internet packet exchange (IPX) and hyper text transfer protocol (HTTP). It should be noted that only the frame body of data frames are encrypted and the entire frame of other frame types are transmitted in the clear, unencrypted (Karygiannis & Owens, 2003). To add an additional integrity check, an initialisation vector (IV) is used in conjunction with the secret encryption key. The IV is used to avoid encrypting multiple consecutive ciphertexts with the same key, and is usually 24 bits long. The shared key and the IV are fed into the RC4 algorithm to produce the key stream. This is XORed with the data to produce the ciphertext, the IV is then appended to the message. The IV of the incoming message is used to generate the key sequence necessary to decrypt the incoming message. The ciphertext, combined with the proper key sequence, yields the original plaintext and integrity check value (ICV) (Tyrrell, 2003). The decryption is verified by performing the integrity check algorithm on the recovered plaintext and comparing the output ICV to the ICV transmitted with the message. If it is in error, an indication is sent back to the sending station. The IV increases the key size, for example, a 104 bit WEP key with a 24bit IV becomes a 128 bit RC4 key. In general, increasing the key size increases the security of a cryptographic technique. Research has shown that key sizes of greater than 80 bits make brute force[1] code breaking extremely difficult. For an 80 bit key, the number of possible keys—$10^{\wedge}24$ which puts computing power to the test; but this type of computing power is not beyond the reach of most hackers. The standard key in use today is 64-bit. However, research has shown that the WEP approach to privacy is vulnerable to certain attacks regardless of key size (Karygiannes & Owens, 2003). Although the application of WEP may stop casual "sniffers," determine hackers can crack WEP keys in a busy network within a relatively short period of time.

WEP's Weaknesses

WEP's major weaknesses relate to three main issues. Firstly, the use of static keys, secondly, the length of the IV, and thirdly, the RC4 algorithm.

Static Keys

When WEP is enabled in accordance with the 802.11b standard, the network administrator must personally visit each wireless device in use and manually enter the appropriate WEP key. This may be acceptable at the installation stage of a WLAN or when a new client joins the network, but if the key becomes compromised and there is a loss of security, the key must be changed. This may not be a huge issue in a small organisation with only a few users, but it can be impractical in large corporations, who typically have hundreds of users (Dismukes, 2002). As a consequence, potentially hundreds of users and devices could be using the same, identical, key for long periods of time. All wireless network traffic from all users will be encrypted using the same key; this makes it a lot easier for someone listening to traffic to crack the key as there are so many packets being transmitted using the same key. Unfortunately, there were no key management provisions in the original WEP protocol.

IV Length

This is a 24 bit initialisation vector WEP appends to the shared key. WEP uses this combined key and IV to generate the RC4 key schedule; it selects a new IV for each packet, so each packet can have a different key. This forms a family of 2^{24} keys. As described, each packet transmission selects one of these 2^{24} keys and encrypts the data under that key. On the surface, this may appear to strengthen protection by lengthening the 40 bit WEP key, however this scheme suffers from a basic problem; if IVs are chosen randomly there is a 50% chance of reuse after less than 5,000 packets (Walker, 2000). The problem is a numerical restriction; because the IV is only 24 bits long, there are a finite number of variations of the IV for RC4 to pick from. Mathematically there are only 16,777,216 possible values for the IV. This may seem like a huge number, but given that it takes so many packets to transmit useful data, 16 million packets can easily go by in hours on a heavily used network. Eventually the RC4 algorithm starts using the same IVs over and over. Thus, someone passively 'listening' to encrypted traffic and picking out the repeating IVs can begin to deduce what the WEP key is. Made easier by the fact that there is a static variable, (the shared key), an attacker can eventually crack the WEP key (iLabs, 2002). For example, a busy AP, which constantly sends 1500 byte packets at 11Mbps, will exhaust the space of IVs after $1500 \times 8/(11 \times 10^6)$ x 2^{24} = 18,000 seconds, or 5 hours. (The amount of time may actually be smaller since many packets are less than 1500 bytes). This allows an attacker to collect two ciphertexts that are encrypted with the same key stream. This reveals information about both messages. By XORing two ciphertexts that use the same key stream would cause the key stream to be cancelled out and the result would be the XOR of the two plaintexts (Vines, 2002).

There is an additional problem that involves the use of IVs, more specifically, weak IVs. Some numbers in the range 0-16,777,215 don't work to well with the RC4 algorithm. When these weak IVs are used, the resulting packet can be run through a series of mathematical functions to decipher part of the WEP key. By capturing a large number of packets an attacker can pick out enough weak IVs to reveal the WEP key (PCQuest, 2003). Tools like Airsnort specifically exploit this vulnerability to allow hackers to obtain the above information relatively easily. The crack process within Airsnort works by collecting packets thought to have been encrypted using a weak IV and then sorting them according to which key byte they help expose. A weak IV can assist in exposing only one key byte. The Flurer attack states that a weak IV has about a 5% chance of exposing the corresponding key byte. So, when a sufficient number of weak IVs have been collected for a particular key byte, statistical analysis will show a tendency towards a particular value for that key byte. The crack process makes a key guess based on the highest ranking values in the statistical analysis. Tests conducted by Stubblefield, Ioannidis, and Rubin (2001) show that between 60 and 256 weak IVs were needed to recover a key (AirSnort FAQ). In addition to the fundamental weaknesses in the WEP security protocol, (which is the primary security measure in WLANs), there are numerous other attacks that can be instigated against WLANs and their devices. Each of these will be discussed in turn in the next chapter; how they are carried out and what impact they could have. Some of these attacks will be carried out against the test WLAN as part of the primary research; this will assess the relative ease with which these attacks can be carried out and how effective they are.

War Driving

Not surprisingly a new "sport" has emerged within the computer hacking world which takes advantage of some of the security weaknesses in WLANs. So called "war driving" is a term used to describe a hacker, who, armed with a laptop, a wireless NIC, an antenna and sometimes a GPS device travels, usually by car, scanning or "sniffing" for WLAN devices, or more specifically unprotected or "open" and easily accessed networks . The name is thought to have come from another hacking technique called War-Dialling, where a hacker programs their system to call hundreds of phone numbers in search of a poorly protected computer dial-up (Poulsen, 2001).

Due to the increased use of WLANs in recent years, it is quite possible that the number of unsecured devices has also risen in tandem, thus providing potential hackers with more choice. After all that has been written about the insecurities of WLAN, some users/organisations still insist on implementing them with their default settings and no encryption (Ulanoff, 2003). A Worldwide WarDrive, held in August to September 2002, discovered that 70% of APs were running without using any encryption, worse still 27% were doing so while using the default SSID that came with the hardware, leaving them wide open for use by anyone in range with a wireless NIC and a note of all vendor's default SSIDs. These figures are rather disturbing figures; leaving an AP at its default settings is the this is the equivalent of putting an Ethernet socket on the outside of the building so anyone passing by can plug into the network (Griffith, 2002). There is a plethora of hacking tools widely available to download from the Internet for any potential war driver to use.

Forms of Attack

This chapter deals with the various attacks that can be performed against WLANs (aside from the WEP crack), how they are carried out and what affect they have in relation to authentication, confidentiality and integrity, the three basic security requirements within networks. All of the attacks can be categorised into two general attack types; passive and active.

Passive Attacks

A passive attack is an attack on a system that does not result in a change to the system in any way; the attack is purely to monitor or record data. Passive attacks affect confidentiality, but not necessarily authentication or integrity. Eavesdropping and traffic analysis fall under this category. When an attacker eavesdrops, they simply monitor transmissions for message content. It usually takes the form of someone listening into the transmissions on a LAN between stations/devices.

Eavesdropping

Eavesdropping is also known as "sniffing" or wireless "footprinting." As mentioned in a previous chapter there are various tools available for download online which allow the monitoring of networks and their traffic; developed by hackers, for hackers. Netstumbler, Kismet, Airsnort, WEPCrack and Ethereal are all well known names in wireless hacking circles, and all are designed specifically for use on wireless networks, with the exception of Ethereal, which is a packet analyser and can also be used on a wired LAN. NetStumbler and Kismet can be used purely for passive eavesdropping; they have no additional active functions, except perhaps their ability to work in conjunction with global positioning systems (GPSs) to map the exact locations of identified wireless LANs. NetStumbler is a Windows-based sniffer, where Kismet is primarily a Linux-based tool. NetStumbler uses an 802.11 Probe Request sent to the broadcast destination address, which causes all APs in the area to issue an 802.11 Probe Response containing network configuration information, such as their SSID, WEP status, the MAC address of the device, name (if applicable), the channel the device is transmitting on, the vendor and the type, either peer or AP, along with a few other pieces of information. Using the network information and GPS data collected, it is then possible to create maps with tools such as StumbVerter and MS Mappoint.

Kismet, although not as graphical or user friendly as NetStumbler, is similar to its Windows counterpart, but it provides superior functionality. While scanning for APs, packets can also be logged for later analysis. Logging features allow for captured packets to be stored in separate categories, depending upon the type of traffic captured. Kismet can even store encrypted packets that use weak keys separately to run them through a WEP key cracker after capture, such as Airsnort or WEPCrack (Sutton, 2002). Wireless network GPS information can be uploaded to a site called Wigle (http://www.wigle.net). Therefore, if wigle data exists for a particular area, there is no need to drive around that area probing for wireless devices; this information can be obtained in advance from the Wigle web site. All that remains is to drive to a location where known networks exist to observe traffic. Wigle currently has a few hundred thousand networks on its database.

Traffic Analysis

Traffic analysis gains intelligence in a more subtle way by monitoring transmissions for patterns of communication. A considerable amount of information is contained in the flow of messages between communicating parties. Airopeek NX, a commercial 802.11 monitoring and analysis tool for Windows, analyses transmissions and provides a useful node view, which groups detected stations and devices by their MAC address and will also show IP addresses and protocols observed for each. The peer map view, within Airopeek NX, presents a matrix of all hosts discovered on the network by their connections to each other. This can make it very easy to visualise AP and client relationships, which could be useful to hackers in deciding where to try and gain access or target for an attack (McClure,

Scambray, & Jurtz, 2003). Some attacks may begin as passive, but and then cross over to active as they progress. For example, tools such as Airsnort or WEPCrack may passively monitor transmissions, but their intent is to crack the WEP key used to encrypt data being transmitted. Ultimately the reasons for wanting to crack the key are so that an unauthorised individual can access a protected network and then launch an active attack of some form or another. These types of attack are classed as passive decryption attacks.

Airsnort, mentioned previously, exploits the key weaknesses and uses this to crack WEP keys, as does WEPCrack. These are tools that put hackers on the first step towards an active attack. However, WEPCrack, unlike Airsnort, must be used in conjunction with a separate packet sniffer as it does not have the ability to capture network traffic. These tools utilise what is known as a Brute Force technique to break codes. Brute Force is a method of breaking a cipher by trying every possible key until the correct key is found. The feasibility of this attack depends on the key length of the cipher, and/or the amount of computational power available to the attacker, and of course time. Another type of passive decryption attack is what is known as a dictionary attack, also a form of the brute force technique. A dictionary attack refers to breaking a cipher, or obtaining a password by running through a list of likely keys, or a list of words. The term dictionary attack initially referred to finding passwords in a specific list, such as an English dictionary. Today, a Brute Force approach can compute likely passwords, such as all five-letter combinations, "on-the-fly" instead of using a pre-built list. The last Brute Force, passive decryption, attack is called a table attack and can be demonstrated with an example that makes reference to IVs. It is a method which involves using the relatively small number of IVs (24 bit) to build decryption tables. Once the contents of a single encrypted packet are known, the hacker can work backwards and build a table of all the keys possible with a particular IV (Franklin, 2001).

Active Attacks

An active attack, also referred to as a malicious attack, occurs when an unauthorised third party gains access to a network and proceeds to perform denial of service (DoS) attack, to disrupt the proper operation of a network, to intercept network traffic and either modify or delete it, or inject extra traffic onto the network. There are many active attacks that can be launched against wireless networks; the following few paragraphs outline almost all of these attacks, how they work and what affect they have (Karygiannis & Owens, 2003). DoS attacks are easily the most prevalent type of attack against 802.11 networks, and can be waged against a single client or an entire WLAN. In this type of attack the hacker usually does not steal information, they simply prevent users from accessing network services, or cause services to be interrupted or delayed. Consequences can range from a measurable reduction in performance to the complete failure of the system. Some common DoS attacks are outlined.

Man-in-the-Middle (MITM) Attack

This attack is carried out by inserting a malicious station between the victim station and the AP, thus the attacker becomes the 'man in the middle'; the station is tricked into believing that the attacker is the AP, and the AP into believing that the attacker is the legitimate station. To being the attack the perpetrator passively monitors the frames sent back and forth between the station and the AP during the initial association process with an 802.11 analyser. As a result, information is obtained about both the station and the AP, such as the MAC and IP address of both devices, association ID for the station and SSID of the network. With this information a rogue station/AP can be set up between the two unsuspecting devices. Because the original 802.11 does not provide mutual authentication, a station will happily re-associate with the rogue AP. The rogue AP will then capture traffic from unsuspecting users; this of course can expose information such as user names and passwords.

After gleaning enough information about a particular WLAN, a hacker can then use a rogue station to mimic a valid one. This enables the hacker to deceive an AP by disassociating the valid station and reassociating again as a rogue station with the same parameters as the valid station. Two wireless cards are typically required for this type of attack (Griffith, 2002). Once the attacker has successfully inserted themselves between the AP and client station, they are free to modify traffic, selectively forward or even delete it completely, while logging every packet that comes through it. In addition, the attacker is also free to explore and use other areas of the network as a legitimate user.

War Driving

The purpose of the war driving was to discover how many wireless devices were in use in the Londonderry area with and without WEP. The research was carried out by driving around the target area, equipped with a Laptop, wireless NIC, an external antenna, and NetStumbler for Windows. We probed for any wireless devices in use within range. Association with open AP's was attempted as was obtaining an Internet connection by proxy. It must be stressed that the research was purely white-hat,[2] no malicious attempts were made against any networks or devices discovered to be lacking in security, no further network penetration attempted either. This would have been unethical and defy the efforts of this chapter to identify weaknesses and present recommendations to help users. The rationale behind this research was to, firstly, discover how many wireless networks were in use, and secondly, observe if they had any security measures in place, namely WEP, or if they were open to attack. Without further network probing it is unclear what other security measures users had in place other than or in addition to WEP. This information was not immediately available. For the purposes of this research it was assumed that when a device was displayed as being open on NetStumbler, it was deemed as having no security measures in place. When a device was displayed in NetStumbler as being protected by WEP, it was assumed that this was the only security measure they were utilising.

War Driving

Over the period of three months, from August to October 2003, initial scans were carried out in the Londonderry area. The first few scans were used to test the software and equipment

Table 1. Wireless devices discovered in the Londonderry area

#	MAC	SSID	DEFAULT	ENCRYPTION	CHANNEL	TYPE
1	0030AB099F8D	Wireless	YES	NO	6	AP
2	02D0D86402D0	Brieco Wireless Network	NO	YES - WEP	9	PEER
3	00022D20CBBD	WaveLAN Network	YES	NO	10	AP
4	00095B43173C	NETGEAR	NO	YES - WEP	11	AP
5	0002B3B140C8	101	NO	NO	11	AP
6	0007408BAB18	0007406B8CF8	NO	NO	11	AP
7	0209D16EF444	KYOCERA	NO	NO	3	PEER
8	00047562B539	3Com	NO	NO	1	AP
9	00E018B29361	default	NO	NO	1	AP
10	000476A7A325	3Com	NO	NO	6	AP
11	4096365501	testlab	NO	NO	7	AP
12	0030AB0B711E	exuswlan27templemore	NO	YES - WEP	11	AP
13	00022D2DEB1C	WaveLAN Network	YES	NO	10,1,2,3,4,5,6,7	AP
14	0030650C7E30	MSHOME	NO	NO	11	UNKNOWN
15	022384D093A8	MSHOME	NO	NO	11	PEER
16	00601D23358C	ANY	NO	NO	6	AP
17	0030AB1E5CAB	Wireless	YES	NO	1	AP
18	000A417D4128	BTOpenzone	NO	NO	7	AP
19	022365DC93A8	MSHOME	NO	NO	11	PEER
20	0223E0D093A8	MSHOME	NO	NO	11	PEER
21	00022D2DDBF8	WaveLAN Network	YES	NO	10	AP
22	00022D1CF3A2	WaveLAN Network	YES	NO	10	AP
23	00022D285F63	WaveLAN Network	YES	NO	10	AP
24	00022D28616B	WaveLAN Network	YES	NO	10	AP
25	00095B4C1E46	Wireless	YES	NO	6	AP
26	000D549B7F4F	Singularity	NO	YES - WEP	10	AP
27	000D549B7F84	Singularity	NO	YES - WEP	11	AP
28	02095639F444	KYOCERA	NO	NO	11,5	PEER
29	020939F7F444	KYOCERA	NO	NO	11	PEER
30	000A417D4128	BTOpenzone	NO	NO	7,1,10,4,3,11	AP

to ensure they were operating correctly, verified by the same information being picked up in the second test as in this first, proving the consistency of the information collected. Table 1 displays the devices discovered in the Londonderry area over this period.

It is worth noting at this stage that 30 devices were detected, out of which only a mere five were protected with WEP; however two of these were BTOpenZone Hotspots. A staggering 83% of the devices detected were open and vulnerable to attack. Even if security measures are implemented further into the network, the fact that the gateway is wide open enabling a connection to be made, provides the first step towards launching an attack. With the exception of the BT Hotspots, internet access was gained through all open devices apart from the six devices with the WaveLAN network SSID; obviously http traffic is disallowed on this

Figure 1. Map of city with wireless devices discovered

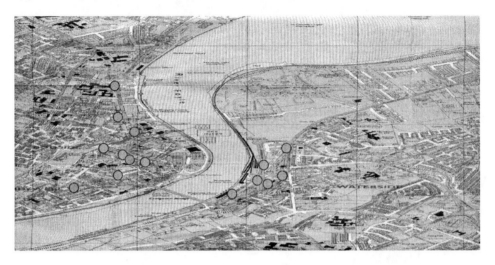

network. These devices are deemed to be part of one overall network due to the similarity in SSID and GPS coordinates; all devices were sensed within a close geographical area within the grounds of one particular set of buildings. The implications of an unknown third party having access to an Internet connection are huge. Because their presence online is disguised by the IP address of the connection they are using they can do whatever they want virtually undetected. This may appear harmless on the surface, but if this person were to use the connection to launch a series of Internet-based DoS attacks or a huge spam-mail campaign, or to use the connection to hack into another network, or worse still, to download and distribute explicit and/or illegal material, the implications could be far reaching. It may be difficult for the owner of the connection to disprove any allegations raised and the consequences could be disastrous. In addition to this, network performance could be affected. Users may notice a real degradation in network bandwidth if third parties are using the connection continuously for downloads. Users with internet-based applications may experience a noticeable reduction in performance, thereby affecting their ability to carry out their job.

Even more disturbing, a total of eight out of the thirty devices discovered were operating under their default settings. This means that the devices were literally taken out of their boxes and plugged in, no further configuration was attempted. As mentioned, this is the equivalent of putting an ethernet connection on the outside of the building, enabling anyone passing by to join the network. The five remaining devices were locked using WEP encryption. Regardless of how weak WEP is, this encryption is a deterrent. Any potential hacker will have to spend time (depending on network traffic loads) outside a building collecting packets and running the risk of being caught. If these networks have relatively low traffic, WEP may be sufficient to protect them. It would take a potential hacker an unjustified length of time before enough packets could be collected to effectively crack the key.

Figure 1 shows one local map where WLAN's were discovered in the war drive. The devices have been plotted on the map as a series of coloured dots. A red dot represents a locked device and a green dot represents an unprotected device. The overwhelming number of greens dots is apparent when plotted in this manner. However, if the network has a heavy traffic load, WEP may not be effective; also mentioned in chapter two, five hours may be all it would take to collect enough packets, less if packets are small and there is considerable traffic.

Active WLAN Hacking

The second stage of the primary research was done on an infrastructure test wireless network which imitated a real world WLAN scenario. The test network consisted of one AP, two workstations with a wireless NICs, and one third-party workstation acting as attacker. The purpose was to demonstrate how easy it would be for an attacker to gain access to a wireless network and the damage they could cause. This will apply to all the devices discovered in the previous section. The AP used offered a few security options which were WEP at varying key lengths, MAC-address-based filtering and SSID hiding. Experiments were done to test the effectiveness of the WEP security protocol as this is what the devices identified in the area were using as protection, along with a few other basic security measures. Airsnort was used to test WEP, and Ethereal and SMAC was used to penetrate the MAC filtering and SSID hiding. In addition to this, the SNMP attack was also attempted to demonstrate how easy it would be for an attacker to gain access and reconfigure the APs identified in the live networks earlier; made even easier by the lack of security. It is assumed that some level of file and service sharing is set up between clients in the live networks as this is the prime rationale for networking, to share resources. Therefore, within the test network a few of the folders on the drive of each PC have been shared for access by other members of the network, as has the printer service.

The nature of files and folders that are typically shared within a network are files that everyone requires access to either for leisure or for business. This could be films or photographs in the home environment or business related documents and records, for example, accounting and customer information, within the office environment. Occasionally whole hard drives are carelessly shared instead of selective folders or files, which is much more than is required. This provides access to everything on the shared PC, including sensitive Operating System files the PC needs in order to function; Windows, for example. For home users, the nature of shared files may not carry the same level of sensitivity, but the dangers are much the same. If the entire hard drive is shared, this leaves the PC vulnerable to changes and the Operating System files are exposed to deletion or alteration. To imitate the real networks discovered, the first level of security was no security. No attacks are required to gain access to an open network. Information obtained from NetStumbler is enough for this. Just a few configuration changes on the PC will allow association with the AP and thus participation in the network. Subsequent to this, a demonstration and description of the damage that could be caused to a network with this type of easy access will be detailed. This will be applicable to those apparently open networks discovered in the Londonderry area. Further attacks are made trivial in environments like this as there is no need to break through any security in order to execute them. These attacks are also possible after the WEP key has been compromised.

For the purposes of this chapter, we define three levels of security. Light might be defined as being easily broken or bypassed. Medium is tougher than light, but not impossible to break and Heavy is the strongest security, hard if not impossible to break. Light may include the following preventions: changing SSID, disabling SSID broadcasts, changing default settings on AP, enabling MAC filtering and enabling WEP. Medium would include the above as well as implementing WPAv1. Heavy would include all of the above along with WPAv2, VPNs, and IDSes.

Software used included NetStumbler, Ethereal, AirSnort and SMAC. While equipment used was three laptop PC's; one Windows/Linux-based, two Windows-based, three wireless NIC's; one with Prism II chipset and one access point (AP).

Attack One: Joining an Unsecured Network

Figure 2 shows the information about the test network, called "WIRELESSOFFICE," detected by NetStumbler. The information contained in NetStumbler's output was enough to enable a PC to be configured to use the WIRELESSOFFICE connection and then join the WIRELESSOFFICE network.

Once an intruder has access they will have the same privileges as legitimate users on the network if no security is in place. If any files/folders are shared on any connected PC's the intruder will have access to these also. They will be able to copy, delete or move these files/folders, with devastating consequences. They are also free to implement any of the attacks mentioned in chapter three. The hard drive of the PC's in the test network were shared in full meaning that both PC's were able to browse, copy, change or delete files on the other. This also meant that the third PC, acting as intruder, was also able to browse, copy, change or delete the files and folders on the two PC's. If an internet connection had been available through the AP, the third PC would also have been able to use this.

Figure 2. Screen shot from NetStumbler showing test network

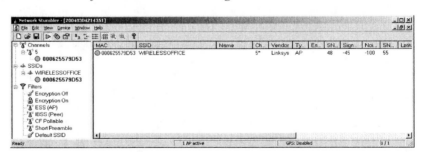

Attack Two: Joining a Network with MAC-Filtering

MAC address-based filtering was enabled on the AP allowing access to only one of the PC's using the hardware MAC address on the wireless NIC. This was verified by the connection on the disallowed PC going down and the connection on the authorised PC coming back up again. The MAC address information was easily obtained using Ethereal packet analyser. Figure 3 shows the MAC address of the authorised card highlighted in blue.

This information was then used to change the MAC address on the other PC to match that of an authorised user. This was done using SMAC, a MAC address changing utility provided by KLC Consulting. Figure 4 provides a sample screen from SMAC showing the original MAC address and the spoofed MAC address.

After the PC was restarted it assumed the MAC address of the authorised PC and was permitted to join the network by the AP. The Physical Address changed on the Buffalo card and it was allowed to connect to the network by the AP. MAC address-based access lists are easily penetrated.

Figure 3. Screen shot from Ethereal

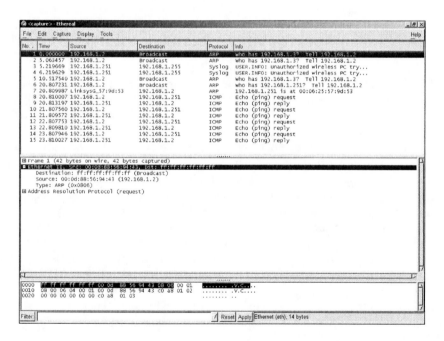

Figure 4. Screen shot from SMAC

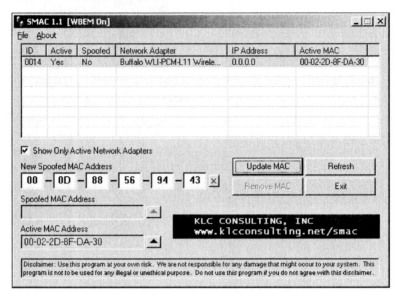

Attack Number Four: Joining a Network with WEP Enabled

WEP was enabled on the AP at 64-bits as this was the lowest key size allowed, 40 was not an option. The cards on the two test network PC's were also configured to use 64-bit WEP encryption. The key was based on a series of numbers, 3145324641, which produced a key of 17BE311175—generated by the AP. This key was then used to configure the PC's. The third PC, acting as attacker, was not configured with the WEP key nor network information and was hence not part of the legitimate network. Instead it was left to run Airsnort on Linux Mandrake 9.1 and monitor all traffic passing over the WIRELESSOFFICE network. NetStumbler was used first to identify which channel the AP and clients were operating on; channel 5. Airsnort was then set to capture packets from this channel. This was a necessity as when Airsnort was set to scan and capture on all channels the system simply froze up and refused to operate. The WIRELESSOFFICE network was detected as soon as the Airsnort capture began, it was also identified that WEP was in use. To speed the crack process up, files were copied between the two PC's in the network. This created network traffic for Airsnort to analyse. After only two hours of traffic and around 4.9 million packets, Airsnort was able to crack the 64-bit key based on the information it had gathered. Figure 5 shows a screen shot of Airsnort showing the number of packets gathered and the WEP key, exactly as detailed above; 17BE311175.

Following this a 128-bit WEP was implemented to test the relative strength of using a longer key. This time the key was based on 314532464156, two digits more than previously, and produced the 26 long character sequence 053DB0F983E36FBF0B308627A2, just over two

Figure 5. Screen shot from Airsnort showing 64-bit key crack

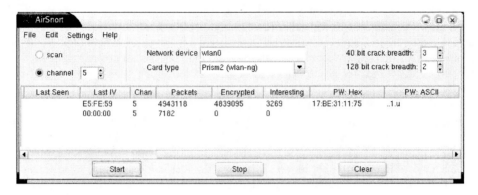

Figure 6. Screen shot from Airsnort showing 128-bit key crack

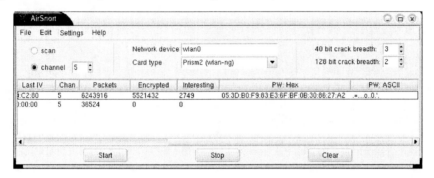

and a half times longer than the sequence produced by the 64-bit number series. After 6.2 million packets had passed over the network, Airsnort was able to provide the crack for the 128-bit key. Surprisingly fewer packets than anticipated. Figure 6 provides depicts the screen shot from this crack clearly showing the number of packets and the exact key.

Airsnort is highly effective in breaking WEP. Testing on a 256-bit key could not be carried out due to hardware limitations. However, on comparison of the number of packets taken to break the 64 and 128-bit keys, it is estimated that the 256-bit key would not take a huge number of packets before its key is also exposed. When WEP is broken an attacker is free to join a network protected in this manner. They can then carry out further attacks using the HostAP driver, like malicious association and de-association. Or worse still they can browse and copy networked files and folders. For the networks that are protected by WEP in the Londonderry area this is a very real threat. The experiment above proves just how weak WEP is and the field research shows that of the networks that were protected in

Londonderry all were using WEP.

Because Airsnort runs on a Linux-based PC it makes it one of the more tricky hacks to run, especially if coming from a Windows-based background. Airsnort is not easy to implement unless you know what you are doing. It is not easy to implement or to get running without some form of Linux knowledge. The wireless NIC requires special drivers to enable it to function under Linux, the wireless card must also have a certain chipset in order for it to be able to be instructed by the special drivers. This chipset is what is known as Prism II and not all cards use this chipset. Indeed it is quite difficult to find out information about a wireless card's chipset as this information does not appear on the manufacturer's packaging or documentation. The only way to determine a card's chipset is to perform searches online in Linux mail archives and related web sites. If the card is new it makes it even more problematic as information online usually relates to older cards that have been tried and tested. Various searches were performed online to find information on how to install and run Airsnort. Once Airsnort has been installed and is running it is relatively simple to use and quick to execute, it can be left to run with little effort required from the hacker. Because it is passive in nature, Airsnort can be run without fear of being detected, unless a network administrator is extremely observant.

Attack Five: Network Admin Username/Password

It is also possible to obtain the information required to gain access to the administrator privileges on the AP and thus make configuration changes which will affect network connectivity for the attached PCs. Using Ethereal packets were gathered as one of the client PC's logged onto the AP to make configuration changes. After examining Ethereal's output the required information was located within a short period of time in packet number 120. The administrator username was 'elaine' and the password was "theSimpsons." This information allows access to the configuration of the AP with network administrator's privileges. The IP address of the AP is also easily obtained from Ethereal, this is also required in order to connect to the AP using Internet Explorer.

For the purposes of comparison and to aid the recommendations, a final test on network traffic was undertaken. This was to assess normal traffic levels and ascertain who long it may be before a certain number of packets was achieved on a network during normal use. Ethereal packet counts were used to gauge traffic loads in various situations within a 10-minute period. The varying situations were continuous traffic achieved by copying a file; intermittent traffic achieved by accessing, browsing, amending and saving files on one PC from the other; and, low traffic achieved by simply having a ten minute period of inactivity. This is to reflect and in some way simulate the traffic patterns of the three groups identified.

The home user would have large periods of inactivity and traffic loads in bursts usually in the early evening and more frequent at the weekends. This can be reflected by mixing part intermittent traffic and inactivity in the ratio of 20/80 based on a 12-hour day. For the small office traffic will be the same as continuous intermittent use throughout normal office hours and then have a large period of inactivity out of office hours. The ratio here would be 60/40 based on a 12-hour day, with 40 representing the period of inactivity. Due to the sheer size of a medium to large organisation and the number of devices on the network, their traffic load can be best reflected by the continuous traffic load detailed above. Their usage will also be usually 60/40 in a 12-hour day, but can also extend towards a full 12-hour day of usage depending on the organisation.

Recommendations

For the purposes of making more specific and accurate recommendations, three categories of user have been identified; home user, small office/home office (SOHO) and medium to large organisations. The following recommendations are based on the findings presented earlier and upon which option is viewed to be most appropriate for each group of user. This is somewhat subjective and does not consider what type of applications each group of user will be using their WLAN for.; that is, type of application and consequent traffic load. It simply assumes that the home user will have relatively low traffic; the SOHO user will have moderate traffic levels, whereas the medium to large organisations will have considerable/heavy traffic loads, mainly due to the sheer number of devices in operation. Further, it is assumed that medium-large organisations will have greater spending power in relation to securing their network, where the home user and SOHO users will not have as much revenue available for spending on security. Additionally, home users will be more inclined to purchase cheaper, low-end equipment as they are viewed as only wanting the service provided at the lowest cost possible, security is not high in their list of priorities when purchasing. This may be because they do not fully understand the implications of each security option or the threats which exist. The following recommendations are aimed at each specific group of user; beginning with the home user, progressing to the SOHO group and medium to large organisations.

Home User Security Recommendations

The home user is viewed as having low levels of traffic and a relatively low security rating due to the nature of data traversing their networks. The data may not be as sensitive as the data travelling over a SOHO or medium to large organisational network. However, this does not mean that it should not be secured. It may be that the home user is simply using their wireless devices to enable sharing of an Internet connection, but if this is unsecured it enables unknown third parties to also share the connection as well as the IP address. This may appear harmless but it depends on what the unknown third party is using the connection for. It could be that they are using it to access or distribute illegal material or to launch Internet-based attacks using the connection and IP address as a proxy which will hide their real identity. The following recommendations, if fully implemented, should be enough to secure the home user network from unauthorised and unknown third parties and from the attacks described in the previous chapter. Below is an overview of the security measures that should be followed:

- Change AP default settings; SSID and administrator password.
- Change the SSID regularly.
- Disable SSID broadcasting.
- Enable MAC address-based filtering.
- Enable WEP.

The home user is perceived as having relatively low levels of traffic, this therefore makes WEP a suitable, and strong, security measure for that group; and by ensuring that the WEP key is as long as possible (dictated by the equipment itself), WEP will deter most, if not all, potential attackers. The home user will consequently not need to change their WEP key too often, but based on the figures in chapter three, it is recommended that it should be changed on a regular basis. At least once a month, or more, depending on the user's own assessment of their traffic load. This will avoid an attacker being able to collect enough information to break the key. If the home user is making use of their network for downloads more than three hours per day, the key should be changed more often, perhaps once every fortnight. Because the home user would not be hugely attractive to a potential hacker, WEP would be a sufficiently strong method of protection. Traffic is typically intermittent during the day and night and an attacker would not wait around long enough to wait for enough traffic to obtain enough to break the key. After all, an attacker has not got much to gain by cracking a home network so it is unlikely that they would spend any great time and effort on this type of network.

SOHO Security Recommendations

The home office has a slightly elevated security status over the purely home user, their traffic load will also be higher than that of the home user and it is assumed that it will be less intermittent and perhaps somewhat steady traffic during normal office hours, depending on the type of business being operated. Eighty percent of the network usage is seen as being business related, with 20% being for leisure. The nature of traffic flowing over a home office network will be more sensitive than the home user's; the home office user should be aware that their business information may be open to eavesdroppers or attackers. This could in turn have a detrimental affect on the business through loss of confidentiality and integrity and through deletion or alteration of documents. In addition, attacks against the operation of the network will also affect the home office user's ability to access the network; these can range from intermittent network failure/degradation in performance, to prolonged DoS attacks.

The small office's network traffic will be 100% business related, but will typically only have traffic during normal office hours. It can have up to 20 wireless devices, all transmitting information on the airwaves. This consequently increases the amount of network traffic, hence the amount of information available to a would-be attacker. Even if WEP is enabled, the possibility of a hacker obtaining the information they require to enable them to break a WEP key is increased and the time taken to do so. Consequently, small offices need to implement something stronger than, or in addition to, WEP and the other basic methods to secure their network and their data. The options available to the small office are numerous, but again, the small office is more than likely to be inhibited by cost; this will subsequently narrow their choices slightly. With this in mind it is recommended that the small office should implement *all* the basic security measures outlined previously with respect to WEP, MAC address filtering, SSIDs, passwords and firewalls. They should also strive to buy hardware with as many built in security features as possible within their spending region; low-end devices are no good. In addition to this they should consider implementing some of the more advanced security options available. The Wi-Fi alliance has provided SOHO users with an alternative security solution aimed specifically at that group; known as Wi-Fi Protected access, version one, pre-shared key (WPA-PSK). It was derived from the upcoming 802.11i standard and addresses the vulnerabilities of WEP and adds user authentication. At this stage it is important to specify why this security option has not been recommended to the home office group. The measures already recommended, if implemented in full, should provide enough protection for the home office; it is also felt that WPA may prove difficult to understand, or perhaps too technical for the home office user, and may even be overkill. WPA addresses the weaknesses in WEP caused by the IVs, it ensures integrity through message integrity check (MIC or "Michael") and uses temporal key integrity protocol (TKIP) to enhance data encryption (Bowman, 2003).

WPA-PSK does not require the use of authentication servers, which makes it extremely suitable for use within the small office environment, where cost is an inhibitor and where the complexity of a server is uncalled for. WPA-PSK is easily introduced into an existing WLAN implementation; it is designed to be a software/firmware upgrade on devices that can support it—usually most Wi-Fi Certified products—thereby preserving investment in equipment. It is also purported to be easy to set up and run, which makes it attractive to more inexperienced users. To set up and use WPA a password, or master key, is entered on the AP and each client device; the password allows only devices with matching passwords to join the network, it is also used to start the TKIP encryption process (Grim, 2002). WPA-PSK strengthens encryption by automatically changing keys (dynamic re-keying) between devices after a specified period of time, or number of packets. These levels should be set in relation to network traffic levels; networks with lower traffic will have a higher threshold and vice versa (Bowman, 2003). It is recommended that the packet threshold is set to change every 500,000 packets regardless of key size. WPA-PSK is the strongest option available to this group of user; the process used to generate the encryption key is very rigorous and the re-keying is done very quickly. This prevents attackers from gathering enough data to break encryption. It significantly increases the effort required to allow passive monitoring and decryption of traffic, foiling Airsnort. TKIP uses the same encryption algorithm as WEP, (RC4), but its dynamic nature makes it considerably more difficult for attackers to crack.

Medium to Large Organisations Security Recommendations

This group is viewed as having the highest traffic load, security rating and spending power, because of this they also have the strongest security options available to them. The following recommendations are the strongest measure available today; due to this group's security status they *must* implement at least one of these options in addition to, or alternative to the basic recommendations made earlier. They are large enough to justify spending on security implementations; simply on the amount of traffic that can traverse their network and the number of users. These options are directed towards this group as they usually require dedicated IT expertise and support to administer and appropriate funding to maintain, which also makes them wholly inappropriate for any other group of user. Larger organisations with more complex WLANs with hundreds of users and APs require more sophisticated access control through incorporating RADIUS servers. It is not feasible for such large organisations to maintain huge lists of MAC addresses to implement filtering and the traffic load would be such that reliance on WEP would be futile. Indeed, on an 802.11b network operating at peek 11Mpbs speeds, a WEP key would need to be changed every few hours, this would become a logistical nightmare in a network of this size. Below is an overview of the security measures recommended for this group of user, followed by a brief description of each method.

WPA for the Enterprise

In the "enterprise," WPA is used in conjunction with an authentication server to provide centralised access control and management. It is scaleable and suitable for hundreds of users. Authentication can be carried out through a number of credentials, including digital certificates, unique usernames and passwords, smartcards, or other forms of secure ID (Peikari & Fogie, 2002). WPA for the enterprise makes use of the IEEE's 802.1x infrastructure to standardise the authentication process, originally intended for wired networks. Implementing WPA for the enterprise will involve, as mentioned, an authentication server, typically RADIUS-based severs, selecting the EAP type that will be supported on all stations, APs and authentication servers, and the software upgrade of client and AP devices to enable them to use WPA (Wi-FI Alliance, February 2003). There are typically four EAP methods in use today; EAP-MD5, EAP-Cisco Wireless (LEAP), EAP-TLS and EAP-TTLS, all of which are unfortunately incompatible with each other. It is important that organisations choose one EAP method and ensure it is applied to *all* equipment throughout the organisation, otherwise roaming between APs will be prohibited. WPA enterprise provides strong security through authentication, when a device requests access to a network, the AP demands a set of credentials, the information supplied is then passed, by the AP, to a RADIUS server for authentication and authorisation (Dismukes, 2002). In addition, RADIUS allows the existence of a centralised database of user profiles which allows certain network privileges for different users, and also the power to deny participation completely; this is a very powerful network management tool. However, because 802.1x primarily handles authentication, the data is still only as secure as its encryption makes it, therefore if WEP is used, organisations are still caught will all of its associated problems. It is recommended that TKIP at a minimum is employed for encryption, with a view to upgrading to AES in the future as part of WPA version 2, which will require new hardware. AES improves upon previous encryption methods by removing use of the RC4 algorithm and using an alternative called the Rijndael algorithm, plus longer keys of 192 and 256 in length, which makes it extremely strong. However, it requires a separate processor to avoid slowing down the network, which means that it will not be backward compatible, so a move to WPA version 2 could mean replacing all equipment in the network and is a decision that should not be taken lightly (Fleishmann, 2002).

Virtual Private Networks (VPNs)

VPNs were originally developed to enable remote clients to securely connect to servers/networks over the public Internet, but are equally useful within the wireless environment. This may be an expensive option, but it is an alternative if not implementing WPA/802.1x. Special VPN software must be purchased and installed on each communicating device, and depending on the number of devices, this could become a huge task in its own. If the number of devices does not run into a few hundred VPN is a feasible option. In addition network administrators are advised to define a VLAN[3] which consists of all APs on the network; then configure a firewall that allows only VPN traffic to access the VLAN. Together, the firewall, VLAN and VPN ensure that wireless users are authenticated and their traffic is encrypted. This requires the skills of a dedicated network administrator, which most medium to large organisations employ. VPNs make use of the IPSec (Internet protocol security) protocol suite. This is a set of authentication and encryption protocols developed by IETF (Internet engineering task force). It encapsulates a packet by wrapping another packet around it and then encrypting everything; this double-encryption forms a secure 'tunnel' across an otherwise un-secure network (McDonald, 2003). This means wireless clients can connect securely to the organisational network through a VPN gateway on the organisational network edge. The gateway can be set up to use PSK or digital certificates; additionally user authentication to the VPN gateway can occur using RADIUS. As mentioned, VPNs can prove expensive and scale poorly. If using digital certificates, these must be purchased and tracked; VPN terminators can also become bottlenecks, depending on the level of traffic, thereby degrading network performance. VPNs would work well with a few wireless users, but if the number of users is expected to be large, VPNs are not recommended. They are better utilised for a small section of users who need mobility, but also need to be part of the wired backbone. Using VPNs to secure wireless users is recommended if new users are being added to an already established VPN infrastructure, WPA/802.1x is recommended above the use of VPNs, but if WPA/802.1x is not utilised VPN is also acceptable.

Intrusion Detection Systems (IDS)

This is an option that can be applied in conjunction with, or in addition to any other security measure, but should not be applied on its own. It is recommended that medium to large organisations implement these systems to monitor their network traffic to discover attempts to hack or cause a DoS. Generally speaking, there are four categories of IDS—network intrusion detection systems (NIDSes), system integrity verifiers (SIVs), log file monitoring (LFM) and deception systems (honeypots). NIDSes, as the name suggests, detects attempts on the network. An example would be to watch for a large number of TCP connection requests to different ports. SIVs monitor system files in an attempt to discover when an intruder changes files, perhaps leaving behind a backdoor for later use. LFUs simply monitor log files (a file that lists actions that have occurred) and looks for patterns that would suggest an intruder is attacking (ISP-Planet). The sole purpose of a deception system is a system designed to be broken in order to lure an intruder way from more valuable systems to log and monitor their activities. Deception systems emulate the type of systems that hackers would normally target, like ftp servers, web servers, and so on. This option is an extravagant one and involves the setup of an entire, false, system, purely for deceptive purposes. Many companies may not want to incur the costs of such a system, thus the use of a deception system is recommended to those organisations who feel that their data is highly sensitive enough to merit this (Schoeneck, 2003). IDSes can be further subdivided into passive and reactive systems. Passive systems detect a potential security breach, log the information and signal an alert; reactive systems respond to suspicious activity by actively logging off a user and denying them further access. It is recommended that the medium to large organisations group should implement a reactive NIDS. NIDSes detect an attempt on the network before it becomes successful, whereas SIVs and LFMs are post-event, the damage may already have been done. As mentioned, the deception system option is as an extreme measure and should only be employed if the sensitivity of the data or company operations merits it. However, it must be noted that IDSes are not foolproof, which is why they are recommended as an additional layer of security. Some intrusion attacks can go un-noticed. IDSes should not be utilised where a high amount of traffic overloads the IDS sensor and intrusion traffic is missed. IDSes should also not be utilised where an NIDS needs to see the traffic on each switch segment because in switched networks there is no ideal location to connect an NIDS, and deploying NIDS on each segment is cost prohibitive in many environments, thereby leaving segments unprotected. If a switched network exists with many segments, perhaps an IDS should be avoided completely, or only implemented on a segment that provides access to the outside world, or on a segment that contains a system attractive to attackers, or on the segment where the wireless LAN meets the wired backbone.

Documented Security Policies and Procedures

Like any business function, it is important that policies and procedures for the use of WLANs are defined, mainly to protect the network, but also to protect its users. It is equally important that any policies or procedures are communicated effectively to staff; staff should be in no doubt about what they are/are not permitted to do. Clearly defined policies can protect a network from un-necessary security breaches as well as performance degradation. They are important for medium to large organisations due to the huge number of employees and devices, thus introducing an element of risk into the organisation. There is a need for centralised, management-backed, policies and procedures that are communicated to all staff. Due to its size, this group is at an increased risk of being exposed by a rogue AP; they are easy to install and provide the mobility that employees seek. Employees may think that installing a device which helps them better utilise their PC is harmless, when in reality, if they don't secure their device properly, or at all, it can become a huge security risk. It is issues like this which can be overcome by a defined and enforced security policy.

It is strongly recommended that the use of APs by employees, other than the network administration team, is completely prohibited. This should be strictly enforced as such devices can blow a huge hole in any carefully planned security measures. In addition, policies should be in place which forbid employees to alter the configuration of APs and wireless NICs, especially in relation to WEP, SSID broadcasts, and so forth. The AP hardware should be placed in a secure room where no one but the network administration team can gain access, this not only minimises un-necessary signal leakage, but means the hardware can be protected from reset to default by an unauthorised individual. Policies which limit transmissions to certain channels, at certain speeds and at certain times make it easier to identify an intruder operating on a different channel from the car park at a lower data rate after office hours (AirDefense, 2003). However, policies are useless unless a network is actively being monitored for breaches, this may be part of the network administrator's job depending on the size of the network. It is this person's responsibility to report any breaches or peculiar behaviour no matter how trivial it may appear.

Conclusion

The aim of this chapter was to investigate WLAN usage in one particular region and ascertain the level and amount of WEP systems in place. Based on the evidence presented here from the field research, there is an apparent and serious lack of security on WLAN devices. Even those users that have implemented WEP may not realise just how weak this protocol is or how their network could be affected, as demonstrated by the second layer of research. Recommendations however were made here for three groups of user. Home users should implement all the security measures their hardware offers them, to include WEP at the longest key length permitted. The home office section of the SOHO group should utilise all the built-in security measures and implement firewalls on all connected PCs and change their WEP key on a weekly basis. The small office section of the SOHO group should implement WPA-SPK; and the Medium to Large Organisations should implement one or more of either WPA Enterprise with a RADIUS server, VPN software, IDSs, and provide documented policies in relation to WLANs and their use.

References

AirDefense. (2003). *5 practical steps to secure your WLAN*. Retrieved January 28, 2004, from http://ssl.salesforce.com/servlet/servlet.EmailAttachmentDownload?q=00m0 000000005af00d0000000hiyd0050000005k8d5

AirSnort FAQ. (2003). *How the crack process works*. Retrieved October 25, 2003, from http://airsnort.shmoo.com/faq.html

Bowman, B. (2003, July 28). WPA wireless security for home networks. *Windows XP Expert Zone Community Column*. Retrieved from http://www.microsoft.com/windowsxp/using/networking/expert/bowman_03july28.mspx

Dismukes, T. (2003). "Azariah." *Wireless Security Blackpaper*. July 2002. Retrieved September 18, 2003, from http://arstechnica.com/paedia/w/wireless/security-1.html

Fleishmann, G. (2002, October 31). Good-bye WEP, hello WPA. *Wi-Fi Net News*. Retrieved from http://www.wifinews.com/archives/2002_10.html

Franklin, C. (2001). *A cracked spec.* Retrieved November 7, 2003, from http://www.inter-netweek.com/reviews01/rev031201-2.htm

Geier, J. (1999). *Wireless LANs, implementing interoperable networks.* MacMillan Network Architecture and Development Series, MacMillan Technical Publishing.

Griffith, E. (2002, June 3). Defending the WLAN air. *WiFi Planet News.* Retrieved from http://www.wi-fiplanet.com/news/article.php/1181601

Grim, C. (2002, November 23). WiFi's protected access wireless: The background. *News-Wireless.net.* Retrieved from http://www.newswireless.net/index.cfm/article/528

Harte, L., Kellog, S., Dreher, R., & Schaffinit, T. (2000). *The comprehensive guide to wireless technologies: Cellular, PCS, paging, SMR and satellite.* APDG Publishing.

iLabs, Wireless Security Team. (2002). *What's wrong with WEP?* Retrieved October 23, 2003, from http://www.nwfusion.com/research/2002/0909wepprimer.html

Karygiannis, T., & Owens, L. (2003). National Institute of Standards and Technology, Special Publication 800-48. Retrieved August 18, 2003, from http://csrc.nist.gov/publications/drafts/draft-sp800-48.pdf

McClure, S., Scambray, J., & Jurtz, G. (2003). *Hacking exposed: Network security secrets and solutions* (4th ed.). Osbourne McGraw-Hill.

PCQuest. (2003). *WEP security cracked.* Retrieved November 7, 2003, from http://www.pcquest.com/content/topstories/wireless/103081102.asp

Peikari, C., & Fogie, S. (2002). *Maximum wireless security.* Sams Publishers.

Poulsen, K. (2001). *War driving by the bay.* Retrieved October 23, 2003, from http://www.theregister.co.uk/content/archive/18285.html

Sikora, A. (2003). *Wireless personal and local area networks.* West Sussex: John Wiley & Sons.

Stubblefield, A., Ioannidis, J., & Rubin, A. (2001, August 21). Using the Fluhrer, Mantin, and Shamir attack to break WEP (ATT Labs Tech. Rep. No. TD4ZCPZZ, Revision 2).

Sutton, M. (2002). *Hacking the invisible network.* iDefense, iAlert White Paper. Retrieved August 18, 2003, from http://www.rootshell.be/~doxical/download/docs/misc/Idefense_Hacking_the_invisible_network_(wireless).pdf

Tourrilhes, J. (2000). *Wireless overview : The MAC level.* Retrieved October 10, 2003, from http://www.hpl.hp.com/personal/Jean_Tourrilhes/Linux/Linux.Wireless.mac.html

Tyrrell, K. (2003). *An overview of wireless security issues.* Retrieved October 19, 2003, from http://www.giac.org/practical/GSCE/Kevin_Tyrrell_GSEC.pdf

Ulanoff, L. (2003). Get free Wi-Fi, while its hot. *PC Magazine, Ziff Davies.*

Vines, R.D. (2002). *Wireless security essentials: Defending mobile systems from data piracy.* Indiana: Wiley.

Walker, J. (2000). *Unsafe at any key size: An analysis of the WEP encapsulation.* Retrieved October 23, 2003, from http://www.dis.org/wl/pdf/unsafe.pdf

Endnotes

1   A method that relies on sheer computing power to try all possibilities until the solution to a problem is found, usually refers to cracking passwords by trying every possible combination of a particular key space.

2   A *white hat* describes a hacker who identifies a security weakness in a computer system but, instead of taking malicious advantage of it, exposes the weakness in a way that will allow the system's owners to fix the breach before it can be taken advantage of by others.

3   VLAN stands for *virtual local area network*. Virtual LANs can only be specified on switch hardware allowing VLANs to be treated as a separate logical LANs.

Chapter XIII

A SEEP Protocol Design Using 3BC, ECC(F_2^m) and HECC Algorithm

Byung Kwan Lee, Kwandong University, Korea

Seung Hae Yang, Kwandong University, Korea

Tai-Chi Lee, Saginaw Valley State University, USA

Abstract

Unlike SET (secure electronic transaction) protocol. This chapter proposes a SEEP (highly secure electronic payment) protocol, which uses ECC (elliptic curve cryptosystem with F_2^m not F_p) (Koblitz, 1987; Miller, 1986; Harper, Menezes, & Vanstone, 1993), SHA (secure hash algorithm) and 3BC (block byte bit cipher) instead of RSA and DES. To improve the strength of encryption and the speed of processing, the public key and the private key of ECC and HECC (Hyper Elliptic Curve Cryptosystem) are used in 3BC (Cho, Shin, Lee, & Lee, 2002; Cho & Lee, 2002) algorithm, which generates session keys for the data encryption. In particular, when ECC and HECC are combined with 3BC, the strength of security is improved significantly. As the process of the digital envelope used in the existing SET protocol is removed by the 3BC algorithm in this chapter, the processing time is substantially reduced. In addition, the use of multiple signatures has some advantages of reducing the size of transmission data as an intermediate payment agent and avoiding the danger of eavesdropping of private keys.

Introduction

Today, electronic data exchange is part of our everyday life. The EC (electronic commerce) has been expanding rapidly in quantity and quality since it started on the Internet. The reason is that it can be done by increasing the reliability of EC with the new development of security technique. The SSL, a security socket layer, which is currently used in EC is being considered the only stable access to the Internet during the transportation, but it can hardly ensure the problem of information security. To some extent, the SET (secure electronic transaction) protocol based on electronic payment has improved message integrity, authentication, and non-repudiation. Such a protocol is related directly to cryptography for security and consists of an asymmetric key algorithm, RSA for authentication and non-repudiation, DES for the message confidentiality, Hash algorithm and SHA for message integrity. But the disadvantage of this protocol is that the speed of processing is slow because of long key size. From this standpoint, ECC (elliptic curve cryptosystem) technique is very important to Cryptography. This chapter proposes a SEEP (highly secure electronic payment) protocol, which uses ECC instead of RSA. To improve the strength of encryption and the speed of processing, the public key and the private key of ECC and HECC are used in the 3BC (block byte bit cipher) algorithm, which generates session keys for the data encryption. Therefore, the digital envelope used in the existing SET protocol can be removed by the 3BC algorithm, which makes SEEP protocol better than SET by simplifying the complexity of dual signature. Some basic concepts of encryption and decryption, ECC, and SET are introduced in a later section. 3BC algorithm and the structure of SEEP protocol are proposed and defined in a following section. The advantages of SEEP protocol vs. SET are discussed in the conclusion.

Basic Concepts

Encryption and Decryption Algorithm

As shown in Figure 1, the user A computes a new key $k_A(k_BP)$ by multiplying the user B's public key by the user A's private key k_A. The user A encodes the message by using this key and then transmits this cipher text to user B. After receiving this cipher text, The user B decodes with the key $k_B(k_AP)$, which is obtained by multiplying the user A's public key, k_AP by the user B's private key, k_B. Therefore, as $k_A(kBP) = k_B(k_AP)$, we may use these keys for the encryption and the decryption (Harper, Menezes, & Vanstone, 1993).

SET (Secure Electronic Transaction) Protocol

With digital signatures, encryption for message, and digital envelope, SET offers confidentiality, data integrity, authentication, and non-repudiation over an open network. But the public key cipher algorithm, which is used in digital signature and digital envelope of SET is slow in processing data. In general, SET uses SHA and RSA for a digital signature and

Figure 1. Concept of en/decryption of ECC

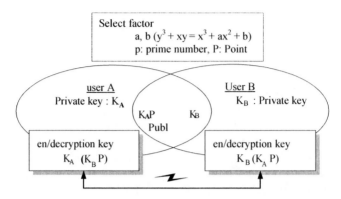

envelope, and DES for encryption and decryption of message. However, RSA has a possibility to be destroyed by factorization, and thus SET can be weak. The procedure of encoding for SET consists of digital signature, encryption for message, and digital envelope. The generation process of digital signature is that it produces a message digest from plaintext by one-way hash function and then signs it with sender's private key. The encryption of message means that original messages, digital signature, and certificate are encoded with session keys. The digital envelope is used for transmitting a session key and is decoded with receiver's public key later.

The decryption of SET is as follows. First of all, the receiver decodes the digital envelope with receiver's private key and then acquires the transmitted session key. Second, the cipher text is decoded and the message of plaintext, digital signature, and certificate are generated. Third, the receiver separately generates a message digest from the message by using a hash function. In addition, in the digital signature there is a message digest that is decoded with sender's public key. A receiver compares the former message digest with the latter and verifies the message integrity and the authentication.

Proposed SEEP (Security Enhanced Electronic Payment) Protocol

The existing SET uses RSA in digital signature and DES in message encryption. Our proposed SEEP protocol uses ECC instead of RSA. Because of this, the strength of encryption and the speed of processing are improved. Besides, in message encryption, SEEP utilizes the 3BC algorithm to generate session keys and cipher text. The encryption and decryption processes are shown in Figures 2 and 3 respectively. First, the public key and private key from ECC and HECC are put into 3BC algorithm and then generates the session keys. Second, the 3BC algorithm encodes the message by applying these keys. Since the receiver has his own private key, SEEP can remove the digital envelope, which enhances the speed for processing a message, and strengthens the security for information. In addition, if digital envelope is removed, SEEP doesn't need to transfer a session key to the other, which may

Figure 2. Encryption of SEEP

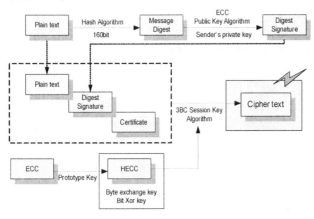

Figure 3. Decryption of SEEP

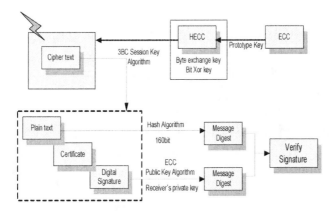

avoid the possibility of being intercepted and it can reduce part of the encryption procedure. Therefore, it simplifies a dual signature and decreases a communicative traffic over a network as compared with the existing SET.

F_2^m ECC (Elliptic Curve Cryptosystem)

Elliptic Curves over F_2^m[5] (Koblitz, 1987; Miller, 1986)

A non-supersingular elliptic curve $E(F_2^m)$ over F_2^m defined by the parameters a, b ε F_2^m, b ≠ 0, is the set of solutions (x, y), x ∈ F_2^m, y ∈ F_2^m, to the equation:

$$y^2 + xy = x^3 + ax^2 + b$$

together with an extra point 0, the point at infinity. The number of points in $E(F_2^m)$ is denoted by $\#E(F_2^m)$. It follows from the Hasse theorem that:

$$q + 1 - 2\sqrt{q} \le \#E(F_2^m) \le q + 1 + 2\sqrt{q},$$

where $q = 2^m$. Furthermore, $\#E(F_2^m)$ is even.

The set of points $E(F_2^m)$ is a group with respect to the following addition rules:

1. $0 + 0 = 0$.
2. $(x, y) + 0 = (x, y)$ for all $(x, y) \in E(F_2^m)$.
3. $(x, y) + (x, x + y) = 0$ for all $(x, y) \in E(F_2^m)$ (i.e., the inverse of the point (x, y) is the point $(x, x + y)$).
4.   Rule for adding two distinct points that are not inverses of each other:

     Let $(x_1, y_1) \in E(F_2^m)$ and $(x_2, y_2) \in E(F_2^m)$ be two points such that $x_1 \ne x_2$.
     Then $(x_1, y_1) + (x_2, y_2) = (x_3, y_3)$, where $x_3 = L + L + x_1 + x_2 + a$, $y_3 = L(x_1 + x_3) + x_3 + y_1$, and $L = (y_1 + y_2) / (x_1 + x_2)$.

5.   Rule for doubling a point:

     Let $(x_1, y_1) \in E(F_2^m)$ be a point with $x_1 \ne 0$. Then $2(x_1, y_1) = (x_3, y_3)$, where $x_3 = L^2 + L + a$, $y_3 = x_1^2 + (L + 1) x_3$, and $L = x_1 + y_1 / x_1$.

Figure 4. Encryption/decryption process of elliptic curve algorithm

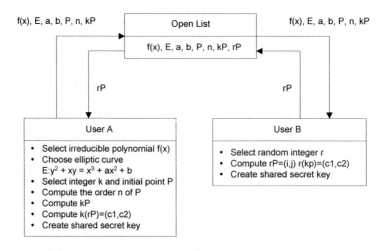

The group $E(F_2^m)$ is abelian, which means that $P + Q = Q + P$ for all points P and Q in $E(F_2^m)$.

The Encryption/Decryption Process of Elliptic Curve Algorithm

The encryption/decryption process of elliptic curve algorithm is as follows:

- **Step 1. User A:** When it is m=4, select the irreducible polynomial $f(x)=x^4+x+1$. Generator g=0010 of F_2^4, The vector values of F_2^4 is shown in Table 1 (IEEE P1363).
- **Step 2. User A:** Choose elliptic curve of the following form and vector values a, b.

E: $y^2+xy = x^3+ax^2+b$, $a,b \in F_2^m$

Find an initial point P on elliptic curve.

- **Step 3. User A:** Compute kP after selecting integer k.
- **Step 4-1. User A:** Register f(x), E, a, b, P and kP to the open list.
- **Step 4-2. User B:** After selecting random integer r as a secret key, register a public key rP of user B, f(x), E, a, b, and P in the open list.
- **Step 5. User B:** Compute $r(kP) = (c_1, c_2)$ using public key kP of user A in the open list.
- **Step 6. User B:** Encrypt message m by $r(kP) = (c_1, c_2)$ and send to user A.
- **Step 7. User A, B:** Change the result to integer and bit string to create shared secret key.

F_2^m HECC (Hyper Elliptic Curve Cryptosystem)

Hyper Elliptic Curves over F_2^m

A hyperelliptic curve C of genus $g(g \geq 1)$ over F is a nonsingular curve that is given by an equation of the following form:

C : $v^2 + h(u)v = f(u)$ (in F[u, v])

where $h(u) \in F[u]$ is a polynomial of degree $\leq g$, and $f(u) \in F[u]$ is a monic polynomial of degree 2g+1.

Table 1. Vector values of F_2^4

Vector values	α^3	α^2	α^1	α^0
$g^0=1$	0	0	0	1
$g^1=\alpha$	0	0	1	0
$g^2=\alpha^2$	0	1	0	0
$g^3=\alpha^3$	1	0	0	0
$g^4=\alpha+1$	0	0	1	1
$g^5=(\alpha+1)\alpha=\alpha^2+\alpha$	0	1	1	0
$g^6=(\alpha^2+\alpha)\alpha=\alpha^3+\alpha^2$	1	1	0	0
$g^7=(\alpha^3+\alpha^2)\,\alpha=\alpha^4+\alpha^3=\alpha^3+\alpha+1$	1	0	1	1
$g^8=(\alpha^3+\alpha+1)\alpha=\alpha^4+\alpha^2+\alpha=\alpha^2+1$	0	1	0	1
$g^9=(\alpha^2+1)\alpha=\alpha^3+\alpha$	1	0	1	0
$g^{10}=(\alpha^3+\alpha)\alpha=\alpha^4+\alpha^2=\alpha^2+\alpha+1$	0	1	1	1
$g^{11}=(\alpha^2+\alpha+1)\,\alpha=\alpha^3+\alpha^2+\alpha$	0	1	1	0
$g^{12}=(\alpha^3+\alpha^2+\alpha)\alpha=\alpha^4+\alpha^3+\alpha^2=\alpha^3+\alpha^2+\alpha+1$	1	1	1	1
$g^{13}=(\alpha^3+\alpha^2+\alpha+1)\alpha=\alpha^4+\alpha^3+\alpha^2+\alpha=\alpha^3+\alpha^2+1$	1	1	0	1
$g^{14}=(\alpha^3+\alpha^2+1)\alpha=\alpha^4+\alpha^3+\alpha=\alpha^3+1$	1	0	0	1
$g^{15}=(\alpha^3+1)=\alpha^4+\alpha=1$	0	0	0	1

In hyperelliptic cryptosystems, Jacobian's subg roup J(F) is used. The group J(F) can be viewed as the set of reduced divisors. Each element of J(F) has a unique representation as a reduced divisor div(a, b), where a, b $\in$ F[u], deg $_u$ a $\le$ g, deg $_u$ b < deg $_u$ a, and hence J(F) is in fact a finite abelian group.

Let D_1 = div(a_1,b_1) and D_2 = div(a_2,b_2) be two reduced divisors, both defined over $F_2{}^m$. Then the following algorithm finds a semi-reduced divisor D=div(a, b), such that D~D_1 + D_2

1.   Using Euclide's algorithm, find polynomials d_1, e_1, e_2 $\in$F[u] where d_1 = gcd(a_1,a_2) and d_1 = e_1a_1 + e_2a_2

2.   Using Euclide's algorithm, find polynomials d_1, f_1, $f_2$$\in$F[u] where d_2 = gcd(d_1,b_1 + b_2 + h) and d_1 = f_1d_1 + f_2(b_1 + b_2 + h)

3.   Let s_1 = f_1e_1, s_2 = f_1e_2, s_3 = f_2, so that d_2 = s_1a_1 + $s_2\,a_2$ + s_3(b_1 + b_2 + h)

4.   Set $a = \dfrac{a_1a_2}{d_2^2}$ and $b = \dfrac{s_1a_1b_2 + s_2a_2b_1 + s_3(b_1b_2 + f)}{d_2}(\bmod\, a)$

5.   Output(div(a, b))

The following algorithm shows the steps to reduce the semi-reduced divisor to an equivalent divisor.

i)   Set a′ = (f − bh − b²)/a and b′=(− h − b)mod a′

ii)   If deg $_u$ a′ > gthen set a←a′, b←b′ and go to step i.

iii)   Let c be the leading coefficient of a′, and set a′←c⁻¹a′

iv)   Output(div(a′, b′))

The Encryption/Decryption Process of Hyperelliptic Curve Algorithm

The encryption/decryption process of hyperelliptic curve algorithm is as follows:

The encryption/decryption process of hyperelliptic curve algorithm is equal to the process of elliptic curve algorithm.

Both ECC and HECC use the same irreducible polynomial. Therefore, the vector values of ECC are equal to the vector values of HECC. In this chapter, the result of ECC is used the initial point of HECC. But, it is converted to the result of ECC by a convert_key algorithm.

The following convert_key algorithm shows the steps to convert the result of ECC algorithm.

3BC (Block Byte Bit Cipher) Algorithm

In this chapter, the proposed 3BC algorithm (Cho, Shin, Lee, & Lee, 2002) consists of two parts, which are session key generation and data encryption. And the data encryption is divided into three phases, which are inputting plaintext into data blocks, byte-exchange between blocks, and bit-wise XOR operation between data and session key.

Session Key Generation

As we know that the value which is obtained by multiplying one's private key by the other's public key is the same as what is computed by multiplying one's public key to the other's private key. The feature of EC is known to be almost impossible to estimate a private and a public key. With this advantage and the homogeneity of the result of operations, the proposed 3BC algorithm uses a 64-bit session key to perform the encryption and decryption. Given the sender's private key $X = X_1 X_2, \ldots X_m$ and the receiver's public key, $Y = Y_1 Y_2, \ldots Y_n$, we concatenate X and Y to form a key N (i.e., $N = X_1 X_2, \ldots X_m Y_1 Y_2, \ldots Y_n$), and then compute the session keys as follows:

1.   If the length (number of digits) of X or Y exceeds four, then the extra digits on the left are truncated. And if the length of X or Y is less than four, then they are padded with 0's on the right. This creates a number $N' = X_1' X_2' X_3' X_4' Y_1' Y_2' Y_3' Y_4'$. Then a new number N'' is generated by taking the modulus of each digit in N' with 8.

2.   The first session key sk1 is computed by taking bit-wise OR operation on N'' with the reverse string of N''.

Figure 5. The encryption/decryption process of hyperelliptic curve algorithm

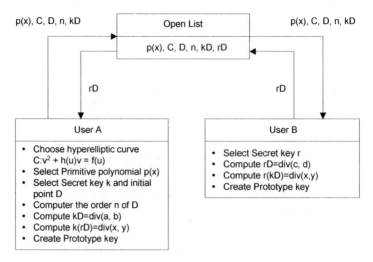

3.   The second session key sk2 is generated by taking a circular right shift of sk1 by one bit. And repeat this operation to generate all the subsequent session keys needed until the encryption is completed

Encryption

The procedure of data encryption is divided into three parts, inputting plaintext into data block, byte-exchange between blocks, and bit-wise XOR operation between data and session key.

Figure 6. The algorithm of convert_key

```
Convert_key(ecc_key(x,y)){
    If(Ispoint(ecc_key(x,y)) == FLASE){
      D(u,                    v) =
search_nearlist_point(ecc_key(x,y));
    }
    a = convert_div(u);
    b = convert_div(v);
    Return(div(a, b));
}
```

Figure 7. Exchange bytes at (row, col) for a selected pair of blocks

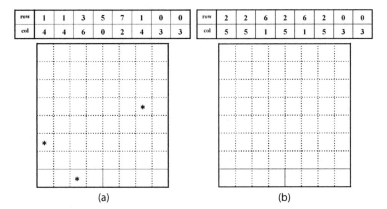

(a)

(b)

Input Plaintext into Data Block

The block size is defined as 64 bytes. A block consists of 56 bytes for input data, 4 bytes for the data block number, and 4 bytes for the byte-exchange block number (1 or 2, see Figure 7). During the encryption, input data stream are blocked by 56 bytes. If the entire input data is less than 56 bytes, the remaining data area in the block is padded with each byte by a random character. Also, in the case where the total number of data blocks filled is odd, then additional block(s) will be added to make it even, and each of those will be filled with each byte by a random character as well. Also, a data block number in sequence) is assigned and followed by a byte-exchange block number, which is either 1 or 2.

Byte-Exchange between Blocks

After inputting the data into the blocks, we begin the encryption by starting with the first data block and select a block, which has the same byte-exchange block number for the byte exchange. In order to determine which byte in a block should be exchanged, we compute its row-column position as follows (Cho & Lee, 2002):

i)   For the two blocks whose block exchange number, n = 1, we compute the following:

byte-exchange row = $(N_i *n) \bmod 8$ (i = 1,2 ...,8)

byte-exchange col = $N_i *n) + 3) \bmod 8$ (i = 1,2 ...,8),

Figure 8. Structure of block

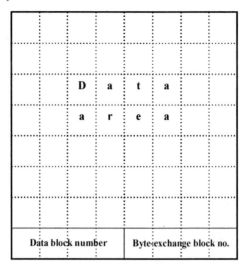

where N_i is a digit in N''. These generate 8 byte-exchange positions. Then for $n = 1$, we only select the non-repeating byte position (row, col) for the byte-exchange between two blocks whose block exchange numbers are equal to 1. Similarly, we repeat the procedure for $n = 2$. The following example illustrate the process of byte-exchange operation.

Example: Given the values of a sender's public key 21135 and a receiver's private key 790, we compute row and col for byte-exchange between as follows:

For $n = 1$, it follows from 3.2.1 that $N'' = 11357900$ (after truncation, padding and concatenation), and row $= ((1,1,3,5,7,9,0,0)*1) \bmod 8 = (1,1,3,5,7,1,0,0)$ and col $= (((1,1,3,5,7,9,0,0)*1 \bmod 8) + 3) \bmod 8 = (4,4,6,0,2,4,3,3)$

This results 8 byte-exchange positions, (1,4), (1,4), (3,6), (5,0), (7,2), (1,4), (0,3) and (0,3). However only the three bytes at (3,6), (5,0), and (7,2) will be selected for byte-exchange between two blocks (see Figure 8 (a)).

For $n = 2$, we have:

row $= ((1,1,3,5,7,1,0,0)* 2) \bmod 8 = (2,2,6,2,6,2,0,0)$ and
col $= (((1,1,3,5,7,1,0,0 * 2) \bmod 8) + 3) \bmod 8 = (5,5,1,5,1,5,3,3)$,

which results 8 byte-exchange positions, (2,5), (2,5), (6,1), (2,5), (6,1), (2,5), (0,3) and (0,3). Since all byte positions are repeating, there will be no byte-exchanges between two blocks as shown in Figure 8 (b).

Bit-Wise XOR between Data and Session Key

After the byte-exchange is done, the encryption proceeds with a bit-wise XOR operation on the first 8 byte data with the session sk1 and repeats the operation on every eight bytes of the remaining data with the subsequent session keys until the data block is finished. Note that the process of byte-exchange hides the meaning of 56 byte data, and the exchange of the data block number hides the order of data block, which needs to be assembled later on. In addition, the bit-wise XOR operation transforms a character into a meaningless one, which adds another level of confusion to the attackers. Figure 9 shows an encryption procedure using session keys as described in a later section deriving from a private key and a public key.

Decryption

Decryption procedure is given as follows. First, a receiver generates a byte exchange block key sk1 and a bit-wise XOR key sk2 by using the sender's public key and the receiver's private key. Second, the receiver decrypts it in the reverse of encryption process with a block in the input data receiving sequence. The receiver does bit-wise XOR operation bit by bit, and then, a receiver decodes cipher text by using a byte-exchange block key sk1 and moves the exchanged bytes back to their original positions. We reconstruct data blocks in sequence by using the decoded data block number.

Multiple Signature

In the proposed SEEP protocol, the multiple signature is used instead of Dual Signature of existing SET protocol.

1. User A generates message digests of OI (order information) and PI (payment information) separately by using hash algorithm, concatenates these two message digests; produces MD_BMD_C; and hash it to generates MD (message digest). Then the user A encrypts this MD by using an encryption key, which is obtained by multiplying the private key of user A to the public key of the receiver. The PI to be transmitted to user C is encrypted by using 3BC algorithm. The encrypted PI is named CPI.

2. User B generates message digest MD_B' with the transmitted OI from user A. After having substituted MD_B' for the MD_B of MD_BMD_C, the message digest MD is generated by using hash algorithm. User B decrypts a transmitted DS_B, and extracts MD from it. User B compares this with MD generated by user B, certificates user A and confirms the integrity of message. Finally, user B transmits the rest of data, MD_BMD_C, CPI, DS_C to user C.

Figure 9. The bit-wise XOR on rows with session keys

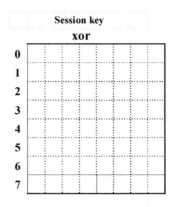

Session keys	xor	Rows in a block
0 0 1 0 1 1 1 1	xor 0	
0 1 0 1 1 1 1 0	xor 1	
1 0 1 1 1 1 0 0	xor 2	
0 1 1 1 1 0 0 1	xor 3	
1 1 1 1 0 0 1 0	xor 4	
1 1 1 0 0 1 0 1	xor 5	
1 1 0 0 1 0 1 1	xor 6	
1 0 0 1 0 1 1 1	xor 7	

Table 2. Example of key to be distributed for SEEP

User	A		B		C	
Open	a, b, P, p					
Private key	K1		K2		K3	
Public key	(K1P)		(K2P)		(K3P)	
Encrypt/ Decrypt key	B	K1(K2P)	A	K2(K1P)	A	K3(K1P)
	C	K1(K3P)	C	K2(K3P)	B	K3(K2P)

3.   User C decrypts the CPI transmitted from user B, extracts PI, and generates message digest (MD$_C$) from this by using hash algorithm; substitutes this for MD$_B$ of MD$_B$MD$_C$ transmitted from user B, and produces message digest (MD) by using Hash algorithm. Then the user C decrypts the DS$_C$ transmitted from user B and extracts message digest (MD). Again, the user C compares this with the MD extracted by user C, verifies the certificate from the user A, and confirms the integrity of the message. Finally, the user C returns an authentication to the user B.

Performance Evaluation

The Comparison of ECC and HECC with RSA

In this chapter, the proposed SEEP protocol uses ECC instead of RSA. In comparison with RSA, the results of the encryption and decryption times are shown in Figure 13 and 14 respectively, which indicate that encryption and decryption time of ECC are much less than those of RSA.

3BC and DES

Figure 15 and 16 show the mean value of encryption time of 3BC and DES by executing every number of block about message twenty times. According to Figure 15, we can conclude that 3BC is faster than the existing DES in encryption time. In addition, the security of 3BC is enhanced by using Byte-exchange and Bit-wise XOR Therefore, the strength of the encryption is improved and more time is saved for encryption and decryption than DES.

Conclusion

The proposed SEEP protocol employees ECC and the 3BC algorithm instead of RSA and DES as used in the existing SET. As a result, it speeds up the encryption process by reducing communication traffic for transmission, simplifying dual signature. In addition, the security for information is strengthened which prevents session keys from being intercepted from attackers on the network. The proposed 3BC, which uses byte-exchange and the bit operation increases data encryption speed. Even though cipher text is intercepted during transmission over the network. Because during the encryption process, the 3BC algorithm performs byte exchange between blocks, and then the plaintext is encoded through bit-wise XOR operation, it rarely has a possibility for cipher text to be decoded and has no problem to preserve a private key.

Figure 10. Encryption of user A

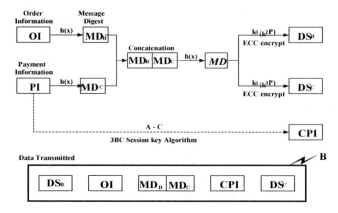

Figure 11. Decryption of user B and data transmitted to C

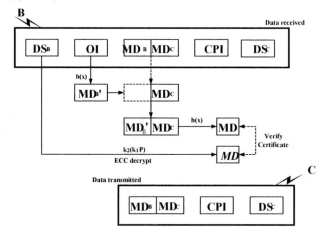

Figure 12. Decryption of user C

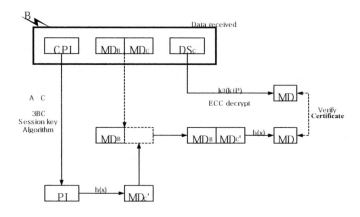

Figure 13. A comparison for encryption time (unit : μs)

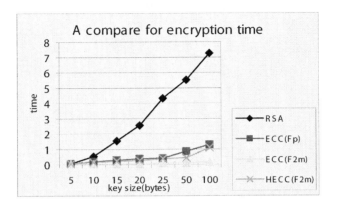

Figure 14. A comparison for decryption time (unit : μs)

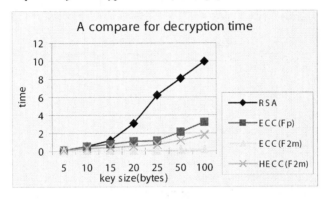

Figure 15. A comparison for encryption time (unit : μs)

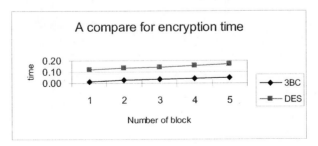

Figure 16. A comparison for decryption time (unit : μs)

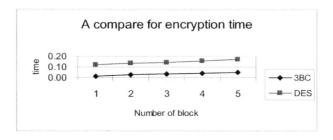

Table 3. Decryption of SEEP protocol

protocol	Digital signature	Encryption for message	Digital envelope
SET	RSA	DES	Use
ECSET	ECC	DES	Use
SEEP	ECC	3BC	Unnecessary

Moreover, the proposed SEEP protocol has a simple structure, which can improve the performance with the length of session key, byte-exchange algorithm, bit operation algorithm, and so on. From the standpoint of the supply for key, the certificate authority (CA) has only to certify any elliptic curve and any prime number for modulo operation, the anonymity and security for information can be guaranteed over communication network. (see Table 3.)

Note

This research was supported by the program for the Training of Graduate Students in Regional Innovation, which was conducted by the Ministry of Commerce, Industry and Energy of the Korean Government.

References

Cho, I. S., & Lee, B. K. (2002). ASEP (advanced secure electronic payment) protocol design, In *Proceedings of International Conference of Information System* (pp. 366-372).

Cho, I. S., Shin, D. W., Lee, T. C., & Lee, B. K. (2002). SSEP (simple secure electronic payment) protocol design. *Journal of Electronic and Computer Science, 4*(1), 81-88.

Ecommercenet. (n.d.). Retrieved from http://www.ezyhealthmie.com/Service/Editorial/set. htm

Harper, G., Menezes, A., & Vanstone, S. (1993). Public-key cryptosystem with very small key lengths. In *Advances in Cryptology-Proceedings of Eurocrypt '92* (LNCS 658, pp. 163-173). Springer-Verlag.

IEEE P1363. (1997, February 6). *Working draft, Appendices* (p. 8).

Koblitz, N. (1987). Elliptic curve cryptosystems. *Math. Comp., 48.* 203-209.

Miller, V.S. (1986). Use of elliptic curve in cryptography. In *Advances in cryptology, Proceedings of Crypto '85* (LNCS 218, pp. 417-426). Springer-Verlag.

Chapter XIV

Fighting the Problem of Unsolicited E-Mail Using a Hashcash Proof-of-Work Approach

Kevin Curran, University of Ulster at Magee, UK

John Honan, University of Ulster at Magee, UK

Abstract

This chapter investigates the problem of e-mail spam, and identifies methods to minimise the volumes. The analysis focuses on the hashcash proof-of-work approach, and investigates the feasibility of a hashcash-based solution. A potential problem with proof-of-work is that disparity across different powered computers may result in some unfortunate users spending a disproportionately long time calculating a stamp. An experiment is carried out to time how long it takes to calculate stamps across a variety of processor speeds. It is concluded from the analysis of the results that due to this problem of egalitarianism, hashcash (or CPU-bound proof-of-work in general) is not a suitable approach as a stand-alone anti-spam solution. It appears that a hybrid anti-spam system in conjunction with a legal and policy framework is the best approach.

Introduction

As a communications medium, e-mail has become very useful and practically universal. However, the usefulness of e-mail and its potential for future growth are jeopardized by the rising tide of unwanted e-mail, both spam and viruses. This threatens to wipe out the advantages and benefits of e-mail. Existing anti-spam measures are not effective against eliminating spam. One problem is that they focus on filtering spam at the recipient end, and do not deter the spammer from sending it in the first place. Current industry proposals present new approaches to anti-spam, including a technical method called "proof-of-work," based on the sender's CPU expending a certain amount of processing power to generate a virtual stamp which is attached to outgoing e-mail. This approach was first proposed by Dwork and Naor (1992) in their seminal paper "Pricing via Processing or Combating Junk Mail."

Proof-of-work is fundamentally different to existing anti-spam methods as it focuses on impacting the spammer's profitability by slowing down their e-mail transmission rate, and therefore deterring them from sending spam in the first place. Adam Back developed Dwork's proposal into a working implementation of proof-of-work based on the SHA-1 algorithm entitled "hashcash" (Back, 1997). Hashcash is currently in the beta test stage of development (Back, 2002), although the code is freely available it has not yet been deployed or accepted by a wider audience. An issue with hashcash is that of disparity of performance across users computers; while calculating stamps may impact a spammers profitability, it may also impact certain users ability to effectively send e-mail. Therefore hashcash may not be a viable universal approach to anti-spam.

How Spammers Operate

This chapter examines how spammers operate. It describes how spammers are able to exploit flaws in simple mail transport protocol (SMTP) to send spam. Spammer profitability, the main reason behind spamming, is discussed. Finally the requirements for an effective anti-spam solution are outlined.

Weaknesses in SMTP

SMTP is the main protocol that e-mail servers use to send and receive e-mail. It was designed and implemented early in the development of the Internet, at a time when spam was unheard of. SMTP has not changed for decades, and the simplicity and openness of the protocol exposes certain weaknesses which are now being exploited by spammers. A major flaw in current e-mail standards (most notably SMTP) is the lack of any technical requirement that ensures the reliable identification of the sender of messages. A message's domain of origin can easily be faked, or "spoofed." Spoofing (Templeton & Levitt, 2003) is a technique often used by spammers to make them harder to trace. Trojan viruses embedded in e-mail messages also employ spoofing techniques to ensure the source of the message is more difficult to locate (Ishibashi, Yamai, Abe, & Matsuura, 2001). Spam filters and virus scanners can only eliminate a certain amount of spam and also risk catching legitimate e-mails. As the SoBig virus (Levy, 2003) has demonstrated, virus scanners themselves actually add to the e-mail traffic through notification and bounceback messages. SMTP is flawed in that it allows these e-mail headers to be faked, and does not allow for the sender to be authenticated as the "real" sender of the message. If this problem can be solved, it will result in a reduction in spam e-mail messages, more security for existing e-mails, and allow e-mail viruses to be tracked down and stopped more effectively (Schwartz & Garfinkel, 1998). This approach is known as "trusted e-mail." Spammers exploit SMTP through a number of flaws in the protocol:

- There is no verification of identify, the SMTP server accepts who you say you are without question.

- There are no consequences for dishonest addressing ("From" line can be anything you want).

- Content filtering requires delivery (the e-mail has to be received by the server before it can be filtered).

- There is nothing on which to base delivery routing options (no generic flags in the header or elsewhere to allow an e-mail to be flagged as an advertisement, adult content, newsletter, or otherwise).

- There are no consequences for dishonest content (where the actual message contents do not match the subject line).

SMTP allows "untrusted" communications to take place (Tserefos, Smythe, Stergiou, & Cvertkovic, 1997). There is no requirement to prove you are who you say you are when an SMTP communication is instigated. SMTP is also very effective at sending e-mail as quickly as possible to its destination, meaning the spammer is only slowed down by the speed of his connection to the internet. These problems offer the spammer two main advantages which allow them to continue spamming unhindered; anonymity and volume of spam (Simpson, 2002).

Remaining Anonymous

Apart from the obvious methods of supplying incorrect information in the e-mail header, many spammers go to great lengths to remain anonymous. Anonymity is important to a spammer, because if they can be tracked down to an ISP they risk having their e-mail servers shut down or their web-hosting account terminated. In light of the new "Can-Spam" anti-spam legislation, spammers are even more determined to remain unaccountable. One additional technique used by spammers is exploitation of open e-mail relays (Cerf, 2005). These are SMTP servers that are incorrectly configured and which allow e-mail to be forwarded to addresses outside of the server's domain. On inspecting the e-mail headers, it appears as if the relay server is the source of the e-mail (Hastings & McLean, 1996). In order to trace the spammer, the owner of the open relay needs to be made aware of the activity. However, some sites are either reluctant to act or willingly abet spammers. Furthermore, even when spammers are identified and an ISP removes their account, they will often open a new one immediately and carry on their activities. Many system administrators are aware of techniques that spammers use and have configured e-mail servers correctly and securely. However, spammers have discovered the capability of using common web mail form handling software as open relays. Many websites provide form applications such as mailto and the FormMail perl scripts to allow users to construct forms, the input to which can be forwarded to a specified e-mail address for collecting information. Spammers write software which exploits security holes in FormMail scripts to enable them to forward e-mail to an address they specify. This results in the spam appearing to originate from the website of the FormMail software, a most undesirable outcome (Simpson, 2002). Spammers e-mail in bulk using automatic e-mail-sending programs. They must first obtain e-mail addresses. Sources for e-mail addresses include (Pfleeger & Bloom, 2005):

- Scavenging for them on Web sites and bulletin boards (using software called robots, spiders, or spam-bots),
- Guessing (using a dictionary attack—pairing randomly generated usernames with known domain names), and
- Purchasing lists of names from brokers (which can contain millions of addresses).

Spammers ensure their spam is not blocked by spam-filtering software by making the spam look like legitimate e-mail, by avoiding excessive use of HTML or exclamation marks, or by misspelling commonly used spam phrases and words (Goodman & Rounthwaite, 2004).

Why Spammers Send Spam

Currently a spammer is only limited by the speed of their uplink and their available hardware as to how many spam messages they can send per day. Spammers are usually specialists in their field. They are employed on a cost per e-mail or sometimes a response commission basis (Boutin, 2004). In order to make it unprofitable for the spammers to stay in business, it is necessary to reduce the amount of spam they send, or make it costly to send each message. It should be possible based on existing knowledge about spammer's business models to calculate how much the rate of spamming needs to be slowed down (this will be calculated in a later section). If the rate of spam transmission can be slowed below a certain number of e-mails transmitted per day, some calculations against expected response rate and profitability should allow the spammers "break-even" point to be determined, in other words, how much they need to be slowed down in order for their activity to become unprofitable.

Requirements of an Anti-Spam Solution

Block All Spam

Ideally, the system should block all spam. In practice this may not be achievable, as there may always be a small quantity of spam that bypasses whatever system is in place. The number of messages getting through should be perhaps one in 1,000. If a person is sent 200 spam e-mails a day, then if one spam gets through to their in-box per five-day working week, this equates to 0.1%, which should be acceptable to most e-mail users.

No False Positives

The system should not block legitimate e-mail. Not receiving e-mail you are expecting, or important e-mail getting blocked by a spam filter is considered worse by many people then receiving large quantities of spam (Deepak & Parameswaran, 2005). It is important therefore that any anti-spam system ensures that 100% of legitimate e-mail gets through (Damiani, De Capitani di Vimercati, Paraboschi, & Samarati, 2004).

Transparent to the User

The system should block spam with little or no user interaction. The spam blocking ideally should happen before the e-mail even reaches the client computer. Any filtering that happens on the client computer means the spam has to be downloaded, which results in additional network traffic for the user, and possibly a noticeable delay while the spam is filtered. The system should ideally exist on the e-mail server itself, not on the client computer. The user should not be aware of any delays in either sending or receiving and filtering e-mail. Users may be tolerant of certain performance issues if they know it is preventing spam reaching their inbox, but they will not be so accepting if this starts affecting their normal day-to-day operation of their PC to send and receive e-mails (Bass & Watt, 1997).

Can be Implemented Universally

Any anti-spam solution should have the ability to be availed of by all e-mail users, regardless of device or method of accessing the internet.

Minimises Network Spam Volume

If spam is filtered at the recipient end, this does not decrease the volume of spam on the internet. If the spam can be stopped at the sender end, or by deterring/preventing the spammer from sending it in the first place, it has the added advantage of minimising spam volumes.

Existing Anti-Spam Methods

Most anti-spam methods currently in use are based on some type of filtering at the recipient end. New proposals attempt to take a different approach to stopping spam, by deterring the spammer from sending the e-mail in the first place; either through impacting their profitability or some other policy/legal/framework approach. This chapter will look at the existing and proposed anti-spam methods in more detail. Filman (2003) identifies three major categories for anti-spam solutions: social evolution, political evolution, and technical evolution.

Figure 1 shows these three categories, with expanded sub-categories branching out. The "technical" category is the one which has attracted the most research and development work in the past few years. This category warrants a more detailed break-down as shown in Figure 2.

An important difference between the filtering methods and stamp (proof-of-work) methods is in the reduction of spam volumes on the network. In most filtering methods, the spammer sends massive volumes of e-mail, which then must be filtered at the recipient end. The recipient's hardware (or their ISP's servers) is where the filtering processes happen. The analysis of existing filter-based approaches to anti-spam show that although they are having an impact on how much spam is reaching in-boxes, they are not impacting the volume of spam being sent. In fact, this continues to increase. With a proof-of-work approach, the e-mail is stamped (i.e., the work is done) at the senders end, before the e-mail is sent. This should result in reduced spam volumes. With existing filtering solutions based at the recipient end, the spammer is not restricted in any way, and will continue to transmit large volumes of spam. Proof of work shifts the burden to the sender. By slowing down the rate of sending spam at the senders end, this lowers overall spam volumes, and leaves the recipient with a very simple stamp validation to perform. All the processing happens with the sender. The technical methods listed in Figure 2 are now explained in more detail (Graham, 2003). We also examine the weaknesses of each method.

Social

Spinello (1999) identifies the ethical implications of sending spam. Spam is different from normal junk mail in that it shifts the burden of cost to the recipient. Social evolution depends

Figure 1. Expanded view of Filman (2003) categories

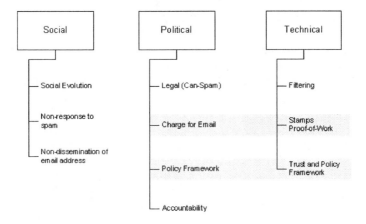

Figure 2. Technical approaches to anti-spam

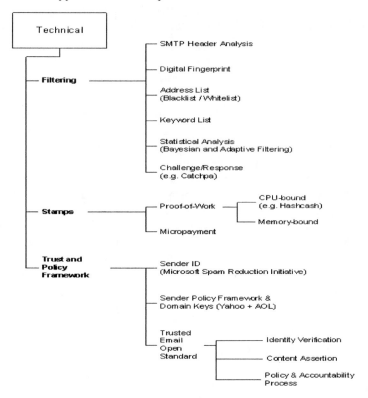

on the internet community as a whole to assume the sense of shared responsibility (Spinello, 1999) for this communications medium and recognise that sending spam is morally and ethically wrong. Holmes (2005) also highlights the importance of understanding the underlying social problems associated with spam; technology alone will not solve the problem. Unfortunately, for as long as spammers remain anonymous, and continue to make money out of sending spam, then social evolution can not be depended on to slow down spam. It only requires a tiny number of respondents to spam to make it worthwhile for spammers (Cerf, 2005). If users of e-mail do not respond to spam, and reduce the spammers response rate to 0%, then it will no longer be profitable for the spammer. However, to educate every e-mail user in the world about not responding to spam is a formidable task. If the spammers know they might still reach a few gullible people and generate some responses, they will just increase their sending volumes and thus clog the network even more.

Political

Description: In 2003 the U.S. Senate passed into law the "Can Spam" act as an attempt to cut down spam (Baker & Kamp, 2003). This is potentially a very effective deterrent against spammers. If a spammer thinks they are going to get taken to court and possibly fined, they might think twice about their activities. However, a loophole in spam laws is usually in the exact definition of "spam." Most spam laws allow the sending of unsolicited e-mail to recipients who have a prior relationship with the sender. This is reasonable, but it must be defined carefully what a prior relationship consists of. There is a type of spammer ("permission-based e-mail marketers") who obtain e-mail addresses by buying them from websites with unethical privacy policies. By calling the site they bought your e-mail address from a "partner" or "affiliate," the spammers can claim that they too have a prior relationship with you, and are therefore exempt from spam laws. In November 2004, (Levine, 2004) the USA held its first criminal trial concerning spam in Leesburg, Virginia with a conviction of Jeremy Jaynes. The case was brought under Virginia's state anti-spam law, not the weaker Federal Can-Spam act. Virginia's law makes it a crime to send unsolicited bulk mail using forgery, so the Commonwealth had to show first that Jaynes sent lots of unsolicited mail and second that it was sent using forgery. While most of society welcomes rulings like in Virginia, it must be noted that spammers are often based in different countries, which have different internet laws. Applying a law on an international basis, or prosecuting spammers in other countries is full of difficulties (Goodman & Heckerman, 2004; Holmes, 2005).

Technical

SMTP Header Analysis

The e-mail header provides some clues which indicate if the received message is a spam. For example, an IP which does not match the domain name indicates that the header may be forged. A forged header is a good indication that an e-mail is spam. Other clues in the header might include; use of distribution list, and the presence of error lines (Pelletier, Almhana, & Choulakian, 2004).

Digital Fingerprint

This method compares incoming e-mails against a signature database of known spam e-mails. The system calculates a checksum signature of an incoming spam message, and adds it to the database. Any incoming e-mails are then compared to this database to see if they are spam. This is an accurate way of matching spam. It can achieve very low "false positives" since only definite spam is matched based on the hash signature of its contents. But in order to be detected as spam, the message will have to exist in the database of pre-sent spam messages first. If the spam is new, it may not exist in the database yet, and therefore won't get blocked (Graham, 2003).

Address List

An IP blacklist is a list of the IP addresses of suspected spammers' mail servers, or relay servers (unsecured servers which allow spammers to forward e-mail). These lists are maintained by volunteer groups and anti-spam organisations. ISPs can then subscribe to these lists and refuse to accept e-mail from any listed IP addresses (Jung & Sit, 2004). This is a very precise method of blocking potential spam. Unfortunately, these blacklists can never hope to list every single IP address that spammers use. Also, they often end up listing legitimate IP addresses, or blacklisting an entire domain (1,000 ordinary users could get blacklisted for the actions of one spammer). The source IP is often spoofed by the spammer, which means they can bypass the blacklist.

Keyword List

Until Bayesian filtering was introduced, this was probably the most flexible method to help identify spam. Rule-based filters look for patterns that indicate spam: specific words and phrases, lots of uppercase and exclamation points, malformed headers, dates in the future or the past, and so on. This is how nearly all spam filters worked until 2002 (Graham, 2003). Again, this method is very easy for the spammer to bypass. The clever spammer even runs their spam through keyword-based filters before sending it to ensure it doesn't trigger the spam alert. Many spammers have now learnt how to make their e-mail not look like spam to the filters, and use techniques to ensure it is at least opened by the recipient when it reaches their inbox. (e.g., making the "From" look like a real persons name, and making the "Subject" something like "Hi" or "Long time no see"). This method is often used in conjunction with Bayesian filtering.

Statistical Analysis

This method uses a statistical analysis technique (typically a Bayesian approach) to analyze the words contained in each received e-mail. It uses predefined lookup tables to determine the probability that an e-mail is spam. For example, the word "Viagra" would have a high weighting, since it commonly appears in spam. Bayesian filtering is a relatively new approach to spam prevention. This approach seems to trigger less false positives than other types of filtering, as it is self-training based on spam it receives. In some cases the user can update the filter if it misclassifies an e-mail, thus improving the detection accuracy (Graham, 2003). Spammers often bypass these types of filters by making the spam look less spammy; using less spam-related words (often making the e-mail read like a personal e-mail from a friend), or putting random non-spam words at the end of the message to cause the Bayesian calculation to misclassify them as non-spam. Another technique spammers use is to misspell spam-related words.

Challenge/Response

When you get an e-mail from someone you haven't had e-mail from before, a challenge-response filter sends an e-mail back to them, telling them they must go to a web page and fill out a form before the e-mail is delivered. Once the sender has verified themselves, they get added to a senders whitelist to ensure any future e-mails get through without requiring verification (Gburzynski & Maitan, 2004). This method ensures you only receive e-mail from people who really want to correspond with you. The chances are that a spammer is not going to spend the time filling out the web form. However, this can be quite inconvenient for the sender, as they have to remember to fill in the form before the recipient gets the e-mail. In some cases the sender might not bother, and this method will always result in e-mail being delayed. This approach has not been widely adopted.

Stamps

Spam has low response rates (on the order of 15 per million) but spammers make up for it with high volumes, sending millions of e-mails per day (Schwartz & Garfinkel, 1998). If you could slow down the rate at which they send e-mail, you could put them out of business. One way to do this would be to make any computer used to send e-mail perform an easily verifiable time-consuming computation before you would accept that e-mail. Whatever these computations are, they should be within acceptable, controllable levels of complexity, because legitimate corporate e-mail servers have to be able to send high volumes of e-mail. And corporate e-mail servers would be running on standard hardware. Many computations can be made hundreds or thousands of times faster by custom hardware. This is the first approach that directly attacks the spammers' profitability model. Instead of trying to block or filter spam that has already been sent it makes it more costly for the spammer to send each message. It also helps reduce false positives caused by other types of spam filtering. It is likely that if an e-mail has a "proof of work" stamp, then it has been sent by a genuine sender, and can bypass the standard Bayesian filters. For this idea to work, you'd need to figure out a kind of computation that couldn't easily be speeded up by custom hardware. Even with a suitable computation, this idea would require new e-mail protocols. Any new protocol has a problem: no one is inclined to adopt it till everyone else does. As a result, it is practically impossible to get a new protocol adopted for anything. How are you going to get system administrators who don't even bother to install patches for years-old security holes to switch to a new e-mail protocol?

Trust and Policy Framework

The approaches outlined above take a "technology only" approach to the spam problem. What is required is an approach which encompasses technology with a policy-based solution. Any approach also needs support from the major ISPs (such as Yahoo, Hotmail, and AOL), and should be aligned with existing anti-spam laws. There are a number of industry proposals, most of which encompass hybrid multi-layer spam blocking/filtering technologies with trust-based systems and often cover the areas of policy as well. Microsoft's proposal covers a number of areas, but the main focus is on a system called Caller ID (Microsoft, 2004). Microsoft and the Internet Engineering Task Force have proposed changes to the way SMTP verifies the sender of an e-mail by looking up the source via DNS. This involves modifications of DNS standards (a central part of the internet itself). Caller ID allows Internet domain owners to publish the Internet protocol (IP) address of their outgoing e-mail servers in an Extensible Markup Language (XML) format e-mail "policy" in the domain name system (DNS) record for their domain. E-mail servers can query the DNS record and match the source IP address of incoming e-mail messages to the address of the approved sending servers. This results in e-mail being verifiable as coming from who it says it's from.

Sender Policy Framework and Domain Keys

These proposals (supported by Yahoo and AOL) are essentially the same as the caller ID proposals. They use a DNS challenge/response mechanism to allow look-up and verification of the sender of the e-mail to ensure they are who they claim to be. Weaknesses are already becoming apparent in this system. It was implemented by Yahoo in the first quarter of 2004, but it has resulted in no reduction in spam volumes to Yahoo e-mail addresses. The spammers are validating themselves as legitimate e-mail senders to ensure their e-mails get through, and legitimate e-mailers are sending from servers who have not actually implemented the domain keys technology. Although the spammers no longer have anonymity on their side, there is no solid legal framework in place, or even a way to prevent them from continuing to send spam if they are using domain keys. Systems like domain keys and caller ID only offer a part of the anti-spam solution. They ensure the e-mail sender can be identified. But they do not offer a way to stop a spammer sending spam (Geer, 2004).

Trusted E-mail Open Standard (TEOS)

In May 2003, the ePrivacy Group announced the trusted e-mail open standard (TEOS) to fight spam, spoofing, and e-mail fraud (Schiavone, Brussin, Koenig, Cobb, & Everett, 2003). TEOS is a staged approach towards a trusted e-mail system built upon and extending the SMTP protocol. TEOS takes a two-track approach comprising an identify verification system, content assertions (flags in the subject line which identify the type of content) in conjunction with a policy-based trust and accountability process. TEOS creates a framework of trusted identity for e-mail senders based on secure, fast, lightweight signatures in e-mail headers, optimized with DNS-based systems for flexibility and ease of implementation. TEOS also provides a common-language framework for making trusted assertions about the content of each individual message. ISPs and e-mail recipients can rely on these assertions to manage their e-mail.

Hybrid Approach

This approach consists of using an intelligent combination of technologies to provide an effective approach by using the strengths of one method to counter the weaknesses of another. There are a quartet of complementary technologies to consider which are; proof of work, signatures with whitelist, domain certificates, and content filters. This cocktail of anti-spam measures is known as the "hybrid" system. A combination of anti-spam solutions which are inadequate when used individually, but when used together can compensate for the inadequacies inherent in each part of the system. First, the incoming mail is checked for a valid hashcash stamp, if it passes this step it goes straight to the inbox. If not, it goes to the next stage to see if the sender is listed on the recipients list of "allowed senders" (i.e., a conversation and level of trust has previously been established between the two parties). If the e-mail is from a whitelisted sender, it can be directed to the user's inbox. Finally, a standard content filter is applied. If an e-mail does not have a stamp and is not from a whitelisted sender, then there is a possibility it might be spam. So, a Bayesian filter check is applied to the contents to check it for "spaminess," if it scores highly on this check (i.e., it is undoubtedly spam) it is routed to the trash folder. Otherwise it is routed to the "suspect" folder for review by the recipient. Hopefully, most spam will be filtered out in step one and two, to minimise the chance of false positives in the final filtering step (the filtering step is the part most likely to introduce false positives in this setup). Camram (Johansson & Dawson, 2003) is an example of a hybrid system, although this is still in the beta/development phase. Camram blends anti-spam solutions to compensate for the weaknesses in each. Hashcash forms the foundation of the Camram system. An all-encompassing anti-spam system needs to address a number of additional areas however, and ideally consists of a multi-layered approach:

- **Policies:** Mass-mailers agree to conform to certain standards.

- **Accountability:** If spammers don't conform, then some sort of internet "sanctions" should be applied.

- **Traceability:** E-mail should be verifiable as coming from who it says it is from, to ensure senders can be traced.

- **Legal:** For repeat or spammers who refuse to comply with any of the policies, then legal discourse can be used as the fall-back position.

- **Technical:** Proof-of-work stamps to minimise spam volumes. Traditional Bayesian filters to trap anything that gets through (this is the point where false positives could occur—so whether Bayesian filters are still required in this model is debatable).

Comparison of Anti-Spam Solutions

Table 2 summarises and compares the technical anti-spam solutions discussed in this chapter. The five main requirements for an anti-spam system are shown, with each method evaluated against each of the requirements. It can be seen that no one method fits all the requirements perfectly.

In the case of "Proof-of-work," specifically hashcash, it is not known if it can be implemented universally in a manner which is transparent to the user. It is suspected that due to the disparity of performance across e-mail devices, hashcash may not be a universal stand-alone solution. Hashcash will now be examined and tested in more detail to determine if it is a feasible stand-alone solution to spam (i.e., to find out if it meets the "transparent" and "universal" requirements).

Table 2. Comparison of technical anti-spam solutions

Method	Type	Spam Blocking Efficiency	Causes False Positives	User Transparency Rating	Universal Solution	Minimise Network Volumes
SMTP Header Analysis	Filtering	Poor	Yes	Good	Yes	No
Digital Fingerprint	Filtering	Poor	Yes	Good	Yes	No
Address List	Filtering	Good	Yes	Good	Yes	No
Keyword List	Filtering	Poor	Yes	Good	Average	No
Statistical Analysis	Filtering	Good	Yes	Good	Average	No
Challenge / Response	Filtering	Average	No	Poor	Average	No
Proof of Work	Stamp	Good	No	Unknown	Unknown	Yes
Micropayment	Stamp	Good	No	Good	Yes	Yes

Hashcash in Detail

A novel proposal to anti-spam is the proof-of-work method called "hashcash." This presents an interesting line of investigation as it is still in development and has not been deployed. There also exist some doubts over its feasibility due mainly to the problem of CPU-bound functions not performing equally across platforms. Hashcash (Dwork & Naor, 1992; Back, 1997, 2002) is a method of adding a textual stamp to the header of an e-mail to prove you have expended a certain amount of CPU time calculating the stamp prior to sending the e-mail. In other words, as you have taken a certain amount of time to generate the stamp and send the e-mail, it is unlikely that you are a spammer. The stamp can be validated quickly at the recipient end. If the stamp is valid, then it is possible to flag the message as "not spam" and direct it straight to the recipient's inbox. Hashcash inserts a X-hashcash: header into the e-mail headers section of the e-mail the user sends. Figure 7 shows an example of an e-mail with a hashcash stamp in the header.

To hashcash-stamp an outgoing e-mail, the recipient e-mail address is supplied to the hashcash minter program together with how many "bits" the stamp should be (larger bit stamps take longer to calculate). The minter program, after a certain amount of calculation time, will return a valid hashcash stamp in the format shown in Figure 7. The stamp is then attached to the header of the e-mail, and the e-mail is sent as usual. This process should happen as a background job so the sender is not even aware a stamp is being generated and attached to the outgoing e-mail. On the recipient end, the server reads the hashcash stamp and performs the following verification:

1.   Is the stamp is the required number of bits?

2.   Is the address in the stamp the person the e-mail is intended for?

3.   Is the date in the stamp today's date?

Figure 7. Hashcash stamp in e-mail header

From: Someone <test@test.invalid>
To: John Honan <jhonan@silveronion.com>
Subject: test Hashcash
Date: Thu, 24 Jun 2004 11:59:59 +0000
X-Hashcash: 0:040624: jhonan@silveronion.com:1fea2abb184ebf0a

blah blah

-Someone

If the above three tests are passed, then the stamp is valid, and the e-mail is directed to the recipients in-box. The important point is that is takes a lot longer to calculate a stamp than to verify it. It could take a number of minutes for the senders PC to calculate a valid stamp, but it only takes a few milliseconds for the recipient's e-mail server to check the stamp is valid. Therefore the "CPU cost" of calculating a stamp is borne at the senders end. Hashcash is based on the SHA-1 hashing algorithm. SHA-1 generates a unique 120 bit number to from any input text. It is easy to validate the input text generates the output hash. This method is often used to check that executable files or documents which are downloaded from the internet are intact and not tampered with when they reach their destination, by validating their SHA-1 hash signature is correct at the receiving end. Even if one character of the input text changes, this results in a drastically different SHA-1 hash. Hashcash makes use of the fact that it is highly unlikely that any two input strings will generate the same output hash signature (120 bit hashes give 2^{120} possible hash combinations)

How Hashcash Computes Hash-Collisions

Basically on the recipient's e-mail address and the date—what hashcash actually does is look for bit collisions on strings such as:

0:040624:jhonan@silveronion.com:1fea2abb184ebf0a

against an all "0" string. The stamp contains a date (040624= Jun 24th 2004), and an e-mail address (jhonan@silveronion.com). The first field (the 0:) is the stamp version number. The last field, a string of random letters, is some random text used to in the collision detection part of the stamp generation process. Lots of different random strings must be tried to find the required bit-collision, approximately 2^{16} attempts for a 16 bit collision. One of the powerful features of hashcash is that it is defined using SHA1, a commonly used and effective hashing algorithm. The above stamp hashed gives:

echo -n **0:040624:jhonan@silveronion.com:1fea2abb184ebf0a** | sha1

00000000c70db7389f241b8f441fcf068aead3f0

It can be seen that the first eight hex digits are 0. Each hex digit is fiur bits. This means the above stamp has a collision on (8*4 bits) = 32 bits. So the above stamp is a 32-bit collision. This is a big collision which would take a high-end 2Ghz PC many hours to compute. But for normal e-mail it is expected to use stamps in the range of 20-25 bits (which will take under a minute to calculate on most hardware). The self-contained nature of a hashcash stamp means that once the stamp is generated, then any tampering to the stamp will result in the collision bit count changing, and thus rendering the stamp useless. This is very important, as it means a spammer cannot just generate one stamp and slot multiple e-mail addresses into it. Also, they cannot generate hundreds of stamps in advance for a single e-mail address, as the date forms part of the stamp. For example, assuming a spammer legitimately generated the following 20-bit stamp:

0:040624:jhonan@silveronion.com:r7rk+dl/34

This stamp can only be attached to an e-mail being sent to "jhonan@silveronion.com" on Jun 24th 2004. Any other recipient will reject this stamp (as it doesn't contain their e-mail address), and if it is sent on any other date to jhonan@silveronion.com, then it will be rejected as the date is incorrect. Now, the spammer decides they want to use the same stamp, but doesn't want to spend the CPU time generating it. So why not just change the stamp slightly?

0:040624:someone@yahoo.com:r7rk+dl/34

The e-mail address has been modified to read "someone@yahoo.com." However, if this stamp is validated with SHA1, it is no longer a 20-bit stamp:

SHA1 (0:040624:someone@yahoo.com:r7rk+dl/34)

= 155DD9CAD53322C7FA119A3AFB6851501D06A7E8

= 3 bit collision (unacceptable)

This is because changing the stamp itself actually results in a different SHA1 hash output. Once the stamp has been generated, it cannot be tampered with. Computing a full hash-collision (finding two text inputs that generate the same 160-bit hash output) is computationally infeasible—there isn't enough computing power on the planet to create one in the next 100 years. Hashcash instead works on the basis of partial-collisions. A full-collision would be that all bits of SHA-1(x) must match SHA-1(y); a k-bit partial collision would be where only the k most-significant bits match. The only way to attempt to calculate these partial collisions is by using a brute force method; this is where the CPU-time expenditure (proof-of-work) takes place. Taking the hash we need to find a match on, loop through a process of appending randomly generated text until checking the output hash gives the required number of collision bits. The loop can take millions of attempts before it finds a matching x-bit collision. And it is this brute force iterative approach that takes so much computational effort to find a collision and therefore generate a valid stamp. There is no other mathematical way of quickly finding hash collisions; this brute-force looping method is the only way.

To take a 20 most significant bits collision as an example (which is a practical target). A 2GHz P4 can compute one in about 1.6 seconds, but this equates to about 1,048,576 (2^{20}) iterations, on average, through the loop. Because hashcash uses a brute-force algorithm to find hash collisions, there is no guarantee as to exactly how many iterations it will take before finding a collision. It might be "lucky" and start the loop close to a successful collision, and thus calculate the collision in a matter of milliseconds. Or, the loop might require a large number of iterations, and actually take longer than expected to achieve the required collision. On average, it will take 2^n attempts to find a collision (RSA Laboratories, 2000), where n is the number of collision bits required. If we know how long each iteration takes (by simply timing the collision detection loop), then we can work out on average how long it will take to calculate the required stamp on that particular hardware. The goal of introducing a proof-of-work system like hashcash is to reduce the amount of spam the average person receives to below some fraction of their legitimate e-mail. Independent testing of the best commercial spam filtering solutions shows that they currently achieve an spam-to-legitimate ratio of 0.06 (Snyder, 2003). There are some[1] who say that hashcash will encourage spammers to utilise large collections of zombie computers, which run malware to send spam unbeknownst to the user. These large networks have a large total computational power, which can be used to generate legitimate hashes for the spam e-mails they send. It can be argued that the extra CPU usage will often be noticed by the owners of the machines, who will be more likely to fix them. Laurie and Clayton (2004) argue that while hashcash for e-mail is attractive, nonetheless spammer profit margins per sale mean that they well be able to afford the PCs to do the proof of work required. This claim will be tested by the spammer profitability analysis later. We believe however that their economic analysis of spammer charge per e-mail and hardware costs are weighed in favour of the spammer (i.e., lower than we would state them) and they themselves mention elsewhere in the paper that spam response rates to date are badly documented.

Evaluating the Hashcash Approach

The aim of the experiment is to determine if the hashcash proof of work approach meets all the requirements of an anti-spam solution. In Table 2, we were able to match some of the requirements, but there is still doubt over the suitability of hashcash as a universal solution. To restate the research question "Is hashcash proof-of-work a single technique which meets all the requirements of an anti-spam solution?" We can deduce by simple analysis of the way hashcash operates that it does meet the following requirements to block all spam, prevent false positives, minimise network spam volume, be transparent to users and be universally implementable. The experiment will be approached in 2 parts:

1.   Calculate spammer profitability and breakeven point to find out how long (in seconds) the hashcash stamp needs to be to deter spammers

2.   Take time measurements of stamp calculation times across for different bit sizes across different devices (processor speeds)

We can then combine and analyse the results of both parts of the experiment and draw conclusions for the "transparent" and "universal" requirements. This chapter narrows down and defines the method and research instruments required for primary data collection.

Choosing a Method

The most common method used in measuring the performance of a filter-based anti-spam system is using a corpus of spam messages, passing them through the system, and measuring success rates and false positive reading (Lai & Tsai, 2004; Kim, Kim, Jung, & Jo, 2004; Stuart, Cha, & Tappert, 2004). This method is particularly useful for evaluating Bayesian and adaptive filtering approaches (discussed in a previous section) and spam testing methodologies are emerging, such as measurements of spam precision, legitimate precision and spam recall (Stuart et al., 2004). However, hashcash takes a different approach to anti-spam, so these testing methods cannot be used. The central concept of hashcash is that it takes a certain amount of time to generate a stamp, which can be attached to any e-mail and then quickly validated at the recipient end. There is no "filtering" as such at the recipient end, just a simple check that the stamp is valid. Every e-mail with a legitimate stamp is accepted, and every e-mail without a stamp, or with an invalid stamp, is rejected. The objective of this experiment is to compare the time taken to generate stamps across platforms, in order to prove that hashcash is not feasible due to the wide disparity of stamp generation times from one system to the next. There are a number of possible approaches to performance testing the hashcash system. For this analysis, we need to measure the following;

•   Calculate (based on spammer profitability) the minimum stamp size required in bits to make hashcash an effective solution

•   Measure how long it takes to calculate various size hashcash stamps on different powered CPUs

  o   Test from the "slowest" CPU to the "fastest" available for testing, and some in-between

  o   Calculate average time (seconds) to generate an n-bit stamp

For the analysis of the data, we can then compare the minimum stamp size required against the slower machines and reach some conclusions about the feasibility of a universal hashcash-based solution.

Various stamp calculation times are to be tested across different types of CPU and operating system in a standalone (i.e., not Internet-connected or part of an SMTP system). It is assumed that a spammer will be willing to invest in a stack of "fast CPUs" running optimised minting code in order to generate stamps as quickly as possible, and comparing this to the "poor" Pentium 2 user who just wants to send e-mail in the most efficient way. Since a collision detection of the required number of bits has an element of "luck," there is no exact measurement of how long it takes to calculate a stamp with a certain bit size. What we do know is that the time taken averages out over a number of samples. The most accurate way of determining the average time per x-bit stamp is to measure the number of collision detections (hashes) per second, and then using the following formula:

Average time taken to calculate X-bit stamp (seconds) = Collisions per second / 2^X

(RSA Laboratories, 2000)

In order to get a like-for-like comparison, a version of the hashcash minter which can run from a DOS command line was used. Hashcash version 0.28[2] was used to run the experiments and obtain the primary data. The "-s" command line flag tells hashcash to calculate and output the number of collision tests per second. The slowest specification machine that the test was run on was an Intel 486 25Mhz, the highest specification machine was the Apple Xserve G5. The data obtained from these machines was the "number of collision tests per second" they can compute. A stamp size parameter range of between 20-bits and 31-bits was selected. In the case of the slower processors, actually running a full stamp generation for a 30-bit stamp was unfeasible as it could take over 2.5 days to calculate. Therefore we calculated how long one hash takes to calculate, and then used the 2^n formula to obtain an average minting time.

Results and Analysis

Part One: Spammer Profitability and Breakeven Point

Proof-of-work is based on the concept that if it takes x seconds for a spammer to stamp and send an e-mail, then if x is large enough it should be possible to impact the spammers profitability enough to deter them from sending spam in the first place. For the first part of the analysis, we need to work out what this breakeven point is. In other words, how long it should take to calculate a hashcash stamp to make sending spam unprofitable. There are only a certain number of seconds in a day, which means the spammer is limited in the maximum amount of stamped e-mail they can send per CPU per day. It should be possible to combine both these ideas together. We need to make some assumptions about average costs to the spammer, and establish some base variables. These base variables are required throughout the calculations which follow.

a.   There are $(3600*24)*365.25 = 31,557,600$ seconds in a year
b.   We will assume the average cost of acquiring, powering, housing, maintaining, and administering one CPU for one year is approximately €200

c. Therefore, we can divide (b) by (a) to determine the cost of running a CPU for one second

Base variables		
a)	Seconds in a year	31,557,600
b)	CPU cost per year	€200.00
c)	CPU cost per second	€0.000006338

Normally, the time taken to transmit one e-mail (without stamping it) is in the fractions of a second. Fast spam programs can send hundreds of e-mails a second.

d. To continue with the calculation, we will assume the spammer has to stamp every mail, and that each stamp takes 15 seconds to calculate (this number will change later on, as we will use goal-seek to find what the minimum value needs to be, but lets say 15 seconds for the moment to demonstrate the formula as a first pass)

e. The CPU cost to send one message is then (cost per second / seconds per message)

Cost of sending one message		
d)	**Seconds per message**	**15**	This is the value we need to find using goal-seek
e)	CPU cost per message	€0.00009506	

Spammer revenue and response rate figures are difficult to obtain. We know that spammers operate different business models with different success rates and profits. Mangalindan (2002) gave real-world examples of spam response rates of 0.013% and 0.0023% (1 response per 7,692 e-mails, and 1 response per 43,478 e-mails). These were obtained through interviews with only one spammer so will have to be viewed as "typical" response rates. Yerazunis (2003) quotes a response rate of 0.01% (one response per 10,000 e-mails). Which appears to uphold Mangalindan's claimed response rates. Overall this secondary data is not very accurate or reliable as it was derived from limited interviews or rough estimates around response rates. Since it is very difficult to obtain exact spammer response rates we will have to use these approximations. Spammers deal with their clients using a variety of models; fixed price per mailing to fixed price per e-mail sent, to pay-per-response, where the spammer gets paid once a recipient clicks on a link to a webpage or actually makes a purchase (Boutin, 2004). We will use the commission-based and click-through based models as examples in the profitability calculations which follow.

- **Click-through model:** The spammer receives a fixed payment for every recipient who clicks on a link in the spam and is taken to a website (regardless of whether they purchase anything or the value of the final item). Since it is easier to get someone to click a link on an e-mail, the response rates could be between one-click-for-every-

Table 4. Approximate parameter range values

	Low	**High**
Click-through rate	1-in-2,000	1-in-10,000
Revenue per click	€1	€2
Conversion rate	1-in-50,000	1-in-100,000
Revenue per conversion	€20	€40

2000-messages-sent and one-click-for-every-10000-messages-sent. However, the revenue-per-click could be quite low, between €1 and €2 per click. Again, these values will vary considerably depending on how successful the spammer is, and what type of campaign they run. However, we will be averaging out these minimum and maximum values, so exact figures are not as critical for this part of the calculation.

- **Commission-based model:** The spammer receives a fixed payment for every completed sale. Fewer recipients will actually see the purchase through to completion once they click through to the website. So we can assume the response rates for this model are lower, say between one-purchase-for-every-50,000-messages-sent and one-purchase-for-every-100,000-messages-sent. But, the payment the spammer gets could be much higher, we will use the range €20-€40 per response for this model. So we now have a broad range of minimum and maximum parameters, summarised in Table 4.

From (e), we know how much it will cost the spammer to send one 15-second stamped message. It can now be derived how much it will cost the spammer to achieve one revenue-generating response:

f.   Messages for 1 response is taken from **Table 4**

g.   Revenue per response is taken from **Table 4**

h.   Cost per response (Messages for 1 response/CPU Cost per message) (f/e)

Total cost needed to achieve one response		Click-based commission		Conversion-based commission	
		Min	**Max**	**Min**	**Max**
f)	Messages for 1 response	2,000	10,000	50,000	100,000
g)	Revenue per response	€1.00	€2.00	€20.00	€40.00
h)	Cost per response	€0.19	€0.95	€4.75	€9.51

i. Revenue minus Cost gives the gross profit per response (i = g – h)

		Click-based commission		Conversion-based commission	
		Min	Max	Min	Max
i)	Gross profit per response	€0.81	€1.05	€15.25	€30.49

However, because of the stamp slow-down there is now a "cap" on the maximum number of messages the spammer can send in one day, this needs to be introduced into the calculation:

j. Max messages sendable in one day = Number of seconds in a day / number of seconds per message (3600*24)/15 (from (d))

j)	Max messages per day		5,760	

		Click-based commission		Conversion-based commission	
		Min	Max	Min	Max
k)	Max responses per day	2.9	0.6	0.1	0.1
l)	Max profit per day	€2.33	€0.60	€1.76	€1.76
m)	Average max profit per day	€1.61			

We can now apply (j) to the gross profit per response calculation, to calculate maximum achievable profit per day for each of the models:

k. Maximum messages per day divided by number of messages for 1 response (j/f)

l. Profit per response (i) multiplied by max number of responses per day (k)

m. Average of 4 values in row (l)

By using the Excel goal-seek function, we now need to make (m) equal to zero by modifying (d) (seconds per message). We know that to make the spammer unprofitable, then we must reduce their profit per day figure (m) to zero, or less than zero. The MS Excel goal-seek function (Making (m) = 0 by changing (d)) provides the results show in Table 5.

It can be seen that with a value of 59 for "(d) seconds per message," the average profit is reduced to zero. Given the uncertainty around the minimum and maximum range values in table, it is safe to round this up to 60 seconds to be sure of making the spammer unprofitable regardless of business model.

Table 5. Spammer stamp breakeven point calculation

	Base variables				
a)	Seconds in a year	31,557,600			
b)	CPU cost per year	€200.00			
c)	CPU cost per second	€0.000006338			

	Cost of sending one message				
d)	**Seconds per message**	**59**			
e)	CPU cost per message	€0.00037447			

Total cost needed to achieve one response

		Click-based commission		Conversion-based commission	
		Min	Max	Min	Max
f)	Messages for 1 response	2,000	10,000	50,000	100,000
g)	Revenue per response	€1.00	€2.00	€20.00	€40.00
h)	Cost per response	€0.75	€3.74	€18.72	€37.45

		Click-based commission		Conversion-based commission	
		Min	Max	Min	Max
i)	Gross profit per response	€0.25	-€1.74	€1.28	€2.55
j)	Max messages per day	1,462			

		Click-based commission		Conversion-based commission	
		Min	Max	Min	Max
k)	Max responses per day	0.7	0.1	0.0	0.0
l)	**Max profit per day**	**€0.18**	**-€0.26**	**€0.04**	**€0.04**

m)	**Average max profit per day**	**€0.00**			

Therefore, in order for hashcash to deter spammers, the minimum time required to calculate one stamp should be 60 seconds.

Part Two: Hashcash Stamping Performance Measurement

Now that the minimum stamp time has been determined, the second part of the experiment sets out to collect data across processor types to find out how long various bit-lengths take to calculate. This part of the experiment involves running hashcash performance measurement tests on a variety of processors and collecting the data for further analysis. The setup consisted of creating a DOS boot disk to boot the PC to a C:\> command line prompt. This was primarily to ensure that all the processing power was available to the hashcash stamp generation, and not interrupted by operating system multi-tasking (which may have introduced inaccuracies). The boot disk also contained a copy of the hashcash executable (hashcash.exe) version 0.28, which was the latest stable build at the time of the experiment. The "hashcash –s" command was executed 10 times in succession and an average of the 10 results was recorded as the result for each processor type. Typical command-line output can be seen in Figure 10.

Results of the Experiment

The results of the experiment are shown in Table 6. "Collision tests per second" was the primary data measurement collected for each processor type.

For example, the P2 400MHz can perform 210,521 collision tests per second compared to the 1,264,580 collision tests per second of the P4 3GHz machine. An n-bit stamp will take on average 2^n collision tests until a partial hash collision is obtained. We now know how many collision tests per second can be performed by each processor type, so it is possible to calculate how many seconds each processor type will take on average to mint a stamp of n-bits.

- To mint a 20-bit stamp, it will take on average $2^{20} = 1,048,576$ collision tests before a partial collision is found.

- The 486 25MHz can perform 5,000 collision tests per second (data obtained from direct measurement)

- Therefore the 486 25MHz will take, on average, $(1,048,576 / 5,000) = $ **209.7 seconds** to find a partial collision for a 20-bit stamp (as seen in the results in Table 6)

Overall the experiment and the results were accurate, and stood up to analysis providing the necessary conclusions for the research question. However, there were two potential problem areas; Different version releases of hashcash, and extrapolation of data. The developer community is continuously working on and optimising the performance of the hashcash code so stamp generation times will be faster from one version release to the next. Although this will speed up the time taken for stamp generation, it will do so equally across all platforms, so the conclusions of this research should not be impacted. However, this variance across software versions should be considered if these tests are to be duplicated. Version 0.28 was used for the experiment as it was the most stable release available at the time. As an example, a later version of hashcash (v0.30) was executed on the Intel P4 3GHz. The result is shown in Table 6. It can be seen that the performance of hashcash for this processor has almost doubled in just two version releases. (1,264,580 per second for v0.28 versus 2,396,776 for v0.30). The data in Table 6 was obtained by extrapolating the collision test per second figures for each processor across the range of bit-lengths (as described in 6.2.3). This was

Table 6. Seconds taken to mint stamps on different processors

		Collision tests / sec	Seconds required to mint stamp of bit value:										
Processor			20	21	22	23	24	25	26	27	28	29	30	31
Intel 486	25MHz	5,000	209.7	419.4	838.9	1,677.7	3,355.4	6,710.9	13,421.8	26,843.5	53,687.1	107,374.2	214,748.4	429,496.7
Intel Pentium	200MHz	77,500	13.5	27.1	54.1	108.2	216.5	433.0	865.9	1,731.8	3,463.7	6,927.4	13,854.7	27,709.5
Intel Pentium 2	400MHz	210,521	5.0	10.0	19.9	39.8	79.7	159.4	318.8	637.6	1,275.1	2,550.2	5,100.4	10,200.8
Intel Pentium 3	750MHz	399,521	2.6	5.2	10.5	21.0	42.0	84.0	168.0	335.9	671.9	1,343.8	2,687.6	5,375.1
Intel Pentium 4	2GHz	658,915	1.6	3.2	6.4	12.7	25.5	50.9	101.8	203.7	407.4	814.8	1,629.6	3,259.1
Intel Pentium 4	3GHz	1,264,580	0.8	1.7	3.3	6.6	13.3	26.5	53.1	106.1	212.3	424.5	849.1	1,698.2
Intel Pentium 4 (opt)	3GHz	2,396,776	0.4	0.9	1.7	3.5	7.0	14.0	28.0	56.0	112.0	224.0	448.0	896.0
Apple G-5 X-Serve Dual	Dual 2.3Ghz	18,000,000	0.1	0.1	0.2	0.5	0.9	1.9	3.7	7.5	14.9	29.8	59.7	119.3

necessary as it would take too long to calculate average minting times for the slower processors within the timescales of the research. To allow these processors to calculate full 31-bit stamps multiple times (for averages) would have meant running the hashcash algorithm for weeks on each machine, which was unfeasible. Hence the extrapolation method was used. One area which the extrapolation method did not allow investigation of was the "variance problem." When a full hashcash stamp is generated we can estimate on average how long it will take (based on the 2^n formula 5.3), in reality it could be either faster or slower (described in 4.4). The "full-stamp" generation results would have demonstrated this variance problem, but would have required lengthy iteration on the slower machines which was not feasible in the project timescales. The average (extrapolated) method was a better fit for the purposes of this analysis.

Analysis of Results

Selected results are shown graphically in Figure 5 which focuses on the generation of a 24-bit stamp, showing how long it takes to mint on various processors. Even before incorporating spammer breakeven data, we can clearly see the disparity between the fastest and the slowest machine.

Taking the full range of results, and incorporating the spammer breakeven point of one minute calculated in 6.1 gives us the chart shown in Figure 6.

The point at which even the fastest processor takes **60 seconds** to generate a stamp is at **30 bits**. So, for hashcash to work as a deterrent for all spammers (assuming spammers are likely to afford fast processors like the Apple G-5), **a global stamp value of 30 bits needs to be used.** Any less than 30 bits and the spammer is profitable (since it now takes him less than 60 seconds to generate a stamp which is below his breakeven point) and by just increasing the number of stamp-generating processors he will soon be sending large volumes of spam again, which would render hashcash useless as a solution. Now, the problem can be seen. With a global stamp value set at 30-bits, the person running the 25MHz 486 will take 60 hours, or 2.5 days, to generate a single stamp. Even for the most patient user, this is unacceptable. Other machines, like the P2 400MHz (a common configuration still in use) would

Figure 5. Time taken to calculate 24 bit stamp on various processors

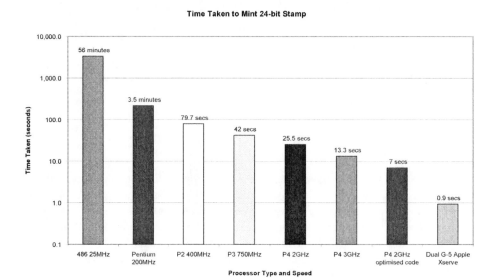

Figure 6. Hashcash minting performance across processors

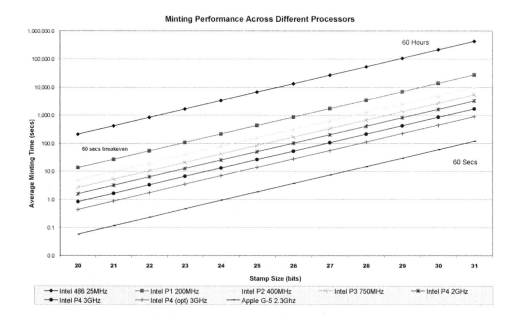

take 5,100 seconds, or over 1.5 hours to generate a stamp. Even is the user was willing to wait this long for the stamp to be generated, it would still limit his e-mail sending to (24/1.5) = 16 e-mails per day, which might not be enough for one user. Moore's law states (roughly) that chip density doubles every eighteen months. This means that memory sizes, processor power, and so forth—all follow the same curve. Therefore in order to keep the stamp calculation times at spammer breakeven levels, it will be necessary to increase the global stamp postage value on a regular basis. To be fully successful as a standalone anti-spam solution the hashcash method will need to be universally adopted. If hashcash is used in isolation as an anti-spam measure, then it will need to be installed across all servers and e-mail clients in order to be successful, otherwise legitimate e-mail senders without hashcash stamps will not be able to send e-mail to hashcash enabled recipients.

Conclusion

Hashcash does not meet all the requirements of a standalone anti-spam system (as defined earlier). Specifically it fails in the areas of "user transparency" as it takes too long to generate the required stamp size on slower machines, and "universally implementable" performance disparity means it would be unfeasible for low-powered devices. It is becoming increasingly clear that a single technology isn't going to solve the problem of spam (Roberts, 2004; Ishibashi et al., 2001). We can concur with this statement, as unfortunately hashcash does not offer a single-technology solution.

In some cases (for example low specification PCs, or other devices used to send e-mail like handheld PDAs or mobile phones) the processing power in the hardware itself would not be enough to generate a reasonable size stamp. It may be possible to move the minting process to a separate minting server. The minting server would have to be powerful enough to handle multiple mint generation requests from multiple clients. And as hashcash is designed to be processor intensive, then a rack of minting servers may be required, depending on the demand. It is important to protect these minting servers from attacks by spammers intent on using the power of these servers to generate stamps. Proof of work could be used as a foundation for signatures. Obviously, it is cheaper for a sender to add a signature than a proof-of-work token, but if a signature relationship hasn't yet been set up, the proof-of-work token is the way to go. Hashcash is a good candidate for the proof-of-work part of a hybrid solution. Content filters are the last line of defence. They should only come into play if a message passes the domain certificate stage but gets an inconclusive result from the signature and proof-of-work filters (perhaps because neither are present). Any hybrid anti-spam solutions such as these discussed in this chapter go far beyond the technically "simple" anti-spam solutions currently in use, in that to be successful they need to be adopted on a global scale. This means the main industry players have to reach agreement on the type of solution to implement, and how it should be implemented. Currently the main stumbling block in any of these proposed industry solutions is achieving agreement between the industry partners on the best way forward. Spammers have learned to adapt to overcome many of the anti-spam measures used against them thus the greater urgency for industry partners to work together sooner to implement a global hybrid solution.

References

Back, A. (1997). *Hashcash*. Retrieved March 1, 2004, from http://www.cypherspace.org/Hashcash/

Back, A. (2002). *Hashcash: A denial of service counter-measure* (Tech. Rep.). Retrieved March 2004, from http://www.cypherspace.org/adam/Hashcash/Hashcash.pdf

Baker, W., & Kamp, J. (2003, December). *Summary of can spam act*. Retrieved August 15, 2004, from http://www.wrf.com/publications/publication.asp?id=1623481222003

Bass, T., & Watt, G. (1997). Simple framework for filtering queued SMTP mail (cyberwar countermeasures). In *Proceedings of IEEE MILCOM97*.

Boutin, P. (2004). Interview with a spammer. *InfoWorld*. Retrieved April 16, 2004, from http://www.infoworld.com/article/04/04/16/16FEfuturerichter_1.html?s=feature

Cerf, V. (2005). Spam, spim, and spit. *Communications of the ACM, 48*(4), 39-43.

Damiani, E., De Capitani di Vimercati, S., Paraboschi, S., & Samarati, P. (2004). P2P-based collaborative spam detection and filtering. In *Proceedings of the Fourth International Conference on Peer-to-Peer Computing (P2P'04)* (pp. 176-183).

Deepak, P., & Parameswaran, S. (2005). Spam filtering using spam mail communities. In *Proceedings of the 2005 Symposium, Applications and the Internet* (pp. 377-383).

Dwork, C., & Naor, M. (1992). Pricing via processing or combating junk mail. In *Crypto'92* (pp. 139-147).

Filman, R. (2003). When e-mail was good. *IEEE Internet Computing*, 4-6.

Gburzynski, P., & Maitan, J. (2004). Fighting the spam wars: A re-mailer approach with restrictive aliasing. *ACM Transactions on Internet Technology, 4*(1), 1-30.

Geer, D. (2004). Will new standards help curb Spam? *IEEE Computer Magazine, 37*(2), 14-16.

Goodman, J., & Rounthwaite, R. (2004). Stopping outgoing spam. *ACM Conference on Electronic Commerce, EC'04*, New York (pp. 20-39).

Goodman, J., & Heckerman, D. (2004). Fighting spam with statistics. *Significance, 1*(2), 69-72.

Graham, P. (2003). Different methods of stopping spam. October 2003. Retrieved January 15, 2004, from http://www.secinf.net/anti_spam/Stopping_Spam.html

Hastings, N., & McLean, P. (1996, March 27-29). TCP/IP spoofing fundamentals. *IEEE IPCCC'96, IEEE International Phoenix Conference on Computers and Communications*, Phoenix, AZ (pp. 218-224).

Holmes, N. (2005). In defense of spam. *Computer IEEE, 38*(4), 86-88.

Ishibashi, H., Yamai, N., Abe, K., & Matsuura, T. (2001). Protection method against unauthorised access and address spoofing for open network access systems. *IEEE 0-7803-7080-5/01,* 10-13.

Johansson, E., & Dawson, K. (2003). *Camram*. Technical paper. Retrieved March 14, 2004, from http://harvee.org:6080/~esj/output/camram.pdf

Jung, J., & Sit, E. (2004, October 25-27). An empirical study of spam traffic and the use of DNS black lists. In *Proceedings of the 4ᵗʰ ACM SIGCOMM Conference on Internet Measurement, Taormina,* Sicily, Italy (pp. 370-375).

Kim, H.J., Kim, H.N., Jung, J.J., & Jo, G.S. (2004). *On enhancing the performance of spam mail filtering system using semantic enrichment* (LNCS 3339, pp. 1095-1100).

Lai, C-C., & Tsai, M-C. (2004). An empirical performance comparison of machine learning methods for spam e-mail categorization. In *Proceedings of the Fourth International Conference on Hybrid Intelligent Systems* (pp. 44-48).

Laurie, B., & Clayton, R. (2004). Proof of work proves not to work. *The Third Annual Workshop on Economics and Information Security (WEIS04),* University of Minnesota, Digital Technology Center.

Levine, J. (2004). Putting a spammer in jail. *CircleID.* Retrieved November 16, 2004, from http://www.circleid.com/article/804_0_1_0_C/

Levy, E. (2003). The making of a spam zombie army. *Security & Privacy Magazine, IEEE, 1*(4), 58-59.

Mangalindan, M. (2002). For bulk e-mailer, pestering millions offers path to profit. *Wall Street Journal.*

Microsoft. (2004, February 13). *The coordinated spam reduction initiative—a technology and policy proposal.* Microsoft Corporation. Whitepaper. Retrieved from http://www.microsoft.com/downloads

Pelletier, L., Almhana, J., & Choulakian, V. (2004, May 19-21). Adaptive filtering of SPAM. In *Proceedings of Communication Networks and Services Research, 2004* (pp. 218-224).

Pfleeger, S.L., & Bloom, G. (2005). Canning spam: Proposed solutions to unwanted e-mail. *Security & Privacy Magazine, IEEE, 3*(2), 40-47.

Roberts, P. (2004, March). Experts question Microsoft's caller ID patents. *InfoWorld.* Retrieved April 20, 2004, from http://www.infoworld.com/article/04/03/05/HNcalleridpatents_1.html

RSA Laboratories (2000). *RSA Laboratories frequently asked questions about today's cryptography (Version 4.1), RSA Security Inc.* Retrieved from July 10, 2005, http://www.rsasecurity.com/rsalabs/node.asp?id=2152

Schiavone, V., Brussin, D., Koenig, J., Cobb, S., & Everett, R. (2003). Trusted e-mail open standard: A comprehensive policy and technology proposal for e-mail reform. *ePrivacy Group.* White paper. Retrieved from January 15, 2004, from http://www.eprivacygroup.net/teos/TEOSwhitepaper1.pdf

Schwartz, A., & Garfinkel, S. (1998). Stopping spam. *O'Reilly.*

Simpson, P. (2002). Putting spam back in the can. *ITsecurity.com.* Retrieved May 13, 2004, at http://www.itsecurity.com/archive/papers/mime6.htm

Snyder, J. (2003). Test: Spam in the wild. *Network World Fusion.* Retrieved from http://www.nwfusion.com/reviews/2003/0915spam.html

Spinello, R.A. (1999). Ethical reflections on the problem of spam. *Ethics and Information Technology, 1*(3), 185-191.

Stuart, I., Cha, S. H., & Tappert, C. (2004). A neural network classifier for junk e-mail (LNCS 3163, pp. 442-450).

Templeton, S., & Levitt, K. (2003). Detecting spoofed packets. *IEEE DARPA Information Survivability Conference and Exposition - I*. Washington, DC.

Tserefos, P., Smythe, C., Stergiou, I., & Cvetkovic, S. (1997). A comparative study of simple mail transfer protocol (SMTP), POP and X.400 e-mail protocols. In *Proceedings of the 22ⁿᵈ Annual IEEE Conference on Local Area Networks*, Minneapolis, MN (pp. 545-55).

Yerazunis, W (2003, January). *Sparse binary polynomial hashing and the CRM114 discriminator*. Spam Conference Presentation. Retrieved from January 15, 2004, from http://crm114.sourceforge.net/crm_slides/img39.html

Endnotes

[1]   http://en.wikipedia.org/wiki/Hashcash

[2]   http://www.Hashcash.org/binaries/win32/

About the Authors

Jairo Gutiérrez is a senior lecturer in the Department of Information Systems and Operations Management at the University of Auckland, New Zealand. He teaches data communications and computer networking, and has supervised the research projects of more than 35 postgraduate students over the past nine years. He is the editor-in-chief of the *International Journal of Business Data Communications and Networking* and has served as a reviewer for several leading academic publications. His current research topics are in network management systems, viable business models for mobile commerce, programmable networks, and quality of service issues associated with Internet protocols. He is also the co-ordinator for the University of the Cisco Networking Academy Program. Dr. Gutiérrez received a systems and computer engineering degree from The University of The Andes (Colombia, 1983), a masters degree in computer science from Texas A&M University (1985), and a PhD in IS from The University of Auckland in 1997.

* * *

Ashraf Ahmad is a PhD researcher with MIS Lab, National Chiao Tung University, Taiwan. His interest area includes MPEG video streaming and multimedia communication. He has published many conference and journal papers of his field of expertise. Ahmad has co-edited several conference proceedings and books. He chaired and organized many special issues in international conferences.

Fernando Beltrán holds a BSc in electrical engineering from the Universidad de Los Andes (Colombia), and an MSc and PhD in applied mathematics from the State University of New York at Stony Brook. Currently, he is a senior lecturer with the Department of Information Systems and Operation Management, University of Auckland, New Zealand.

Noel Broderick is an MSc graduate of the University of Ulster, UK. He has worked for a number of years in the telecommunications industry and his research interests include distributed systems, mobile systems, low level protocols, and Internet technologies.

Youssef Chahir earned an MSc in fundamental computer science from the University of Technology of Compiegne (1986), and a PhD in signal and image processing from the Centrale Lyon (2000). Since September 2000, he has been an assistant professor with the Departement of Computer and Information Science at the University of Caen, France. He is a researcher in the GREYC Laboratory at this same university. His research interests include data mining and knowledge discovery in images and video, image processing, statistical pattern recognition, and classification.

Liming Chen received a BSc in mathematics and computer science from Université de Nantes (1984). He earned a master's degree in 1986 and a PhD in computer science from the University of Paris 6. He first served as an associate professor at Université de Technologies de Compiègne, and then joined Ecole Centrale de Lyon, France as a professor where he has been leading an advanced research team on multimedia analysis. As author of more than 90 publications in the multimedia indexing field, his current research interest includes cross media analysis, multimedia indexing and retrieval, face detection and recognition, and image. He is a member of the IEEE Computer Society.

Kevin Curran is a lecturer at the University of Ulster, Northern Ireland. He is a senior member of the IEEE. He has written over 170 academic papers to date. Curran is a member of the editorial committee of *The Technology Source*, *Computers and Education* and the *Journal of Universal Computer Science* (JUCS). His research interests include distributed computing especially emerging trends within wireless ad-hoc networks, dynamic protocol stacks, multimedia transport protocols, and mobile systems.

Subhankar Dhar is an assistant professor in the Department of Management Information Systems at San José State University, USA. Dr. Dhar's research interest is distributed, mobile, and pervasive computing. In addition, he is also interested in information technology outsourcing. He teaches a variety of courses including telecommunications, data communications and networks, and distributed information systems. His publications have appeared in reputed international journals and gave presentations to various international conferences. He serves as a member of the editorial board of the *International Journal of Business Data Communications and Networking*. He is a reviewer of papers for various international journals, conferences, and scholarly publications. He also served as a member of the organizing committee of various international conferences like International Conference on Broadband Networks (BroadNets) and International Workshop on Distributed Computing (IWDC). Dr. Dhar has several years of industrial experience in software development, consulting for Fortune 500 and high-tech industries including product planning, design, and information systems management.

César García-Díaz holds a BSc in industrial engineering from the Pontificia Universidad Javeriana (Colombia), and an MSc in industrial engineering from the Universidad de Los Andes (Colombia). Currently, he is a PhD candidate at the Department of International Economics and Business at the University of Groningen, The Netherlands.

John Goh received his Bachelor of Information Technology, and subsequently Master of Information Technology at Monash University, Australia. Goh is currently undertaking his third year of PhD research in knowledge extraction from mobile users. Goh is interested in learning and developing innovative methods which have the ultimate result of generating patterns that allows decision makers to better understand the behavior of mobile users. He has since published a few conference and journal papers in this research area. Goh also teaches project management courses as an assistant lecturer, both at undergraduate and postgraduate level at Monash University. He aims to become a full time academic upon graduation.

Mohamed Hammami obtained a PhD in computer science from Ecole Centrale at the Lyon Research Center for Images and Intelligent Information Systems (LIRIS) associated to the French research institution CNRS as UMR 5205. His research interest is in combining techniques of data mining and image analysis in order to resolve different classification problems such as image classification and Web site filtering. He was a staff member in RNTL-Muse project. He has served on technical conference committees and as reviewer in many international conferences.

John Honan is a student with the Open University. He is also completing an MSc in distributed computing. His research interests include distributed systems, hashcash, and spam filtering systems.

Bryan Houliston recently completed a master's degree in IT, to go with his bachelor's degree in commerce. In between, he spent 10 years as a professional software developer. Houliston has since returned to professional practice. When time allows, his current research interests include mobile ad-hoc wireless networks. His master's dissertation is on the application of RFID technology in hospitals. He is a member of the ACM, IEEE, and New Zealand Computer Society.

Ismail Khalil Ibrahim is a senior researcher and lecturer at the Institute of Telecooperation at Johannes Kepler University Linz, Austria. He currently teaches, consults, and conducts research in mobile multimedia, norm-based computing, and ubiquitous intelligence and is also interested in the broader business, social, and policy implications associated with the emerging information technologies. Dr. Ibrahim holds a BSc in electrical engineering (1985), and an MSc (1998) and PhD (2001) in computer engineering and information systems. Before joining Johannes Kepler University of Linz in October 2002, he was a research fellow at the Intelligent Systems Group at Utrecht University, The Netherlands (2001-2002) and a senior researcher and project manager at the Software Competence Center Hagenberg - Austria (2000-2001). His work has been published at various books, journals, and conferences. He is also a reviewer and PC member for several conferences and journals.

Byung Kwan Lee received a BS from Pusan National University in 1970, an MS in computer science from Chung-Ang University in 1986 and a PhD in computer science from Chung-Ang University in 1990. He has been on the faculty of the Department of Computer Science and Engineering, Kwandong University, Kang-Won-Do, Korea since 1988. He has been a visiting processor in Saginaw Valley State University, Michigan, for two years since 2000. He is a permanent member of the KISS and KIPS. His current research interests are distributed and network management, and network security.

Tai-Chi Lee received a BS in mathematics from the National Taiwan Normal University, Taipei (1965), an MS in electrical engineering and computer science from University of Illinois at Chicago (1986), and a PhD in applied mathematics from the University of Utah (1975). He has been on the faculty at Saginaw Valley State University, USA, since 1988. He is currently a professor of computer science and his research interests include computer architectures, database systems design, image compression, and cryptography and network security.

Say Ying Lim is currently a postgraduate student in Monash University, Australia, under the School of Computer Science and Software Engineering. She has completed her Bachelor of Business Systems and Master of Business systems by projects, both also in Monash University.

Ted Chia-Han Lo is a data warehouse analyst / developer with Metcash Trading Ltd. (Sydney). He has a master's degree in commerce from the University of Auckland (Department of Information Systems & Operations Management), New Zealand, and a bachelor's degree in commerce (information systems and marketing majors). His current research interests are in OLAP, data warehousing and data mining.

June Park is the chief technology officer, chief knowledge officer, and executive vice president of service delivery support at Samsung SDS Company Limited, Seoul, South Korea. Dr. Park earned his PhD from Ohio State University. Prior to joining Samsung SDS, Dr. Park taught in the Department of Management Science at the University of Iowa for more than

10 years. He has published extensively in the area of telecommunication network modelling and design in *Management Science, European Journal of Operational Research, Journal of Heuristics* and *Telecommunication Systems.*

Nurul Sarkar is a senior lecturer in the School of Computer and Information Sciences at the Auckland University of Technology, New Zealand. He has more than 10 years of teaching experience in universities at both undergraduate and postgraduate level, and has taught a range of subjects including: computer networking, data communications, computer hardware and e-commerce. At the University of Auckland, he is currently completing his PhD in wireless communication networks. Sarkar has been published in a number of journals and conferences, and has contributed chapters to several edited research compilations. His research interests include wireless communication networks, simulation and modelling of computer and data communication networks, and tools to enhance methods for teaching and learning computer networking and hardware concepts. Sarkar is a member of IEEE Communications Society.

Elaine Smyth (BA, MSc) is currently studying for a PhD at the University of Ulster, UK. Her research interests include 802.11 security, distributed systems, pattern matching and audio streaming protocols. She is currently working on a PhD which seeks to develop a system which constructs a real-time musical structural analysis with MPEG-7 definition description language (DDL) compliant output based on automated similarity measurements which detect musical sections (and modulated sections) in real-time.

Varadharajan Sridhar is a professor in the information management area at the Management Development Institute, Gurgaon, India. He received his PhD in MIS from the University of Iowa. He was on the faculty of Ohio University, Athens and American University, Washington, DC. He also taught for four years at the Indian Institute of Management, Lucknow. His current research interests include telecommunications management and policy, global electronic commerce, and global virtual teams. He has published articles in a number of journals including *Annals of Cases on Information Technology, European Journal of Operational Research, Information Resource Management Journal, International Journal of Business Data Communications and Networking, Journal of Global Information Management, Journal of Heuristics,* and *Telecommunication Systems.* He is an associate editor of *International Journal of Business Data Communications and Networking.*

Bala Srinivasan is a professor of IT in the School of Computer Science and Software Engineering, Faculty of Information Technology, Monash University, Melbourne, Australia. He was formerly an academic staff member with the Department of Computer Science and Information Systems at the National University of Singapore and the Indian Institute of Technology, Kanpur. He has authored and jointly edited six technical books and authored and co-authored more than 150 international refereed publications in journals and conferences in the areas of multimedia databases, data communications, data mining, and distributed systems. He is a founding chairman of the Australasian database conference. He was awarded the Monash vice-chancellor medal for post-graduate supervision. He holds a

Bachelor of Engineering Honours degree in electronics and communication engineering, a master's degree and a PhD, both in computer science.

David Taniar received his bachelor's (Hon.), master's, and PhD—all in computer science, with a particular speciality in databases. His research now expands to data mining and mobile databases. He has published research papers in these fields extensively including a recent book *Object-Oriented Oracle*. Dr. Taniar now works at Monash University, Australia. He is editor-in-chief of international journals, including *Data Warehousing and Mining*, *Business Intelligence and Data Mining*, *Web Information Systems*, *Web and Grid Services*, *Mobile Multimedia*, and *Mobile Information Systems*. He is a fellow of the Institute for Management Information Systems (FIMIS).

Agustinus Borgy Waluyo is a PhD candidate at School of Computer Science and Software Engineering (SCSSE), Monash University, Australia. During his three years candidature, he has published over 20 refereed conference and journal publications. His research interest includes context-awareness, query processing, data management, data broadcasting and caching management in mobile/wireless computing environment.

Seung Hae Yang received his BS from Kwandong University in 2000 and his MS in computer science from Kwan-Dong University in 2003. He is currently working towards his doctorate degree in Kwan-Dong University of Korea. His current research interests are distributed and network management, network security and e-commerce.

Index

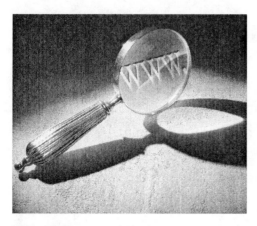